YO-CDI-225

Short Papers
on Scripture Subjects

by

C. H. Mackintosh

Published by
BELIEVERS BOOKSHELF INC.
5205 Regional Road #81, Unit #3
Beamsville, Ontario L0R 1B3
Canada

2nd Printing – Revised Version

2,000 hardback and
4,000 paperback vol. 1 – pages 1-126
4,000 paperback vol. 2 – pages 127-251
4,000 paperback vol. 3 – pages 252-379
4,000 paperback vol. 4 – pages 380-478

ISBN 0-88172-205-7

1995

BELIEVERS BOOKSHELF INC.

5205 Regional Road #81, Unit #3
Beamsville, Ont. L0R 1B3 Canada

P. O. Box 261, Sunbury, Pennsylvania 17801 USA

Distributed by:

Scripture Truth
30 South Road
WOOLER, Northumberland
NE71 6SP ENGLAND

Chapter Two
13 Plum Lane, LONDON
SE18 3AF
ENGLAND

Words of Truth
P. O. Box 147
BELFAST
BTB 4TT N. IRELAND

Christliche Schriftenverbreitung
An der Schlossfabrik 30
D-42499 HÜCKESWAGEN
GERMANY

Printed in U.S.A.

Table of Contents

EDITOR'S INTRODUCTION
TO THE 1995 EDITION

Charles Henry Mackintosh was well known for both his spoken ministry and his written ministry which spanned 50 years. In style and character, his writings, often under the initials C.H.M., clearly showed his very deep love for the Lord Jesus and for His saints. He believed in and wrote about the narrow pathway the Christian is called to walk by the Word of God, but for a need of a large heart of love and grace while never giving up or failing to practice any truth found in that Word. Although he wrote a number of years ago, his writing seems very up-to-date in speaking of deteriorating world political and moral conditions – a giving up of the truth of the Word of God even by professed Christians.

Many of CHM's writings were in the form of short articles and letters to persons who asked him questions. We are thankful to those who, in the past, have collected these articles and letters for publication and arranged them in the published order. Although this order is generally random, some which naturally fall together are placed together.

This 1995 edition of Short Papers retains about 98% of CHM's original words, but for the modern reader, a number of words, little used today, have been changed to their modern equivalents. Some very long sentences and paragraphs have been broken up to enhance readability, and much of the heavy punctuation has been lightened. A few references to events or publications no longer relevant today have been removed. The King James Translation is used, unchanged, except for updating the word "charity" to "love" and capitalizing pronouns referring to deity.

Believers Bookshelf sends forth this 1995 edition with the prayer that these writings will be a blessing to a whole new generation of readers around the world. We thank the unnamed ones who spent many hours reviewing, finalizing and typesetting this manuscript. We commend it to you with the Scriptural admonition to "prove all things, hold fast the good" (1 Thes.5:21).

July 1995

A WORD TO OUR READERS

Dearly Beloved in the Lord,

We desire to offer you a few earnest words on a subject which we believe to be of commanding interest and importance; it is this: The divine sufficiency and supreme authority of Holy Scripture and the urgent need of submitting ourselves absolutely to its guidance in all things.

In thus stating our thesis, we would not have you to suppose for a moment that we undervalue human writings in their proper place. Nothing is further from our thoughts. Indeed it would ill become us to speak disparagingly of a branch of Christian ministry so largely used of God in all ages of His Church's history, and specially in this our own day.

No, beloved, we prize human writings more than we can attempt to say. We receive them as streams from the Fountain Head. Further, we would add that we have rarely met anyone who claimed to despise Christian writings, on the plea of reading nothing but the Bible, who was not crude, shallow and contracted. We might just as well say that we would not listen to a brother speaking to us in the assembly, as refuse to read what God had given him to write, provided we had time to do so. How often has a book or tract been made a rich blessing to the soul, either in bringing one to Christ or building up or helping on in Him! How often may we have read some passage of Scripture and seen nothing in it until the Lord used some paragraph in a human writing to unlock its treasures to our hearts! None of us are self-sufficient. We are dependent one on another. We grow by that which every joint supplies. We need all the "helps" which God has set in the body for our common profit and blessing.

Having said this to guard against misunderstanding and to put human writings in their right place, we return to our special object in this brief paper.

There is but one supreme and paramount authority, and that is the Word of God. All human writings are interesting as references, valuable as aids, but they are worthless, yea mischievous as authority. Scripture is all-sufficient. We want absolutely nothing in the way of guidance and authority beyond what we possess in the sacred canon of Scripture. No doubt, it is only by the Holy Spirit we can understand, appreciate or be guided by Scripture. God may use a human voice or a human pen to help us, but Scripture is divinely sufficient. It can make a child wise unto salvation and it can make a man perfect unto all good works. See 2 Timothy 3:15-17.

Now, having such a guide, such an authority, what becomes us as Christians – as children of God and servants of Christ? Clearly, to submit ourselves absolutely and unreservedly to its teaching in all things! We are bound by every argument and every motive which can possibly sway the heart, to test everything in which we are engaged or with which we stand associated, by the holy standard of the Word of God, and if we find anything, no matter what, which will not stand that test, to abandon it at once and forever.

It is precisely here that we feel there is such serious failure in the professing Church. As a rule, we do not find the conscience under the immediate action and government of the Word. Human opinions bear sway. Human creeds and confessions of faith govern the heart and form the religious character. Human traditions and habits of thought are allowed a formative influence over the soul. If it be merely a question of personal salvation, profit or blessing, Scripture will be listened to. People are glad and thankful to hear how they can be saved and blessed. Everything that bears upon the individual conditions and destiny will be welcomed.

But the moment it becomes a question of Christ's authority over us in spirit, soul and body; when the Word of God is brought to bear upon our entire practical career, upon our personal habits, our domestic arrangements, our commercial pursuits, our religious associations, our ecclesiastical position, then, alas! it becomes apparent how completely the authority of Holy Scripture is virtually thrown overboard. In point of fact, the enemy seems to succeed as completely in robbing professing Christians of the real value, power and authority of the Word of God, as when, during that long and dreary period of the middle ages, it was wrapped in the shroud of a dead language and buried in the dark cloisters of Rome. It is appalling when one comes in contact with the actual condition of things among professing Christians, to observe the ignorance of Scripture and the carelessness about it. Nor can any thoughtful person doubt that the latter is the cause of the former. "If any man *will* do His will, he shall know of the doctrine." But if the Word of God be neglected and practically ignored as an authority, need we marvel when we find people ignorant of its precious contents?

We have been much struck of late in our dealings with Christian professors, in noticing the little moral weight which Scripture seems to possess. You will rarely meet with anyone who is prepared to start with this one grand point, that the voice of the Holy Spirit in Scripture is absolutely conclusive, that it admits of no appeal, that it closes all discussion. We speak not now of man's interpretation of Scripture – of anything in which it can be said, "That is your opinion." We speak only of the written Word of God which we possess and to which we are individually responsible to submit ourselves in all things. God has put His Word into our hands. And He has put His Spirit into our hearts, and by that Spirit we can understand the Word; and we are solemnly bound to be guided and governed by that Word in all the details of our practical career.

It is this we feel imperatively called upon to press home upon the hearts and consciences of our readers. In looking to Him for the theme, we got this answer, "Press upon your readers the sufficiency and authority of Holy Scripture and the necessity of absolute subjection to it in all things." This we have sought to do, and now we leave it with our readers to consider as before the Lord their personal responsibility in this weighty matter. We would entreat them, as they love the Lord Jesus Christ, to examine in the light of Scripture, their entire position and path, and by the grace of God and for His glory, to abandon at once and forever all that is not in perfect accord with that holy standard. Thus shall their path be as the shining light that shines more and more unto the perfect day. Oh! may the true language of all our hearts be, "Speak, Lord; for Thy servant heareth." "Lord, what wilt Thou have me to do?" God grant it, for Christ's sake.

HOW TO STUDY SCRIPTURE

It is a very difficult for anyone to attempt to prescribe for another the proper method of studying Scripture. The infinite depths of Holy Scripture, like the exhaustless resources that are in God and the moral glories of the Person of Christ, are only unfolded to faith and need. This makes it so very simple. It is not cleverness or intellectual power we need, but the simplicity of a little child. The One who composed the Holy Scriptures must open our understandings to receive their precious teaching. And He will do so, if only we wait on Him in real earnestness of heart.

We must never lose sight of the weighty fact that it is as we act on what we know that our knowledge shall increase. It will never do to sit down like a bookworm to read the Bible. We may fill our intellect with biblical knowledge, we may have the doctrines of the Bible and the letter of Scripture at our finger-tips without one particle of unction or spiritual power. We must go to Scripture as a thirsty man goes to a well; as a hungry man goes to a meal; as a mariner goes to a chart. We must go to it because we cannot do without it. We go, not merely to study, but to feed. The instincts of the divine nature lead us to the Word of God as the newborn babe desires the milk by which he is to grow. It is by feeding on the Word that the new man grows.

Hence we may see how very real and practical is this question of how to study Scripture. It is intimately connected with our entire moral and spiritual condition, our daily walk, our actual habits and ways. God has given us His Word to form our character, to govern our conduct and shape our course. Therefore, if the Word has not a formative influence and a governing power over us, it is the height of folly to think of storing up a quantity of scriptural knowledge in the intellect. It can only puff us up and deceive us. It is a most dangerous thing to traffic in unfelt truth; it brings on a heartless indifference, levity of spirit, insensibility of conscience, which is appalling to people of serious piety. There is nothing that tends so to throw us completely into the hands of the enemy as a quantity of head knowledge of truth without a tender conscience, a true heart, an upright mind. The mere profession of truth which does not act on the conscience and come out in the life, is one of the special dangers of the day in which our lot is cast. Better by far only to know a little in reality and power, than profess a quantity of truth that lies powerless in the region of the understanding, exerting no formative influence upon the life. I would much rather be honestly in Romans 7 than fictitiously in chapter 8. In the former case I am sure to come right, but in the latter there is no telling what I may come to.

As to the question of making use of human writings to help us in the study of Scripture, great caution is needed. No doubt the Lord may and does make use of the writings of His servants, just as He uses their oral ministry for our instruction and edification. Indeed, in the present broken and divided state of the Church, it is wonderful to mark the Lord's rich grace and tender care in feeding His beloved people with the writings of His servants.

But, we repeat, great caution is needed, earnest waiting on the Lord, that we may not abuse so precious a gift, that it may not lead us to trade on borrowed capital. If we are really dependent upon God, He will give us the right thing; He will put the right book into our hands; He will feed us with food suitable for us. Thus we receive it from Himself and hold it in communion with Himself. It is fresh, living, powerful, formative; it tells on the heart and shines in the life; and we grow in grace and in the knowledge of our Lord and Savior Jesus Christ. Precious growth! Would there were more of it!

Finally, we have to remember that Holy Scripture is the voice of God and the written Word is the transcript of the living Word. It is only by the Holy Spirit's teaching we can really understand Scripture, and He reveals its living depths to faith and need. Let us never forget this.

QUESTIONS; AND HOW TO MEET THEM

I have been very much interested of late in looking at the excellent way in which John the Baptist met the various questions which came before him, for there were many questions in his day, as there are in ours.

What I specially refer to now is presented to us in chapters 1 and 3 of John's Gospel. The first question which this dear and honored servant of Christ was called to answer had respect to himself, and of this he makes very short work indeed. "This is the record of John, when the Jews sent priests and Levites from Jerusalem to ask him, Who art thou?"

It is unwelcome to any right-minded person to be asked to speak about himself. So, I doubt not, John found it. He readily told them that he was not the Messiah, that he was not Elijah, that he was not even the prophet. But they wanted a *positive* answer. "They said unto him, Who art thou? that we may give an answer to them that sent us. What sayest thou of thyself?" Little indeed had he to say of himself. "I" had a very small place in John's thoughts. "A voice." Was this all? Yes; this was all. The Spirit in the prophet had spoken; John quotes the words and there he leaves it. Blessed servant! Honored witness! Would we had more of his excellent spirit, more of his method of answering questions!

But these Pharisees were not satisfied. John's self-hiding spirit was entirely beyond them. "They asked him, and said unto him, Why baptizest thou then, if thou be not the Christ, nor Elias, neither the prophet?"

Here again the Baptist makes short work. "John answering them, saying, I baptize with water; but there standeth One among you whom ye know not. He it is who, coming after me, is preferred before me, whose shoe's latchet I am not worthy to unloose."

Thus, as to himself, he was merely a voice. And, as to his work, he baptized with water, and he was only too glad to retire behind that blessed One whose shoe's latchet he felt himself utterly unworthy to unloose.

This is uncommonly fine. I feel assured, my beloved friend, that the lovely spirit displayed by this most illustrious servant of Christ is what you earnestly covet for yourself. And I think I am one with you. I do long to know more and more of this self-hiding – this losing sight of self and its doings, this retiring spirit. Truly it is much needed in this day of egotistical boast and pretension.

Turn with me for a moment to John 3. Here we have another kind of question. It is not now about himself or his work, but about purifying. "There arose a question among some of John's disciples and the Jews about purifying. And they came to John and said unto him, Rabbi, He that was with thee beyond Jordan, to whom thou bearest witness, behold, the same baptizeth and all come to Him."

Now this was a mistake, for "Jesus Himself baptized not, but His disciples." But this is not the point here. What strikes me is John's mode of settling all questions, right or wrong. He finds a perfect solution for all in the presence of his Lord. "John answered and said, A man can receive nothing except it be given him from heaven."

How true! How simple! How perfectly obvious! What a complete settlement of every question! If a man has anything at all, from where did it, where could it, come? Surely only from heaven. What a perfect cure for strife, envy, jealousy and emulation! "Every good gift and every perfect gift is from above, and cometh down from the Father of lights." What a tale this tells of earth. What a record it bears to heaven and to God! Not one atom of good on earth but what comes from heaven. Not an atom of good in man but what comes from God. Why then should anyone boast or be jealous or envious? If all goodness is from above, let there be an end of all strife and let all hearts go up in praise to "the Father of lights."

Thus it was the Baptist met the questions of his day. He let all the questioners know that their questions had little interest for him. And more than that, he let them know where all his interests lay. This blessed servant found all his springs in the Lamb of God, in His precious work, in His glorious Person. The voice of the Bridegroom was enough for him, and having heard that, his joy was full. The question of purifying might be interesting enough in its place, and like all other questions, it had its right and its wrong side, but for John, the Bridegroom's voice was enough. In His presence he found a divine answer to every question, a divine solution for every difficulty. He looked up to heaven and saw every good thing coming from there. He looked into the Bridegroom's face and saw every moral glory centered there. This was enough for him. Why trouble him with questions of any kind – questions about himself or his work, or about purifying? He lived far beyond the region of questions, in the blessed presence of his Lord, and there he found all his heart could ever need.

Now, my much loved friend, it seems to me that you and I would do well to take a leaf out of John's book as regards all this. I need not remind you that in this our day there are questions agitating men's minds. Yes, and some of us are called to account for not expressing ourselves more decidedly on some of these questions. But I believe the devil is doing his utmost to alienate our hearts from Christ and from one another by questions. We ought not to be ignorant of his devices. He does not come openly and say, "I am the devil and I want to divide and scatter you by questions." Yet this is precisely what he is seeking to do.

Now, it matters not whether the question be right or wrong in itself; the devil can make use of a right question just as effectively as of a wrong one, provided he can succeed in raising that question to undue prominence, causing it to come between our souls and Christ, and between us and our brethren. I can understand a difference in judgment on various minor questions. Christians have differed about such for long centuries and they will continue to differ until the end of time. It is human weakness. But when any question is allowed to assume undue prominence, it ceases to be mere human weakness and becomes a wile of Satan. I may have a very decided judgment on any given point, and so may you. But what I long for now is a thorough sinking of all questions and a rejoicing together in hearing the Bridegroom's voice and going on together in the light of His blessed countenance. This will confound the enemy. It will effectively deliver us from prejudice and partiality and from cliques. We shall then measure one another, not by our views of any particular question, but by our appreciation of the Person of Christ and our devotion to His cause.

In a word, my beloved and valued friend, what I long for is that you and I, and all our dear brethren throughout the whole world, may be characterized by a deep-toned, thorough devotion to the name and truth and cause of Christ. I long to cultivate broad sympathies that can take in every true lover of Christ, even though we don't see eye to eye on all minor questions. At best "we know but in part," and we can never expect people to agree with us about questions. But if Christ be our one absorbing object, all other things will assume their right place, their relative value, their proper proportions. "Let us, therefore, as many as be perfect (as many as have Christ for their one object) be thus minded: and if in anything ye be otherwise minded, God shall reveal even this unto you. Nevertheless, whereto we have already attained, let us walk by the same rule (Christ), and mind the same thing" (Christ). The moment anything else but Christ is introduced as a rule to walk by, it is simply the work of the devil. Of this I am as sure as I hold this pen in my hand.

May the Lord keep us all close to Himself, walking together, not in sectarianism, but in true brotherly love, seeking the blessing and prosperity of all who belong to Christ and promoting in every possible way His blessed cause until He come!

EPAPHRODITUS

We want the reader to turn with us to Philippians 2 and study the brief sketch of the interesting character of Epaphroditus. There is great moral beauty in it. We are not told very much about him, but in what we are told, we see a great deal of what is truly lovely and pleasant – much that makes us long for men of the same stamp in this our day. We cannot do better than quote the inspired record concerning him; and may the blessed Spirit apply it to our hearts and lead us to cultivate the same lovely grace which shone so brightly in that dear and honored servant of Christ!

"I supposed it necessary," says the blessed apostle, "to send to you Epaphroditus, my brother and companion in labor, and fellow-soldier, but your messenger and he that ministered to my wants. For he longed after you all and was full of heaviness, because that ye had heard that he had been sick. For indeed he was sick nigh unto death; but God had mercy on him, and not on him only, but on me also, lest I should have sorrow upon sorrow. I sent him therefore the more carefully, that when ye see him again, ye may rejoice, and that I may be the less sorrowful. Receive him therefore in the Lord with all gladness; and hold such in reputation, because for the work of Christ he was nigh unto death, not regarding his life, to supply your lack of service toward me" (Phil. 2:25-30).

Now it is quite possible that some of us, on reading the above, may feel disposed to inquire if Epaphroditus was a great evangelist or teacher or some highly gifted servant of Christ, seeing the inspired apostle bestows upon him so many high and honorable titles, styling him his "brother and companion in labor, and fellow-soldier."

Well, we are not told that he was a great preacher or a great traveler or a profound teacher in the Church of God. All we are told about him in the above touching narrative is that he came forward in a time of real need to supply a missing link, to "fill a gap," as we say. The beloved Philippians had it upon their hearts to send help to the revered and aged apostle Paul in his prison at Rome. He was in need and they longed to supply his need. They loved him, and God had laid it upon their loving hearts to communicate with his necessities. They thought of him, though he was far away from them, and they longed to minister to him of their substance.

How lovely was this! How pleasing to the heart of Christ! Hearken to the glowing terms in which the dear old prisoner speaks of their precious ministry. "But I rejoiced in the Lord greatly, that now at the last your care of me hath flourished again; wherein ye were also careful, but ye lacked opportunity.... Notwithstanding, ye have well done that ye did communicate with my affliction. Now, ye Philippians, know also that in the beginning of the gospel, when I departed from Macedonia, no church communicated with me as concerning giving and receiving, but ye only. For even in Thessalonica ye sent once and again unto my necessity. Not because I desire a gift, but I desire fruit that may abound to your account. But I have all, and abound; I am full, having received of Epaphroditus the things from you, an odor of a sweet smell, a sacrifice acceptable, well pleasing to God" (Phil. 4:10, 14-18).

Here we see the place which Epaphroditus filled in this blessed business. There lay the beloved apostle in his prison at Rome, and there lay the loving offering of the saints at Philippi. But how was it to be conveyed to him? These were not the days of banks checks and post-office money orders. No, nor of railway traveling. It was no easy matter to get from Philippi to Rome in those days. But Epaphroditus, that dear, unpretending, self-surrendering servant of Christ, presented himself to supply the missing link, to do the very thing that was needed and nothing more; to be the channel of communication between the assembly at Philippi and the apostle at Rome. Deep and real as was the apostle's need, precious and seasonable as was the Philippians' gift, yet an instrument was needed to bring them both together, and Epaphroditus offered himself for the work. There was a manifest need and he filled it. He did not aim at doing some great showy thing, something which would make him very prominent and cause his name to be blazed abroad as some wonderful person. Ah! no, Epaphroditus was not one of the pushing, self-confident, extensive class. He was a dear, self-hiding, lowly servant of Christ, one of that class of workmen to whom we are irresistibly attracted. Nothing is more charming than an unpretending, retiring man who is content just to fill the empty niche; to render the needed service, whatever it is; to do the work cut out for him by the Master's hand.

There are some who are not content unless they are at the head and tail of everything. They seem to think that no work can be rightly done unless they have a hand in it. They are not satisfied to supply a missing link. How repulsive are all such! How we retire from them! Self-confident, self-sufficient, ever pushing themselves into prominence. They have never measured themselves in the presence of God, never been broken down before Him, never taken their true place of self-abasement.

Epaphroditus was not of this class at all. He put his life in his hand to serve other people; and when at death's door, instead of being occupied with himself or his ailments, he was thinking of others. "He longed after you all and was full of heaviness" – not because he was sick, but – "because ye had heard that he had been sick." Here was true love. He knew what his beloved brethren at Philippi would be feeling when informed of his serious illness, an illness brought on by his willing-hearted service to them.

All this is morally lovely. It does the heart good to contemplate this exquisite picture. Epaphroditus had evidently studied in the school of Christ. He had sat at the Master's feet and drunk deeply into His spirit. In no other way could he have learned such holy lessons of self-surrender and thoughtful love for others. The world knows nothing of such things; nature cannot teach such lessons. They are altogether heavenly, spiritual, divine. Would that we knew more of them! They are rare among us with all our high profession. There is a most humiliating amount of selfishness in all of us, and it looks so hideous in connection with the name of Jesus. It might agree well enough with Judaism, but its inconsistency with Christianity is terribly glaring.

Notice the very touching manner in which the inspired apostle commends Epaphroditus to the assembly at Philippi. It seems as if he could not make enough of him, to speak after the manner of men. "He longed after you all, and was full of heaviness, because that ye had heard that he had been sick. For indeed he was sick nigh unto death, but God had mercy on him, and not on him only, but on me also, lest I should have sorrow upon sorrow." How deeply affecting! What a tide of divine affection and sympathy rolled in upon that unpretending, self-sacrificing servant of Christ! The whole assembly at Philippi, the blessed apostle and above all, God Himself all engaged in thinking about a man who did not think about himself. Had Epaphroditus been a self-seeker, had he been occupied about himself or his interests, or even his work, his name would never have shone on the page of inspiration. But no; he thought of others, not of himself. Therefore God and His apostle and His Church thought of him.

Thus it will ever be. A man who thinks much of himself saves others the trouble of thinking about him. But the lowly, the humble, the modest, the unpretending, the retiring, the self-emptied, who think of and live for others, who walk in the footsteps of Jesus Christ, these are the persons to be thought of and cared for, loved and honored, as they ever will be by God and His people.

"I sent him therefore the more carefully," says the beloved apostle, "that when ye see him again ye may rejoice, and that I may be the less sorrowful. Receive him therefore in the Lord with all gladness; and hold such in reputation. Because for the work of Christ he was nigh unto death, not regarding his life, to supply your lack of service toward me" (Phil. 2:28-30).

Thus it was with this most dear and honored servant of Christ. He did not regard his life, but laid it at his Master's feet, just to supply the missing link between the church of God at Philippi and the suffering and needy apostle at Rome. Therefore, the apostle calls upon the Church to hold him in reputation, and the honored name of Epaphroditus has been handed down to us by the pen of inspiration, and his precious service has been recorded and the record of it read by untold millions, while the names and the doings of the self-seekers, the self-important, the pretentious of every age and every clime and every condition are sunk – and deservedly so – in eternal oblivion.

SELF-SURRENDER
(PHILIPPIANS 2)

It is delightful to contemplate the moral triumphs of Christianity – the victories which it gains over self and the world, and the marvelous way in which such victories are obtained. The law said, "Thou shalt do this; and thou shalt not do that." But Christianity speaks a totally different language. In it, we see life bestowed as a free gift – life flowing down from a risen and glorified Christ. This is something entirely beyond the range of the law. The language of the law was, "The man that doeth these things shall live in them." Long life in the land was all the law proposed to the man who could keep it. Eternal life in a risen Christ was something utterly unknown and unthought of under the legal system.

But Christianity not only gives eternal life; it gives also an object with which that life can be occupied – a center round which the affections of that life can circulate – a model on which that life can be formed. Thus it gains its mighty moral triumphs. Thus it gains its conquests over a selfish nature and a selfish world. It gives divine life and a divine center; and as the life moves round that center we are taken out of self.

This is the secret of self-surrender. It cannot be reached in any other way. The unconverted man finds his center in self, and hence to tell him not to be selfish is to tell him not to be at all. This holds good even in the matter of mere religiousness. A man will attend to his religion in order, as he thinks, to promote his eternal interest. But this is quite a different thing from finding an object and a center outside himself. Christianity alone can supply these. The gospel of the grace of God is the only thing that can effectively meet man's need and deliver him from the selfishness which belongs to him. The unrenewed man lives for himself. He has no higher object. The life which he possesses is alienated from the life of God. He is away from God. He moves around another center altogether, and until he is born again, until he is renewed, regenerated, born of the Word and Spirit of God, it cannot be otherwise. Self is his object, his center in all things. He may be moral, amiable, religious, benevolent, but until he is converted, he has not done with himself as to the ground of his being or as to the center round which that being revolves.

The foregoing train of thought naturally introduces us to the striking and beautiful illustration of our theme afforded in Philippians 2. In it we

15

have a series of examples of self-surrender, commencing with a divinely perfect One, the Lord Himself.

Before we proceed to gaze upon this exquisite picture, it may be well to enquire what it was that rendered it needful to present such a picture before the Philippian saints. The attentive reader will observe in the course of this most charming epistle, certain delicate touches from the inspired pen, leading to the conclusion that the keen and vigilant eye of the apostle detected a certain root of evil in the bosom of the beloved and cherished assembly gathered at Philippi. To this he addresses himself, not with a sledge-hammer or a long whip, but with a refinement and delicacy far more powerful than either the one or the other. The mightiest moral results are reached by those delicate touches from the hand of God the Holy Spirit.

What was the root to which we have referred? It was not a splitting into sects and parties as at Corinth. It was not a return to the law and ritualism as at Galatia. It was not a hankering after philosophy and the rudiments of the world as at Colosse. What was it then? It was a root of envy and strife. The sprouting of this root is seen distinctly in the collision between those two sisters, "Euodias and Syntyche" (chap. 4:2), but it is glanced at in earlier portions of the epistle, and a divine remedy supplied.

It is a great point with a medical man not only to understand what is wrong with his patient, but also to understand the true remedy. Some physicians are clever in discovering the root of the disease, but they do not so well know what remedy to apply. Others are skilled in the knowledge of medicine, the powers of various drugs, but they do not know how to apply them to individual cases. The divine Physician knows both the disease and its remedy. He knows exactly what is the matter with us and He knows what will do us good. He sees the root of the matter and He applies a radical cure. He does not treat cases superficially. He is perfect in diagnosis. He does not guess at our disease from mere surface-symptoms. His keen eye penetrates at once to the very bottom of the case and His skillful hand applies the true remedy.

Thus it is in the epistle to the Philippians. Those saints held a very large place in the large heart of the apostle. He loved them much, and they loved him. Again and again he speaks in grateful words of their fellowship with him in the gospel from the very first. But all this did not and could not shut his eyes to what was wrong among them. It is said that "love is blind." In one sense, we look upon this saying as a libel upon love. If it were said that "love is superior to faults," it would be nearer the truth. What should anyone give for blind love? Of what use would it be to be loved by one who only loved us because he was ignorant of our blots and blemishes? If it be meant that love will not see our blots, it is blessedly true (Nu. 23:21), but no one would care for a love that was not at once aware of and superior to our failures and infirmities.

Paul loved the saints at Philippi and rejoiced in their love to him, and tasted the fragrant fruit of that love again and again. But then he saw that it was one thing to love and be kind to a distant apostle, and quite another thing to agree among themselves. Doubtless, Euodias and Syntyche both contributed to send a present to Paul, though they were not pulling harmoniously together in the wear and tear of daily life and service. This is no uncommon case. Many sisters and brothers too are ready to contribute of their substance to help some distant servant of Christ, but they do not walk pleasantly together. How is this? There is a lack of self-surrender. This, we may rest assured, is the real secret of much of the "strife and vainglory" so painfully manifest in the very midst of the people of God. It is one thing to walk alone and it is another thing to walk in company with our brethren in the practical recognition of that great truth of the unity of the body and in the remembrance that "we are members one of another."

Christians are not to regard themselves as mere individuals, as isolated atoms, as independent persons. This cannot be, seeing that Scripture declares, "There is one body" and we are members thereof. This is a divine truth – a grand fact – a positive reality. We are not to stand out in lonely individuality. We are living members of a living body, each one having to do with other members with whom we are connected by a bond which no power of earth or hell can sever. In a word, there is a relationship formed by the presence of the Holy Spirit who not only dwells in each individual member, but is the power of the unity of the one body. It is the presence of God the Spirit in the Church that constitutes that Church as the one living body of the living Head.

It is when we are called to walk in the actual acknowledgement of this great truth that there is a demand for self-surrender. If we were merely solitary individuals, treading each in his own self-chosen path, carrying out his own unique thoughts, walking in the sparks of his own kindling, pursuing his own unique line of things, indulging his own will, then indeed a quantity of self might be retained. If Euodias and Syntyche could have walked alone, there would have been no collision – no strife. But they were called to walk together, and here was the demand for self-

17

surrender. And be it ever remembered that Christians are not members of a club, of a sect or of an association; they are members of a body, each connected with all, and all connected by the fact of the indwelling of the Holy Spirit with the risen and glorified Head in heaven.

This is an immense truth, and the practical carrying out of it will cost us not only all we have, but all we are. There is no place in all the universe where self will be so pulled to pieces as in the Assembly of God. And is it not well? Is it not a powerful proof of the divine ground on which that Assembly is gathered? Should we not be glad to have our hateful self thus pulled to pieces? Shall we or ought we run away from those who do it for us? Are we not glad – do we not often pray to get rid of self? And shall we quarrel with those who are God's instruments in answering our prayers? True, they may do the work roughly and clumsily, but never mind that. Whoever helps me to crush and sink self does me a kind turn, however awkwardly he may do it. One thing is certain, no man can ever rob us of that which, after all, is the only thing worth having, namely Christ. This is a precious consolation. Let self go and we shall have the more of Christ. Euodias might lay the blame on Syntyche, and Syntyche on Euodias; the apostle does not raise the question of who was right or who was wrong, but he beseeches both to be "of the same mind in the Lord."

Here lies the divine secret. It is self-surrender. But this must be a real thing. There is no use in talking about sinking self while at the same time, self is fed and patted on the back. We sometimes pray with fervor to be enabled to trample self in the dust, and the very next moment, if anyone seems to cross our path, self is like a porcupine with all its quills up. This will never do. God will have us real. Surely we can say with all our weakness and folly, we want to be real – real in everything and therefore real when we pray for the power of self-surrender. But, most assuredly, there is no place where there is a more urgent demand for this lovely grace than in the bosom of the assembly of God.

We may range through the wide domain of inspiration and not find a more exquisite model of self-surrender than that which is presented to us in the opening lines of Philippians 2. It is impossible for anyone to breathe the holy atmosphere of such a scripture and not be cured of the sore evils of envy and jealousy, strife and vain glory. Let us approach the marvelous picture and, gazing intently upon it, seek to catch its inspiration.

"If there be therefore any consolation in Christ, if any comfort of love, if any fellowship of the Spirit, if any bowels and mercies, fulfill ye my joy that ye be likeminded, having the same love, being of one accord, of one mind. Let nothing be done through strife or vain glory, but in lowliness of mind, let each esteem other better than themselves. Look not every man on his own things, but every man also on the things of others. Let this mind be in you which was also in Christ Jesus, who, being in the form of God, thought it not robbery to be equal with God; but made Himself of no reputation and took upon Him the form of a servant, and was made in the likeness of men: and being found in fashion as a man, He humbled himself and became obedient unto death, even the death of the cross" (vv. 1-8.)

Here then is the divine remedy for envy and jealousy, strife and vain glory – for self-occupation in all its hideous forms. The inspired penman introduces to our hearts the self-emptied, humble, obedient Man, Christ Jesus. Here was One who possessed all power in heaven and earth. Divine majesty and glory belonged to Him. He was God over all, blessed forever. By Him all things were made and by Him they subsist. And yet He appeared in this world as a poor man – a servant – one who had nowhere to lay His head. The foxes and the fowls, the creatures of His formation, were better provided for than He, their Maker. They had a place to rest. He had none. He thought of others, cared for them, labored for them, wept with them, ministered to them, but He never did a thing for Himself. We never find Him taking care to supply Himself with anything. His was a life of perfect self-surrender. He who was everything, made Himself nothing. He stood in perfect contrast to the first Adam who being but a man, thought to make himself like God, and became the serpent's slave. The Lord Jesus, the Most High God, took the very lowest place among men. It is utterly impossible that any man can ever take so low a place as Jesus. The word is, "He made himself of no reputation." He went so low that no one could possibly put Him lower. "He became obedient unto death, even the death of the cross."

Be it observed that the cross is here viewed as the consummation of a life of obedience – the completion of a work of self-surrender. It is what we may call, to use a Levitical term, the burnt-offering aspect of the death of Christ rather than the sin offering. True it is that the self-same act which consummated a life of obedience, also put away sin, but in the passage now before us, sin-bearing is not so much the thought as self-surrender. Jesus gave up all. He laid aside His glory and came down into this poor world. When He came, He shunned all human pomp and grandeur and became a poor man. His parents were poor. They were only able to procure the lowest grade of sacrifice which the law allowed for the poor;

not a bullock, not a lamb, but a pair of turtle doves. Compare Leviticus 15:29 and Luke 2:24. He Himself worked and was known as a carpenter. Nor are we to miss the moral force of this fact by saying that every Jew was brought up to some trade. Our Lord Jesus Christ really took a low place. The very town where He was brought up was a proverb of reproach. He was called "The Nazarene." And it was asked, with a sneer of contempt, "Is not this the carpenter?" He was a root out of a dry ground. He had no form nor comeliness, no beauty in man's eye. He was the despised, neglected, self-emptied, meek and lowly Man from first to last. He gave up all, even to life itself. His self-surrender was complete.

Mark the result. "Wherefore God also hath highly exalted Him and given Him a name which is above every name; that at the name of Jesus every knee should bow, of things in heaven and things in earth and things under the earth; and that every tongue should confess that Jesus Christ is Lord, to the glory of God the Father."

The blessed Lord Jesus took the very lowest place, but God has given Him the very highest. He made Himself nothing, but God has made Him everything. He said, "I am a worm and no man," but God has set Him as Head over all. He went into the very dust of death, but God has placed Him on the throne of the Majesty in the heavens.

What does all this teach us? It teaches us that the way to get up is to go down. This is a grand lesson and one which we very much need to learn. It would effectively deliver us from envy and jealousy, from strife and vain glory, from self-importance and self-occupation. God will assuredly exalt those who, in the spirit and mind of Christ, take the low place. On the other hand, He will as assuredly abase those who seek to be somebody.

Oh! to be nothing! This is true liberty – true happiness – true moral elevation. What intense power of attraction in one who makes nothing of himself! On the other hand, how repulsive is a pushing forward, elbowing, self-exalting spirit! How utterly unworthy of one bearing the name of Him who made Himself of no reputation! It is a fixed truth that ambition cannot possibly live in the presence of One who emptied Himself. *An ambitious Christian is a flagrant contradiction.*

There are other samples of self-surrender presented to us in Philippians 2; inferior to the divine model at which we have been gazing, for in this as in all things else, Jesus must have the pre-eminence. Still, though inferior and imperfect, they are deeply interesting and valuable to us. Look at Paul. See how deeply he had drunk into his Master's spirit of self-surrender. Hear the following words from one who, naturally, would have allowed none to outstrip him in his career of ambition. "Yea," he says, "and if I be poured forth [as a drink offering] upon the sacrifice and service of your faith, I joy and rejoice with you all" (v. 17).

This is uncommonly fine. Paul was ready to be nothing – to be spent – to be poured forth as a drink offering upon the Philippians' sacrifice. It mattered not to him who presented the sacrifice or who performed the service, provided the thing was done. Does not this put some of us to shame? How little do we know of this excellent spirit! How prone we are to attach importance to work if we ourselves have anything to do with it! How little we are able to joy and rejoice with others in *their* sacrifice and service! Our work, our preaching, our writings, have an interest in our view quite different from those of anyone else. In a word, self, self, detestable self, creeps in even in that which seems to be the service of Christ. We are drawn to those who think well of us and of our work, and retire from those who think otherwise. All this needs to be judged. It is unlike Christ and unworthy of those who bear His holy Name. Paul had so learned Christ as to be able to rejoice in the work and service of others as well as in his own; and even where Christ was preached of contention, he could rejoice.

Then look at Paul's son, Timothy. Hearken to the glowing testimony borne to him by the pen of inspiration. "But I trust in the Lord Jesus to send Timotheus shortly unto you, that I also may be of good comfort when I know your state. For I have no man likeminded, who will naturally care for your state. For all seek their own, not the things which are Jesus Christ's. But ye know the proof of him, that as a son with the father, he hath served with me in the gospel" (vv. 19-22).

Here was self-surrender. Timothy naturally cared for the saints; and that, too, at a moment when all sought their own things. And yet, dear as Timothy was to Paul's heart – valuable as such a self-denying servant must have been to him in the work of the gospel, he was willing to part with him for the sake of the Church. Timothy, likewise, was willing to be separated from his invaluable friend and father in the faith in order to ease his anxious mind in reference to the state of the Philippians. This was indeed giving proof of real devotedness and self-surrender. *Timothy did not talk of these things; he practiced them.* He did not make a parade of his doings, but Paul by the Holy Spirit engraved them on a tablet from which they can never be erased. This was infinitely better. Let another praise you and not yourself. Timothy made nothing of himself, but Paul made a great deal of him. This is divine. The sure way to get up is to go down. Such is the law of the heavenly road.

A man who makes much of himself saves others the trouble of doing so. There is no possible use for two persons doing the same thing. Self-importance is a noxious weed nowhere to be found in the entire range of the new creation. It is, alas, often found in the ways of those who profess to belong to that blessed and holy creation, but it is not of heavenly growth. It is of fallen nature – a weed that grows luxuriantly in the soil of this world. The men of this age think it laudable to push and make way for themselves. A bustling, self-important, pretentious style takes with the children of this generation. But our heavenly Master was the direct opposite of all this. He who made the worlds, stooped to wash the disciples' feet (John 13); and if we are like Him, we will do the same. There is nothing more foreign to the thoughts of God, the mind of heaven, the spirit of Jesus, than self-importance and self-occupation. On the other hand, there is nothing that savors so of God, of heaven and of Jesus as self-surrender.

Look once more at our picture in Philippians 2. Examine with special care that figure which occupies a very prominent place. It is Epaphroditus. Who was he? Was he a great preacher – a very eloquent speaker – a pre-eminently gifted brother? We are not told. But this we are told, and told powerfully and touchingly; he was one who exhibited a lovely spirit of self-surrender. This is better than all the gifts and eloquence, power and learning that could possibly be concentrated in any single individual. Epaphroditus was one of that illustrious class who seek to make nothing of themselves. As a consequence the inspired apostle spares no pains to exalt him. See how he writes in detail about the actings of this singularly attractive person. "Yet I supposed it necessary to send unto you Epaphroditus, my brother and companion in labor, and fellow soldier, but your messenger, and he that ministered to my wants."

What a cluster of dignities! What a brilliant array of titles! How little did this dear and unpretentious servant of Christ imagine that he was to have such a monument erected to his memory! But the Lord will never permit the fruits of self-sacrifice to wither, nor the name of the self-emptied to sink into oblivion. Hence it is that the name of one who, otherwise, might never have been heard of, shines on the page of inspiration as the brother, companion and fellow soldier of the great apostle of the Gentiles.

What did this remarkable man do? Did he spend a princely fortune in

the cause of Christ? We are not told, but we are told what is far better –
he spent himself. This is the grand point for us to seize and ponder. It was
not the surrender of his fortune merely, but the surrender of himself. Let
us listen to the record concerning one of the True David's mighty men.
"He longed after you all, and was full of heaviness." Why? Was it because
he was sick? Because of his pains and aches and privations? Nothing of
the sort. Epaphroditus did not belong to the generation of whiners and
complainers. He was thinking of others. "He was full of heaviness,
because that ye had heard that he had been sick." How lovely! He was
occupied with the Philippians and their sorrow about him. The only thing
that affected him in his illness was the thought of how it would affect
them. Perfectly exquisite! This honored servant of Christ had brought
himself to death's door to serve others, and when there, instead of being
occupied about himself and his ailments, he was thinking of the sorrow
of others. "He was sick and nigh unto death: but God had mercy on him;
and not on him only, but on me also, lest I should have sorrow upon sorrow."

Can anything be more morally beautiful than this? It is one of the
rarest pictures ever presented to the human eye. There is Epaphroditus
near to death for the sake of others, but he is full of sorrow about the
Philippians, and the Philippians are full of sorrow about him; Paul is full
of sorrow about both, and God comes and mingles Himself with the
scene and in mercy to all, raises up the loved one from the bed of death.

Then mark the tender care of the blessed apostle. It is like some tender
mother sending her darling son away and committing him with fond
earnestness to the care of some friend. "I sent him therefore the more carefully, that, when ye see him again, ye may rejoice, and that I may be the
less sorrowful. Receive him therefore in the Lord with all gladness; and
hold such in reputation." Why? Was it because of his gifts, his rank or his
wealth? No; but because of his self-surrender. "Because for the work of
Christ he was nigh unto death, not regarding his life, to supply your lack of
service toward me." Oh! dear Christian reader, let us think on these things.
We have introduced you to a picture and we leave you to gaze upon it. The
grouping is divine. There is a moral line running through the entire scene
and linking the figures into one striking group. It is like the anointing of the
true Aaron, and the oil flowing down to the skirts of his garments. We have
the blessed Lord, perfect in His self-surrender, as in all beside; and then we
have Paul, Timothy and Epaphroditus, each in his measure exhibiting the
rare and lovely grace of self-surrender.

RESTORATION
(JOHN 21:1-19)

A careful study of these verses will enable us to trace in them distinct kinds of restoration, namely restoration of conscience, restoration of heart and restoration of position.

The first of these, *restoration of conscience,* is all-important. It would be utterly impossible to over-estimate the value of a sound, clear, uncondemning conscience. A Christian cannot get on if there is a single blot on his conscience. He must walk before God with a pure conscience – a conscience without stain or sting. Precious treasure! May my reader ever possess it.

It is obvious that Peter possessed it in the touching scene "at the sea of Tiberias." Yet he had fallen – shamefully, grievously fallen. He had denied his Lord with an oath, but he was restored. One look from Jesus had broken up the deep fountains of his heart and drawn forth floods of bitter tears. Yet it was not his tears, but the love that drew them forth, which formed the ground of his thorough restoration of conscience. It was the changeless and everlasting love of the heart of Jesus – the divine effectiveness of the blood of Jesus – and the all-prevailing power of the advocacy of Jesus that imparted to Peter's conscience the boldness and liberty so strikingly and beautifully exhibited on the memorable occasion before us.

The risen Savior is seen in these closing chapters of John's Gospel, watching over His poor, foolish, feeble, erring disciples, hovering about their path, presenting Himself in various ways before them – taking occasion from their very necessities to make Himself known in perfect grace to their hearts. Was there a tear to be dried, a difficulty to be solved, a fear to be hushed, a bereaved heart to be soothed, an unbelieving mind to be corrected? Jesus was present in all the fullness and variety of His grace to meet all these things. So also when, under the guidance of the ever-forward Peter, they had gone forth to spend a night in fruitless toil, Jesus had His eye upon them. He knew all about the darkness and the toil and the empty net, and there He was on the shore to kindle a fire and prepare a dinner for them. Yes, the selfsame Jesus who had died on the cross to put away their sins, now stood on the shore to restore them from their wanderings, gather them round Himself and minister to all their need. "Have ye any meat?" developed the fruitlessness of their night's toil. "Come and dine" was the touching expression of the tender thoughtful, all-providing love of the risen Savior.

Let us note the evidences of a thoroughly restored conscience as exhibited by Simon Peter. "Therefore that disciple whom Jesus loved, saith unto Peter, It is the Lord. Now when Simon Peter heard that it was the Lord, he girt his fisher's coat unto him (for he was naked) and did cast himself into the sea." He could not wait for the ships or for his fellow disciples, so eager was he to get to the feet of his risen Lord. He did not say to John or to the others, "You know how shamefully I have fallen, and although I have since then seen the Lord and heard Him speak peace to my soul, yet I think it more becoming in one who has so fallen to keep back. You therefore go first and meet the blessed One and I shall follow after." Rather, he flings himself boldly into the sea as much as to say, "I must be the very first to get to my risen Savior; none has such a claim on Him as poor, stumbling, failing Peter."

Now, here was a perfectly restored conscience – a conscience without a single spot – a conscience basking in the sunlight of unchanging love. Peter's confidence in Christ was unclouded, and this, we may boldly affirm, was pleasing to the heart of Jesus. Love likes to be trusted. Let us always remember this. No one need imagine that he is honoring Jesus by standing afar off on the plea of unworthiness; yet it is very hard for one who has fallen or backslidden to recover his confidence in the love of Christ. Such an one can see clearly that a sinner is welcome to Jesus, no matter how great or many his sins may have been, but then he thinks the case of a backsliding or stumbling Christian is entirely different.

Should these lines be scanned by one who has backslidden or fallen, we would earnestly press upon him the importance of immediately returning to Jesus. "Return, ye backsliding children, and I will heal your backslidings." What is the response to this pathetic appeal? "Behold, we come unto Thee; for Thou art the Lord our God." "If thou wilt return, O Israel, saith the Lord, return unto Me" (Jer. 3:22; 4:1). The love of the heart of Jesus knows no change. We change but He is "the same yesterday, today, and forever," and He delights to be trusted. The confidence of Peter's heart was a rich feast to the heart of Christ. No doubt, it is sad to fall, to err, to backslide, but it is sadder still, when we have done so, to distrust the love of Jesus or His gracious readiness to take us to His bosom again.

Beloved reader, have you fallen? Have you erred? Have you backslidden? Have you lost the sweet sense of divine favor, the happy consciousness of acceptance with God? If so, what are you to do? Simply this, Return! This is God's own special word to the backslider. Return in self-judgment and in the fullest confidence in the boundless, changeless love of the heart of Christ. Do not, we beseech you, keep away in the distance of your own unbelief. Do not measure the heart of Jesus by your own thoughts. Let Him tell you what is in His heart toward you. You have sinned, you have failed, you have turned aside, and now, it may be, you are afraid or ashamed to turn your eyes toward the One whom you have grieved and dishonored. Satan also is suggesting the darkest thoughts, for he would seek to keep you at a chilling distance from that precious Savior who loves you with an everlasting love. But you have only to fix your gaze upon the blood, the advocacy, the heart of Jesus, to get a triumphant answer to all the enemy's terrible suggestions and to all the infidel reasonings of your own heart. Do not, therefore, go on another hour without seeking to get a thorough settlement of the question between your soul and Christ. Remember, "His is an unchanging love, free and faithful, strong as death." Remember also His own words, "Return, ye backsliding children" – "Return to Me." Finally, remember that Jesus loves to be trusted.

Secondly, the *heart* has to be restored as well as the conscience. Let this not be forgotten. It often happens in the history of souls that though the conscience may be perfectly clear as to certain acts which we have done, yet the roots from where those acts have sprung have not been reached. The acts appear on the surface of daily life, but the roots are hidden down deep in the heart, unknown to ourselves and others, but thoroughly exposed to the eye of Him with whom we have to do.

Now, these roots must be reached, exposed and judged before the heart is in a right condition in the sight of God. Look at Abraham. He started on his course with a certain root in his heart, a root of unbelieving reserve in reference to Sarah. This thing led him astray when he went down into Egypt. Although his conscience was restored and he got back to his altar at Bethel, yet the root was not reached for years afterwards in the affair of Abimelech, king of Gerar.

All this is deeply practical and most solemn. It finds its illustration in Peter as well as in Abraham. Mark the exquisitely delicate way in which our blessed Lord proceeds to reach the roots in the heart of His dear and honored servant, Peter. "So when they had dined." Not till then. There was no allusion to the past, nothing that might cause a chill to the heart or bring a cloud over the spirit while a restored conscience was fasting in company with a love that knows no change. This is a fine moral trait. It characterizes the dealings of God with all His saints. The conscience is set at rest in the presence of infinite and everlasting love, before there is the most distant illusion to the roots of things in the heart. When Simon Peter, in the full confidence of a restored conscience, flung himself at the feet of his risen Lord, he was called to listen to that gracious invitation, "Come and dine." But "when they had dined," Jesus took Peter apart to let in upon his soul the light of truth, so that by it he might discern the root from where all his failure had sprung. That root was self-confidence which had led him to place himself above his fellow-disciples and say, "Though all should deny Thee, yet will not I."

This root had to be exposed. Therefore, "When they had dined, Jesus saith to Simon Peter, Simon son of Jonas, lovest thou Me more than these?" This was a pointed and strong question, and it went right to the very bottom of Peter's heart. Three times Peter had denied his Lord and three times his Lord now challenges the heart of Peter, for the roots must be reached if any permanent good is to be done. It will not do merely to have the conscience purged from the effects which have been produced in practical life, there must also be the moral judgment of that which produced them. This is not sufficiently understood and attended to. Hence, again and again the roots spring up and bring forth fruit, and scatter their seed a thousand-fold around us, thus cutting out for us the most bitter and sorrowful work which might all be avoided if the roots of things were thoroughly judged and kept under.

Christian reader, our object in this article is entirely practical. Let us exhort one another to judge our roots, whatever they may be. Do we know our roots? Doubtless, it is very hard to know them. They are deep and many; pride, personal vanity, covetousness, irritability, ambition – these are some of the roots of character, the motive-springs of action, over which a rigid censorship must ever be exercised. We must let nature know that the eye of self-judgment is continually upon it. We have to carry on the struggle without stopping. We may have to lament over occasional failure, but we must maintain the struggle, for *struggle* is the evidence of life. May God the Holy Spirit strengthen us for the ceaseless conflict.

Lastly, we shall close with a brief reference to restoration as bearing upon the soul's position or path. The conscience being thoroughly purged and the heart with its varied roots, judged, there is moral preparedness for our proper path. The perfect love of Jesus had expelled all fear from Peter's conscience; His threefold question had opened up the roots in Peter's heart, and now He says to him, "Verily, verily, I say unto thee, when thou wast young, thou girdest thyself and walkedst whither thou wouldest: but when thou shalt be old, thou shalt stretch forth thy hand and another shall gird thee and carry thee whither thou wouldest not. This spoke He, signifying by what death he should glorify God. And when He had spoken this, He saith unto him, follow Me."

Here we have in two words the path of the servant of Christ. "Follow Me." The Lord had just given Peter the sweetest pledges of His love and confidence. He had, notwithstanding all past failure, entrusted him with the care of all that was dear to His loving heart in this world, even the lambs and sheep of His flock. He had said to him, "If you have affection for Me, feed My lambs, shepherd My sheep," and now, in one brief but comprehensive utterance, He opens before him his proper path. "Follow Me." This is enough. It includes all beside.

If we want to follow Jesus, we must keep the eye continually upon Him; we must mark His footprints and tread therein. Yes, mark them and walk in them; and when tempted like Peter to "turn about" to see what this one or that one has to do, or how he does it, we may hear the correcting words, "What is that to thee? Follow thou Me." This is to be our one grand and all-absorbing business, come what may. A thousand things may arise to distract and hinder. The devil will tempt us to look here and there, to look at this one and that one, to imagine we could do better here than there or there than here, to be occupied with and imitate the work of some fellow-servant. All this is met by those pointed words, "Follow Me."

There is immense danger in the present day of following in the wake of others, of doing certain things *because* others do them, or doing things *as* others do them. All this has to be carefully guarded. It will be sure to come to nothing. What we really want is a broken will – the true spirit of a servant who waits on the Master to know His mind. Service does not consist in doing this or that, or running here and there; it is simply doing the Master's will, whatever that may be. "They serve who stand and wait." It is easier to be busy than to be quiet. When Peter was "young," he went where he would, but when he got "old" he went where he would not. What a contrast between the young, restless, ardent, energetic Peter, going where he would, and the old, matured, subdued, experienced Peter going where he would not. What a mercy to have the will broken! To be able to say from the heart, "*What* Thou wilt, *as* Thou wilt, *where* Thou wilt, *when* Thou wilt." "Not My will, but Thine, O Lord, be done."

"Follow Me." Precious words! May they be engraved on our hearts, beloved reader. Then shall we be steady in our course and effective in our service. We shall not be distracted or unsettled by the thoughts and opinions of men. It may be we will get very few to understand us or sympathize with us – few to approve or appreciate our work. It matters not. The Master knows all about it. Let us only be sure of what He has told us to do, and *do* it. If a master tells one of his servants to go and do a certain thing or occupy a certain post, it is his business to go and do that thing, or occupy that post, no matter what his fellow-servants may think. They may tell him he ought to be somewhere else or to do something else. A proper servant will not listen to them, for he knows his master's mind and has to do his master's work.

Would it were more thus with all the Lord's servants! Would that we all knew more distinctly and carried out more decidedly the Master's will respecting us. Peter had his path and John had his. James had his work and Paul had his. So it was of old, the Gershonite had his work and the Merarite had his; and if one had interfered with the other, the work could not have been done. The Tabernacle was carried forward or set up by each man doing his own proper work. Thus it is in this our day. God has varied workmen in His house and in His vineyard. He has quarrymen, stone-squarers, masons and decorators. Are all quarrymen? Surely not, but each has his work to do, and the building progresses by each one doing his own appointed work. Should a quarryman despise a decorator or a decorator look down with contempt upon a quarryman? Assuredly not. The Master wants them both, and whenever the one interferes with the other, as we so often do, the faithful correcting word falls on the ear, "What is that to thee? Follow thou Me."

DELIVERANCE

When a Christian dies and goes to heaven he is completely delivered from the power of sin. It is manifestly impossible that sin can have any power or authority over a dead man. But it is not so readily seen or admitted that the believer, even now, is as thoroughly delivered from the *power* of sin as though he were dead and gone to heaven. Sin has no more dominion over a Christian than over a man who is actually dead and buried.

We speak of the *power* of sin, not of its presence. Let the reader carefully note this. Regarding the question of sin, there is this material difference between a Christian here and hereafter. Here, he is delivered only from the power of sin; hereafter he will be freed from its presence. In his present condition sin dwells in him, but it is not to reign. By-and-by, it will not even dwell. The reign of sin is over and gone. The reign of grace has begun. "Sin shall not have dominion over you, for ye are not under law, but under grace."

And, be it carefully observed, the apostle is not speaking in Romans 6 of the forgiveness of sins, which he treats in chapter 3. Blessed be God, our sins are all forgiven – blotted out – eternally cancelled. But in chapter 6 the theme is not forgiveness of sins, but complete deliverance from sin as a ruling power or principle.

How do we obtain this immense favor? By death. We have died to sin – died in the death of Christ. Is this true of every believer? Yes, of every believer beneath the canopy of heaven. Is it not a matter of attainment? By no means! It belongs to every child of God, every true believer. It is the common standing of all. Blessed, holy standing! All praise to Him who has earned it for us and brought us into it! We live under the glorious reign of grace – "grace which reigns through righteousness, unto eternal life, by Jesus Christ our Lord."

This liberating truth is little understood by the Lord's people. Very few get beyond the forgiveness of sins, if they even get that far. They do not see their full deliverance from the power of sin. They feel its pressure, and arguing from their painful feeling instead of reckoning themselves to be what God tells them they are, they are plunged into doubt and fear as to their conversion. They are occupied with their own inward self-consciousness instead of with Christ. They are looking at their *state* in order to get peace and comfort, and thus they are and must be miserable. We will never get peace if we seek it in our spiritual state or condition. The way to get peace is to believe that I've died with Christ, was buried with Him, was raised with Him, am justified in Him, accepted in Him. In short that, "As He is so are we in this world" (1 John 4:17).

This is the solid basis of peace. And not only so, but it is the only divine secret of a holy life. We are dead to sin. We are not called to make ourselves dead. We are so in Christ. A monk, a lover of beauty, or an ardent striver after sinless perfection may try to put sin to death by various bodily exercises. What is the inevitable result? Misery! Yes, misery in proportion to the earnestness. How different is Christianity! We start with the blessed knowledge that we are dead to sin, and in the blessed faith of this we count as dead, not the body but its "deeds."

May the reader enter by faith into the power of this full "deliverance!"

THE LAW AND THE GOSPEL
(READ LUKE 10:25-35)

We desire to dwell for a little upon two grand questions which are suggested and answered in our Lord's interview with the lawyer, namely, What is written in the law? What is revealed in the gospel? These questions have only to be named to secure the attention and awaken the interest of every intelligent and thoughtful reader. It is surely most needful to understand the object, nature and range of the law; and in no way can these things be so clearly seen as when examined in contrast with the glorious gospel of God's free grace in Christ. Let us then proceed to enquire,

WHAT IS WRITTEN IN THE LAW?

This question may be very simply answered. The law reveals what man ought to do. This is what is written in the law. We often hear it said that "The law is the transcript of the mind of God." This definition is altogether defective. What idea should we have of God were we to regard "the ten words" uttered on the top of Mount Sinai, mid thunderings and lightnings, blackness, darkness and tempest, as the transcript of His mind? How should we know God if "the ministration of death and condemnation, written and engraven in stones," is the transcript of His mind? May we not, with great justice, inquire of the framers of the above most objectionable definition, "Is there nothing in the mind of God except death and condemnation? Is there nothing in the mind of God except thou shalt and thou shalt not? If there be more than these, then it is a mistake to affirm that "The law is the transcript of the mind of God." If it be said that "The law declares the mind of God as to what man ought to do," we have no objection to offer, for that is what we hold the law to be. But then, let the reader remember that the declaration of what man ought to do and the revelation of what God is, are two totally different things. The former is the law, the latter is the gospel. Both are perfect – divinely perfect – but they stand in vivid contrast; the one is perfect to condemn, the other is perfect to save.

Let us see how this point is unfolded in the scripture before us. "And, behold, a certain lawyer stood up and tempted him, saying, Master, what shall I do to inherit eternal life? He said unto him, what is written in the law? How readest thou? And he answering said, Thou shalt love the Lord thy God with all thy heart, and with all thy soul, and with all thy strength, and with all thy mind; and thy neighbor as thyself. And He said unto him, Thou hast answered right: this do, and thou shalt live."

It in no wise interferes with the teaching of this passage to say that the lawyer stood up with the wicked intention of tempting Christ, or that he could flippantly and unfeelingly repeat what was written in the law. What we have to see is this, that the great law-question, "What must I do?" is here proposed and answered. If a man is to get life by keeping the commandments, he must keep them. There is no mystery about this. It is so plain that the question is, "How readest thou?" A man has only to read Exodus 20 to know his duty toward God and his duty toward his neighbor.

But, then, dear reader, the solemn inquiry is, "Have I done my duty? Have I loved God with all my heart and my neighbor as myself?" Alas! Alas! I have not; far, very far from it. I have proved times without number that I loved many things which are quite contrary to God; that I have indulged in lusts and pleasures which God condemns; that my will is most thoroughly opposed to God's will; that I hate the things which He loves, and love the things which He hates. In a word, it is perfectly manifest that I have not loved God with all my heart, that I have not given Him a single affection of my heart. And as to my neighbor, have I loved him as myself? Have I, at all times and under all circumstances, as carefully sought to promote my neighbor's interests as though they were my own? Have I rejoiced as unfeignedly in his prosperity as in my own? I dare not answer in the affirmative. I have only to bow my head and confess that I have utterly and shamefully failed in my duty both toward God and toward my neighbor. I own it most fully to be my duty to love God with all my heart and my neighbor as myself, but I own as fully that I have done neither the one nor the other.

What then can the law do for me? Curse me and slay me on the spot! Is there no mercy? Not in the law! There is no mercy at Mount Sinai. If a man stands before that fiery mount, the tremendous alternative is duty or damnation. There is no middle ground. "This do, and thou shalt live" is the solemn, conclusive and emphatic language of the law. "The man that doeth these things shall live in them," but on the other hand, "cursed is everyone (without a single exception) that continueth not in all things which are written in the book of the law to do them" (Gal. 3:10). "He that despised Moses' law died without mercy under two or three witnesses" (Heb. 10:28).

The law makes no provision for imperfect obedience, however sincere. It makes no allowance for infirmity. Its one brief, pointed inquiry is, "Have you continued in all things?" If you say No (and who can say otherwise?) it can only curse you. Why? *Because it is perfect.* Were it to pass over a single transgression, it would not be a perfect law. Its very perfection insures the condemnation of the transgressor. "As many as are of works of law (that is, as many as work on the principle, stand on the ground, occupy the platform of works of law) are under the curse," and cannot possibly be anything else. This establishes the point unanswerably. The law can only prove to be a ministration of death and condemnation to the sinner, simply because he is a sinner and "the law is holy, and just, and good." It is no use for a man to say, "I am not looking to the law for life or justification, but merely as a rule and for sanctification." As a rule for what? For the sanctification of what? If you say, "for my old nature," the answer is, so far from being "a rule of life," it is "a ministration of death;" and so far from sanctifying the flesh, it condemns it, root and branch. If, on the other hand, you say it is for the new nature, then is your mistake equally obvious, since the apostle expressly declares that "the law is not made for a righteous man" (1 Tim. 1:9).

This is plain enough for anyone who is content to take the Holy Scriptures as his guide. The law can neither be the ground of life nor the rule of life to a fallen creature; neither can it be the ground of righteousness nor the power of sanctification. "By deeds of law there shall no flesh be justified in his sight: for by the law is the knowledge of sin" (Rom. 3:20). This one passage is conclusive both as to justification and sanctification. No flesh can be justified in God's sight by the law; and as to sanctification, how can I ever become holy by means of that which only shows me my ungodliness? If I measure a short board by a true measure I must prove it short. A true measure cannot make a short board the proper length, it can only show what it is. Just so with the law and the sinner. Again, "The law worketh wrath" (Rom. 4:15). How is this? Because it is pure and I am impure.

The law and the sinner are complete opposites – wholly irreconcilable. I must get a new nature, stand upon new ground, be in the new creation, before I can delight in the law of God. "I delight in the law of God *after the inward man*" (Rom. 7:22). But how do I get this "inward man," this new nature? How do I get into the new creation? Not by works of law of any shape or description, but by faith of Jesus Christ. I become united to Christ in the power of a new and endless life, upon which the law has no claim. I died in Christ. Hence the law has no further demand on me. If a man is in prison for murder and dies there, the law is done with him, inasmuch as the life in which the crime was committed is gone. Thus it is with the sinner who believes in Jesus. God sees him to be dead. His old man is crucified. The sentence of the law has been put into execution upon him in the Person of Christ. Had it been executed upon himself, it would have been death eternal, but having been executed upon Christ, His death is of infinite, divine and eternal effectiveness. Moreover, having the power of eternal life in Himself, He rose, as a Conqueror from the tomb after having met every claim. And wonderful to declare, the believer, having died in Him, now lives in Him forever. Christ is his life; Christ is his righteousness; Christ is his rule of life; Christ is his model; Christ is his hope; Christ is his all and in all (Rom. 6, 7; Gal. 2:20-21; 3, 4; Eph. 2:4-6; Col. 2:10-15).

Some may feel disposed to inquire, "If the law cannot yield life, furnish righteousness or promote sanctification, then for what end was it given?" The apostle anticipates and answers this question. "Wherefore then the law? It was added because of transgression, till the seed should come to whom the promise was made" (Gal. 3:19). We also read, "Moreover, the law entered (or came in by the way, between the promise and the accomplishment) that the offense might abound" (Rom. 5:20). These two passages declare in simplest terms the object of the law. It is not said, "the law entered in order that we might get life, righteousness or sanctification by it," but quite the opposite. It was "because of transgression" and "that the offense might abound." Where is it said in Scripture that the law was given that we might get life, righteousness or sanctification by it? Nowhere. But it is expressly declared that "the law was added because of transgression" and that "it came in by the way that the offense might abound." It is not possible to conceive two objects more diverse.

The legal system speaks of life, righteousness and sanctification by law; the Scripture, on the contrary, speaks of "offense," "transgression" and "wrath." Why? Because we are sinners and the law is holy. It demands strength and we are weak; it demands life in order to keep it, and we are dead; it demands perfection in all things, and we are perfect in nothing; it is holy and just and good, and we are unholy, unjust and bad. Thus it stands between us and the law; and it matters not in the least, regarding the principle of the law, whether we are regenerate or unregenerate, believers or unbelievers, saints or sinners. The law knows nothing of any such distinctions. It is addressed to man in the flesh, in his old-Adam condition, in his old-creation standing. It tells him what he ought to do for God, and inasmuch as he has not done that, it curses him:

it cannot do anything else. It shows him no mercy, but leaves him in the place of death and condemnation.

Thus much as to "what is written in the law." Let us now proceed to inquire in the second place,

WHAT IS IN THE GOSPEL?

This is unfolded with uncommon beauty and power in the touching parable of "the Good Samaritan." The lawyer, like all legalists, "willing to justify himself," sought to ascertain who was his neighbor. In reply, our blessed Lord draws a picture in which is most vividly presented the true condition of every sinner, be he lawyer or else. "A certain man went down from Jerusalem to Jericho and fell among thieves, which stripped him of his raiment and wounded him and departed, leaving him half dead." What a picture of man's career and man's condition! "A certain man" – the writer or the reader of these lines – "went down." How true! Reader, is it not so? Has not your course ever been a downward one? Have you ever, when left to yourself, taken a step upward, a step in the right direction? There is no use in generalizing, in making statements about mankind, the whole human race, Adam's posterity and the like. What we want is to bring the matter home to ourselves and say, each for himself, "I am the 'certain man' of this beautiful parable; it is myself that appears in the foreground of this masterly picture; my course has been a downward one; I have gone down from the innocency of childhood to the folly of youth, and from the folly of youth to the matured wickedness of manhood, and here I am, stripped of every shred in which I might wrap myself; wounded in every region of my moral being; and having the painful consciousness that death has already begun its terrible work in me."

Such is the career, such the condition of every sinner – his career, downward – his condition, death. What is to be done? Can he keep the law? Alas! he is not able to move. Can the "priest" do anything for him? Nothing! He has no sacrifice and no ability to rise and get one. Can the "Levite" not help him? No! He is so polluted with his wounds and bruises that neither Levite nor priest could touch him. In a word, neither law nor ordinances can meet his case. He is utterly ruined. He has destroyed himself. The law has flung him overboard as a defiled, good-for-nothing, condemned thing. It is useless talking to him about the law or asking him will he take it as a means of justification, a rule of life or the power of sanctification. It has cursed, condemned and set him aside altogether, and he has only to cry out from the profound and awful depths of his moral ruin, "O wretched man that I am! Who shall deliver me from the body of this death?"

Now, it is when a man is really brought to this point that he is in a position to see the moral grandeur of the gospel. It is when he has discovered his own guilt, misery and ruin, and also his entire inability to meet the just and holy claims of the law, or profit in any wise by the appliances of the legal system in its most attractive forms, that he is prepared to appreciate the ample provisions of the grace of God.

These facts are most strikingly illustrated in the scene before us. When the poor man had gone down from Jerusalem to Jericho, from the city of God to the city of the curse (Josh. 6:26; 1 Ki. 16:33-34); when he lay stripped, wounded and half-dead; when both priest and Levite had turned from him and gone their way; it was just then that he was in a position to prove the grace of the Good Samaritan who assuredly is none other than the blessed Lord Jesus Himself, blessed forever be His precious name! He appears in the form of a Samaritan only to enhance the grace that breathes forth upon our souls in this lovely scene. "The Jews have no dealings with the Samaritans." Hence, had the Jew in this parable had sufficient strength, he would not, we may safely affirm, have permitted the stranger to touch him. But he was so far gone, so powerless, so under the power of death, that the gracious Samaritan had it all his own way. And what a tender way it was!

"But a certain Samaritan, as he journeyed, came where he was: and when he saw him, he had compassion, and went to him, and bound up his wounds, pouring in oil and wine, and set him on his own beast, and brought him to an inn, and took care of him. And on the morrow when he departed, he took out two pence and gave them to the host and said unto him, Take care of him; and whatsoever thou spendest more, when I come again, I will repay thee."

Here is what is revealed in the gospel. Man has ruined himself. He has gone down from God. He has fallen under the power of the enemy. He is the victim of Satan, the slave of sin, the subject of death. His case is hopeless, so far as he is concerned. But, blessed be God, the true Samaritan has come down into all the ruin. The Son of God left His Father's bosom, His eternal dwelling-place, came down into this world to remedy our ruin, to bear our guilt, to endure the wrath of God in our place. All this He did, beloved reader, as the expression of His own tender compassion and love. "He had compassion" and came to bind up our wounds, to pour

37

"the wine and oil" of His own most precious grace into our souls, to heal, restore and bless us, to put us into His own position according to the power which had brought Him into ours, to make ample provision for all our need until that bright and happy moment when we shall be ushered into His presence to go no more out forever.

The page of inspiration does not present a more touching picture than that which the Master's pen has drawn for us in "The Good Samaritan." It is perfectly beautiful and beautifully perfect. It is divine. Every expression is filled with exquisite moral loveliness. "He came where he was" – not half-way or nine-tenths of the way, but all the way. "And when he saw him," what then? Did he turn away in disgust at his appearance and despair of his condition? Ah! no; "He had compassion on him." His tender heart yearned over him. He cared not what he was or who he was. Jew or Gentile, it mattered not; the streams of tender compassion came gushing up from the deep fountains of a heart that found its own delight in ministering to every form of human need. Was this "compassion" a mere movement of sentimentality – a momentary feeling uttering itself in empty words and then passing away? No; it was a real, living, acting thing, expressing itself in the most unmistakable manner. "He went to him." For what? To meet his every need and not to leave him until he had placed him in a position of security, rest and blessing.

Nor was this all. Not only did this gracious stranger fully meet the wounded one's present need, but before leaving, he spoke these touching words, "Take care of him." How this must have melted the poor man's heart. Such kindness! And all from a stranger, from one with whom he would naturally have "no friendly dealings."

Finally, as if to complete the picture, he says, "when I come again." He awakens in the heart by these last words, "the blessed hope" of seeing him again. What a lovely picture! And yet it is all a divine reality. It is the simple story of our blessed Jesus who, in His tender compassion, looked upon us in our low and utterly hopeless condition, left His eternal dwelling-place of light and love, took upon Himself the likeness of sinful flesh, was made of a woman, made under the law, lived a spotless life, and fulfilled a perfect ministry down here for 33 years, and finally died on the cross as a perfect atonement for sin so that God might be just and the Justifier of any poor, ungodly, convicted sinner that simply trusts in Jesus.

Yes, dear reader, whoever you are, high or low, rich or poor, learned or unlearned, Jesus has done all this; and He is now at the right hand of the

Majesty in the heavens. The One who was nailed to the cross for us, is now on the throne. Eternal Justice has wreathed His sacred brow with the wreath of victory, and that, be it remembered, on our behalf. Nor is this all. He has said, "I will come again." Precious words! Would *you* be glad to see Him? Do you know Him as the Good Samaritan? Have you felt His loving hand binding up your spiritual wounds? Have you known the healing virtues of His oil, and the restoring, invigorating, and cheering influence of His wine! Have you heard Him speak the thrilling words, "Take care of him?" If so, then, surely, you will be glad to see His face: you will cherish in your heart's tender affections the blessed hope of seeing Him as He is and of being like Him and with Him forever. The Lord grant it may be so with you, beloved reader, and then you will be able to appreciate the immense difference between the law and the gospel – between what we ought to do for God and what God has done for us – between what we are to Him and what He is to us – between "do and live" and "live and do" – between "the righteousness of the law" and "the righteousness of faith."

May the blessing of the Father, of the Son and of the Holy Spirit rest upon the reader of these lines, now, henceforth and forevermore!

DEAD TO THE LAW

"For I through law, am dead to law, that I might live to God" (Gal. 2:19). This is a weighty word and much needed just now. The spiritual apprehension of the truth set forth will preserve the soul from two errors which are very common in the professing Church – legality on the one hand and licentiousness on the other. Were we to compare these two evils, were we compelled to choose between them, we would undoubtedly prefer the former. We would much rather see a man under the authority of the law of Moses than one living in lawlessness and self-indulgence. Of course, we know that neither is right and that Christianity gives us something quite different, but we have much more respect for a man who, seeing nothing beyond Moses and regarding the law of Moses as the only divine standard by which his conduct is to be regulated, bows down in a spirit of reverence to its authority, than for one who seeks to get rid of that law so he may please himself. Thank God, the truth of the gospel gives us the divine remedy for both cases. But how? Does it teach us that the law is dead? No! What then? It teaches that the *believer* is dead. "I through law am dead to law." And to what end? That I may please myself? That I may seek my own profit and pleasure? By no means, but "that I may live to God."

Here lies the grand and all-important truth – a truth lying at the very base of the entire Christian system, and without which we can have no just sense of what Christianity is at all. So in Romans 7 we read, "Wherefore, my brethren, ye also have become dead to the law (not the law is dead) by the body of Christ, in order that ye may be to another (not to yourselves, but) even to Him that was raised from the dead, that ye might bring forth fruit unto God" (v. 4). Again, "But now ye are delivered from the law, being dead to that wherein ye were held, that ye might serve in newness of spirit and not in oldness of letter" (v. 6).* Mark, it is that we may serve, not that we may please ourselves. We have been delivered from the intolerable yoke of Moses that we may wear the "easy yoke of Christ," not that we may give a loose run to nature.

---

* The marginal reading of verse 6 is doubtless the correct one. It is well to note this, as also the difference between the way in which the apostle uses the illustration. It is the husband who dies, but in the application, it is the believer, not the law. Not seeing this had led many into the error of teaching that the law is dead, whereas in 1 Timothy 1:8, the apostle expressly declares, not that the law is dead, but the very reverse; "We know that the law is good, if a man use it lawfully." And how is it to be used lawfully? "Knowing this, that the law is not made for a righteous man, but for the lawless." It is of the utmost importance that the reader should be clear as to this.

There is something shocking to a serious mind in the thought of men appealing to certain principles of the gospel to establish a plea for the indulgence of the flesh. They want to fling aside the authority of Moses, not that they may enjoy the authority of Christ, but merely to indulge self. But it is vain. It cannot be done with any shadow of truth, for it is never said in Scripture that the law is dead or abrogated, but it is said – and urged repeatedly – that the believer is dead to the law and dead to sin so he may taste the sweetness of living unto God, of having his fruit unto holiness, and the end everlasting life.

We earnestly commend this weighty subject to the attention of the reader. He will find it fully unfolded in Romans 4 and 5, Galatians 3 and 4. A right understanding of it will solve a thousand difficulties and answer a thousand questions, and deliver the soul from a vast mass of error and confusion. May God give His own Word power over the heart and conscience!

GRACE AND HOLINESS

Thank God we are under grace. But does this blessed fact weaken in any way the truth that "Holiness becometh God's house forever?" Has it ceased to be true that "God is greatly to be feared in the assembly of his saints; and to be held in reverence of all those who are about Him?" Is the standard of holiness lower for the Church of God now than it was for Israel of old? Has it ceased to be true that "our God is a consuming fire?" Is evil to be tolerated because "we are not under law, but under grace?" Why were many of the Corinthians weak and sickly? Why did many of them die? Why were Ananias and Sapphira struck dead in a moment? Did that solemn judgment touch the truth that the Church was under grace? Assuredly not. But neither did grace hinder the action of judgment. God can no more tolerate evil in His assembly now, than He could in the days of Achan.

You say, "We must not draw comparisons between God's dealings with His earthly people and His dealings with His Church." What is the meaning of the following words in 1 Corinthians 10? "Moreover, brethren, I would not that ye should be ignorant, how that all our fathers were under the cloud, and all passed through the sea; and were all baptized unto Moses in the cloud and in the sea; and did all eat the same spiritual meat; and did all drink the same spiritual drink; for they drank of that spiritual Rock that followed them; and that Rock was Christ. But with many of them God was not pleased; for they were overthrown in the wilderness. Now these things were our examples, to the intent we should not lust after evil things as they also lusted.... Now all these things happened unto them for examples; and they are written for our admonition, upon whom the ends of the world are come."

Is not this drawing a comparison between God's dealings with His earthly people and His Church now? Yes indeed; and well will it be for us all to ponder and be admonished by the comparison. It would be sad indeed if we were to plead from the pure and precious grace in which we stand to lower the standard of holiness. We are called to purge out the old leaven on the blessed ground that "Christ our passover is sacrificed for us." Is not this "drawing a comparison?" The assembly at Corinth was commanded – woe be unto them if they had refused – to put away from among them the wicked person, to deliver him to Satan for the destruction of the flesh.

True, they were not called to stone him or to burn him; and here we have a contrast rather than a comparison. But they had to put him out from among them if they would have the divine presence in their midst. "Thy testimonies are very sure; holiness becometh Thy house, O Lord, *forever*." Can you not praise Him for the holiness as well as the grace? Can you not, as the standard of holiness rises before you, add your doxology, "Blessed be His name forever and ever! Amen and amen?" We trust you can.

We must never forget that, while we stand in grace, we are to walk in holiness; and as regards the assembly, if we refuse to judge bad doctrine and bad morals, we are not on the ground of the Assembly of God at all. People say we must not judge; God says we must. "Do not ye judge them that are *within*? But them that are *without* God judgeth. Therefore put away from among yourselves that wicked person." If the assembly at Corinth had refused to judge that wicked person, it would have forfeited all title to be regarded as the assembly of God, and all who feared the Lord would have had to leave it. It is a very solemn matter indeed to take the ground of the Assembly of God. All who do so have to bear in mind that it is not at all a question of whom we can receive or what we can tolerate, but what is worthy of God? We hear a great deal now-a-days about the "broad" and the "narrow;" *we have just to be as broad and as narrow as the Word of God.*

ISOLATION

It is one of our great difficulties at the present moment – indeed it has ever been a difficulty – *to combine a narrow path with a wide heart.* There is very much on all sides tending to produce isolation. We cannot deny it. Links of human friendship seem so fragile; so many things crop up to shake confidence; so many things which one cannot possibly sanction, that the path becomes more and more isolated.

All this is unquestionably true. But we must be very careful as to how we meet this condition of things. We have little idea how much depends on the spirit in which we carry ourselves in the midst of scenes and circumstances which, all must admit, are uniquely trying.

For example, I may retreat in upon myself and become bitter, gloomy, severe, repulsive, withered up, having no heart for the Lord's people, for His service, for the holy and happy exercises of the assembly. I may become barren of good works, having no sympathy with the poor, the sick, the sorrowful. I may live in the narrow circle in which I have withdrawn, thinking only of myself and my personal and family interests.

What can be more miserable than this? It is the most deplorable selfishness, but we do not see it because we are blinded by our inordinate occupation with other people's failures.

Now it is a very easy matter to find flaws and faults in our brethren and friends. But the question is, How are we to meet these things? Is it by retreating in upon ourselves? Never! To do this is to render ourselves as miserable in ourselves as we are worthless, and worse than worthless, to others. There are few things more pitiable than what we call "a disappointed man." He is always finding fault with others. He has never discovered the real root of the matter or the true secret of dealing with it. He has retired, but within himself. He is isolated, but his isolation is utterly false. He is miserable; and he will make all who come under his influence – all who are weak and foolish enough to listen to him – as miserable as himself. He has completely broken down in his practical career; he has succumbed to the difficulties of his time and proved himself wholly unequal to meet the stern realities of actual life. Then, instead of seeing and confessing this, he retires into his own narrow circle and finds fault with everyone except himself.

How truly delightful and refreshing to turn from this dismal picture to the only perfect Man who ever trod this earth! His path was indeed an isolated one – none more so. He had no sympathy with the scene around Him. "The world knew Him not." "He came unto His own [Israel], and His own received Him not." "He looked for some to take pity, but there was none; and for comforters, but He found none." Even His own beloved disciples failed to sympathize with, or understand Him. They slept on the mount of transfiguration in the presence of His glory and they slept in the Garden of Gethsemane in the presence of His agony. They roused Him out of His sleep with their unbelieving fears and were continually intruding upon Him with their ignorant questions and foolish notions.

How did He meet all this? In perfect grace, patience and tenderness. He answered their questions; He corrected their notions; He hushed their fears; He solved their difficulties; He met their need; He made allowance for their infirmities; He gave them credit for devotedness in the moment of desertion; He looked at them through His own loving eyes and loved them, notwithstanding all. "Having loved His own which were in the world, He loved them unto the end."

Christian reader, let us seek to drink into our blessed Master's spirit and walk in His footsteps. Then our isolation will be of the right kind, and though our path may be narrow, the heart will be large.

A WORKMAN'S MOTTO

"Therefore, my beloved brethren, be ye steadfast, immovable, always abounding in the work of the Lord, forasmuch as ye know that your labor is not in vain in the Lord" (1 Cor. 15:58).

Here we have an uncommonly fine motto for the Christian workman, and every Christian ought to be a workman. It presents a most valuable balance for the heart. We have immovable stability linked with unceasing activity.

This is of the utmost importance. There are some of us who are such sticklers for what we call *principle* that we seem almost afraid to embark in any scheme of large-hearted Christian activity. On the other hand, some of us are so bent on what we call *service* that in order to reach desired ends and realize noticeable results, we do not hesitate to overstep the boundary line of sound principle.

Now, our motto supplies a divine antidote for both these evils. It furnishes a solid basis on which we are to stand with steadfast purpose and immovable decision. We are not to be moved the breadth of a hair from the narrow path of divine truth, though tempted to do so by the most forcible argument of a plausible expediency. "To obey is better than sacrifice; and to hearken, than the fat of rams."

Noble words! May they be engraved in characters deep and broad on every workman's heart. They are absolutely invaluable, and particularly so in this our day when there is such willfulness in our mode of working, such erratic schemes of service, such self-pleasing, such a strong tendency to do that which is right in our own eyes, such a practical ignoring of the supreme authority of Holy Scripture.

It fills the thoughtful observer of the present condition of things with the very gravest apprehensions as he sees the positive and deliberate throwing aside of the Word of God, even by those who professedly admit it to be the Word of God. We are not speaking of the insolence of open and avowed infidelity, but of the heartless indifference of respectable orthodoxy. There are millions who profess to believe the Bible is the Word of God, who, nevertheless, do not have the smallest idea of submitting themselves absolutely to its authority. The human will is dominant. Human reason bears sway. Expediency commands the heart. The holy principles of divine revelation are swept away like autumn leaves or the dust of the threshing-floor before the vehement blast of popular opinion.

How immensely valuable and important in view of all this, is the first part of our workman's motto! "Therefore, my beloved brethren, be ye steadfast and immovable." The "therefore" throws the soul back upon the solid foundation laid in the previous part of the chapter in which the apostle unfolds the most sublime and precious truth that can possibly engage the Christian's heart – truth which lifts the soul completely above the dark and chilling mists of the old creation and plants it on the solid rock of resurrection. It is on this rock we are exhorted to be steadfast and immovable. It is not an obstinate adherence to our own notions – to some favorite dogma or theory which we have adopted – or to any special school of doctrine. It is not anything of this kind, but a firm grasp and faithful confession of the whole truth of God of which a risen Christ is the everlasting Center.

But we have to remember the other side of our motto. The Christian workman has something more to do than to stand firmly on the ground of truth. He has to cultivate the lovely activities of grace. He is called to be "always abounding in the work of the Lord." *The basis of sound principle must never be abandoned, but the work of the Lord must be diligently carried on.* There are some who are so afraid of doing mischief that they do nothing; and others, who rather than not be doing something, will do wrong. Our motto corrects both. It teaches us to set our faces as a flint where truth is involved; while on the other hand, it leads us to go forth in largeness of heart and throw all our energies into the work of the Lord.

Let the Christian reader specially note the expression, "The work of the Lord." We are not to imagine for a moment that all which engages the energies of professing Christians is entitled to be designated "the work of the Lord." It is far from it! We see a mass of things undertaken as service for the Lord with which a spiritual person could not possibly connect the holy name of Christ. We desire to have the conscience exercised as to the work in which we embark. We deeply feel how needful it is in this day of willfulness, laxity and wild liberalism, to own the authority of Christ in all that we put our hands to, in the way of work or service. Blessed be His name, He permits us to connect Him with the most trivial and commonplace activities of daily life. We can even eat and drink in His holy name and to His glory. The sphere of service is wide enough; it is only limited by that weighty clause, "The work of the Lord." The Christian workman must not engage in any work which does not place itself under that most holy and all-important heading. He must, before he enters upon any service, ask himself this great practical question, "Can this honestly be called the work of the Lord?"

AUTHORITY AND POWER

If ever there was a moment in the history of the professing Church in which it was vital for people to have divine authority for their path and divine power to pursue it, this is the moment. There are so many conflicting opinions, so many jarring voices, so many opposing schools, so many contending parties, that we are in danger at all points of losing our balance and being carried we know not where. We find the very best of men ranged on opposite sides of the same question – men who seem to have a single eye to the glory of Christ and who take the Word of God as their sole authority in all things.

What is an unlearned soul to do? How is one to get on in the face of all this? Is there no peaceful haven in which to anchor one's tiny boat, away from the wild tossing of the stormy ocean of human opinion? Yes, blessed be God, there is; and the reader may know the deep blessedness of casting anchor there this very moment. *It is the sweet privilege of the very simplest child of God, the merest babe in Christ, to have divine authority for his path and divine power to pursue it – authority for his position and power to occupy it – authority for his work and power to do it.*

What is it? Where is it? The authority is found in the divine Word; the power is found in the divine presence. Each and all may know it – ought to know it for the stability of their path and the joy of their heart.

In contemplating the present condition of professing Christians generally, one is struck with this very painful fact, that so very few are prepared to face Scripture on all points and in all matters, personal, domestic, commercial and ecclesiastical. If the question of the soul's salvation be settled – and alas! how rarely it is settled – then people consider themselves at liberty to break away from the sacred domain of Scripture and launch forth upon the wild watery waste of human opinion and human will where each one may think for himself, choose for himself and act for himself.

Now, nothing is more certain than this, that where it is merely a question of human opinion, human will or human judgment, there is not a shadow of authority – not a particle of power. No human opinion has any authority over the conscience, nor can it impart any power to the soul. It may have some worth, but it has neither authority nor power for me. I must have God's Word and God's presence, else I cannot move forward. If anything, no matter what, comes between my conscience and the Word of God, I do not know where I am, what to do or where to turn. And if anything, no matter what, comes between my heart and the presence of God, I am perfectly powerless. The Word of my Lord is my only guide; His dwelling in me and with me, my only power. "Have not I commanded thee? Lo, I am with thee."

The reader may ask, "Is it really true that the Word of God contains ample guidance for all the details of life? Does it tell me, for instance, where I am to go on the Lord's day and what I am to do from Monday morning till Saturday night? Does it direct me in my personal path, in my domestic relationships, in my business position, in my religious associations and opinions?"

Most assuredly. The Word of God furnishes you thoroughly for all good works, and any work for which it does not furnish you is not good but bad. Hence, if you cannot find authority for where you go on Lord's day – no matter where it is – you must at once give up going. And if you cannot find authority for what you do on Monday, you must at once cease to do it. "To obey is better than sacrifice; and to hearken, than the fat of rams." Let us honestly face Scripture. Let us bow down to its holy authority in all things. Let us humbly and reverently yield ourselves to its heavenly guidance. Let us give up every habit, every practice, every association, be it what it may, or be it sanctioned by whom it may, for which we do not have the direct authority of God's Word and in which we cannot enjoy the sense of His presence.

This is a point of the gravest importance. Indeed, it would be impossible for human language to set forth with due force or in adequate terms, the importance of absolute and complete submission to the authority of Scripture in *all* things.

One of our greatest practical difficulties in dealing with souls arises from the fact that they do not seem to have any idea of submitting in all things to Scripture. They will not face the Word of God or consent to be taught exclusively from its sacred pages. Creeds and confessions, religious formularies, the commandments, the doctrines, the traditions of men – these things will be heard and yielded to. Our own will, our own judgment, our own views of things will be allowed to bear sway. Expediency, position, reputation, personal influence, usefulness, the opinion of friends, the thoughts and example of good and great men, the fear of grieving or giving offense to those whom we love and esteem and with whom we may have been long associated in our religious life and service; the dread of being thought presumptuous, intense shrinking from the appearance of judging or condemning many at whose feet we would willingly sit – all these things operate and exert a most harmful influence upon the soul and hinder full surrender of ourselves to the paramount authority of God's Word.

May the Lord graciously stir up our hearts in reference to this weighty subject! May He lead us by His Holy Spirit to see the true place and the real value and power of His Word! May that Word be set up in our souls as the one all-sufficient rule so that everything, no matter what, may be unhesitatingly and utterly rejected that is not based upon its authority. Then we may expect to make progress. Then will our path be as the path of the just, like a shining light that shines more and more unto the perfect day. May we never rest satisfied until, in reference to all our habits, all our ways, all our associations, our religious position and service, all we do and all we do not do, where we go and where we do not go, we can truly say we have the sanction of God's Word and the light of His presence. Here and here alone lies the deep and precious secret of *Authority and Power.*

OBEDIENCE AND DEPENDENCE

We saw in the previous article that our God has, in His infinite mercy, provided for His people in this dark and evil world both authority and power – the authority of His Word and the power of His Spirit – for the path which they are called to tread and the work they are called to do. We have ample guidance in the Word, and we have the power of God to count upon for all the difficulties and demands of the scene through which we have to pass home to our eternal rest above. We have authority and power for all.

But we must remember that if God has furnished us with authority, we must be obedient. And if He has provided the power, we must be dependent. Of what use is authority if we do not obey it? I may give my employee the plainest and fullest directions as to where he is to go, what he is to do and what he is to say, but if, instead of acting simply upon my directions, he begins to reason and think and draw conclusions, to use his own judgment and act according to his own will, of what use are my directions? None whatever, except to show how entirely he has departed from them. Clearly, the business of an employee, of a servant, is to obey, not to reason – to act according to his master's directions, not according to his own will or judgment. If he only does exactly what his master tells him, he is not responsible for the consequences.

The one grand business of a servant is to obey. This is the moral perfection of a servant. Alas! how rare! There has been only one absolutely obedient and perfectly dependent servant in the entire history of this world – the man Christ Jesus. His food and His drink were to obey. He found His joy in obedience. "Sacrifice and offering Thou didst not desire; Mine ears hast Thou opened: burnt-offering and sin-offering hast Thou not required. Then said I, Lo, I come: in the volume of the book it is written of Me, I delight to do Thy will, O My God: yea, Thy law is within My heart" (Ps. 40:6-8).

Our blessed Lord Jesus found the will of God to be His only motive for action. There was nothing in Him that needed to be restrained by the authority of God. His will was perfect and His every movement was of necessity – the very necessity of His perfect nature – in the current of the divine will. "Thy law is within My heart," "I delight to do Thy will," "I came down from heaven, not to do Mine own will, but the will of Him that sent Me."

Now, what could Satan do with such a Man as this? Absolutely nothing. He tried to withdraw Him from the path of obedience and the place of dependence, but in vain. "If Thou be the Son of God, command these stones to be made bread." Surely God would give His Son bread. No doubt, but the perfect Man refuses to make bread for Himself. He had no command, no authority, and therefore no motive for action. "It is written, Man shall not live by bread alone, but by every word that proceedeth out of the mouth of the Lord." So throughout the entire temptation. Nothing could withdraw the blessed One from the path of simple obedience. "It is written" was His one unvarying answer. He would not, could not act without a motive, and His only motive was found in the will of God. "I delight to do Thy will, O My God; yea, Thy law is within My heart."

Such was the obedience of Jesus Christ – an obedience perfect from first to last. And not only was He perfectly obedient, but perfectly dependent. Though God over all, blessed forever, yet, having taken His place as a Man in this world, He lived a life of perfect dependence on God. He could say, "I clothe the heavens with blackness, and I make sackcloth their covering. The Lord God hath given Me the tongue of the learned, that I should know how to speak a word in season to him that is weary: He wakeneth morning by morning, He wakeneth Mine ear to hear as the learned. The Lord God hath opened Mine ear and I was not rebellious, neither turned away back. I gave My back to the smiters and My cheeks to them that plucked off the hair: I hid not My face from shame and spitting. For the Lord God will help Me; therefore shall I not be confounded: therefore have I set My face like a flint, and I know that I shall not be ashamed" (Isa. 50.) And again, "Preserve Me, O God, for in Thee do I put My trust." And again, "I was cast upon Thee from the womb." He was wholly and continually cast upon God from the manger of Bethlehem to the cross of Calvary; and when He had finished all, He surrendered His spirit into the Father's hand and His flesh rested in hope. His obedience and dependence were divinely perfect throughout.

We must now ask the reader to turn with us to two examples of the very opposite of all this – two cases in the which, through lack of obedience and dependence, the most disastrous results followed. Let us first turn to 1 Kings 13. Doubtless, the case is familiar to us, but let us look at it in connection with our present theme.

"And, behold, there came a man of God out of Judah by the word of the Lord, unto Bethel: and Jeroboam stood by the altar to burn incense. And he cried against the altar in the word of the Lord." Thus far all was right. He spoke by the Word of God and the power of God accompanied the testimony. The spirit of the king was humbled and subdued for the moment.

More than this, the man of God was enabled to refuse the king's invitation to come home with him and refresh himself and receive a reward. "And the man of God said unto the king, If thou wilt give me half thine house, I will not go in with thee, neither will I eat bread nor drink water in this place. For so it was charged me by the word of the Lord, saying, Eat no bread nor drink water, nor turn again by the same way that thou camest."

All this was lovely – perfectly delightful to dwell upon. The feet of the man of God stand firm in the bright and blessed path of obedience, and all is victory. The offers of the king are flung aside without a moment's hesitation. Half the royal house cannot tempt him off the narrow, holy, happy path of obedience. He rejects every overture and turns to pursue the straight path opened before him by the word of the Lord. There is no reasoning, no questioning, no hesitation. The word of the Lord settles everything. He has but to obey, regardless of consequences. And so far he does, and all is well.

But mark the sequel. "Now there dwelt an old prophet in Bethel." Beware of old prophets! This old prophet followed the man of God and said unto him, "Come home with me and eat bread." This was the devil in a new shape. What the word of a king had failed to do, the word of a prophet might accomplish. It was a wile of Satan for which the man of God was evidently unprepared. The garb of a prophet deceived him and threw him completely off his guard: we can at once perceive his altered tone. When replying to the king he speaks with vividness, force and bold decision: "If thou wilt give me half thine house, I will not go in with thee." And then he adds, with equal force, his reason for refusing: "For so was it charged me by the word of the Lord."

But in his reply to the prophet, there is manifest decline in the way of energy, boldness and decision. He says, "I may not return with thee nor go in with thee." And in assigning the reason, instead of the forcible word "charged," we have the feeble expression, "It was said to me."

In short, the whole tone is lower. The Word of God was losing its true place and power in his soul. That Word had not changed. "For ever, O Lord, Thy Word is settled in heaven", and had that Word been hidden in the heart of the man of God, had it been dwelling richly in his soul, his answer to the prophet would have been as distinct and decided as his answer to the king. "By words of Thy lips, I have kept me from the paths of the destroyer." The spirit of obedience is the great moral safeguard against every scheme and every snare of the enemy. The enemy may shift his ground, he may change his tactics, he may vary his agency, but obedience to the plain and simple Word of God preserves the soul from all his wicked schemes and crafty devices. The devil can do nothing with a man who is absolutely ruled by the Word of God and refuses to move the breadth of a hair without divine authority.

Note how the enemy urges his point with the man of God. "He said unto him, I am a prophet also as thou art: and an angel spoke unto me by the Word of the Lord, saying, Bring him back with thee into thine house."

What should the man of God have said to this? If the Word of his Lord had been abiding in him, he would at once have said, "If ten thousand prophets and ten thousand angels were to say, bring him back, I should regard them all as liars and emissaries of the devil sent forth to allure me from the holy, happy path of obedience." This would have been a wonderful reply. It would have the same heavenly ring about it as exhibited in these glowing words of the apostle: "Though we, or an angel from heaven, preach any other gospel unto you than that which we have preached, let him be anathema."

But, alas! the man of God stepped off the path of obedience. Then the very man whom Satan had used to draw him off, became the mouthpiece of Jehovah to announce in his ears the terrible consequence. He lied when Satan used him. He spoke truth when God used him. The erring man of God was slain by a lion because he disobeyed the word of the Lord. Yes; he stepped off the narrow path of obedience into the wide field of his own will, and there he was slain.

Reader, let us beware of old prophets and angels of light! Let us, in the true spirit of obedience, keep very close to the Word of our God. We shall find the path of obedience both safe and pleasant, holy and happy.

Now, let us glance at Joshua 9, which records for our admonition the manner in which even Joshua was ensnared through lack of simple dependence upon God. We do not quote the passage or enter into any detail. The reader can turn to the chapter and ponder its contents.

Why was Israel beguiled by the craft of the Gibeonites? Because they leaned to their own understanding and judged by the sight of their eyes instead of waiting upon God for guidance and counsel. He knew all about the Gibeonites. He was not deceived by their tattered rags and moldy bread; and neither would Israel have been, had they only looked to Him.

But here they failed. They did not wait on God. He would have guided them. He would have told them who these crafty strangers were. He would have made all clear for Israel had they simply waited on Him in the sense of their own ignorance and feebleness. But no; they would think for themselves and judge for themselves, and reason from what they saw and draw their own conclusions. All these things they would do. Hence the tattered garments of the Gibeonites accomplished what the frowning bulwarks of Jericho had failed to do.

We may be quite sure that Israel had no thought of making a league with any of the Canaanites. No, they were in terrible indignation when they discovered that they had done so. But they did it and had to abide by it. It is easier to make a mistake than to rectify it, and so the Gibeonites remained as a striking memorial of the evil of not waiting on God for counsel and guidance.

May the Holy Spirit teach us, from all that has passed before us, the solemn importance of "obedience and dependence."

STABILITY AND PEACE
(JOSHUA 1:9)

"Have not I commanded thee? Be strong and of a good courage; be not afraid, neither be thou dismayed; for the Lord thy God is with thee wheresoever thou goest."

Here lies the true secret of stability and peace at all times and under all circumstances. The authority of God for the ground we occupy, and His presence with us thereon – the Word of the Lord as the warrant for what we are doing, and the light of His countenance in the doing of it. There is no possibility of getting on without these two things. It will not do merely to be able to give chapter and verse for a certain position which we have taken up; we must realize the Lord's own presence with us. And it will not do to say we have the Lord's presence with us, unless we can give a divine warrant, a "Thus saith the Lord" for what we are doing and for the path we are treading.

Joshua could never have faced the difficulties of his day without these two things. And although we may not have to meet the same things that lay in his path, yet we may rest assured of this, we shall never get on in these days without the Word of God as our authority and His presence as our strength. Our lot is cast in a time of special confusion. A multitude of conflicting voices fall on the ear. Men are taking sides. We see apparently the best and holiest, the most devoted and intelligent men ranged on opposite sides of the same question and pursuing opposite ways, though professing to follow the same Lord. What are we to think? What are we to do? What do we want? We want to hear, deep down in our very inmost soul, these two weighty and imperishable sentences, "Have not I commanded thee?" – "Lo, I am with thee." These are grand realities which the feeblest and most unlettered saint may enjoy, and without which none can possibly make headway against the tide of evil at present rising around us.

Never, perhaps, in the annals of Christianity was there a moment which more imperatively demanded the most direct personal dealing of the soul with God and His truth. It will not do for anyone to pin his faith to the sleeve of another. God is testing souls in a very remarkable manner. The sieve is doing its solemn work in the midst of the Church. Those who are enabled to go through the sifting and testing with God will reap a rich harvest of blessing, *but we must go through it.* It is being made manifest just now in a very special way, whose faith is standing merely in the wisdom of men and whose in the power of God. All that is hollow is being exposed and will be so more and more, but God will keep those whose hearts are true to the name of Jesus. "Thou wilt keep him in perfect peace whose mind is stayed on Thee, because he trusteth in Thee."

This is the soul's unfailing refuge at all times. It was to this the apostle Paul directed the elders of Ephesus at the close of his touching and pathetic address in Acts 20. "And now, brethren, I commend you to *God* and to the *Word* of His grace." He does not commend them to any order of men, not even to apostles or their successors, or to general councils or their decrees, or to fathers or their traditions, or to doctors or their dogmas. No, none of these would avail in the presence of the "grievous wolves" which were about to enter in among them, and amid the "perverse things" which some from among themselves would give utterance to. Nothing but God Himself and the Word of His grace could stand in an evil day, or enable a soul to stand.

There is something beautiful in the jealous care of the apostle Paul lest any should lean upon him or upon anything except the living God Himself. Hearken to the following glowing passage, "For this cause also thank we God without ceasing, because, when ye received the Word of God which ye heard of us, ye received it not as the word of men, but as it is in truth, the Word of God which effectually worketh also in you that believe" (1 Thes. 2:13). That devoted, single-hearted workman only sought to connect souls with God by means of His Word. This is the object of all true ministry. Where the ministry is not true, not of God, it will connect souls with itself; and in that case human influence will be brought to bear – weight of character, education, mental power, wealth, position, a thousand things which are all used to form a foundation for the soul's confidence and shut it out from God. Thus the faith of the soul is made to rest in the wisdom of men and not in the power of God.

Christian reader, we want you to ponder this matter deeply. Be assured it demands your serious attention. See that your soul is resting on the deep and solid foundation of God's Word – that you have His direct and positive authority for where you are and what you are doing. And then see also that you have His presence with you. These two things will impart sweet peace to your spirit and holy stability to your path, come what may. "Have not I commanded thee?" – "Lo, 1 am with thee." It is your happy privilege to know the reality of these things, just as fully and just as distinctly in your day as did Joshua in his day,

Jeremiah in his day, and the apostles in their day. The measure of apprehension may vary – the circumstances may differ – but the ground of principle is the same always.

Do not, therefore, we entreat you, be satisfied with anything less than God's authority and God's presence. Be not troubled or perplexed about the conflicting opinions of men. You must expect these. They are nothing new. But remember that, far above all the din and confusion, the strife and controversy, the opposition of sects and parties – far above all these things, in the clear light of the divine presence, in the calmness of the inner sanctuary, faith can hear with distinctness those precious, soul-sustaining words, "Have not I commanded thee?", "Lo, I am with thee."

These things can never fail: they are imperishable. See that you possess them just now. Be able, in the calm dignity of a faith that rests only in the power and on the authority of God, to give a reason for the path you tread, the work you do, the niche you fill. This is not highmindedness or haughtiness, dogmatism or pride, self-confidence or vainglory. It is the very reverse. It is self-denial and confidence in God. "With the lowly is wisdom." Precious truth! May we all remember it! It is the lowly mind that really possesses heavenly wisdom. It is not the learned, the astute, the intelligent or clear-headed among men who can thread their way through the labyrinths of the present moment. No, it is the lowly, the simple, the self-distrusting, the childlike, the unpretending. These are they who will have wisdom to guide them in darkest times. These are they who will possess peace in their souls and stability in their ways. May God's Spirit lead us into these things!

OBEDIENCE: WHAT IS IT?
AND ARE WE OBEDIENT?

It is of the greatest importance for the Christian to have a clear apprehension of the true character of Christian obedience. It is evident that I must be a Christian before ever I can obey Christ. A child can understand this. I must be in a position in order to discharge the duties which belong to it. I must be in a relationship before I can know, feel or display the affections which flow out of it.

If we keep this simple principle in our minds, it will prevent our attaching a legal idea to obedience. There is not, and cannot be, a single trace of legality in the obedience to which we are called as Christians, seeing that, before we can take a step in that most blessed path, we must have divine life. And how do we get this life? "Not by works of righteousness," not by legal efforts of any kind whatsoever, but by the free gift of God, all praise and thanks to His holy name! "The gift of God is eternal life through Jesus Christ our Lord." And how is this life communicated? How are we quickened or born again? By the Word and Spirit of God, and in no other way. We are by nature "dead in trespasses and sins." There is not in any son or daughter of Adam a single pulsation of divine life. Take the very best specimen of mere nature – take the most refined, cultivated, moral and amiable person in the very highest circle of social life; take the most religious and devout person in mere nature, and there is not so much as one spark of divine or spiritual life.

This is very humbling to the human heart, but it is the plain truth of Holy Scripture which must be constantly maintained and faithfully set forth. We are by nature alienated from God, enemies in our minds by wicked works, and hence we have neither the will nor the power to obey. There must be a new life, a new nature, before a single step can be taken in the blessed pathway of obedience, and this new life is communicated to us by the free grace of God through the operation of the Spirit who quickens us by the Word.

A passage or two of Holy Scripture will set this matter clearly before the mind of the reader. In John 3 we read, "Except a man be born of water and of the Spirit, he cannot enter the kingdom of God." Here we have the Word presented under the figure of water, as we read in Ephesians 5 of "the washing of water by the Word." Again, in James 1 we read, "Of His own will begat He us, by the Word of truth." It is not possible to conceive anything more entirely independent of human effort than the new birth as here set forth. It is wholly of God, of His own will and by His own power. What has a man to do with his natural birth? Surely nothing. What, then, can he have to do with his spiritual birth? It is of God exclusively, from first to last. All praise to Him that it is so!

Take one more passage on this great subject. In 1 Peter 1:23 we read, "Being born again, not of corruptible seed, but of incorruptible, by the Word of God which liveth and abideth forever. For all flesh is as grass, and all the glory of man as the flower of grass. The grass withereth and the flower thereof falleth away. But the Word of the Lord endureth forever. And this is the Word which by the gospel is preached unto you."

Nothing can be more precious than this. When the glad tidings of salvation fall with power upon the heart, that is the birth moment. The Word is the seed of divine life, deposited in the soul by the Holy Spirit. Thus we are born again. We are renewed in the very deepest springs of our moral being. We are introduced into the blessed relationship of sons, as we read in Galatians 4. "When the fullness of the time was come, God sent forth His Son" – marvelous grace! – "made of a woman, made under the law, to redeem them that were under the law, that we might receive the adoption of sons. And because ye are sons, God hath sent forth the Spirit of His Son into your hearts, crying, Abba, Father. Wherefore thou art no more a servant, but a son; and if a son, then an heir of God through Christ."

Here, then, we have the true ground of obedience clearly and fully set before us. It is eternal life possessed and eternal relationship enjoyed. There can be no legality here. We are no more servants on legal ground, but sons on the blessed and elevated ground of divine love.

We must remember we are called to obedience. "Lord, what wilt Thou have me to do?" is the very first breathing of a new-born soul. It was the question which came from the broken and penitent heart of Saul of Tarsus when smitten to the ground by the manifested glory of the Son of God. Up to that moment, he had lived in rebellion against that blessed One, but now he was called to yield himself, body, soul and spirit, to a life of unqualified obedience. Was there anything of the legal element in this? Not a trace from beginning to end. "The love of Christ," he says, "constraineth us; because we thus judge, that if one died for all, then were all dead. And that He died for all, that they which live should not henceforth live unto themselves, but unto Him who died for them, and rose again" (2 Cor. 5).

Here, beloved Christian reader, lies the grand motive-spring of all

Christian obedience. *Life* is the ground; *love* the spring. "If ye love Me, keep My commandments." And again, "He that hath My commandments, and keepeth them, he it is that loveth Me; and he that loveth Me shall be loved of My Father, and I will love him and will manifest Myself to him." How precious! Who can adequately set forth the blessedness of this manifestation of Christ to the obedient heart? Should we not earnestly long to know more of it? Can we expect it if we are living in the habitual neglect of His holy commandments? It is "he that hath My commandments *and keepeth them,* he it is that loveth Me."

Have we His commandments? Are we keeping them? How utterly worthless is mere lip profession! It is like the son in the parable who said, "I go, sir, and went not." It is empty, hollow, contemptible mockery. What father would care for loud profession of affection on the part of a son who didn't care to carry out his wishes? Could such a son expect to enjoy much of his father's company or confidence? Surely not; indeed it is questionable if he could value either the one or the other. He might be ready enough to accept all that the father's hand could bestow to meet his personal wants, but there is a big difference indeed between receiving gifts from a father's hand and enjoying fellowship with that father's heart.

It is this latter we should ever seek, and it is the precious fruit of loving obedience to our Father's words. "If a man love Me, he will keep My words; and My Father will love him, and We will come unto him and make Our abode with him. He that loveth Me not, keepeth not My sayings." Can anything this side of heaven be more precious than to have the Father and the Son coming to us and making their "mansion" (abode) with us? Do we know what it means? Do we enjoy it? Is it common to all? By no means! It is known only to those who know and have and keep the words of Jesus. He speaks of "His commandments" and "His words." What is the difference? The former set forth *our* holy duty; the latter are the expression of *His* holy will. If I give my child a commandment, it is his duty to obey, and if he loves me he will delight to obey. But supposing he has heard me saying, "I like so-and-so," and so he does that thing without being directly commanded to do it. He thus gives me a much more touching proof of his love and of his affectionate interest in all my wishes. This is most pleasing to a loving father's heart, and he will respond to this loving obedience by making the obedient child his companion and the depositary of his thoughts.

But there is more than this. In John 15 we read, "If ye abide in Me and My words abide in you, ye shall ask what ye will, and it shall be done unto you. Herein is My Father glorified, that ye bear much fruit; so shall ye be My disciples. As the Father hath loved Me, so have I loved you." Amazing truth! "Continue [or abide] ye in My love." How is this to be done? "If ye keep My commandments, ye shall continue [or abide] in My love; even as I have kept My Father's commandments and abide in His love."

Here we learn the wondrous truth that we are called to the very same kind of obedience as that which our adorable Lord and Savior rendered to the Father when He walked as a Man on this earth. We are brought into full fellowship with Himself, both in the love wherewith we are loved and in the obedience which we are privileged to render. This is most blessedly confirmed by the Spirit in 1 Peter where Christians are spoken of as "elect according to the foreknowledge of God the Father, through sanctification of the Spirit, unto obedience and sprinkling of the blood of Jesus Christ" (ch. 1:2).

Let the reader carefully note this. We are elected of the Father and sanctified by the Spirit to obey as Jesus obeyed. Such is the plain teaching of the passage. That blessed One found His food and drink in doing the Father's will. His only motive for acting was the Father's will. "I delight to do Thy will, O My God." There was no opposing element in Him as there sadly is in us. But, blessed be His name, He has linked us with Himself and called us into blessed fellowship, both in the Father's love to Him and in His obedience to the Father.

Marvelous privilege! Would that we appreciated it more! Oh, that we rendered a more loving obedience to all His precious commandments and sayings, so He might manifest Himself to us and make His abode with us. Blessed Lord, do make us more obedient in all things!

PREACHING CHRIST: WHAT IS IT?

"Philip went down to Samaria and preached Christ unto them" (Acts 8). This brief and simple statement embodies in it a grand characteristic feature of Christianity – a feature which distinguishes it from every system of religion that now exists or ever was propounded in this world. Christianity is not a set of abstractions – a number of dogmas – a system of doctrines. It is preeminently a religion of living facts, of divine realities – a religion which finds its center in a divine Person, the Man Christ Jesus. He is the foundation of all Christian doctrine. From His divine and glorious Person all truth radiates. He is the living fountain from which all the streams issue forth in fullness, power and blessing. "In Him was life, and the life was the light of men." Apart from Him all is death and darkness. There is not one atom of life, not one ray of light in all this world except what comes from Him. A man may possess all the learning of the schools; he may bask in the most brilliant light that science can pour upon his understanding and his pathway; he may garnish his name with all the honors which his fellow mortals can heap upon him, but if there is the breadth of a hair between him and Jesus – if he is not in Christ and Christ in him – if he has not believed on the Name of the only begotten Son of God, he is involved in death and darkness. Christ is "the true Light which lighteneth every man that cometh into the world." Hence no man can, in a divine sense, be termed an enlightened man except "a man in Christ."

It is well to be clear as to this. It is needful to press it, in this day of man's pride and pretension. Men are boasting of their light and intelligence, of the progress of civilization, of the research and discovery of the age in which our lot is cast, of the arts and sciences and what has been done and produced by their means. We do not want to touch these things. We are quite willing to let them stand for what they are really worth, but we are arrested by these words which fell from the Master's lips, "I am the light of the world; he that followeth Me shall not walk in darkness, but shall have the light of life." Here it is, "He that followeth Me." Life and light are only to be had in Jesus. If a man is not following Jesus, he is plunged in death and darkness, even though he is possessed of the most commanding genius and enriched with all the stores of science and knowledge.

We will be deemed narrow-minded in thus writing. We will by many, be regarded as men of very contracted views indeed – men of one idea, and even that one idea presented in a one-sided way. Well, be it so. We are men of one idea; and we heartily desire to be more so. But what is that one idea? Christ! He is God's grand idea, blessed be His Name forevermore. Christ is the sum and substance of all that is in the mind of God. He is the central object in heaven, the grand fact of eternity, the object of God's affection – of angels' homage – of saints worship – of demons' dread – the alpha and the omega of the divine counsels – the keystone of the arch of revelation – the central sun of God's universe.

All this being so, we need not marvel at Satan's constant effort to keep people from coming to Christ and to draw them away from Him after they have come to Him. He hates Christ and will use anything and everything to hinder the heart in getting hold of Him. Satan will use cares or pleasures, poverty or riches, sickness or health, vice or morality, profanity or religion; in short, he cares not what it is, provided he can keep Jesus out of the heart.

On the other hand, the constant object of the Holy Spirit is to present Christ Himself to the soul. It is not something *about* Christ, doctrines respecting Him, or principles connected with Him merely, but His own very self in living power and freshness. We cannot read a page of the New Testament without noticing this. The whole book, from the opening lines of Matthew to the close of the Revelation, is simply a record of facts respecting Jesus. It is not our purpose to follow out this record; to do so would be interesting beyond expression, but it would lead us away from our immediate thesis to which we must now address ourselves. May it be unfolded and applied in the power of the Holy Spirit!

In studying Scripture in connection with our subject, we shall find the Lord Jesus Christ presented in three ways – as a test, as a victim and as a model. Each of these points contains in itself a volume of truth, and when we view them in their connection, they open to our souls a wide field of Christian knowledge and experience. Let us then consider what is meant when we speak of

CHRIST AS A TEST

In contemplating the life of the Lord Jesus as a Man, we have the perfect exhibition of what a man ought to be. We see in Him the two grand creature perfections, namely, obedience and dependence. Though God over all, the Almighty Creator and Sustainer of the wide universe; though He could say, "I clothe the heavens with blackness, and I make sackcloth their covering," yet so thoroughly and absolutely did He take the place of a Man on this earth that He could say, "The Lord God hath given Me the tongue of the learned, that I should know how to speak a word in season to him that is weary: He wakeneth morning by morning, He wakeneth Mine ear to hear as the learned. The Lord hath opened Mine ear, and I was not rebellious, neither turned away back" (Isa. 1:4-5).

The Lord never moved one step without divine authority. When the devil tempted Him to work a miracle to satisfy His hunger, His reply was, "It is written, Man shall not live by bread alone, but by every word that proceedeth out of the mouth of the Lord." He would readily work a miracle to feed others, but not to feed Himself. Again, when tempted to cast Himself from the pinnacle of the temple, He replied, "It is written, Thou shalt not tempt the Lord thy God." He had no command from God to cast Himself down, and He could not act without it; to do so would be a tempting of Providence. So also, when tempted with the offer of all the kingdoms of this world, on condition of doing homage to Satan, His reply was, "It is written, Thou shalt worship the Lord thy God, and Him only shalt thou serve."

The Man Christ Jesus was perfectly obedient. Nothing could tempt Him to diverge the breadth of a hair from the narrow path of obedience. He was the obedient Man from first to last. It was the same to Him where He served or what He did. He would act by the authority of the divine Word. He would take bread from God; He would come to His temple when sent of God, and He would wait for God's time to receive the kingdoms of this world. His obedience was absolute and uninterrupted from the manger to the cross, and in this He was well pleasing to God. It was creature perfection; and nothing in any wise different from this could be agreeable to God. If perfect obedience is pleasing to God, then disobedience must be hateful. The life of Jesus, in this one feature of it, was a continual feast to the heart of God. His perfect obedience was continually sending up a cloud of the most fragrant incense to the throne of God.

Now, this is what a man *ought* to be. We have here a perfect test of man's condition, and when we look at ourselves in the light of this one ray of Christ's glory, we must see our entire departure from the true and only proper place of the creature. The light that shines from the character and ways of Jesus reveals, as nothing else could reveal, the moral darkness of our natural state. We are not obedient; we are willful; we do our own pleasure; we have cast off the authority of God; His Word does not govern us. "The carnal mind is enmity against God; it is not subject to the law of God; neither indeed can be" (Rom. 8).

It may be asked, "Did not the law make manifest the wilfulness and enmity of our hearts?" No doubt, but who can fail to see the difference between a law *demanding* obedience and the Son of God, as Man, *exhibiting* obedience? Well then, in so far as the life and ways of the blessed Lord Jesus Christ transcend in glory the entire legal system, and in so far as the Person of Christ transcends in glory and dignity the person of Moses, just so far does Christ, as a test of man's condition, exceed in moral power the law of Moses. And the same holds good of every test that was ever applied and every other standard that was ever set up. The Man Christ Jesus, viewed in the one point of perfect obedience, is an absolutely perfect test by which our natural state can be tried and made manifest.

Take another ray of Christ's moral glory. He was as absolutely dependent upon God as He was obedient to Him. He could say, "Preserve Me, O God, for in Thee do I put My trust" (Ps. 16). And again, "I was cast upon Thee from the womb" (Ps. 22). He never for one moment abandoned the attitude of entire dependence upon the living God. It is befitting to be dependent upon God for everything. The blessed Jesus ever was! He breathed the very atmosphere of dependence from Bethlehem to Calvary. He was the only Man who ever lived a life of uninterrupted dependence upon God, from first to last. Others have depended partially, He did it perfectly. Others have occasionally or even mainly looked to God; He never looked anywhere else. He found *all* His springs, not some of them or most of them, in God.

This, too, was most pleasing to God. To have a Man on this earth whose heart was never, for one single moment of time, out of the attitude of dependence, was very precious to the Father. Hence, again and again, heaven opened and the testimony came forth, "This is My beloved Son in whom I am well pleased."

Since this dependence in the perfect life of the Man Christ Jesus was infinitely agreeable to the mind of God, it also furnishes an infinitely powerful test of the natural state of man. We can here see, as we can see nowhere else, our apostasy from the creature's only proper place – the place of dependence. True, the inspired historian informs us in Genesis 3 that the first Adam fell from his original place of obedience and dependence. True also, the law of Moses makes manifest that Adam's descendants are, every one of them, in a condition of revolt and independence, but who can fail to see with what superior power all this is brought out in this world by the life and ways of Jesus? In Him we see a Man perfectly obedient and perfectly dependent in the midst of a scene of disobedience and independence, and in the face of every temptation to abandon the position which He occupied.

Thus the life of Jesus in this one particular point of perfect dependence, tests man's condition and proves his entire departure from God. Man in his natural state always seeks to be independent of God. We need not go into any detailed proof of this. This one ray of light, emanating from the glory of Christ and shining into man's heart, lays bare every chamber thereof, and proves beyond all question – proves in a way that nothing else could prove – man's departure from God and the haughty independence which marks our natural condition.

The more intense the light which you bring to bear upon an object, the more perfectly you can see what it is. There is a vast difference between looking at a picture in the dim morning twilight and examining it in broad daylight. Thus it is in reference to our real state by nature. We may view it in the light of the law, in the light of conscience, in the light of the loftiest standard of morality known among men, and in so viewing it, we may see that it is not what it ought to be, but it is only when we view it in the full blaze of the moral glory of Christ that we can see it as it really is. It is one thing to say, "We have done those things which we ought not to have done, and left undone those things which we ought to have done," and it is another thing altogether to see ourselves in that perfect light which makes everything manifest. It is one thing to look at our ways in the light of law, conscience or morality, and another thing to look at our nature in the light of that all-powerful test, namely, the life of the Man Christ Jesus.

We will refer to one more feature in the character of Christ, and that is His perfect self-emptiness. He never once sought His own interest in anything. His was a life of constant self-sacrifice. "The Son of Man has come to serve and to give." These two words "serve" and "give" formed the motto of His life and were written in letters of blood upon His cross. In His marvelous life and death, He was the Servant and the Giver. He was ever ready to answer every form of human need. We see Him at Sychar's lonely well, opening the fountain of living water to a poor thirsty soul. We see Him at the pool of Bethesda, imparting strength to a poor impotent cripple. We see Him at the gate of Nain, drying the widow's tears and giving back to her bosom her only son.

All this and much more we see, but we never see Him looking after His own interests. No, never! We cannot too deeply ponder this fact in the life of Jesus, nor can we too thoroughly scrutinize ourselves in the light which this wondrous fact emits. If in the light of his perfect obedience, we can detect our terrible wilfulness; if in the light of His absolute dependence, we can discern our pride and haughty independence; then surely, in the light of His self-emptiness and self-sacrifice, we may discover our gross selfishness in its ten thousand forms, and as we discover it, we must loathe and abhor ourselves. Jesus never thought of Himself in anything He ever said or did. He found His food and His drink in doing the will of God and in meeting the need of man.

What a test is here! How it proves us! How it makes manifest what is in us by nature! How it sheds its bright light over man's nature and man's world, and rebukes both the one and the other! For what, after all, is the great root-principle of nature and of this world? Self! "Men will praise thee when thou doest well to thyself" (Ps. 49). Self-interest is really the governing principle in the life of every unrenewed man, woman and child in this world. Nature may clothe itself in very amiable and attractive forms; it may assume a very generous and benevolent aspect; it can scatter as well as hoard; but of this we may rest assured that the unregenerate man is wholly incapable of rising above self as an object. In no way could this be made so thoroughly manifest – in no way could it be developed with such force and clearness – in no way could its vileness and hideousness be so fully detected and judged as in the light of that perfect test presented in the self-sacrificing life of our blessed Lord Jesus Christ. It is when that penetrating light shines upon us that we see ourselves in all our true depravity and personal vileness.

The Lord Jesus came into this world and lived a perfect life – perfect in thought, perfect in word, perfect in action. He perfectly glorified God, and not only so, but He perfectly tested man. He showed what God is, and He showed also what man ought to be – showed it not merely in His doctrine, but in His walk. Man was never so tested before. Therefore, the Lord Jesus could say, "If I had not come and spoken unto them, they had not had sin; but now they have no cloak for their sin. He that hateth Me, hateth My Father also. If I had not done among them the works which none other man did, they had not had sin; but now have they both seen and hated both Me and My Father" (Jn. 15:22-24).

Again, He says, "I judge no man; and yet if I judge, My judgment is true" (Jn. 8:15-16). The object of His mission was not judgment but salvation, yet the effect of His life was judgment upon everyone with whom He came in contact. It was impossible for anyone to stand in the light of Christ's moral glory and not be judged in the very center and source of His being. When Peter saw himself in that light, he exclaimed, "Depart from me for I am a sinful man, O Lord" (Lk. 5).

Such was the certain result of a man's seeing himself in the presence of Christ. Not all the thunderings and lightnings of Mount Sinai, not all the condemnations of the legal system, not all the voices of the prophets could produce such an effect upon a sinner as one single ray of the moral glory of Christ darting into his soul. I may look at the law and feel I have not kept it, and own I deserve its curse. Conscience may terrify me and tell me I deserve hell-fire because of my sins. All this is true, but the very moment I see myself in the light of what Christ is, my whole moral being is laid bare – every root, every fiber, every motive spring, every element, all the sources of thought, feeling, desire, affection and imagination are exposed to view, and I abhor myself. It cannot possibly be otherwise. The whole book of God proves it. The history of all God's people illustrates it. To cite cases would fill volumes.

True conviction is produced in the soul when the Holy Spirit lets in upon it the light of the glory of Christ. Law is a reality, conscience is a reality, and the Spirit of God may and does make use of the former to act on the latter, but it is only when I see myself in the light of what Christ is, that I get a proper view of myself. Then I am led to exclaim with Job, "I have heard of Thee by the hearing of the ear, but now mine eye seeth Thee; therefore I abhor myself."

Reader, have you ever seen yourself in this way? Have you ever really tested yourself by the perfect standard of the life of Christ? It may be you have been looking at your fellow man and comparing yourself with that imperfect standard, and trying yourself by that imperfect test. This will never do. Christ is the true standard, the perfect test, the divine touchstone. God cannot have anything different from Christ. You must be like Him – conformed to His image – before you can find your place in the presence of God. Do you ask, "How can this ever be?" By knowing Christ as the Victim and by being formed after Him as the Model!

It is most needful, before we proceed with the subject which has been engaging our attention, that the whole world and each human heart should be seen and judged in the light of the moral glory of Christ – that divine and perfect test by which everyone and everything must be tried. Christ is God's standard for all. The more fully and faithfully the world and self are measured thereby, the better. The grand question for the whole world and for each human heart is this, "How has Christ been treated? What have we done with Him?" God sent His only begotten Son into the world as the expression of His love to sinners. He said, "It may be they will reverence My Son when they see Him." Did they do so?

Sadly, no. "They said, This is the heir; come let us kill Him." This is how the world treated Christ.

Be it observed, it was not the world in its dark pagan form that so treated the blessed One. No; it was the world of the religious Jew and of the polished and cultivated Greek. It was not into the dark places of the earth, as men speak, that Jesus came, but into the very midst of His own highly favored people "who were Israelites; to whom pertained the adoption, and the glory, and the covenants, and the giving of the law, and the service of God, and the promises." It was to them He came in meekness, lowliness and love. It was among them He lived and labored and "went about doing good, healing all who were oppressed of the devil, for God was with him." How did they treat Him? This is the question; let us ponder it deeply, and ponder the answer. They preferred a murderer to the holy, spotless, loving Jesus. The world got its choice. Jesus and Barabbas were set before it and the question was put, "Which will you have?" What was the answer – the deliberate, determined answer? "Not this man, but Barabbas. Now Barabbas was a robber."

Tremendous fact! – a fact little weighed, little understood, little entered into – a fact which stamps the character of this present world and tests and makes manifest the state of every unrepentant, unconverted heart beneath the canopy of heaven. If I want a true view of the world, of nature, of the human heart, of myself, where shall I turn? To police reports? To the calendars of our Grand Juries? To the various statistics of the social and moral condition of our cities and towns? No; all these may set before us facts which fill us with horror, but let it be distinctly seen and deeply felt that all the facts ever recorded of crime in its most fearful forms, are not to be compared with that one fact, the rejection and crucifixion of the Lord of glory. This crime stands out in bold relief from the background of man's entire history and fixes the true condition of the world, of man, of nature, of self.

Now, it is this we are anxious to urge upon the heart of the reader before we proceed to the second division of our subject. It is the only way to get a right sense of what the world is and of what the human heart is. Men may speak of the vast improvement which has taken place in the world and of the dignity of human nature, but the heart turns back to that hour in when the world, when called to make a choice between the Lord of glory and a murderer, deliberately selected the latter and nailed the former to a tree, between two thieves. This crime of crimes remains, so far as the world is concerned, uncancelled, unforgiven. It stands recorded on the eternal page. Not only is this so as regards the world as a whole, but it also holds good for the unrepentant, unconverted reader of these lines. The solemn question still remains to be answered – answered by the world – answered by the individual sinner – "What have you done with the Son of God? What has become of Him? How have you treated Him?"

Of what use is it to point to the progress of the human race, to the march of civilization, to the advance of the arts and sciences, to improvements in transportation and communication, to modern weapons, to the ten thousand forms in which human genius has tasked itself in order to minister to human lust, luxury and self-indulgence? All these things are far outweighed by the misery, the moral degradation, the squalid poverty, the ignorance and vice in which more than nine-tenths of the human race are involved.

But we do not attempt to put barbarism against civilization, poverty against luxury, grossness against refinement, ignorance against intelligence. We have only one test, the one standard, the one gauge, and that is the cross to which Jesus was nailed by the representatives of this world's religion, its science, its politics and its civilization.

It is here we take our stand and ask this question, Has the world ever yet repented of this act? No; for had it done so, the kingdoms of this world would have become the kingdoms of our Lord and of His Christ. It is here we take our stand and ask the reader, Have *you* repented of this act? He may say, "I never did it. It was done by wicked Jews and wicked Romans nearly 2000 years ago. How could I be counted guilty of a crime which was committed so many centuries before I was born?"

We reply, It was the act of the world and you are either part of that world which stands before God under the guilt of the murder of His Son, or you have, as a repentant and converted soul, found refuge and shelter in the pardoning love of God. There is no middle ground, and the more clearly you see this the better, for in no way can you have a just sense of the condition of this world or of your own heart except in the light which is cast thereon by the life and death of Christ *as a test.* We cannot stop short of this mark if we would form a true estimate of the character of the world, the nature of man and the condition of the unconverted soul. As to the world, there can be no real improvement in its condition, no radical change in its state, until the sword of divine judgment has settled the question of its treatment of the Son of God. As far as the individual sinner is concerned, the divine testimony is, "Repent and be converted that your sins may be blotted out." This leads us, in the second place, to contemplate

CHRIST AS A VICTIM

This is a much more pleasing subject to dwell upon, though the other must never be omitted in preaching Christ. It is too much lost sight of in our preaching. We do not sufficiently press home upon the conscience of the sinner, Christ both in life and death, as a test of nature's true condition and a proof of its irremediable ruin. The law may be used, and rightly so, to do its testing work in the conscience. Yet, through the blindness and folly of our hearts, we may attempt to take up that very law to work out a righteousness for ourselves – that law by which, when rightly viewed, is the *knowledge* of sin. But it is impossible for anyone to have his eyes opened to see the death of Christ as the terrible exhibition of the enmity of the heart against God, and not be convinced that he is utterly and hopelessly ruined and undone. This is true repentance. It is the moral judgment, not merely of my acts, but of my nature in the light of the cross as the only perfect test of what that nature really is.

All this is fully brought out in the preaching of Peter in the earlier chapters of the Acts. Look at the second chapter where we find the Holy Spirit presenting Christ both as a test and as a victim. "Ye men of Israel, hear these words: Jesus of Nazareth, a Man approved of God among you by miracles and wonders and signs, which God did by Him, in the midst of you, as ye yourselves also know. Him, being delivered by the determinate counsel and foreknowledge of God, ye have taken and by wicked hands have crucified and slain; whom God hath raised up, having loosed the pains of death; because it was not possible that He should be holden of it ... Therefore let all the house of Israel know assuredly that God hath made that same Jesus, whom ye have crucified, both Lord and Christ."

Here we have solemn and bitter dealing with conscience as to the way they treated the Lord's Anointed. It was not merely that they had broken the law; that was true; nor yet that they had merely rejected all the witnesses that had been sent to them; that was equally true, but that was not all. They had actually crucified and slain "a Man approved of God," and that Man was none other than the Son of God Himself. This was the naked and startling fact which the inspired preacher urges home with solemn emphasis upon the consciences of his hearers.

Mark the result! "Now, when they heard this, they were pricked in their hearts, and said unto Peter and to the rest of the apostles, Men and brethren, what shall we do?" No marvel that they were pierced to the very heart. Their eyes were opened and what did they discover? Why, that they were actually against God Himself – the God of Abraham, Isaac and

Jacob. And about what were they at issue? About the law? No. About the prophets? No. About the rites and ceremonies, the statutes and institutions of the Mosaic economy? No. All this was true and bad enough. But there was something far beyond all this. Their guilt had reached its culmination in the rejection and crucifixion of Jesus of Nazareth. "The God of Abraham, and of Isaac, and of Jacob, the God of our fathers, hath glorified His Son Jesus, whom ye delivered up, and denied Him in the presence of Pilate, when he was determined to let Him go. But ye denied the Holy One and the Just, and desired a murderer to be granted unto you; and killed the Prince of Life, whom God hath raised from the dead; whereof we are witnesses."

This truly was and is the climax of man's guilt, and when brought home in the mighty energy of the Holy Spirit to any heart in all this world, it must produce true repentance and evoke from the depths of the soul, the earnest inquiry, "Men and brethren, what shall I do?" "Sirs, what must I do to be saved?" It is not merely that we have failed in keeping the law, in doing our duty to God and our duty to our neighbor in living as we should. Sadly, all this is too true. But oh! we have been guilty of the dreadful sin of crucifying the Son of God. Such is the measure of human guilt, and such was the truth pressed home by Peter on the consciences of the men of his time.

What then? When the sharp edge of this powerful testimony had penetrated the hearts of the hearers, when the arrow from the quiver of the Almighty had pierced the soul and drawn forth the bitter penitential cry, "What shall we do?," what was the answer? What had the preacher to say? "Repent and be baptized, every one of you in the name of Jesus Christ for the remission of sins, and ye shall receive the gift of the Holy Spirit." So also in the third chapter, he says, "And now, brethren, I know that through ignorance ye did it, as did also your rulers. But those things which God before had showed by the mouth of all His prophets, that Christ should suffer, He hath so fulfilled. Repent ye therefore, and be converted, that your sins may be blotted out, when the times of refreshing shall come from the presence of the Lord."

Here we have the two things very distinctly presented, namely, Christ as a test and Christ as a victim – the cross as the exhibition of man's guilt and the cross as the exhibition of the love of God. "Ye killed the Prince of life." Here was the arrow for the conscience. "But those things which God before had showed that Christ should suffer, He hath so fulfilled." Here was the healing balm. It was the determinate counsel of God that

Christ should suffer, and while it was true that man had displayed his hatred of God in nailing Jesus to the cross, yet no sooner is any soul made to see this and thus is brought to divine conviction, than the Holy Spirit holds up to view that very cross as the foundation of the counsels of redeeming love and the ground of the full remission of sins to every true believer.

Thus it was in that most touching scene between Joseph and his brethren as recorded in Genesis 44 and 45. The guilty brethren are made to pass through deep and painful exercises of heart, until they stand in the presence of their injured brother with the arrow of conviction piercing their inmost soul. Then, but not until then, these soothing words fall upon their ears, "Now, therefore, be not grieved nor angry with yourselves, that ye sold me hither; for God did send me before you to preserve life.... So now it was not you that sent me hither, but God."

Exquisite, matchless grace! The moment they entered the place of confession, Joseph was in the place of forgiveness. This was divine. "He spoke roughly to them" when they were thoughtless as to their sin, but no sooner did they say these words, "We are verily guilty concerning our brother," than they were met by the sweet response of grace, "It was not you, but God."

Thus it is, beloved reader, in every case. The very instant the sinner takes the place of contrition, God takes the place of full and free forgiveness; and most assuredly, when God forgives, the sinner is forgiven. "I said, I will confess my transgressions unto the Lord, and Thou forgavest the iniquity of my sin" (Ps. 32).

Would we have it otherwise? Surely not. An hard heart, an unbroken spirit, an unreached conscience could not understand or make a right use of such words as, "Be not grieved; it was not you, but God." How could it? How could an unrepentant heart appreciate words which are only designed to soothe and tranquilize a broken and contrite spirit? Impossible. To tell a hard-hearted sinner not to be grieved, would be fatally false treatment. Joseph could not possibly have said to his brethren, "Be not grieved with yourselves" until they had said and felt "We are verily guilty."

Such is the order, and it is well to remember it. "I will confess and Thou forgavest." The moment the sinner takes his true place in the presence of God, there is not one syllable said to him about his sins except it be to tell him that they are all forgiven and all forgotten. "Their sins and iniquities will I remember no more." God not only forgives but forgets. The convicted sinner stands and gazes upon the cross, and sees himself in the light of the glory of Christ as the divine and perfect test, and cries out, "What shall I do?" How is he answered? By the unfolding of Christ as a victim, slain by the determinate counsel and foreknowledge of God, to put away sin by the sacrifice of Himself.

Who can define the feelings of a soul that has been convicted of desiring a murderer and crucifying the Son of God, when he learns that that very crucified One is the channel of pardon and life to him – that the blood which was shed puts away forever the guilt of shedding it? What language can adequately set forth the emotion of one who has seen his guilt, not merely in the light of the ten commandments, but as shown out in the cross of a world-rejected Jesus; and yet knows and believes that his guilt is all and forever put away? Who could attempt to embody in language the feelings of Joseph's brethren when they felt his tears of affection dropping upon them? What a scene! Tears of contrition and tears of affection mingled! Precious mixture! The mind of God alone can duly estimate its value and sweetness.

But here let us just guard against misunderstanding. Let no one suppose that tears of contrition are the *cause* of pardon or the meritorious ground of peace. Far, far away be the thought from the reader's mind! All the tears of contrition that ever gushed forth from the fountains of broken hearts, from the days of Joseph's brethren to the days of the third of Acts and to the present moment, could not form the just foundation of a sinner's acceptance and peace with God or wash away a single stain from the human conscience. The blood of the divine Victim and that alone, in prospect from the fall of man to Calvary and in retrospect, from Calvary till this moment – nothing except that precious blood, that atoning death, that peerless sacrifice – could justify a holy God in forgiving one sin. But, blessed be God, so perfectly has that sacrifice vindicated and glorified His Name, that the moment any sinner sees his true state, his guilt, his rebellion, his enmity, his base ingratitude, his hatred of God and of His Christ; the very moment he takes the place of true contrition in the divine presence – the place of one utterly broken down, without plea of moderation – that moment, infinite grace meets him with those healing, soothing, tranquilizing words, "Be not grieved," "your sins and iniquities will I remember no more," "Go in peace."

Some might suppose that we attach undue importance to the measure of contrition, or that we mean to teach that everyone must feel the same character or degree of conviction as was produced by Peter's powerful appeal in Acts 2. Nothing is further from our thoughts. We believe there must and there will be conviction and contrition. Further, we believe the cross is the only adequate measure of human guilt – that it is only in the light of that cross that anyone can have a just sense of the vileness, sinfulness and loathsomeness of his nature. But all may not see this. Many never think of the cross as a test and proof of their guilt, but merely as the blessed ground of their pardon. They are bowed down under a sense of their many sins and shortcomings, and they look to the cross of Christ as the only ground of pardon. Most surely they are right! But there is a deeper view of sin, a deeper sense of what human nature in its fallen state really is, a deeper conviction of the utterly godless and christless condition of the heart. Where is this to be reached? At the cross and there alone. It will never do to look back at the men of the first century and say what terrible sinners they were to crucify the living embodiment of all that was holy and good, gracious and pure. No; what is needed is to bring the cross forward into our century and measure nature, the world and self thereby.

This, be assured of it, reader, is the true way to judge the question. There is no real change. "Crucify Him! Crucify Him!" is as positively the cry of the world of today as it was of the world of the first century. The cross was then and is now the only true measure of human guilt. When anyone, man, woman or child, is brought to see this, he has a far deeper sense of his condition than ever he can have by looking at his sins and shortcomings in the light of conscience or of the ten commandments.

And to what will all this lead the soul? What will be the effect of seeing self in the light which the cross, as a test, throws upon it? The deepest self-abhorrence. Yes, and this holds good in the case of the most refined moralist and amiable religionist who ever lived, just as much as in the case of the grossest and vilest sinner. It is no longer a question of grades and shades of character, to be settled by the graduated scale of human conscience or the moral sense. Oh no; the cross is seen as the only perfect standard. Nature, the world, the heart, self, is measured by that standard, and its true condition reached and judged.

We are intensely anxious that the reader should thoroughly enter into this point. He will find it to be of immense moral power in forming his convictions, both as to his own heart and as to the real character of the world through which he is passing – its moral foundations, its framework, its features, its principles, its spirit, its aim, its end. We want him to take the cross as the perfect measure of himself and all around him. Let him not listen to the suggestions of Satan or to the thoughts that spring up in his own heart, to the vaporings of philosophy and science, falsely so-called, to the infidel vauntings of this preeminently infidel age. Let him listen to the voice of Holy Scripture which is the voice of the living God. Let him use the test which Scripture furnishes – a crucified Christ. Let him try all that and see where it will lead him. One thing is certain, it will lead him down in his own self-consciousness into those profound depths where nothing can avail him except Christ as the divine Victim who bore the judgment of God against sin and opened heaven to the sinner.

Having sought to present Christ as a test and Christ as a victim, we shall now, in dependence upon divine guidance and teaching, proceed to consider Him as

THE MODEL

to which the Holy Spirit seeks to conform every true believer. This will complete our subject and open up a wide field of thought to the Christian reader. God has predestinated His people to be conformed to the image of His Son, that He might be the firstborn among many brethren (Rom. 8). But how can we ever be formed after such a model? How can we ever think of being conformed to such an image? The answer to these questions will unfold more fully the blessedness and infinite value of the truth which has already passed before us.

If the reader has followed the line of thought we have been pursuing; if he has experimentally entered into it or if it has entered into him in the power of the Spirit of God; if he has made it his own, he will see and feel and own that in himself, by nature, there is not a single atom of good, not one point on which he can rest his hopes for eternity. He will see that, so far as he is concerned, he is a total wreck. He will see that the divine purpose as revealed in the gospel is not to reconstruct this moral wreck, but to erect an entirely new thing. Of this new thing, the cross of Christ is the foundation.

The reader cannot ponder this too deeply. Christianity is not the old nature made better, but the new nature implanted. "Except a man be born again, he cannot see the kingdom of God" (Jn. 3). "If any man be in Christ, he is a new creation; old things are passed away; behold, all things are become new. And all things are of God who hath reconciled us to Himself by Jesus Christ, and hath given to us the ministry of reconciliation" (2 Cor. 5).

The effect of the mission of Christ to this world was to prove, as nothing else could have proved, man's totally irremediable ruin. When man rejected and crucified the Son of God, his case was proved to be hopeless. It is of the deepest importance to be thoroughly clear as to this. It solves a thousand difficulties and clears the prospect of many a dark and heavy cloud. As long as a man is possessed with the idea that he must improve his nature by any process whatever, he must be a total stranger to the fundamental truth of Christianity.

Sadly, there is a fearful amount of darkness and error in the professing Church as to this simple truth of the gospel. Man's total ruin is denied or reasoned away in one way or another, and the very truths of Christianity as well as the institutions of the Mosaic economy, are made use of to improve fallen nature and fit it for the presence of God. Thus the true nature of sin is not felt; the claims of holiness are not understood; the free, full and sovereign grace of God is set aside; and the sacrificial death of Christ is thrown overboard.

The sense of all this makes us long for more earnestness, power and faithfulness in setting forth those foundation truths which are constantly affirmed and maintained in the New Testament. We believe it to be the solemn duty of every writer and every speaker, of all authors, editors, preachers and teachers to take a firm stand against the strong current of opposition to the simplest truths of divine revelation, so painfully and alarmingly apparent in every direction. There is an urgent demand for faithfulness in maintaining the standard of pure truth, not in a spirit of controversy, but in meekness, earnestness and simplicity. We want to have Christ preached as a test of all that is in man, in nature, in the world. We want Christ preached as a victim, bearing all that was due to our sins; and we want Him preached as a model on which we are to be formed in all things.

This is Christianity. It is not fallen nature trying to work out righteousness by keeping the law of Moses. Neither is it fallen nature striving to imitate Christ. No; it is the complete setting aside of fallen nature as an utterly good-for-nothing thing and the reception of a crucified and risen Christ as the foundation of all of our hopes for time and eternity. How could the unrenewed sinner get righteousness by keeping the law, by the which is the knowledge of sin? How could he ever set about to imitate Christ? Utterly impossible! "He must be born again." He must get new life in Christ before he can exhibit Christ. This cannot be too strongly insisted upon. For an unconverted man to think of imitating the example or walk in the footsteps of Jesus, is the most hopeless thing in the world. Ah! no; the only effect of looking at the blessed example of Jesus is to put us in the dust in self-abasement and true contrition. And when from this place we lift our eyes to the cross of Calvary to which Jesus was nailed as our surety, our sin-bearer, our substitute, we see pardon and peace flowing down to us through His most precious sacrifice. Then, but not until then, we can calmly and happily sit down to study Him as our model.

If I look at the life of Jesus apart from His atoning death; if I measure myself by that perfect standard; if I think of working myself into conformity to such an image, it must plunge me into utter despair. But when I behold that perfect, spotless, holy One bearing my sins in His own body on the tree – when I see Him laying in His death and resurrection the everlasting foundation of life and peace and glory for me – then, with a peaceful conscience and liberated heart, I can look back over the whole of that marvelous life and see therein how I am to walk, for "He has left us an example that we should follow His steps."

Thus, while Christ as a test shows me my guilt, Christ as a victim cancels that guilt, and Christ as a model shines before the vision of my soul as the standard at which I am to aim continually. In a word, Christ is my life and Christ is my model, and the Holy Spirit, who has taken up His abode in me on the ground of accomplished redemption, works in me for the purpose of conforming me to the image of Christ. True, I must always feel and own how infinitely short I come of that lofty standard, but still, Christ is my life, though the manifestation of that life is sadly hindered by the infirmities and corruptions of my old nature. The life is the same, as the apostle John says, "which thing is true in him and in you, because the darkness is past and the true light now shineth" (1 Jn. 2:8). We can never be satisfied with anything less than "Christ our life, Christ our model." "For me to live is Christ." It was Christ reproduced in the daily life of Paul by the power of the Holy Spirit.

This is true Christianity. It is not flesh turned religious and leading a pious life. It is not unrenewed, fallen, ruined nature trying to recover itself by rites and ceremonies, prayers, alms and vigils. It is not the old man turning from "wicked works" to "dead works," exchanging the beer parlor, the theatre, the gaming table and the race course, for the monastery, the pew, the meeting house or the lecture hall. No reader, it is "Christ in you, the hope of glory," and Christ reproduced in your daily life by the powerful ministry of God the Holy Spirit.

Be not deceived! It is of no possible use for fallen nature to clothe itself in forms of religion. It may become involved in the attractive things of ritualism, sacred music, pious pictures, sculpture, architecture, dim religious light. It may scatter the fruits of a large-hearted benevolence: it may visit the sick, feed the hungry, clothe the naked, shed on all around the sunshine of a genial philanthropy. It may read the Bible and go through every form of religious routine. It may even attempt a hollow imitation of Christ: schoolmen may discipline it, others may subdue it, mystics may enwrap it in their cloudy reveries and lead it into quiet meditation with nothing to contemplate. In short, all that religion, morality and philosophy can do for it and with it, may be done *but all in vain,* inasmuch as it still remains true that, "That which is born of the flesh is flesh." "It cannot see or enter the kingdom of God," for "ye must be born again."

Here lies the deep and solid, the divine and eternal foundation of Christianity. There must be the life of Christ in the soul – the link with "the Second Man, the last Adam." The first man has been condemned and set aside. The Second Man came and stood beside the first. He proved him and tested him, and showed most fully that there was not a single ingredient in his nature, his character or his condition which could be made available in that new creation, that heavenly kingdom which was about to be introduced – that not a single stone or timber in the old building could be worked into the new – that "in my flesh dwelleth no good thing" – and that the ground must be thoroughly cleared of all the rubbish of ruined humanity, and the foundation laid in the death of the Second Man who in resurrection has become, as the last Adam, the Head of the new creation. Apart from Him there can be no life. "He that hath the Son hath life; he that hath not the Son of God hath not life" (1 Jn. 5:12).

Such is the conclusive language of Holy Scripture, and this language must hold good in spite of all the reasonings of those who boast themselves in their liberal and enlightened views, in their intellectual powers and in the breadth of their theology. It matters little what men may think or say; we have only to hearken to the Word of our God which must stand forever, and that Word declares, "Ye must be born again." Men cannot alter this. There is a kingdom which can never be moved. In order to see or enter this heavenly kingdom, we must be born again. Man has been tried in every way and proved wanting. Now, "Once, in the end of the ages, hath Christ appeared to put away sin by the sacrifice of Himself" (Heb. 9:26).

This is the only ground of life and peace. When the soul is firmly settled thereon, it can find its delight in studying Christ as its model. It is finished with all its own poor efforts to obtain life, pardon and the favor of God. It flings aside its "deadly doings;" it has found life in Jesus, and now its grand business is to study Him, to mark His footsteps and walk therein – to do as He did, to aim always at being like Him, to seek in everything to be conformed to Him. The great question for the Christian on all occasions is not, "What harm is there in this or that?" but, "Is this like Christ?" He is our divine pattern. Are husbands exhorted to love their wives? It is "As Christ loved the Church." What a model! Who can ever come up to it? No one, but we are still to keep it before us. Thus we shall enter into the truth of those lines of our own poet,

> *"The more Thy glories strike mine eyes,*
> *The humbler I shall lie,*
> *Thus while I sink, my joys shall rise*
> *Immeasurably high."*

The Christian reader will at once perceive what a wide field of practical truth is opened up by this closing point in our subject. What an unspeakable privilege to be able, day by day, to sit down and study the life and ways of our Great Example to see what He was; to mark His words, His spirit, His style; to trace Him in all the details of His marvelous path; to note how "He went about doing good"; how it was His food and His drink to do the will of God and to minister to the need of man. And then to think that He loves us, that He died for us, that He is our life, that He has given us of His Spirit to be the spring of power in our souls to subdue all that is of the old root of self and produce in our daily life the expression of Christ.

What mortal tongue can unfold the preciousness of all this? It is not living by rules and regulations. It is not pursuing a dead round of duties. It is not subscribing to certain dogmas of religious belief. No; it is union with Christ and the manifestation of Christ. This we repeat and reiterate and would impress upon the reader. This and nothing less, nothing different, is true, genuine, living Christianity. Let him see that he possesses it, for if not, he is dead in trespasses and sins, he is far from God and far from the kingdom of God. But if he has been led to believe on the name of the only begotten Son of God, if as a consciously ruined and guilty sinner he has fled for refuge to the blood of the cross, then Christ is his life, and it should be his one unvarying object, day by day, to study his model, to fix his eye on the headline and aim at coming as near to that as possible. This is the true secret of all practical godliness and sanctification. This alone constitutes a living Christianity. It stands in vivid contrast with what is commonly called "a religious life" which, alas! very often resolves itself into a mere dead routine, a rigid adherence to lifeless forms, a barren ritualism which, far from exhibiting anything of the freshness and reality of the new man in Christ, is a distortion of nature itself.

Christianity brings a living Christ into the heart and into the life. It diffuses a divine influence all around. It enters into all the relations and associations of human life. It teaches us how to act as husbands and wives, as fathers and mothers, as masters, as children, as servants. It does not teach us by dry rules and regulations, but by setting before us, in the Person of Christ, a perfect model of what we ought to be. It presents to our view the very One who, as a test, left us without a single plea, and as a victim, left us without a single stain, and who now, as our model, is to be the subject of our admiring study and the standard at which we are ever and only to aim. It does not matter where we are or what we are, provided Christ is dwelling in the heart and exhibited in the daily life. If we have Him in the heart and before the eye, He will regulate everything; if we don't have Him, we have nothing.

We will here close our paper, not because our theme is exhausted, but because it is inexhaustible. We believe that the Spirit of God alone can open the subject and apply it in living power and freshness to the soul of the reader and thus lead him into a higher type of Christianity than is ordinarily exhibited in this day of worldly profession. May the Lord stir up all our hearts to seek greater nearness to Himself and more faithful conformity to Him in all our ways! May we be enabled to say with a little more truth and sincerity, "Our citizenship is in heaven; from whence also we look for the Savior, the Lord Jesus Christ; who shall change the body of our humiliation, that it may be fashioned like unto His body of glory, according to the working whereby He is able even to subdue all things unto Himself."

JONATHAN
(1 SAMUEL 18:1-4)

"And it came to pass, when he had made an end of speaking unto Saul, that the soul of Jonathan was knit with the soul of David: and Jonathan loved him as his own soul.... Then Jonathan and David made a covenant because he loved him as his own soul. And Jonathan stripped himself of the robe that was upon him and gave it to David, and his garments, even to his sword, and to his bow and to his girdle."

What an exquisite picture we have here! A picture of love stripping itself to clothe its object. There is a vast difference between Saul and Jonathan in this scene. Saul took David home with him to magnify himself by keeping such an one near to himself in his house. But Jonathan stripped himself to clothe David. This was love in one of its charming activities. Jonathan, in common with the many thousands of Israel, had watched the scene in the valley of Elah. He had seen David go forth, single handed, to meet the terrible foe Goliath, whose height, demeanor and words had struck terror into the hearts of the people. He had seen that haughty giant laid low by the hand of faith. He participated with all in the splendid victory.

But there was more than this. It was not merely the victory but the *victor* who filled the heart of Jonathan – not merely the work done, but the one who had done it. Jonathan did not rest satisfied with saying, "Thank God, the giant is dead and we are delivered and may return to our homes and enjoy ourselves." Ah! no; he felt his heart drawn and knit to the conqueror. It was not that he valued the victory less, but he valued the victor more. Therefore, he found his joy in stripping himself of his robes and his armor in order to put them upon the object of his affection.

Christian reader, there is a lesson here for us, and not only a lesson but a rebuke. How prone are we to be occupied with redemption rather than the Redeemer, with salvation rather than with the Savior! No doubt we should rejoice in our salvation, but should we rest there? Should we not, like Jonathan, seek to strip ourselves in order to magnify the Person of Him who went down into the dust of death for us? Assuredly we should, and all the more because He does not demand anything of us. David did not ask Jonathan for his robe or his sword. Had he done so, it would have robbed the scene of all its beauty. No, it was a purely voluntary act. Jonathan forgot himself and thought only of David. Thus it should be with us and the true David. Love delights to strip itself for its object. "The love of Christ constraineth us." And again. "But what things were gain to me, those I counted loss for Christ. Yea, doubtless, and I count all things but loss for the excellency of the knowledge of Christ Jesus my Lord: for whom I have suffered the loss of all things and do count them but dung that I may win Christ" (Phil. 3:7-8).

Oh! for more of this spirit! May our hearts be drawn out and knit more and more to Christ in this day of hollow profession and empty religious formality! May we be so filled with the Holy Spirit that with purpose of heart we may cling to our Lord and Savior Jesus Christ!

THE ALABASTER BOX
(MATTHEW 26:6-13)

It is needful to bear in mind in this day of busy doing and restless activity that God looks at everything from one standpoint, measures everything by one rule, tries everything by one touchstone, and that touchstone, that rule that standpoint is Christ. He values things just so far as they stand connected with the Son of His love, and no farther. Whatever is done to Christ, whatever is done for Him, is precious to God. Everything else is valueless. A large amount of work may be done and a great deal of praise drawn forth thereby, from human lips, but when God comes to examine it, He will simply look for one thing and that is the measure in which it stands connected with Christ. His great question will be, has it been done *in* and *to* the Name of Jesus? If it has, it will stand approved and be rewarded; if not, it will be rejected and burned up.

It does not matter in the least what men's thoughts may be about any particular piece of work. They may praise a person to the skies for something he is doing; they may parade his name in the public journals of the day; they may make him the subject of discourse in their circle of friends; he may have a great name as a preacher, a teacher, a writer, a philanthropist, a moral reformer, but if he cannot connect his work with the name of Jesus – if it is not done for Him and to His glory – if it is not the fruit of the constraining love of Christ, it will all be blown away like the chaff of the summer threshing floor, and sink into eternal oblivion.

A man may pursue a quiet, humble, lowly path of service, unknown and unnoticed. His name may never be heard, his work may never be thought of, but what has been done, has been done in simple love to Christ. He has worked in obscurity with his eye on his Master. The smile of his Lord has been quite enough for him. He has never thought for one moment of seeking man's approval; he has never sought to catch man's smile or shun his frown; he has pursued the even tenor of his way, simply looking to Christ and acting for Him. His work will stand. It will be remembered and rewarded, though he did not do it for remembrance or reward, but from simple love to Jesus. It is work of the right kind, a genuine coin which will abide the fire of the day of the Lord.

The thought of all this is very solemn, yet very comforting. It is solemn for those who are working in any measure under the eye of their fellows, but comforting for all those who are working beneath the eye of their Lord.

It is an unspeakable mercy to be delivered from the time-serving, men-pleasing spirit of the present day and to be enabled to walk before the Lord – to have all our works begun, continued and ended in Him.

Let us look at the lovely and most touching illustration of this, presented to us in "the house of Simon the leper" and recorded in Matthew 26. "Now when Jesus was in Bethany, in the house of Simon the leper, there came unto Him a woman having an alabaster box of very precious ointment, and poured it on His head as He sat at meat."

If we enquire as to this woman's object as she walked to Simon's house, what was it? Was it to display the exquisite perfume of her ointment or the material and form of her alabaster box? Was it to obtain the praise of men for her act? Was it to get a name for extraordinary devotedness to Christ in the midst of a little group of personal friends of the Savior? No, reader, it was none of these things. How do we know? Because the Most High God, the Creator of all things, who knows the deepest secrets of all hearts and the true motive of every action was present, and He weighed her action in the balances of the sanctuary and affixed to it the seal of His approval. He was there in the person of Jesus of Nazareth – He the God of knowledge by whom actions are weighed. He sent her action forth as a genuine coin of the realm. He would not, He could not, have done this if there had been any alloy, any admixture of base metal, any false motive, any undercurrent. His holy and all-penetrating eye went right down into the very depths of this woman's soul. He knew, not only what she had done, but how and why she had done it, and He declared, "She hath wrought a good work upon Me."

In a word, Christ Himself was the immediate object of this woman's soul, and it was this which gave value to her act and sent the odor of her ointment straight up to the throne of God. Little did she know or think that untold millions would read the record of her deep personal devotedness. Little did she imagine that her act would be engraved by the Master's hand on the very pages of eternity, and never be obliterated. She thought not of this. She neither sought nor dreamed of such marvelous notoriety; had she done so, it would have robbed her act of all its beauty and deprived her sacrifice of all its fragrance.

But the blessed Lord to whom the act was done, took care that it should not be forgotten. He not only vindicated it at the moment, but handed it down into the future. This was enough for the heart of this woman. Having the approval of her Lord, she could well afford to bear the "indignation" even of "the disciples" and to hear her act pronounced "waste." It was sufficient for her that His heart had been refreshed. All the rest might go for what it was worth. She had never thought of securing man's praise or of avoiding man's scorn. Her one undivided object from first to last, was Christ. From the moment she laid her hand upon that alabaster box, until she broke it and poured its contents upon His sacred Person, it was of Himself alone she thought. She had an intuitive perception of what would be suitable and pleasing to her Lord in the solemn circumstances in which He was placed at the moment, and with exquisite tact she did that thing. She had never thought of what the ointment was worth; or, if she had, she felt that He was worth ten thousand times as much. As to "the poor," they had their place and their claims also, but she felt that Jesus was more to her than all the poor in the world.

In short, the woman's heart was filled with Christ, and it was this that gave character to her action. Others might pronounce it "waste," but we may rest assured that nothing is wasted which is spent for Christ. So the woman judged, and she was right. To put honor upon Him at the very moment when earth and hell were rising up against Him, was the very highest act of service that man or angel could perform. He was going to be offered up. The shadows were lengthening, the gloom was deepening, the darkness thickening. The cross with all its horrors was at hand; this woman anticipated it all and came beforehand to anoint the body of her adorable Lord.

Mark the result. See how immediately the blessed Lord comes to her defense and shields her from the indignation and scorn of those who ought to have known better. "When Jesus understood it, He said unto them, Why trouble ye the woman? for she hath wrought a good work upon Me. For ye have the poor always with you, but Me ye have not always. For in that she hath poured this ointment on My body, she did it for My burial. Verily, I say unto you, Wheresoever this gospel shall be preached in the whole world, there shall also this, that this woman hath done, be told for a memorial of her."

Here was a glorious vindication in the presence of which all human indignation, scorn and misunderstanding must pass away like the vapor of the morning before the beams of the rising sun. "Why trouble ye the woman? for she hath wrought a good work upon Me." It was this that stamped the act – "a good work upon Me." This marked it off from all else. Everything must be valued according to its connection with Christ. A man may traverse the wide world to carry out the noble objects of philanthropy; he may scatter with a princely hand the fruits of a large-hearted benevolence; he may give all his goods to feed the poor; he may go to the utmost possible length in the wide range of religiousness and morality and yet never do one single thing of which Christ can say, "It is a good work upon Me."

Reader, whoever you are or however you are engaged, ponder this. See that you keep your eye directly upon the Master in all you do. Make Jesus the immediate object of every little act of service, no matter what. Seek to do your every work so He may be able to say, "It is a good work upon Me." Do not be occupied with the thoughts of men as to your path or as to your work. Do not mind their indignation or their misunderstanding, but pour your alabaster box of ointment upon the person of your Lord. See that your every act of service is the fruit of your heart's appreciation of Him. Then be assured He will appreciate your work and vindicate you before assembled myriads.

Thus it was with the woman of whom we have been reading. She took her alabaster box and made her way to the house of Simon the leper with one object in her heart, namely, Jesus and what was before Him. She was absorbed in Him. She thought of none beside, but poured her precious ointment on His head. As a result, her act has come down to us in the gospel record, coupled with His blessed Name. No one can read the gospel without reading also the memorial of her personal devotedness. Empires have risen, flourished and passed away into oblivion. Monuments have been erected to commemorate human genius, greatness and philanthropy, and these monuments have crumbled into dust, but the act of this woman still lives and shall live forever. The hand of the Master has erected a monument to her, which shall never perish. May we have grace to imitate her; and in this day when there is so much of human effort in the way of philanthropy, may our works, whatever they are, be the fruit of our heart's appreciation of an absent, rejected, crucified Lord!

There is nothing which so thoroughly tests the heart as the doctrine of the cross – the path of the rejected, crucified Jesus of Nazareth. This probes man's heart to its deepest depths. If it be merely a question of religiousness, man can go an amazing length, but religiousness is not Christ. We need not travel farther than the opening lines of our chapter (Mt. 26) to see a striking proof of this. Look at the palace of the high priest and what do you see? A special meeting of the heads and leaders of the people. "Then assembled together the chief priests and the scribes, and the elders of the people, unto the palace of the high priest who was called Caiaphas."

Here you have religion in a very imposing form. We must remember that these priests, scribes and elders were looked up to by the professed people of God as the great depositories of sacred learning, as the sole authority in all matters of religion and as holding office under God in that system which had been set up of God in the days of Moses. The assembly in the palace of Caiaphas was not composed of the pagan priests and prophets of Greece and Rome, but of the professed leaders and guides of the Jewish nation. What were they doing in their solemn meeting? They were "consulting that they might take Jesus by subtlety, and kill Him."

Reader, ponder this. Here were religious men, men of learning, men of weight and influence among the people; and yet these men hated Jesus, and they met in council to plot His death – to take Him craftily and kill Him. Now those men could have talked to you about God and His worship, about Moses and the law, about the Sabbath and all the great ordinances and solemnities of the Jewish religion. But they hated Christ. Remember this most solemn fact. Men may be very religious; they may be the religious guides and teachers of others and yet hate the Christ of God. This is one grand lesson to be learned in the palace of Caiaphas the high priest. Religiousness is not Christ; on the contrary, the most zealous religionists have often been the most bitter and vehement haters of that blessed One.

But, it may be said, "Times have changed. Religion is now so intimately associated with the Name of Jesus, that to be a religious man is, of necessity, to be a lover of Jesus. You could not now find anything answering to the palace of Caiaphas." Is this really so? We cannot believe it for a moment. The name of Jesus is as thoroughly hated in Christendom now as it was in the palace of Caiaphas. And those who seek to follow Jesus will be hated too. We need not go far to prove this. Jesus is still a rejected one in this world. Where will you hear His name? Where is He a welcome theme? Speak of Him where you will, in the drawing-rooms of the wealthy and the fashionable, in the railway car, in the saloon of a cruise-boat, in the coffee-house or the dining hall, in short, in any of the resorts of men, and you will, in almost every case, be told that such a theme is out of place.

You may speak of anything else – politics, money, business, pleasure, nonsense. These things are always in place, everywhere; Jesus is never in place anywhere. We have seen in our streets, times without number, the public thoroughfares interrupted by German bands, ballad-singers and puppet-shows, and they have never been molested, reproved or told to move on. But let a man stand in such places to speak of Jesus and he will be insulted or told to move on and not interfere with traffic. In plain language, there is room everywhere in this world for the devil, but no room for the Christ of God. The world's motto as to Christ is, "Oh! breathe not His Name."

But, thank God, if we see around us much that answers to the palace of the high priest, we can also see here and there, that which corresponds with the house of Simon the leper. There are, blessed be God, those who love the name of Jesus and who count Him worthy of the alabaster box. There are those who are not ashamed of His precious cross – those who find their absorbing object in Him and who count it their chief joy and highest honor to spend and be spent for Him in any little way. It is not with them a question of work, of religious machinery, of running here and there, of doing this or that: No, it is Christ, it is being near Him and being occupied with Him; it is sitting at His feet and pouring the precious ointment of the heart's true devotion upon Him.

Reader, be well assured that this is the true secret of power both in service and testimony. A proper appreciation of a crucified Christ is the living spring of all that is acceptable to God, whether in the life and conduct of an individual Christian or in all that goes on in our public assemblies. Genuine attachment to Christ and occupation with Him must characterize us personally and collectively, else our life and history will prove of little worth in the judgment of heaven, however it may be in the judgment of earth. We know of nothing which imparts such moral power to the individual walk and character as intense devotion to the Person of Christ. It is not merely being a man of great faith, a man of prayer, a deeply taught student of Scripture, a scholar, a gifted preacher or a powerful writer. No; it is being a lover of Christ.

So as to the Assembly; what is the true secret of power? Is it gift, eloquence, fine music or an imposing ceremonial? No; it is the enjoyment of a present Christ. Where He is, all is light, life and power. Where He is not, all is darkness, death and desolation. An assembly where Jesus is not, is a tomb, though there be all the fascination of oratory, all the attraction of fine music and all the influence of an impressive ritual. All these things may exist in perfection, and yet the devoted lover of Jesus may have to cry out, "Alas! they have taken away my Lord and I know not where they have laid Him." But, on the other hand, where the presence of Jesus is realized – where His voice is heard and His very touch felt by the soul – there is power and blessing, though to man's view, all may seem the most thorough weakness.

Let Christians remember these things, let them ponder them, let them see to it that they realize the Lord's presence in their public assemblies, and if they cannot say with full confidence that the Lord is there, let them humble themselves and wait upon Him, for there must be a cause. He has said, "Where two or three are gathered together in My name there am I in the midst" (Mt.18:20). But let us never forget that, in order to reach the divine result, there must be the divine condition met.

RESPONSIBILITY AND POWER

The question of man's responsibility seems to perplex many minds. They find it difficult, if not impossible, to reconcile it with the fact of his total lack of power. If, it is argued, man is completely powerless, how can he be responsible? If he cannot of himself repent or believe the gospel, how can he be responsible? And if he is not responsible to believe the gospel, on what ground can he be judged for rejecting it?

Thus the mind reasons and argues. Sadly, theology does not help to solve the difficulty but, on the contrary, increases the mist and confusion. On the one hand, a certain school of divinity teaches, and rightly so, man's utter powerlessness, that he will and cannot come if left to himself, that it is only by the mighty power of the Holy Spirit that anyone ever does come – that, were it not for free, sovereign grace, not a single soul would ever be saved, for if left to ourselves, we would only go wrong and never do right.

From the above, this school infers that man is not responsible. Its teaching is right, but its inference is wrong. Another school of divinity teaches, and rightly so, that man is responsible; that he will be punished with everlasting destruction for rejecting the gospel; that God commands all men everywhere to repent; that He beseeches sinners, all men, the world, to be reconciled to Him; that He will have all men to be saved and to come to the knowledge of the truth.

From this, the second school infers that man has power to repent and believe. Its teaching is right; its inference, wrong. Hence it follows that neither human reasonings nor the teachings of mere theology can ever settle the question of responsibility and power. The Word of God alone can do this, and it does it in a very simple and conclusive manner. It teaches, proves and illustrates from the opening of Genesis to the close of Revelation, man's utter powerlessness for good, his ceaseless proneness to evil. It declares in Genesis 6 that every imagination of the thoughts of man's heart is only and continually evil. It declares in Jeremiah 17 that the heart is deceitful above all things and desperately wicked. It teaches us in Romans 3 that there is none righteous, no, not one; there is none that understandeth, there is none that seeketh after God. They are all gone out of the way, they are together become unprofitable; there is none that doeth good, no, not one.

Further, not only does Scripture teach the doctrine of man's utter and hopeless ruin, his incorrigible evil, his complete powerlessness as to good and his invariable proneness to evil, but it furnishes us with an array of unanswerable evidence in the shape of facts and illustrations drawn from man's actual history, to prove the doctrine. It shows us man in the Garden of Eden, believing the devil, disobeying God and driven out. It shows him, when thus driven out, going on in wickedness until God had to send the flood. Then in the restored earth, man gets drunk and degrades himself. Man is tried without law and proves himself a lawless rebel. He is tried under law and becomes a wilful transgressor. Prophets are sent, he stones them; the Baptist is sent, he beheads him; the Son is sent, he crucifies Him; the Holy Spirit is sent, he resists Him.

Thus, in every volume of man's history – the history of the human race – in every section, every page, every paragraph, every line, we read of his total ruin, his utter alienation from God. We are taught in the most distinct manner possible that, if left to himself, he never could and never would – though most surely he should – turn to God and do works proper for repentance. And in perfect keeping with all this, we learn from our Lord's parable of the great supper in Luke 14 that not so much as a single merely invited guest will be found at the table. All who sit down there are "brought" or "compelled." Not one ever would come if left to himself. Grace, free grace, must *force* them in; and so it does, blessed forever be the God of all grace!

On the other hand, side by side with all this, and taught with equal force and clearness, stands the solemn and weighty truth of man's responsibility. In creation, under the law and in the gospel, man is addressed as a responsible being, for such he is. Further, his responsibility is in every case measured by his advantages. Thus, in the opening of the Epistle to the Romans, the Gentile is viewed as without law, but responsible to listen to the testimony of creation, which he has not done. The Jew is viewed as under law and responsible to keep it, which he has not done. Then in chapter 11, Christendom is viewed as responsible to continue in the goodness of God, which it has not done. And in 2 Thessalonians 1 we read that those who obey not the gospel of our Lord Jesus Christ shall be punished with everlasting destruction. Finally in Hebrews 2, the apostle urges home this most solemn question, "How shall we escape if we neglect so great salvation?"

The Gentile will not be judged on the same ground as the Jew, nor the Jew on the same ground as the nominal Christian. Each will be dealt with on his own distinct ground and according to his light and privilege. There will be the few stripes and the many stripes as in Luke 12. It will be "more tolerable" for some than for others, as in Matthew 11. The Judge of all the earth will do right, but man is responsible and his responsibility is measured by the light and advantage afforded him. All are not huddled together carelessly, as though they were all on one common ground. On the contrary there is the most accurate discrimination, and no one will ever be condemned for slighting and refusing advantages which were not within his reach. But the very fact that there will be a judgment at all, proves, even were there no other proof, that man is responsible.

By whom is the very highest type of responsibility incurred? By the rejecter or the neglecter of the gospel of the grace of God! The gospel brings out all the fullness of the grace of God. All His resources are there displayed – the love of God, the precious work and glorious Person of the Son, the testimony of the Holy Spirit. Moreover, God is seen in the gospel, in the marvelous ministry of reconciliation, actually beseeching sinners to be reconciled to Him.* Nothing can exceed this. It is the very highest and fullest display of the grace, mercy and love of God. Therefore all who reject or neglect it incur the most solemn responsibility and bring down upon themselves the very heaviest judgment of God. Those who refuse the testimony of creation are guilty. Those who break the law are guiltier still, but those who refuse God's freely-offered grace are the guiltiest of all.

Will any still object and say they cannot reconcile the two things, man's powerlessness and man's responsibility? Let them bear in mind that it is none of our business to reconcile them. God has done that for us by placing them side by side in His own eternal word. It is ours to submit and believe, not to reason. If we listen to the conclusions and deductions of our own minds, or to the dogmas of conflicting schools of divinity, we shall be ever in a muddle and a jumble, perplexed and confused. But if we simply bow to Scripture we shall know the truth. Men may reason and rebel, but the question is whether man is to judge God or

---

* Some teach that the expression, "We pray, in Christ's stead, be ye reconciled to God," refers to Christians who are exhorted to be reconciled to the dealings of God. What a mistake! What a complete overlooking of the plain sense and actual terms of the passage! God was in Christ, not reconciling believers to His dealings, but reconciling the world unto Himself. And now the word of reconciliation is committed to Christ's ambassadors, who are to beseech sinners to be reconciled unto God. The force and beauty of this most lovely passage are sacrificed to support a certain school of doctrine which cannot face the full teaching of Holy Scripture. How much better to abandon every school and every system of theology, and come like a little child to the boundless and bottomless ocean of divine inspiration.

God to judge man? Is God sovereign or is He not? If man is to sit in judgment on God, then God is no longer God. "O man, who art thou that repliest against God?"

This is the great question. Can we answer it? The plain fact is, this difficulty as to the question of power and responsibility is a complete mistake, arising from ignorance of our own true condition and our lack of absolute submission to God. Every soul in a right moral condition will freely own his responsibility, his guilt, his utter powerlessness, his exposure to the just judgment of God, and that were it not for the sovereign grace of God in Christ, he should inevitably be damned. Anyone who does not own this from the very depths of his soul, is ignorant of himself and virtually sitting in judgment upon God. Thus it stands if we are to be taught by Scripture.

Take a case. A certain man owes me a hundred pounds, but he is unprincipled and extravagant and thus has rendered himself quite unable to pay me. And not only is he unable, but he is unwilling. He has no desire to pay, no desire to have anything to do with me. If he sees me coming along the street, he slips away down the first alley to avoid me. Is he responsible? And am I justified in taking legal proceedings against him? Does his total inability to pay do away with his responsibility?

Further, I send my servant to him with a kind message; he insults him. I send another; he knocks him down. I send my son to beg of him to come to me and to own himself my debtor, to confess and take his proper place, and that I will not only forgive him his debt, but take him into partnership with myself. He insults my son in every possible way, heaps all sorts of indignity upon him and finally murders him.

All this is only a very feeble illustration of the actual condition of things between God and the sinner, yet some will reason and argue about the injustice of holding man responsible. It is all a fatal mistake, and such it will yet be found to be in every case. There is not a soul in hell that has any difficulty in the matter. And, most surely, there is no difficulty felt by any in heaven. All who find themselves in hell will own that they received the due reward of their deeds, and all who find themselves in heaven will own themselves "debtors to mercy alone." The former will have to thank themselves; the latter will have to thank God. Such we believe to be the only true solution to the question of responsibility and power.

PRIVILEGE AND RESPONSIBILITY
(READ DEUTERONOMY 20:1-9)

Privilege and responsibility! Yes, this is the divine order, and how important it is in dealing with the things of God to place them in the order in which He places them and leave them there! The human mind is ever prone to displace things. Hence it is that we so frequently find the responsibilities which belong to the people of God, pressed upon those who are yet in their sins. This is a great mistake. I must be in a position before I can fulfill the responsibilities attaching thereto. I must be in a relationship before I can know the affections which belong to it. If I am not a father, how can I know or exhibit the affections of a father's heart? Impossible. I may speak about them and attempt to describe them, but in order to feel them I must be a father.

Thus it is in the things of God. I must be in a position before I can enter into the responsibilities which belong to it. I must be in a relationship before I can understand the affections which flow out of it. Man has been tested in every possible way. He has been tried in creation. He has been tried under divine government. He has been tried under law. He has been tried with ordinances. He has been tried by the ministry of the prophets. He has been tried by the ministry of righteousness in the person of John the Baptist. He has been tried by the ministry of grace in the person of Christ. He has been tried by the ministry of the Holy Spirit. What has been the result? Total failure! An unbroken chain of testimony from Paradise to Pentecost has only tended to make manifest man's utter failure in every possible way. In every position of responsibility in which man has been set, he has broken down. Not so much as a single exception can be shown.

So much for man's responsibility. He has proven himself unfaithful in everything. He has not a single inch of ground to stand upon. He has destroyed himself, but in God is his help. Grace has come in, in the Person of Christ, and perfectly met man's desperate case. The cross is the divine remedy for all the ruin, and by that cross the believer is introduced into a place of divine and everlasting privilege. Christ has met all the need, answered all the demands, discharged all the responsibilities, and having done so by His death upon the cross, He has become in resurrection, the basis of all the believer's privileges. We have all in Christ, and we get Him, not because we have fulfilled our responsibilities, but because God loved us even when we had failed in everything. We find ourselves, unconditionally, in a place of unspeakable privilege. We did not work ourselves into it, we did not weep ourselves into it, we did not pray ourselves into it, we did not fast ourselves into it. We were taken up from the depth of our ruin, from that deep pit into which we had fallen as a result of having failed in all our responsibilities. We have been set down by God's free grace in a position of unspeakable blessedness and privilege, of which nothing can ever deprive us. Not all the powers of hell and earth combined, not all the evil of Satan and his emissaries, not all the power of sin, death and the grave, arrayed in their most terrific form, can ever rob the believer in Jesus of that place of privilege in which, through grace, he stands.

My reader cannot be too simple in his apprehension of this. We do not reach our place of privilege as the result of faithfulness in the place of responsibility. Quite the reverse. We have failed in everything. "All have sinned and come short of the glory of God." We deserved death, but we have received life. We deserved hell, but we have received heaven. We deserved eternal wrath, but we have received eternal favor. Grace has entered the scene and it "reigns through righteousness unto eternal life, by Jesus Christ our Lord."

Hence, in the economy of grace, *privilege* becomes the basis of responsibility, and this is beautifully illustrated in the passage of Scripture which stands at the head of this paper. I shall quote it for my reader. "When thou goest out to battle against thine enemies, and seest horses and chariots, and a people more than thou, be not afraid of them, for the Lord thy God is with thee, which brought thee up out of the land of Egypt. And it shall be, when ye are come nigh unto the battle, that the priest shall approach and speak unto the people and shall say unto them, Hear, O Israel; ye approach this day unto battle against your enemies; let not your hearts faint; fear not and do not tremble, neither be ye terrified because of them; for the Lord your God is He that goeth with you, to fight for you against your enemies, to save you."

Here we have Israel's privileges distinctly set forth. "The Lord thy God is with thee," and that in the very character in which He had brought them out of the land of Egypt. He was with them in the power of that sovereign grace which had delivered them from the iron grasp of Pharaoh and the iron bondage of Egypt, which had conducted them through the sea and led them across "the great and terrible wilderness." This made victory sure. No enemy could possibly stand before Jehovah acting in unqualified grace on behalf of His people.

Let my reader note carefully that there is not a single condition proposed by the priest in the above quotation. He states in the most absolute way, the relationship and consequent privilege of the Israel of God. He does not say, "The Lord thy God will be with you, *if* you do so and so." This would not be the proper language of one who stood before the people of God as the exponent of those privileges which grace had conferred upon them. Grace proposes no conditions, raises no barriers, makes no stipulations. Its language is, "The Lord thy God is with thee... He goeth with you... to fight for you... to save you." When Jehovah fights for His people they are sure of victory. "If God be for us, who can be against us?" Grant me but this, that God is with me, and I argue full victory over every spiritual foe.

Thus much as to the question of privilege. Let us now turn to the question of responsibility.

"And the officers shall speak unto the people, saying, What man is there that hath built a new house and hath not dedicated it? Let him go and return to his house lest he die in the battle and another man dedicate it. And what man is he that hath planted a vineyard and hath not yet eaten of it? Let him also go and return to his house, lest he die in the battle and another man eat of it. And what man is there that hath betrothed a wife and hath not taken her? Let him go and return unto his house, lest he die in the battle and another man take her. And the officers shall speak further unto the people, and they shall say, What man is there that is fearful and fainthearted? Let him go and return unto his house, lest his brethren's heart faint as well as his heart."

There is uncommon moral beauty in the order in which the priest and the officer are introduced in this passage. The former is the exponent of Israel's privileges; the latter, of Israel's responsibilities. How interesting it is to see that, before the officers were permitted to address the assembly on the question of responsibility, the priest had established them in the knowledge of their precious privilege. Imagine the case reversed. Suppose the officer's voice had first been heard. What would have been the result? Fear, depression and discouragement! To press responsibility before I know my position – to call for affections before I am in the relationship – is to place an intolerable yoke upon the neck, an insufferable burden upon the shoulder. This is not God's way. If you search from Genesis to Revelation, you will find, without so much as a single exception, that the divine order is privilege and then responsibility. Set me upon the rock of privilege and I am in a position to understand and fulfill my responsibility, but talk to me of responsibility while yet in the pit of ruin, the mire of legality or the ditch of despondency, and you rob me of all hope of ever rising into that hallowed sphere upon which the sunlight of divine favor pours itself in living luster, and where alone responsibilities can be discharged to the glory of the name of Jesus.

Some talk to us of "gospel conditions." Whoever heard of a gospel fenced with conditions? We can understand law-conditions, but a gospel with conditions is "a different gospel" (Gal. 1:6-7). Conditions to be fulfilled by the creature pertain not to the gospel, but to the law. Man has been tried under all possible conditions. And what has been the result? Failure! Yes, failure only, failure continually. Man is a ruin, a wreck, bankrupt. Of what use can it ever be to place such an one under conditions, even though you call them "gospel conditions?" None whatever!

Man, under any kind of conditions, can only prove unfaithful. He has been weighed in the balance and found wanting. He has been condemned, root and branch. "They that are in the flesh cannot please God." It does not say, "they who are in the *body*." No, but "they that are in the *flesh*." The believer is not in the flesh, though in the body. He is not looked at in his old creation standing, in his old Adamic condition in which he has been tried and condemned. Christ has come down and died under the full weight of his guilt. He has taken the sinner's place with all its liabilities, and by His death settled everything. He lay in the grave after having answered every claim and silenced every enemy – justice, law, sin, death, wrath, judgment, Satan, everything and everyone. There lay the divine Surety in the silent tomb, and God entered the scene, raised Him from the dead, set Him at His own right hand in the heavens, sent down the Holy Spirit to testify to a risen and exalted Savior, and to unite to Him, as thus risen and exalted, all who believe in His name.

Here, then, we get onto new ground altogether. We can now listen to the officer as he tells out in our hearing the claims of Christ upon all those who are united to Him. The priest has spoken to us and told us of the imperishable ground which we occupy, the indestructible relationship in which we stand, and now we are in a position to listen to the one who stands before us as the exponent of our high and holy responsibilities. Had "the officer" come first, we should have fled from his presence, discouraged and dismayed by the weight and solemnity of his words, and giving utterance to the despairing inquiry, "Who then can be saved?" But, inasmuch as "the priest" – the minister of grace, the exponent of privilege – has set us upon our feet in the new creation and strengthened our hearts by unfolding the unconditional grace in which we stand, we can listen to the "commandments" of the officer and find them "not grievous," because they come to us from off the mercy-seat.

And what does the officer say to us? Just this: "No man that warreth entangleth himself with the affairs of this life." This is the sum and substance of the officer's message. He demands on the part of God's warriors, a disentangled heart. It is not a question of salvation, of being a child of God, of being a true Israelite. It is simply a question of ability to wage an effective warfare, and clearly, a man cannot fight well if his heart is entangled with "a house," "a vineyard" or "a wife."

It was not a question of *having* such things. By no means. Thousands of those who went forth to tread the battlefield and gather the spoils of victory, had houses and lands and domestic ties. The officers had no quarrel with the possessors of these things. The only point was, not to be *entangled* with them. The apostle does not say, "No man that warreth engages in the affairs of this life." Had he said this, we should all have to live in idleness and isolation, whereas he distinctly teaches us, elsewhere, that, "If any man will not work, neither shall he eat." The grand point is to keep the heart disentangled. God's warriors must have free hearts, and the only way to be free is to cast all our care upon Him who cares for us. I can stand in the battlefield with a free heart when I have placed my house, my vineyard and my wife in the divine keeping.

Further, God's warriors must have courageous hearts as well as free hearts. "The fearful and the faint-hearted" can never stand in the battle or wear the laurel of victory. Our hearts must be disentangled from the world and be bold by reason of our absolute confidence in God. Be it well remembered that these things are not "gospel conditions," but gospel results – a deeply-important distinction. What a mistake to speak of gospel conditions! It is simply the old leaven of legality presented in a new and strange form, and dubbed with a name which is a contradiction. If those precious clusters which are the result of union with the Living Vine, be set forth as the necessary conditions of that union, what must become of the sinner? Where shall we get them if not in Christ? And how do we become united to Christ? Is it by conditions? No, but by faith.

May the Holy Spirit instruct my reader as to the divine order of "privilege and responsibility!"

EXHORTATION

There are few things less understood than the real nature of exhortation. We are apt to attach an idea of legal effort to that word which is quite foreign to it. Divine exhortation always assumes that a certain relationship exists, that a certain standing is enjoyed, that certain privileges are understood. The Spirit never exhorts except on a divine basis. For example, "I beseech you, therefore, brethren, by the mercies of God" (Rom. 12:1). Here we have an excellent example of divine exhortation. "The mercies of God" are first put before us in all their fullness, brightness and preciousness, before we are called to hear the voice of exhortation.

Again, "grieve not the Holy Spirit of God whereby ye are sealed unto the day of redemption" (Eph. 4:30). Here we are exhorted on the settled ground of our being "sealed." He does not say, "Grieve not the Spirit, lest ye be eternally lost." Such would not be in keeping with the true character of divine exhortation. We "are sealed," not as long as we behave ourselves, but "until the day of redemption." It is absolutely done, and this is the powerful reason why we are not to grieve the Holy Spirit. If that which is the eternal seal of God, set upon us until the day of redemption, be the Holy Spirit, how careful should we be not to grieve Him.

Again, "*Since* ye then are risen with Christ, seek those things which are above" (Col. 3:l). As those who are risen, what should we seek but "things above?" We do not seek these things in order to be risen, but because we *are* risen. In other words the solid basis of our standing is laid down by the Spirit of grace, before ever the voice of exhortation falls on the ear. This is divine. Anything else would be mere legality. To call upon a man to set his affections upon things above, before he knows upon divine authority that he is "risen with Christ," is to begin at the wrong end and to lose your labor. It is only when I believe that precious emancipating truth that when Christ died, I died; when He was buried, I was buried; when He rose, I rose; it is only when this grand reality takes possession of my soul that I can lend an open ear and an understanding heart to exhortation's heavenly voice.

It is well for my reader to understand this thoroughly. There is no need whatever for a multitude of words. Let him simply take his New Testament and beginning with the epistle to the Romans, trace throughout the exhortations of the Spirit of God. He will find without a single exception, that they are as completely divested of the legal element as are the promises which glitter like gems on the page of inspiration. This subject is not fully understood. Exhortation in the hands of man is widely different from what it is in the hands of the Holy Spirit. How often do we hear men exhorting us to a certain line of action so we may reach certain privileges. The way of the Spirit is the reverse of this. He sets before us our standing in Christ in the first place, and then He unfolds the walk. He first speaks of privilege – free, unconditional privilege – and then He sets forth the holy responsibility connected therewith. He first presents the settled and unalterable relationship in which free grace has set us, and then dwells upon the affections belonging thereto.

There is nothing so hateful to the Spirit of God as legality, that hateful system which casts us as *doers* back upon self, instead of casting us as lost sinners over upon Christ. Man would eagerly do something, but he must be brought to the end of himself and to the end of all beside, and then as a lost sinner, find his rest in Christ – a full, precious, all-sufficient Christ. In this way alone can he ever expect solid peace and true happiness. Only then will he ever be able to yield an intelligent response to the Spirit's "word of exhortation."

THE TWO LINKS

There are two very important links in Christianity which we should seek to understand. First is the link of everlasting life; secondly, the link of personal communion. These links, being distinct, should never be confounded, and being intimately connected, should never be separated. The former is the *ground* of our security; the later, the secret *spring* of our enjoyment and the source of all our fruitfulness. The first can never be broken; the second may be snapped by a thousand things.

Seeing that these links are of such immense importance, let us reverently and prayerfully enter upon the examination of them in the divine light of inspiration.

First, as to the precious link of everlasting life, we cannot possibly do better than quote a few plain passages of Scripture, setting forth from where it comes, what it is, when and how it is formed.

First of all, it must be distinctly borne in mind that man in his natural state knows nothing of this link. "That which is born of the flesh is flesh." There may be much that is truly amiable – great nobility of character, great generosity, strict integrity – but there is no eternal life. The first link is unknown. It matters not how you cultivate and elevate nature, you cannot form the grand link of everlasting life. You may make it moral, learned, religious, but so long as it is mere nature, there is no eternal life. You may select all the very finest moral virtues and concentrate them in one individual, and that individual may never have felt so much as a single pulsation of everlasting life.

It is not that these virtues and qualities are not good and desirable in themselves; no one in his senses would question that. Whatever is morally good in nature is to be estimated at its proper value. No one would think for a moment of placing a sober, industrious, amiable, well-principled man on a level with a drunken, idle spendthrift. Looked at from a social and moral point of view, there is a wide and very material difference. But, be it clearly understood and well-remembered that we can never by the finest virtues and noblest qualities of the old creation purchase a place in the new. We can never by all the excellencies of the first Adam, even if concentrated in one individual, establish a title to membership in the second. The two are totally distinct, the old and the new, the first and the second. "That which is born of the flesh is flesh; and that which is born of the Spirit is spirit." "Therefore, if any man be in Christ he is a new creation; old things are passed away; behold all things are become new."

Nothing can be more explicit, nothing more conclusive than the last quoted passage from 2 Corinthians 5. "Old things," of whatever kind, "are passed away." They are not recognized as having any existence in the new creation wherein "all things are of God." The old foundation has been completely removed and new foundations laid in redemption. Nor is there so much as a single particle of the old material worked up into the new. "All things are become new", "All things are of God." The old creation "bottles" have been flung aside and redemption-bottles set in their stead. The old creation "garment" has been cast away and the new, the spotless robe of redemption, substituted. In this fair robe, man's hand never wove a thread nor set a stitch. How do we know? How can we speak with such confidence and authority? For the best of all reasons, because the divinely authoritative and therefore absolutely conclusive voice of Holy Scripture declares that in the new creation, "All things are of God." The Lord be praised that it is so! It is this that makes all so secure, that places all so entirely beyond the reach of the enemy's power. He cannot touch anything or anyone in the new creation.

Death is the limit of Satan's domain. The grave forms the boundary of his dominion. But the new creation begins at the other side of death. It opens upon our enraptured gaze at heaven's side of that tomb where the Prince of Life lay buried. It pours the brilliant beams of its glories around us in the midst of a scene where death can never enter, where sin and sorrow are unknown, where the hiss of the serpent can never be heard, nor his hateful trail be seen. "All things are of God."

It would remove a host of difficulties and perplexities, and simplify matters amazingly, if this point of the new creation were clearly understood. If we look around on what is called the religious-world or the professing Church, what do we see? A large amount of effort to improve man in his Adamic, his natural or old creation condition. Philanthropy, science, philosophy, religion, are all brought into play. Every species of moral leverage is brought to bear for the purpose of raising man in the scale of existence. What do men mean when they talk of "elevating the masses?" How far can they go in their operations? To what point can they elevate them? Can they raise them into the new creation? Clearly not, seeing that in that creation all things are of God.

Further, who or what are these "masses" that men seek to elevate? Are they born of the flesh or born of the Spirit? Of the flesh confessedly and assuredly! Well then, "That which is born of the flesh is flesh." You may elevate it as high as you please. You may apply the most powerful lever and raise it to the very loftiest point attainable. Educate, cultivate, sublimate it as you will. Let science, philosophy, religion (so-called) and philanthropy bring all their resources to bear, and what has been done? You cannot make it spirit. You cannot bring it into the new creation. You cannot form the first grand link of everlasting life. You have done absolutely nothing towards man's best, his spiritual, his eternal interests. You have left him still in his old Adamic state, his old creation circumstances. You have left him in his liabilities, his responsibilities, his sins, his guilt. You have left him exposed to the righteous wrath of a sin-hating God. He may be more cultivated in his guilt, but he is guilty all the while. Cultivation cannot remove guilt, education cannot blot out sins, civilization cannot remove from man's horizon the dark and heavy clouds of death and judgment.

Let us not be misunderstood. We do not want to belittle education or civilization, true philanthropy or true philosophy. We say distinctly, let them go for what they are really worth, let them be estimated at their true value. We are ready to allow as large a margin as may be demanded in which to insert all the possible advantages of education in all its branches; and having done so, we return with accumulated force to our grand thesis, namely, that in "elevating the masses," you are elevating that which has no existence before God, no place in the new creation. We repeat with emphasis and urge it with energy, that until you get the soul into the new creation, you have done absolutely nothing for it with respect to eternity, to heaven and to God.

True, you may smooth man's way through this world, you may remove some of the roughnesses from the highway of human life, you may place the flesh in the delusive lap of luxury and ease. You may wreath man's brow with every species of laurel that ever was won in the various arenas in which men have carried on the competitive struggle for fame. You may adorn his name with all the titles that ever were bestowed by mortal upon his fellow mortal, and after all this, you leave him in his sins and exposed to death and eternal damnation. If the first grand link is not formed, the soul is like a vessel broken from her moorings and driven over the watery waste, without either rudder or compass.

We most earnestly desire to press this point upon the attention of the reader. We deeply feel its immense practical importance. We believe there is hardly any truth to which the devil offers more fierce and constant opposition than the truth of the new creation. He knows well its mighty moral influence, its power to lift the soul up out of present things, to produce deadness to the world, and practical and habitual elevation above the things of time and sense. Hence his effort is to keep people ever engaged in the hopeless work of trying to elevate nature and improve the world. He has no objection to morality, to religion as such, in all its forms. He will even use Christianity itself as a means of improving the old nature. Indeed his masterpiece is to tack on the Christian religion as a "new piece" upon the "old garment" of fallen nature. You may do what you like, provided you leave man in the old creation, for Satan knows full well that as long as you leave him there, you have left him in his clutches.

All in the old creation is in the grasp of Satan and within the full range of his guns. All in the new creation is beyond him. "He that is born of God keepeth himself and that wicked one toucheth him not." It is not said that the believer keeps himself and the wicked one touches him not. The believer is a complex being, having two natures – the old and the new, the flesh and the Spirit – and if he does not watch, "that wicked one" will speedily touch him, upset him and cut out plenty of sorrowful work for him. But the divine nature, the new creation, cannot be touched, and so long as we walk in the energy of the divine nature and breathe the atmosphere of the new creation, we are perfectly safe from all the assaults of the enemy.

Now, let us proceed to enquire how we get into the new creation, how we become possessed of the divine nature, how this link of everlasting life is formed. A quotation or two from the Word will be sufficient to open this point to us. "God so loved the world, that He gave His only begotten Son, that whosoever believeth in Him should not perish, but have everlasting life." Mark these words, reader, observe the connection, "Believeth in Him" ... "Have everlasting life." This is the link: simple faith. Thus it is we pass from the old creation with all its belongings, into the new creation with all its belongings. This is the precious secret of the new birth – faith wrought in the soul by the grace of God the Holy Spirit; faith that takes God at 'His word, that sets to its seal that God is true; faith that links the soul with a risen Christ, the Head and beginning of the New Creation.

Take another quotation, "Verily, verily, I say unto you, he that heareth My words and believeth on Him that sent Me, hath everlasting life and shall not come into judgment, but is passed from death unto life." Here is the link again. "Believeth on Me" ... "Hath everlasting life." Nothing can be more simple. By natural birth we enter the precincts of the old creation and become heirs of all that pertained to the first Adam. By spiritual birth we enter the precincts of the new creation and become the heirs of all that pertains to the Second Adam. And if it be asked, what is the secret of this great mystery of the spiritual birth? the answer is, "Faith." "He that believeth on Me." Hence, if the reader is one who believes in Jesus, according to the language of the above passages, he is in the new creation. He is a possessor of the divine nature. He is linked on to Christ by a link which is perfectly indissoluble. Such an one can never perish. No power of earth or hell, men or demons, can ever snap that link of everlasting life which connects all Christ's members with their risen Head in glory, and with one another.

Let the reader note particularly that, in reference to the link of eternal life and its formation, we must take God's thoughts in place of our own. We must be governed exclusively by the Word of God and not by our own vain reasonings, foolish imaginings and ever changing feelings. Moreover, we must be careful not to confound the two links which, though intimately connected, are completely distinct. We must not displace them, but leave them in their divine order. The first does not depend upon the second, but the second flows out of the first. The second is as much a link as the first, but it is second and not first. All the power and malice of Satan cannot snap the first link; the weight of a feather may snap the second. The first link endures forever; the second may be broken in a moment. The first link owes its permanency to the work of Christ for us, which was finished on the cross, and to the Word of God to us, which is settled forever in heaven; the second link depends upon the action of the Holy Spirit in us, which may be and sadly is interfered with by a thousand things in the course of a single day. The former is based upon Christ's victory *for* us; the latter is based upon the Spirit's victories *in* us.

Now, it is our firm conviction that thousands get shaken as to the reality and perpetuity of the first link of everlasting life, by reason of failure to maintain the second link of personal communion. Something occurs to snap the latter, and they begin at once to question the existence of the former. This is a mistake, but it only serves to show the immense importance of holy vigilance in our daily walk so the link of personal communion may not be broken by sin in thought, word or deed; or if it should be broken, of having it instantly restored by self-judgment and confession, founded upon the death and advocacy of Christ. It is an undeniable fact, confirmed by the sad experience of thousands of true saints of God, that when the second link is snapped, it is next to impossible to realize the first. And this, though so vitally important to us, is in reality only a secondary thing; for surely, the suspension of our communion is a small thing when compared with the dishonor done to the cause of Christ and the grief given to the Holy Spirit by that which occasioned the suspension.

May the Spirit of God work in us mightily to produce watchfulness, prayerfulness, seriousness and earnestness, that nothing may occur to interrupt our communion, but that the two links may be understood and enjoyed in their due place and order, to the glory of God by us, the stability of our peace in Him, and the integrity and purity of our walk before Him!

In order to unfold somewhat more fully on the subject of "the two links," we would like to call our reader's attention to a very important passage in 1 Corinthians 5. "For even Christ our passover is slain for us; therefore let us keep the feast." In this brief quotation we have a wide range of truth presented. We have, first, a great fact stated, "Christ our passover is slain." Secondly, we have an earnest appeal, "let us keep the feast." In the former, we have the *ground* of our security, in the latter, the true secret of personal holiness.

Here again, we have the two links in their proper distinctness and yet in their proper order. We have a sacrifice and a feast, two things quite distinct, but yet intimately connected. The sacrifice is complete, but the feast is to be celebrated. Such is the divine order. The completeness of the sacrifice secures the believer's title, and the celebration of the feast involves the whole of the believer's practical life.

We must be careful not to confound these things. The feast of unleavened bread was founded upon the death of the paschal lamb. It typified that practical holiness which is to characterize the whole of a Christian's life down here. "Christ is slain." This secures everything as to title. "When I see the blood, I will pass over you." God as a *Judge* was fully met and satisfied by the blood of the lamb. The destroying angel passed through the land of Egypt at the midnight hour with the sword of judgment in his hand, and the only means of escape was the sprinkled blood. This was divinely sufficient. God had declared, "When I see the blood, I will pass over." Israel's salvation rested on God's estimate of the blood of the lamb. This is a most precious truth for the soul to dwell upon. Man's salvation rests upon God's satisfaction. The Lord be praised! "Christ our passover is slain for us." Mark the words "is slain" and that, "for us." This settles everything as to the great and all-important question of salvation from judgment and wrath. Thus the precious link of salvation is formed, a link which can never be broken. The link of eternal life and the link of eternal salvation is one and the same. The Lord Jesus Christ – the living

Savior, the risen Head – maintains and ever will maintain this link in unbroken integrity. He says, "Because I live, ye shall live also." "If when we were enemies, we were reconciled to God by the death of His Son, much more, being reconciled, we shall be saved by His life." "He ever liveth to make intercession for us."

Now a word or two as to the exhortation of the apostle, "therefore let us keep the feast." Christ keeps us, and we are to keep the feast. He was slain to spread a feast for us, and that feast is a life of personal holiness – practical separation from all evil. Israel's feast was composed of three things – a roasted lamb, bitter herbs and unleavened bread. Precious ingredients! They set forth in typical language, first, Christ as having endured the wrath of God for us; second, those deep, spiritual exercises of heart which flow from our contemplating the cross; and third, personal holiness or practical separation from evil. Such was the feast of God's redeemed, and such is our feast now. Oh that we may have grace to celebrate it according to its due order! May our loins be girded, our feet shod and our pilgrim staff in hand.

Be it remembered, it is not a feast celebrated in order to reach a sacrifice, but a sacrifice slain to provide a feast. We must not reverse this order. We are very prone to reverse it because we are apt to regard God as an *exacter* instead of a *giver* – to make duty the basis of salvation instead of making salvation the basis of duty. An Israelite did not put away leaven in order to be saved from the sword of the destroyer, but because he *was* saved. In other words, there was first the blood-stained lintel and then the unleavened bread. These things must not be confounded, neither must they be separated. We are not saved from wrath by unleavened bread, but by a blood-stained lintel, but we can only enjoy the latter as we are diligently and jealousy maintaining the former. The two links are ever to stand in their divine order and in their inseparable connection. Christ Himself infallibly maintains the one; we by the grace of His Spirit, are to maintain the other. May He enable us so to do!

FOUR POINTS OF KNOWLEDGE
(READ DEUTERONOMY 8:1-9)

In these verses we have four valuable points of knowledge connected with our walk through the wilderness, namely the knowledge of ourselves, the knowledge of God, the knowledge of our relationship, and the knowledge of our hope.

First, as to the knowledge of self, we read, "Thou shalt remember all the way which the Lord thy God led thee these forty years in the wilderness, to humble thee and to prove thee, to know what was in thine heart." Here is a wondrous point of knowledge. Who can say it? Who can penetrate the depths of a human heart? Who can tell its windings and labyrinths? The details of a wilderness life tend to bring out much of the evil that is in us. At the beginning of our Christian career, we are apt to be so occupied with the present joy of deliverance that we know very little of the real character of nature. It is as we get on, from stage to stage of our desert course, that we become acquainted with self.

Secondly, we are not to suppose that, as we grow in self-knowledge, our joy must decline. Quite the opposite. This would be to make our joy depend upon ignorance of self, whereas it really depends upon the knowledge of God. In point of fact, as the believer advances in the knowledge of himself, his joy becomes deeper and more solid, since he is led more thoroughly out of and away from himself, to find his sole object in Christ. He learns that nature's total ruin is not merely a true doctrine of the Christian faith, but a deep reality in his own experience. He also learns that divine grace is a reality; that salvation is a deep, personal reality; that sin is a reality; the cross a reality; the advocacy of Christ, a reality. He learns the depth, the fullness, the power, the application of God's gracious resources. "He humbled thee and suffered thee to hunger," not that you might be driven to despair, but that He might "feed thee with manna which thou knewest not, neither did thy fathers know, that He might make thee to know that man doth not live by bread only, but by every word that proceedeth out of the mouth of the Lord doth man live. Thy raiment became not old upon thee, neither did thy foot swell, these forty years."

Touching and beautiful appeal! "Forty years" of evidence of what was in the heart of God toward His redeemed people. "Six hundred thousand footmen" clothed, fed, kept and cared for during "forty years" in "a vast howling wilderness!" What a noble and soul-satisfying display of the fullness of divine resources! How is it possible that, with the history of Israel's desert wanderings lying open before us, we could ever harbor a single doubt or fear? Oh! that our hearts may be more completely emptied of self, for this is true humility, and more completely filled with Christ, for this is true happiness and true holiness. "For the Lord thy God hath blessed thee in all the works of thy hand; He knoweth thy walking through this great wilderness: these forty years the Lord thy God hath been with thee, *thou hast lacked nothing*" (Deut. 2:7).

Thirdly, all we have been dwelling upon flows out of another thing, and that is the relationship in which we stand. "Thou shalt also consider in thine heart that as a man chasteneth his son, so the Lord thy God chasteneth thee." This accounts for all. The hunger and the food, the thirst and the water, the trackless desert and the guiding pillar, the toil and the refreshment, the sickness and the healing – all tell of the same thing, a Father's hand, a Father's heart. It is well to remember this "lest we be weary and faint in our minds" (Heb. 12). An earthly father will have to use the rod of discipline as well as to imprint the kiss of affection, to administer the rebuke as well as express his approval, to chasten as well as minister supplies. Thus it is with our heavenly Father. All His dealings flow out of that marvelous relationship which He stands towards us. He is a "Holy Father." All is summed up in this. Our Father is the "Holy One;" "the Holy One" is our Father. To walk with, lean on and imitate Him "as dear children," must secure everything in the way of genuine happiness, real strength and true holiness. When we walk with Him, we are happy; when we lean on Him, we are strong; and when we imitate Him, we are practically holy and gracious.

Finally, in the midst of all the exercises, the trials, the conflicts, and even the mercies and privileges of the wilderness, we must keep the eye steadily fixed on that which lies before us. The joys of the kingdom are to fill our hearts and give vigor and buoyancy to our steps as we pass across the desert. The green fields and vine-clad hills of the heavenly Canaan, the pearly gates and golden streets of the New Jerusalem are to fill the vision of our souls. We are called to cherish the hope of glory, a hope which will never make ashamed. When the sand of the desert tries us, let the thought of Canaan cheer us. Let us dwell upon the "inheritance incorruptible, undefiled, and that fadeth not away, reserved in heaven for us" (1 Pet. 1:4). "For the Lord thy God bringeth thee into a good land, a land of brooks of water, of fountains and depths, that spring out of valleys and hills; a land of wheat and barley and vines and fig-trees and pomegranates; a land of oil olive and honey; a land wherein thou shalt eat bread without scarceness, thou shalt not lack anything in it; a land whose stones are iron, and out of whose hills thou mayest dig brass." Bright and blessed prospect! May we dwell upon it and upon Him who will be the eternal source of all its brightness and blessedness!

> "To Canaan's sacred bound
>   We haste with songs of joy,
> Where peace and liberty are found,
>   And sweets that never cloy;
>   Hallelujah!
>   We are on our way to God!
>
> "How sweet the prospect is!
>   It cheers the pilgrim's breast;
> We're journeying through the wilderness,
>   But soon we'll gain our rest.
>   Hallelujah!
>   We are on our way to God!"

"IF THE LORD TARRY"

My Beloved Friend,

Since our last conversation, I have been thinking a good deal of the subject which was then before us, and the more I think of it, the more disposed I am to doubt the moral fitness of the use so frequently made of the sentence which stands at the head of my letter. I have never been able to adopt the phrase, either in writing or speaking. In fact, it is not according to Scripture, though it seems lately to have become a favorite expression with many Christian people who desire to speak and act as in the divine presence and according to the direct teaching of Holy Scripture.

I trust I need not assure you, my friend, that in raising an objection to this special form of speech, I would not want to weaken in any heart the sense of the nearness of the Lord's coming, that most blessed hope which ought each day to become brighter and brighter in the vision of our souls. Far be the thought! That hope abides in all its moral power and in no wise depends on the using or not using of any set form of words.

Suppose I say, "If the Lord tarry, I mean to go to London next week." I make my going to London dependent upon the Lord's tarrying, whereas He may tarry and yet it may not be His will that I should go at all. Hence I ought to place all my movements, all my actions, all my plans, under the commanding influence of my Lord's will.

Is not this in direct accordance with Scripture? What does the inspired apostle James say on the point? "Go to now, ye that say, Today or tomorrow we will go into such a city and continue there a year, and buy and sell and get gain; whereas ye know not what shall be on the morrow. For what is your life? It is even a vapor that appeareth for a little time and then vanisheth away. For that ye ought to say, If the Lord will, we shall live and do this or that" (James 4).

Here, the Spirit of God furnishes us with the proper form of words to be used in all our acts and ways. Surely we cannot find anything better than what He graciously deigns to give. "If the Lord will" includes everything which is to regulate our movements, whether the Lord is pleased to tarry or not.

But in writing this I have no thought of judging anyone in his use of any particular phrase. I am merely giving you my reasons for not adopting the form in question. And I may just add, in conclusion, that whether we say, "If the Lord tarry" or "If the Lord will," we should ever seek, most earnestly, to be in the present power of the words we use and thus avoid everything bordering in the remotest degree upon mere empty phraseology or religious cant. May the Lord make us very real in all our words and ways!

Most affectionately yours, C.H.M.

GOD PREACHING PEACE

"The word which God sent unto the children of Israel, preaching peace by Jesus Christ: He is Lord of all" (Acts 10:36).

One of the most momentous questions which can be put to a human being is this, "Have you peace with God?" It is a question of the deepest solemnity, and it claims a direct and immediate answer from every heart. There is no reason why any truly anxious soul should continue for one moment without settled peace with God. Christ has made peace by the blood of His cross. God is preaching peace by Jesus Christ, and here we have the solid foundation of the believer's peace – Christ's finished work received on the authority of God's Word by the power of the Holy Spirit.

This is the divine basis of peace. The more simply we build thereon, the more solid our peace will be. The reason why so many are in a state of miserable uncertainty is because they do not rest in absolute faith on God's foundation. They are occupied with themselves instead of building exclusively on Christ. They are looking to *experience* rather than to a risen Savior. Feelings and attainments engage them instead of Christ. They are vainly hoping to find some sort of improvement in themselves, and not finding it to their satisfaction – for what honest soul ever does? – they are filled with gloomy doubts. The heart is oppressed with anxious fear and the spirit is overcast with heavy clouds. They have no divine certainty, so they try to find comfort in the exercises of a religious life. Inasmuch as imperfection attaches to their very best and most pious exercises, they are ever kept in a condition of spiritual darkness and bondage. Neither in our inward feelings and experiences, nor in our outward exercises – of whatsoever kind these may be – have we the true ground of our peace in the divine presence. God did not send to the children of Israel, nor does He now send to us Gentiles, peace by spiritual experiences or by religious exercises, but simply by Jesus Christ.

The reader cannot be too simple in laying hold of this great truth. He may rest assured that it is God's gracious desire that his soul should find peace. If not, why should God send, preach, proclaim, announce peace. If God sends us a message of peace, He surely means that we should have it. He has provided it for us by the precious atoning death of His Son, and He declares it unto us by His Spirit in the Holy Scriptures. Thus it is all of God from first to last. Hence it is called the peace of God. It comes forth from His heart. It bears the imprint of His hand and it is to the praise of His own eternal Name. We have nothing to do but to receive with all thankfulness, this precious peace, and let it flow like an even river through our souls.

Here we would turn directly to the reader and press home upon his soul this grand question, "Do you have peace with God?" Do not, we beseech you, put it aside. It is a question of eternal importance – a question, in comparison with which all mere earthly questions dwindle into utter insignificance.

It may be that someone whose eye scans these lines feels really anxious about this grand question, and would give worlds, if he possessed them, for a full, clear and satisfactory answer. Such an one may feel disposed to ask, "What is the ground of this peace and how may I have it for myself?" Two deeply important questions, most surely – questions which we shall seek, by the grace of God, to answer.

First, as to the real ground of the soul's peace. If the reader will turn to the last verse of Romans 4 he will find it set forth in two brief but weighty sentences. In this passage the inspired apostle, in speaking of our Lord Jesus Christ, declares that "He was delivered for our offenses, and raised again for our justification."

Here, we have the solid and imperishable foundation of the sinner's peace, the divine ground on which God can preach peace. Jesus Christ was delivered for our offenses. Let this be carefully noted. Let us mark particularly who was delivered, who delivered Him, and for what He was delivered. All these are essential to our enjoyment of peace.

Who was delivered? The Holy One, the spotless One, the Lamb, the Christ, the Son of God, that blessed One who lay in the bosom of the Father from all eternity, the object of the Father's supreme delight from everlasting, the Eternal Son. This blessed One who lay in the bosom from before all worlds, lay in the womb of the virgin, in the manger of Bethlehem, was baptized in Jordan, was tempted in the wilderness, was transfigured on the Mount, was bowed down in the garden, was nailed to a tree, buried in the grave, raised from the dead and is now seated on the throne of the Majesty in the heavens.

This is He who was "delivered." He stood with our offenses. He represented us on the cross. He stood in our place and received from the hand of Eternal Justice all that we deserved. There was a transfer of all our guilt, all our offenses, all our iniquities, all our transgressions to Him who knew no sin, who had no more to do with sin than we had to do with righteousness. He died in our place. The One whose whole human life

116

was a sweet odor always ascending to the throne of God, was delivered up to death, charged with all our offenses.

Who delivered Him? This is a vital question. Who delivered Jesus up to the death of the cross? Isaiah 53 and 2 Corinthians 5 furnish the answer: "It pleased *Jehovah* to bruise Him." Such is the language of the inspired prophet. And now hear the apostle: "God hath made Him (Christ) to be sin for us." God has done it. It will not do to say that "we lay our sins on Jesus." We want much more than this. If it were merely a question of our laying our sins on Jesus, we could never have peace with God, seeing we do not know the extent of our sin, the depth of our guilt, the true amount of our liabilities as God knows it. To have peace with God, I must know that *He* is satisfied. *God* was the offended party, the grieved One, and He must be satisfied. Well, blessed be His name, He is satisfied, for He Himself has found the ransom. He has laid our sins, according to *His* estimate of them, on the head of the divine Sin-bearer.

All that was needful, not merely to meet our condition, but to satisfy His claims, vindicate His majesty and glorify His name, He Himself has provided in the atoning death of His own Son. Thus He is satisfied. Hence He can preach peace to us by Jesus Christ, Lord of all. The spotless Christ was judged on the cross in our place. God hid His face from that blessed One, turned away His countenance, closed His ear and forsook Him for the moment. Why? Because He was delivered for our offenses. God forsook Him that He might receive us. He treated Him as we deserved in order that He might treat us as He deserved. Jesus took our place in death and judgment, that we might take His place in life, righteousness and everlasting glory.

Now, let us ask, for *what* was the precious Savior delivered? "For our offenses." For how many? For all, most surely. When Jesus hung on the cross, all the believer's offenses were laid upon and imputed to Him. Yes, all. Then, they all were future when Christ bore them on the cross, yet there is no such distinction as past, present or future with Him who spans eternity as a moment. All our sins were laid on Jesus. He answered for them and put them away forever, so they are gone out of God's sight. Instead of our sins, there is nothing before God except the Christ who bore them and blotted them out forever, and was raised for our justification. Who raised Him? Even the same one who delivered Him. And why did He raise Him? Because all was settled for which He had been delivered. Christ glorified God in the putting away of our sins, and God glorified Christ by raising Him from the dead and crowning Him with glory and honor. Most marvelous, most precious truth! Christ forsaken on the cross because our sins were laid on Him. Christ crowned on the throne because our sins are put away. "He was delivered for our offenses and raised again for our justification." Such is the true, the solid, the everlasting ground of a sinner's peace in the presence of God.

Now one word as to the question of how the sinner can have this peace for himself. The answer is as simple as God can make it. What is it? Has the sinner to do anything? Has he to be anything but what he is – a poor lost, worthless, guilty creature? No. He has simply to believe God's Word – to receive into his heart, not merely into his head, the blessed message which God sends to him; to rest in Christ; to be satisfied with that which has satisfied God. God is satisfied with Christ without anything else whatever. Is the reader satisfied or is he waiting for something more, something of his own – his vows and resolutions, his feelings and experiences? If so, he cannot get peace. To be satisfied with Christ is to have peace with God.

> The Lord of Life in death hath lain,
> To clear me from all charge of sin;
> And, Lord, from guilt of crimson stain
> Thy precious blood hath made me clean.

"RIVERS OF LIVING WATER"

"In the last day, that great day of the feast, Jesus stood and cried, saying, If any man thirst, let him come unto Me and drink. He that believeth on Me, as the Scripture hath said, out of his belly shall flow rivers of living water" (Jn. 7:37-38).

The feast referred to in this lovely scripture was "the feast of tabernacles," called at the opening of the chapter, "The Jews' feast." This stamped its character. It could no longer be called, as in Leviticus 23, "A feast of Jehovah." The Lord could not own it. It had become an empty formality, a powerless ordinance, a piece of barren routine – something in which man could boast himself while God was entirely shut out.

This is nothing uncommon. There has ever been a strong tendency in the human mind to perpetuate forms when the power is gone. Power may clothe itself in a certain form, and so long as the form is the expression of the power, it is all right and good. But the danger lies in going on with the mere outward form without a single particle of inward power. Thus it was with Israel of old, and thus it is with the professing Church now. We have all to watch against this snare of the devil. He will use a positive ordinance of God as a means of deceiving the soul and shutting out God altogether. But where faith is in lively exercise, the soul has to do with God in the ordinance, whatever it is, and thus the power and freshness are duly maintained.

The reader may have noticed that in the opening chapters of John's Gospel, the inspired writer invariably designates the feasts as *feasts of the Jews*. Not only so, but we find the Lord Jesus displacing one after another of these feasts and offering Himself as an object for the heart. Thus at the opening of chapter 7 we read, "After these things Jesus walked in Galilee, for He would not walk in Jewry, because the Jews sought to kill Him. Now the Jews' feast of tabernacles was at hand." Terrible anomaly! Deadly delusion! Seeking to murder the Son of God, and yet keeping the feast of tabernacles! Such is religious man without God. "His brethren therefore said unto Him, Depart hence, and go into Judea, that Thy disciples also may see Thy works that Thou doest. For there is no man that doeth anything in secret, and he himself seeketh to be known openly. If Thou do these things, show Thyself to the world. For neither did His brethren believe on Him."

Near as His brethren were to Him according to the flesh, they knew

Him not, they believed not on Him. They wanted Him to make a display of Himself before the world. They knew not His object. He had not come from heaven to be gazed at and wondered after. "All the world will wonder after the beast" by-and-by, but the blessed Son of God came to serve and to give. He came to hide Himself, to glorify God and to serve man.

He therefore refused to exhibit Himself at the feast. "Then Jesus said unto them, My time is not yet come, but your time is always ready. The world cannot hate you, but Me it hateth, because I testify of it that the works thereof are evil. Go ye up unto this feast: I go not up yet to this feast, for My time is not yet fully come. When He had said these words unto them, He abode still in Galilee. But when His brethren were gone up, then went He also up unto the feast, not openly, but as it were in secret."

And for what did He go up? He went up to serve. He went up to glorify His Father and to be the willing Servant of man's necessity. "Now about the midst of the feast, Jesus went up into the temple and taught. And the Jews marveled, saying, How knoweth this man letters, having never learned? Jesus answered them, saying, My doctrine is not Mine, but His that sent Me." Here His moral glory, as the self-hiding Servant, shines out. "My doctrine is not Mine." Such was His answer to those who wondered where He got His learning. Alas! they knew Him not. His motives and His objects lay beyond the reach of carnal and worldly-minded men. They measured Him by their own standard; hence all their conclusions were utterly false. "If any man will do His will he shall know of the doctrine, whether it be of God or whether I speak of Myself. He that speaketh of himself seeketh his own glory, but He that seeketh His glory that sent Him, the same is true and no unrighteousness is in Him."

The blessed One did not speak from Himself, as if He were independent of the Father, but as One who lived in absolute and complete dependence and in unbroken communion, drawing all His springs from the living God, doing nothing, saying nothing, thinking nothing apart from the Father.

We have the same truth with reference to the Holy Spirit in John 16. "Howbeit, when He the Spirit of truth is come, He will guide you into all truth, for He shall not speak of Himself, but whatsoever He shall hear, that shall He speak; and He will show you things to come." The Holy Spirit did not speak from Himself as independent of the Father and the Son, but as One in full communion with them.

We must turn to the words which form the special subject of this paper.

"In the last day, that great day of the feast, Jesus stood and cried, saying, If any man thirst, let him come unto Me and drink." Here we have set before us a truth of infinite preciousness and immense practical power. The Person of Christ is the divine spring of all freshness and spiritual energy. It is in Him alone the soul can find all it really needs. It is to Him we must go for all our personal refreshment and blessing. If at any time we find ourselves dull, heavy and barren, what are we to do? Make efforts to raise the tone? No, this will never do. What then? Let him "Come unto Me and drink."

Mark the words. It is not, "Come unto Me and draw." We may draw for others and be dry ourselves, but if we drink, our own souls are refreshed with "rivers of living water."

Nothing is more miserable than the restless efforts of a soul out of communion. We may be very busy; our hands may be full of work; our feet may run here and there; the head may be full of knowledge; but if the heart is not livingly occupied with the Person of Christ, it will – it must be – all barrenness and desolation so far as we are personally concerned. Also, there will be no "rivers of living water" flowing out for others. If we are to be made a blessing to others, we must feed upon Christ for ourselves. We do not "drink" for other people; we drink to satisfy our thirst, and as we drink, the rivers flow. Show us a man whose heart is filled with Christ and we will show you a man whose hands are ready for work and his feet ready to run, but unless we begin with heart communion, our running and our doing will be a miserable failure. There will be no glory to God, no rivers of living water.

Yes, reader, we must begin in the very innermost circle of our own moral being and there be occupied by faith with a living Christ, else all our service will prove utterly worthless. If we want to influence others, if we would be made a blessing in our day and generation, if we desire to bring forth any fruit to God, if we would shine as lights amid the moral gloom around, if we would be a channel of blessing in the midst of a sterile desert, then we must hearken to our Lord's words in John 7:37. We must drink at the fountain head. And what then? Drink still, drink always, drink largely, and then the rivers must flow. If I say, "I must try and be a channel of blessing to others" I shall only prove my own folly and weakness. But if I bring my empty vessel to the fountain-head and get it filled there, then without the smallest effort, the rivers will flow.

A FRAGMENT ON WORSHIP

It is deeply important that the Christian reader should understand the true character of the worship God looks for and in which He delights. God delights in Christ. Hence it should be our constant aim to present Him to God. Christ should ever be the material of our worship, and He will be in the proportion we are led by the Holy Spirit. How often it is otherwise with us! Both in the assembly and in the closet, how often is the tone low and the spirit dull and heavy! We are occupied with self instead of with Christ. Then the Holy Spirit, instead of being free to do His own proper work, which is to take of the things of Christ and show them unto us, is obliged to occupy us with ourselves in self-judgment because our ways have not been right.

All this is to be deeply deplored. It demands our serious attention both as assemblies and as individuals, in our public meetings and in our private devotions. Why is the tone of our public meetings frequently so low? Why such feebleness, such barrenness, such wandering? Why are the hymns and prayers so often wide of the true mark? Why is there so little that really deserves the name of worship? Why is there so little in our midst to refresh the heart of God? Why is there so little that He can speak of as "My bread for My sacrifices made by fire, for a sweet savor unto Me?" We are occupied with self and its surroundings – our wants, our weakness, our trials, our difficulties – and we leave God without the bread of His sacrifice. We actually rob Him of His due and of that which His loving heart desires.

SEPARATION: NOT FUSION

"Therefore, thus saith the Lord, If thou return, then will I bring thee again, and thou shalt stand before Me; and if thou take forth the precious from the vile, thou shalt be as My mouth; let them return unto thee; but return not thou unto them" (Jer. 15:19).

The principle laid down in the foregoing passage is of the deepest possible importance to all who desire to walk with God. It is by no means a popular principle; very far from it. But this does not detract from its value in the judgment of those who are taught of God. In an evil world the popular thing is almost sure to be the wrong thing, and whatever has the most of God, the most of Christ, the most of pure truth, is sure to be most unpopular. This is an axiom in the judgment of faith inasmuch as Christ and the world are at opposite points of the moral compass.

Now, one of the most popular ideas of the day is fusion or amalgamation, and all who desire to be accounted men of broad sympathies and liberal sentiments go in for this grand object. But we do not hesitate to clearly state that nothing can be more opposed to the revealed mind of God. We make this statement in the full consciousness of its opposition to the universal judgment of Christendom. For this we are quite prepared. Not that we court opposition, but we have long since learned to distrust the judgment of what is called the religious world, because we have so constantly found *its* judgment to be diametrically opposed to the plainest teaching of Holy Scripture. It is our deep and earnest desire to stand with the Word of God against everything and everyone, for we are well assured that nothing can abide forever except that which is based upon the imperishable foundation of Holy Scripture.

What then does Scripture teach on the subject of this paper? Is it separation or fusion? What was the instruction to Jeremiah in the passage quoted above? Was he told to try and amalgamate with those around him? Was he to seek to mingle the precious with the vile? The very reverse! Jeremiah was taught of God first of all to return himself, to stand apart even from those who were the professed people of God, but whose ways were contrary to His mind. And what then? "I will bring thee again, and thou shalt stand before Me."

Here we have Jeremiah's personal path and position most clearly laid down. He was to return and take his stand with God in thorough separation from evil. This was his required duty, regardless of the thoughts of men or of his brethren. They might deem and pronounce him narrow, bigoted, exclusive, intolerant, and the like, but with that he had nothing whatever to do. His one grand business was to obey. Separation from evil was the divine rule, not amalgamation with it. The latter might seem to offer a wider field of usefulness, but mere usefulness is not the object of a true servant of Christ: it is simply obedience. The business of a servant is to do what he is told, not what *he* considers right or good. If this were better understood, it would simplify matters amazingly. If God calls us to separation from evil, but we imagine we can do more good by amalgamation with it, how shall we stand before Him? How shall we meet Him? Will He call that "good" which resulted from positive disobedience to His Word? Is it not plain that our first, our last, our *only* duty is to obey? Assuredly! This is the foundation; yes, it is the sum and substance of all that can really be called good.

But was there not something for Jeremiah to do in his narrow path and circumscribed position? There was. His practice was defined with all possible clearness. What was it? "If thou separate the precious from the vile, thou shalt be as My mouth." He was not only to stand and walk in separation himself, but he was to try to separate others also. This might give him the appearance of a proselytizer or of one whose object was to draw people over to his way of thinking. But here again he had to rise above all the thoughts of men. It was far better, far higher, far more blessed for Jeremiah to be as God's mouth than to stand well with his fellows. What are man's thoughts worth? Just nothing. When his breath goes out of him, in that very hour his thoughts perish. But God's thoughts shall endure forever. If Jeremiah had set about mingling the precious with the vile, he would not have been as God's mouth; he would have been as the *devil's* mouth. Separation is God's principle; fusion is Satan's.

It is counted liberal, large-hearted and charitable to be ready to associate with all sorts of people. Confederacy, association, limited liabilities, are the order of the day. The Christian must stand apart from all such things, not because he is better than other people, but because God says, "Be not unequally yoked together with unbelievers." It was not because Jeremiah was better than his brethren that he had to separate himself, but simply because he was commanded to do so by Him whose Word must ever define the course, govern the conduct and form the character of His people. Further, we may rest assured, it was not in sourness of temper or severity of spirit, but in profound sorrow of heart and humility of mind that Jeremiah separated himself from those around him. He could weep

124

day and night over the condition of his people, but the necessity of separation was as plain as the Word of God could make it. He might tread the path of separation with broken heart and weeping eyes, but tread it he must if he would be as God's mouth. Had he refused to tread it, he would have been making himself to be wiser than God. Though those around him, his brethren and friends, might not be able to understand or appreciate his conduct, with this he had nothing whatever to do. He might refer them to Jehovah for an explanation, but his business was to obey, not to explain or apologize.

Thus it is always. "Be ye not unequally yoked together with unbelievers, for what fellowship hath righteousness with unrighteousness? And what communion hath light with darkness? And what concord hath Christ with Belial? Or what part hath he that believeth with an infidel? And what agreement hath the temple of God with idols? For ye are the temple of the living God; as God hath said, I will dwell in them and walk in them; and I will be their God and they shall be My people. Wherefore come out from among them and be ye separate, saith the Lord, and touch not the unclean; and I will receive you, and will be a Father unto you, and ye shall be My sons and daughters, saith the Lord Almighty" (2 Cor. 6:14-18).

It may seem very plausible and very popular to say, "We ought not to judge other people. How can we tell whether people are believers or not? It is not for us to set ourselves up as holier than others. It is charitable to hope the best. If people are *sincere*, what difference does it make as to creeds? Each one is entitled to hold his own opinions. It is only a matter of views after all."

To all this we reply, God's Word commands Christians to judge, to discern, to discriminate, to come out, to be separate. This being so, all the plausible arguments and reasonings that can possibly be presented are, in the judgment of a true-hearted, single-eyed servant of Christ, lighter by far than dust.

Hearken to the following weighty words from the blessed apostle Paul to his son Timothy – words bearing down with unmistakable clearness upon all the Lord's people at this very moment. "Nevertheless, the foundation of God standeth sure, having this seal, the Lord knoweth them that are His. And let every one that nameth the name of Christ depart from iniquity. But in a great house there are not only vessels of gold and silver, but also of wood and of earth; and some to honor and some to dishonor. If a man purge himself from these (the dishonorable vessels), he shall be a vessel unto honor, sanctified and meet for the

Master's use, and prepared unto every good work" (2 Tim. 2:19-21).

Here we see that if any man desires to be a sanctified vessel, fit for the Master's use and prepared unto every good work, he must separate himself from the iniquity and the dishonorable vessels around him. There is no getting over this without flinging God's Word overboard; and surely to reject God's Word is to reject Himself. His Word commands me to purge myself, to depart from iniquity, to turn away from those who have a form of godliness, but deny its power.

TWO IMPOSSIBLES
(HEBREWS 6)

There are few who have set out to follow the Lord Jesus who have not, at some time or other, gone through painful exercise of heart in connection with the opening verses of Hebrews 6. While, in the long run, they have no reason to regret the exercise, yet it is always needful to distinguish between the Spirit's using a scripture to search us, and Satan's abusing it to stumble us. Searching is good for us. It is most healthful. We all need it, and we have to be thankful when we get it, but we are so prone to be light and superficial and to retire from anything that probes the conscience.

Still, we have not the slightest doubt that many true and earnest souls, many to whom Hebrews 6:4-6 has no application whatever, have been stumbled and discouraged through not understanding the true force and bearing of the passage. It is to help such that we pen the following, for we can truly say there is no work in which we have a more intense interest than in taking the stumbling-blocks out of the way of God's beloved people. We feel most fully assured it is work which He delights to have done, inasmuch as He has given express commandment to His servants to do it. We have just to take care lest, in our desire to remove the stumbling-blocks, we should in any wise disturb the land-marks. May the blessed Spirit graciously help us to a right understanding of this sadly misunderstood passage of Holy Scripture!

So we inquire who are they of whom the inspired writer speaks in verses 4-6 – those of whom he declares, "It is impossible to renew them again to repentance?" A correct answer to this question will remove much of the difficulty felt in respect to this portion of Hebrews. In reaching this answer there are two things to be borne in mind. First, in verses 1 and 2 there is not a single feature belonging to Christianity as distinct from Judaism; secondly, in verses 4 and 5 there is not a single expression that rises to the height of the new birth or the sealing of the Spirit.

Let us quote the apostle's words: "Therefore, leaving the principles of the doctrine of Christ," or as the margin reads it, "The word of the beginning of Christ, let us go on to perfection; not laying again the foundation of repentance from dead works, and of faith toward God, of the doctrine of baptisms or washings, and of laying on of hands, and of resurrection of the dead and of eternal judgment."

Now it must be plain to the reader that the apostle could never exhort those professing Hebrew Christians to *leave* anything belonging to Christianity. There is not a single fact in that glorious economy from first to last – not a single stone in that glorious superstructure from foundation to topstone; not a single principle in that magnificent system from beginning to end – that we could afford to leave or dispense with for a moment. What is the grand foundation of Christianity? The cross. And what are its two characteristic facts? A Man glorified in heaven and God dwelling in man on the earth. Could we leave these? God forbid! To whom or to what should we go? It is impossible that we could leave or give up a single fact, feature or principle of our glorious Christianity.

What then are we to leave in Hebrews 6:1-2? Simply those elements of truth contained in the Jewish system which, in so far as they possessed any permanent value, are reproduced in Christianity, but *as a system* were to be abandoned forever. Where is there a word unique to Christianity in this passage? Can we not see at a glance that the apostle has Judaism before his mind? It is this he exhorts his brethren to leave and to go on to Christianity which he here calls "perfection."

It is a commonly believed idea that the words "Let us go on to perfection" refer to our leaving the earlier stages of the divine life and getting on to the higher. This is a total mistake. As to what is called "the higher Christian life," there is in reality no such thing. If there be a higher life, there must be a lower one, but we *know* that Christ is our life, the life of each, the life of all. There cannot be anything higher than that. The merest babe in Christ has as high a life as the most matured and profoundly-taught member of the Church of God.

There is *progress* in the divine life, growth in grace, faith growing exceedingly. All this we own most fully and would charge ourselves to seek after it most earnestly. But it is not the subject of Hebrews 6:1-2. It is not a question of going from one form in the school of Christ to another, but of leaving the school of Moses to enter fully, heartily and intelligently into the school of Christ. It is not a question of going from one stage of Christian life to another, but of abandoning Judaism to go on to Christianity. We could not abandon a single atom of Christianity without abandoning Christ Himself, for He is the foundation, the source, the center, the spring of it all.

But the reader may feel disposed to ask, Have we not got "repentance, faith, resurrection and eternal judgment" in Hebrews 6:1-2?* True, but only as elements of the Jewish system. There is not a word about "faith in our Lord Jesus Christ", not a word about Christ at all. It is simply Judaism, to which some of the Hebrew professors were in danger of returning, but from which the apostle earnestly urges them to go on.

Let us now turn for a moment to verses 4 and 5. "For it is impossible for those who were once enlightened and have tasted of the heavenly gift, and were made partakers of the Holy Spirit, and have tasted the good Word of God and the powers of the world to come (of the coming millennial age), if they shall fall away, to renew them again unto repentance."

The reader will notice that, as in verses 1 and 2, we have not a single clause specially characteristic of Christianity. Also in verses 4 and 5, we have not a single clause that rises to the height of the new birth or the sealing of the Holy Spirit. A person might be all that is here spoken of and yet never have been born again, never sealed by the Holy Spirit. How many thousands have been "enlightened" by the gospel without being converted by it! Wherever the gospel has been preached, wherever the Bible has been received and read, an enlightening influence has gone forth, altogether irrespective of any saving work wrought in souls. Look at the nations of Europe since the Reformation. In all those countries that have received the Bible, we see the moral effect produced in the way of intelligence, civilization and refinement, apart altogether from the question of the conversion of individual souls. On the other hand those countries which have refused the Bible, exhibit the depressing results of ignorance, moral darkness and degradation. In a word, there may be enlightenment of the understanding without any divine work in the conscience or in the heart.

But what means the "tasting the heavenly gift?" Does not this imply the new birth? By no means. Many have gotten a taste of the new, the heavenly things set forth in the glorious gospel of God, and yet never have passed from death unto life, never have been broken down before God about their sins – never have received Christ into their hearts. *Tasting* of the heavenly gift and passing by new birth into the heavenly kingdom, are totally different things.

Also many were made "*partakers* of the Holy Spirit" so as to speak with tongues, prophesy and the like, who nevertheless were never born of

---

* Resurrection, as seen in Christianity, is not merely "resurrection of the dead," but, "resurrection from *among* the dead."

the Spirit. When the Holy Spirit came down on the day of Pentecost, His presence pervaded the whole Assembly. His power was felt by all, converted or unconverted. The word rendered "partakers" does not express intelligent fellowship. This makes it all the more clear that there is not the slightest thought of new birth or sealing.

Further, as to "*tasting* the good Word of God," do we not all know too well that unconverted people can in a certain sense enjoy the Word of God and have a measure of delight in hearing a full, free gospel preached? Have we not often heard persons who furnished no evidence of divine life, speak in highly appreciative terms of what they call the savory doctrines of grace? There is a wide and very material difference indeed between a person *tasting* the good Word of God and the Word of God entering the soul in living, quickening, convicting and converting power.

Finally, a person might *taste* "the power of the coming age" – the age when Messiah will set up His kingdom. He might heal diseases and cast out demons; he might take up serpents and drink poison; he might speak with tongues. He might do all these things and yet never have been born again. "Thus," as a recent writer has solemnly and forcibly put it, "we may fairly give the fullest force to every one of these expressions. Yet, write them out ever so largely, they fall short both of the new birth and of sealing with the Holy Spirit. There is everything except inward spiritual life in Christ or the indwelling seal of it. One may have the very highest endowments and privileges in the way both of meeting the mind and also of exterior power, and yet all may be given up and the man become so much more the enemy of Christ. Indeed such is the natural result. It had been the mournful fact as to some. They had fallen away. Hence renewal to repentance is an impossibility – declared to be so by the authoritative and conclusive testimony of the Holy Spirit – "seeing they crucify to themselves the Son of God and put him to an open shame."

Why impossible? The case supposed is not anyone who ever possessed a single spark of divine life in his soul; no, nor yet anyone with the very feeblest desire after Christ or one atom of true repentance or desire to flee from the wrath to come. The case is of persons, after the richest proof and privilege, turning aside as apostates from Christ, to take up Judaism once more. As long as that course is pursued, there cannot be repentance. Supposing a man had been the adversary of Messiah here below, as for example, Paul himself, the very writer of the epistle. There was still the opening for him of grace from on high. It was possible that the very man that had slighted Christ here below, might have his eyes opened to see and receive Christ above, but this abandoned, there is no fresh condition in which He could be presented to men. Those who rejected Christ in the fullness of His grace and in the height of His glory in which God had set Him as Man before them – not merely on earth, but in heaven as attested by the Holy Spirit sent down from the ascended and glorified Man on the throne of the Majesty in the heavens – what was there to fall back upon? What possible means to bring them to repentance after that? There is none. What is there but Christ coming in judgment?"*

For one who, from amid the full blaze of gospel light and privilege, could deliberately go back to the darkness of Judaism, there remains nothing but hopeless impenitence, hardness of heart, judicial blindness and eternal judgment.

It is not, be it carefully observed, a child of God falling into sin and getting at a distance from God. Such an one will, most surely, be brought back and restored, though it may be through sore affliction under the chastening hand of God. It is not an anxious soul earnestly seeking the way of life and peace. It is not the case of a poor soul ignorant and out of the way. To none of these does the "impossible" of Hebrews 6:4 apply. There is not a single anxious, earnest soul beneath the canopy of heaven whose case is impossible. There is just one case that approaches awfully near to Hebrews 6:4 and that is one who has gone on sinning against light, refusing to act on the plain Word of God, knowingly and deliberately resisting the truth because of the consequences of acting upon it.

This is indeed most solemn. No one can take it upon him to say at what depths of darkness, blindness and hardness of heart, a case of this kind may arrive. It is a terrible thing to trifle with light and to go on with what we know to be wrong because of worldly advantage, to please friends, to avoid persecution and trial, or for any reason whatsoever. "Give glory to the Lord your God before He cause darkness, and before your feet stumble on the dark mountains, and while ye look for light, He turn it into the shadow of death and make it gross darkness" (Jer. 13:16).

Having sounded this warning note for any whose case may need it, we close this part of our subject by presenting to any troubled soul whose eye may scan these lines, that precious word at the very end of the inspired volume – a word issuing forth from the very heart of God and the heart of Christ, "Whosoever will, let him take the water of life *freely.*"

---

* *Lectures Introductory to Paul's Epistle,"* by W. Kelly.

Let us now look at other warnings and consolations. In reading the Epistle to the Hebrews, we can hardly fail to notice the way in which the most solemn words of warning stand side by side with words of deepest comfort and consolation. Thus, for example, chapter 4 opens with "Let us therefore fear," and closes with "Let us therefore come boldly." When we think of who we are, what we are and where we are, we have reason to fear. But when we think of God – His grace, His goodness, His tender mercy, His faithfulness – we may cherish the most fearless confidence. When we think of the world with all its dangers, temptations and snares, we may well be on our guard. But when we think of "the throne of grace" with its exhaustless provisions, and of our most merciful, faithful and sympathizing High Priest, we can draw near with holy boldness and find an ample supply to meet our deepest need.

So also in chapter 10, we have the same striking contrast of the warning voice and the sweet words of comfort and encouragement. Hearken to the former. "If we sin wilfully after that we have received the knowledge of the truth, there remaineth no more sacrifice for sins, but a certain fearful looking for of judgment and fiery indignation which shall devour the adversaries. He that despised Moses' law died without mercy under two or three witnesses; of how much sorer punishment, suppose ye, shall he be thought worthy who hath trodden under foot the Son of God and hath counted the blood of the covenant wherewith he was sanctified, an unholy thing, and hath done despite unto the Spirit of grace? For we know Him that hath said, Vengeance belongeth unto Me, I will recompense, saith the Lord. And again, The Lord will judge His people. It is a fearful thing to fall into the hands of the living God."

How awfully solemn is all this! How searching! Should we seek to blunt the edge of the warning? God forbid! We should only see that it has its true direction, its proper application. Can it ever touch an anxious inquirer or a true-hearted, earnest follower of Christ? Assuredly not, except indeed that it may deepen the earnestness of the follower and quicken the pace of the inquirer, for only see, reader, how close the word of comfort and encouragement stands to the awful note of warning and admonition. "But call to remembrance the former days in which, after ye were illuminated, ye endured a great fight of afflictions, partly whilst ye were made a gazing-stock, both by reproaches and afflictions; and partly whilst ye became companions of them that were so used. For ye had compassion of me in my bonds and took joyfully the spoiling of your goods, knowing in yourselves that ye have in heaven a better and an enduring substance. Cast not away therefore your confidence, which hath great recompense of reward. For ye have need of patience, that, after ye have done the will of God, ye might receive the promise. For yet a little while and He that shall come will come, and will not tarry. Now the just shall live by faith, but if any man draw back, My soul shall have no pleasure in him. But we are not of them that draw back unto perdition, but of them that believe to the saving of the soul."

Thus we see how the inspiring Spirit connects, in this epistle, the most precious consolation with the most solemn warning. Both are needed and therefore both are given, and it will be our wisdom to seek to profit from both. We need never be afraid to trust Scripture. If we find a difficulty, in stead of puzzling over it, let us quietly wait on God for further light, meanwhile calmly resting in the assurance that no one part of the Word of God can ever contradict another. All is in the most perfect harmony. The apparent discrepancies are entirely owing to our ignorance. Hence, instead of putting forth our gratuitous efforts to reconcile things, we should just allow each passage of Scripture to come home in all its moral force to the heart and conscience, and produce its divinely-appointed result in the formation of our character.

Read such words as "My sheep hear My voice, and I know them, and they follow Me; and I give unto them eternal life and they shall never perish, neither shall any pluck them out of My hand. My Father which gave them to Me is greater than all; and no one is able to pluck them out of My Father's hand. I and My Father are one." It is our sweet privilege to take them in, in all their divine simplicity and heavenly clearness, and rest in them in calm confidence. There is no difficulty, no obscurity, no vagueness about them. All Christ's sheep are as safe as He can make them, as safe as He is Himself. The hand that would touch them must touch Him. They are divinely and eternally secure. Persons may imagine or profess themselves to be His sheep, who are not so in reality. They may fall away from their mere profession, bring much reproach on the cause of Christ, cause the way of truth to be evil spoken of, and lay a stumbling-block in the way of honest inquirers by leading them to think that true Christians can fall away and be lost. All this may be true, but it leaves wholly untouched the precious and most comforting words of our good and faithful Shepherd, *that His sheep have eternal life and shall never – can never – perish.* No passage of Holy Scripture can, by any possibility, contradict the plain statement of our Lord.

But then there are other passages designed to search the conscience, to make us watchful, to produce holy circumspection in our ways, to lead us to judge ourselves, to induce self-denial. Take the following weighty and most searching scripture: "Know ye not that they which run in a race, run all, but one receiveth the prize? So run that ye may obtain. And every man that striveth for the mastery is temperate in all things. Now they do it to obtain a corruptible crown, but we an incorruptible. I therefore so run, not as uncertainly; so fight I, not as one that beateth the air, but I keep under my body and bring it into subjection, lest that by any means, when I have preached to others, I myself should be a castaway" (1 Cor. 9:24-27).

Now, will anyone attempt to place 1 Corinthians 9 in opposition to John 10? Far be the thought! What then? We are simply to receive both in all their divine force and allow them to act upon us according to the divine purpose in giving them to us – the latter on our hearts for comfort and consolation; the former on our consciences for admonition and warning! How terrible it would be for anyone to say or to think that, because he is a sheep of Christ, he may walk in self-indulgence since he can never perish – that he need not seek to keep his body under, but may give loose rein to his desires, because nothing can separate him from the love of Christ! Surely such an one would afford most sad evidence that he is anything but a sheep of the flock of Christ.

But we must return to Hebrews 6 and dwell for a moment upon our second "Impossible." The first, as we have seen, had respect to man; the second has respect to God. Man, with the very highest advantages, with the very rarest privileges, with the most powerful array of evidence, will turn his back upon God and Christ. He will deliberately apostatize from Christianity, give up the truth of God, go back into darkness, and plunge into a condition from which the Holy Spirit declares "it is impossible to renew him again to repentance."

But as usual in this marvelous epistle, the "strong consolation" stands in close and most gracious proximity to the awful warning. And, blessed be God, this same strong consolation is designed for us in connection with the very smallest measure of living faith in the Word of God. It is not a question of great attainments in knowledge, experience or devotedness; no, it is simply a matter of having even that measure and character of faith and earnestness pictured by the man-slayer as he flew to the city of refuge to escape the avenger of blood. How precious is this for every true and earnest soul! The very feeblest spark of divinely-given faith secures eternal life, strong consolation and everlasting glory, because "it is impossible for God to lie." He cannot and will not deny Himself, blessed forever be His name! He has pledged His word and added His oath, the "two immutable things." Where is the power, human or demonic, that can touch these two things?

We close with another quote from William Kelly, from his "Lectures Introductory to Paul's Epistles."

Another point of interest which may be remarked here in Hebrews 6 is the intimation at the end, compared with the beginning of the chapter. We have seen the highest external privileges – and they were merely external – not only the mind of man, as far as it could, enjoying the truth, but the power of the Holy Spirit making the man an instrument of power, not a subject of grace, even though it be to his own shame and deeper condemnation afterwards. In short, man may have the utmost conceivable advantage and the greatest external power, even of the Spirit of God Himself, and yet all come to nothing.

How solemnizing! But the very same chapter which affirms and warns of the possible failure of every advantage, shows us the weakest faith that the whole New Testament describes coming into the secure possession of the best blessings of grace. How consolatory! How truly encouraging! Who but God could have dictated that this same chapter should depict the weakest faith that the New Testament ever acknowledges? What can look feebler, what more desperately pressed, than a man fleeing for refuge? It is not a soul as coming to Jesus; it is not as one whom the Lord meets and blesses on the spot, but here is a man hard-pushed, fleeing for his very life (evidently a figure drawn from the man-slayer fleeing from the avenger of blood), yet eternally saved and blessed according to the acceptance of Christ – the very lowest character of faith met by the very fullest, richest and most permanent blessing!

There was no reality found in the persons referred to in verses 4 and 5, though so highly favored. Hence, as there was no conscience before God, no sense of sin, no clinging to Christ, that everything came to nought. But here, in the end of the chapter, there is the fruit of faith, feeble indeed and sorely tried, but in the light that appreciates the judgment of God against sin. Hence, although it be only fleeing in an agony of soul for refuge, what is it that God gives to one in such a state? Strong consolation, and that which enters within the veil. Impossible that the Son should be shaken from His place on the throne of God. And it is as impossible that the very least and weakest believer should come to any hurt whatsoever! The weakest of saints is more than conqueror.

Well may we exclaim, in view of all this surpassing grace, "Hallelujah!" Beloved Christian reader, may our whole life be spent in praising our ever blessed and most gracious Savior-God!

"RECONCILED AND SAVED"

"For if, when we were enemies, we were reconciled to God by the death of His Son, much more, being reconciled, we shall be saved by His life" (Rom. 5:10).

If ever there was a moment in which it was important to set forth the great foundation truths of Christianity, it is now. The enemy is seeking by every means in his power to loosen the foundations of our faith – to weaken the authority of Holy Scripture over the heart and conscience – to introduce, in the most specious and fascinating forms, deadly error to draw away the soul from Christ and His Word.

It may be said, "This is an old story." It is as old as 2 Timothy, 2 Peter and Jude. But it is a new story also; and while we do not feel it to be our work to grapple in a controversial way with popular errors and evils, we do believe it to be our sacred duty to set forth and maintain constantly those grand, solid, fundamental truths which are our only safeguard against every form of doctrinal error and moral depravity.

Hence it is that we feel called upon to draw the attention of our readers to that very weighty passage which stands at the head of this paper. It is one of the fullest and most comprehensive statements of foundation doctrine to be found within the compass of the Volume of God. Let us meditate for a little upon it.

In examining the context in which this passage stands, we find four distinct terms by which the inspired writer sets forth the condition of man in his unconverted state. He speaks of him as "without strength." This is what we may call a negative term. Man is utterly powerless, wholly incapable of doing anything toward his own deliverance. He has been tried in every possible way. God has tested him and proved him, and found him absolutely good for nothing. When placed in Eden in the midst of the ten thousand delights which a beneficent Creator had poured around him, he believed the devil's lie rather than the truth of God (Gen. 3). When driven out of Eden, we see him pursuing a career of evil – "evil only" – evil continually – until the judgment of God falls upon the whole race with one solitary exception – Noah and his family (Gen. 6-8). Further, when in the restored earth man is entrusted with the sword of government, he gets drunk and exposes himself to contempt in the very presence of his sons. When entrusted with the holy office of the priesthood, man offers strange fire (Lev. 10). When entrusted with the high office of king and enriched with untold wealth, he marries foreign wives and worships the idols of the heathen (2 Chron. 11).

Thus, wherever we trace man – the human race – we see nothing but the most humiliating failure. Man is proved to be good for nothing, "without strength."

But there is more than this. Man is "ungodly." He is not only power-less as to all that is holy and good, but also without one single moral or spiritual link with the living and true God. Examine the unrenewed heart from its center to its circumference, and you will not find so much as one true thought about God or one right affection toward God. There may be a great deal that is amiable and attractive in the way of nature – much that is morally lovely in the eyes of men such as many social virtues and excellent qualities. Human nature, even in its ruins, may exhibit much of all these, just as the visible creation – this earth on which we live – dis-plays, in spite of its ruined and groaning condition, many splendid traces of the master hand that formed it.

All this is perfectly true and perfectly obvious. Moreover, it must ever be taken into account in dealing with the great question of man's stand-ing and condition. There is an extreme way of speaking of the sinner's state which is more likely to stumble and perplex the mind than to con-vict the conscience or break the heart. This should be carefully avoided. We should always take account of all that is really good in human nature. If we look at the case of the rich young ruler in Mark 10, we see that the Lord recognized something lovable in him, for we read that "Jesus beholding him, loved him," though we have no warrant whatever to sup-pose there was any divine work in his soul, seeing he turned his back upon Christ and preferred the world to Him. But there was evidently something most attractive in this young man, something different from those gross, coarse and degraded forms in which human nature often clothes itself.

We cannot but judge that the man who, in writing or speaking about the sinner's moral and spiritual state, would ignore or lose sight of those moral and social distinctions, does positive damage to the cause of truth and neutralizes the very object which he has in view. If, for example, we approach an amiable, upright, frank and honorable person, and in a sweeping manner place him in the same category with a crooked, schem-ing, dishonest, contemptible character, we only drive him away in irrita-tion and disgust. Whereas, if we recognize whatever is really good; if we allow, as Scripture most surely does, a sufficient margin in which to set down all that is morally and socially excellent even in fallen humanity, we are much more likely to gain our end, than by injudiciously ignoring those distinctions. Inasmuch as they clearly exist, it is the height of folly to deny them. Still, it holds good – and let the reader solemnly consider the weighty fact – that man, the very best, the very fairest specimen is "without strength" and "ungodly." Nor is this all. The apostle does not rest in mere negatives. He not only tells us what man is not, but he goes on to tell us what he is. He gives us both sides of this great question. He not only declares that, "When we were without strength, in due time Christ died for the ungodly," but he adds that "God commendeth His love toward us, in that, while we were yet sinners, Christ died for us."

Here we have the positive activity of evil, the actual energy of self-will. For, be it remembered, sin is doing our own will in whatever line that will may travel, whatever form it may assume. It may present itself in the shape of the grossest moral depravity or it may array itself in the garb of a cultivated and refined taste, but it is self-will all the while, and self-will is sin. It may be only like the acorn, the mere seed, but the acorn contains the wide spreading oak. Thus the heart of the newly born infant is a little seed-plot in which may be found the germ of every sin that ever was committed in the world. True, each seed may not germinate or bring forth fruit, but the seed is there and only needs circumstances or influences to unfold it.

If anyone be kept from gross outward sins, it is not owing to a better nature, but simply to the fact of his surroundings. All men are sinners. All by nature do their own will. This stamps their character. "All have sinned and come short of the glory of God." From the days of fallen Adam to this moment – about 6000 years – there has been but one solitary exception to this solemn and terrible rule. There was only One who never sinned, never did His own will, and that is the blessed Lord Jesus Christ. Though God over all blessed forever, yet having become a Man, He surrendered His own will completely and did always and only the things that pleased His Father. From the manger to the cross, He was ruled in all things by the will and the glory of God. He was the only perfect spotless Man who ever trod this sin-stained earth. He was the only fair untainted sheaf that ever appeared in the field of this world – "the Man Christ Jesus" who died for us "sinners" and "suffered for sins, the Just for the unjust, to bring us to God."

What marvelous grace! What soul-subduing love! What amazing mercy! Oh! how it should melt these hearts of ours! Think, dear reader, think deeply of this love, this grace, this mercy. Dwell upon it until your soul is absorbed in the contemplation of it. We are painfully insensible and indifferent. Indeed there is nothing more humbling than our guilty, shameful indifference to a Savior's love. We seem content to take salvation as the result of His cross and passion, His agony and grief, His inexpressible sorrow, while at the same time, our hearts are cold and indifferent to Him. He left the bright heavens and came down into this dark and sinful world for us. He went down into the gloomy depths of death and the grave. He endured the hiding of God's countenance, which involved more intense anguish to His precious soul than all that men and demons, earth and hell could do. He sank in deep waters, and went down into the horrible pit and into the miry clay. He did all this for us "sinners" when we were "ungodly" and "without strength." Yet how little we think of it! How little we dwell upon it! How little we are moved by the record of it!

The remembrance of this should humble us in the dust before our precious Savior-God. The hardness of our hearts in the presence of the profound mystery of the cross and passion of our Lord Christ is, if possible, a more remarkable and striking proof of our depravity than the sins for which He died. But we have rather anticipated what may yet come before us in the further unfolding of our subject. And now a brief reference to the fourth term by which the apostle sets forth our condition in nature. This is contained in the verse which forms our present thesis. "We were enemies." What a thought! We were not merely powerless, godless, sinful, but actually hostile – in a state of positive enmity against God.

Nothing can possibly exceed this. To be the enemy of God gives the most appalling idea we can possibly have of a sinner's state. Yet such is the actual condition of the unconverted reader of these lines. He is an enemy of God. He may be amiable, polite, attractive, refined, cultivated, educated, moral and even outwardly religious. He may occupy the very highest platform of religious profession. He may be a church member, a regular communicant, a worker in the vineyard, a Sunday School teacher, a preacher, a minister, and all the while be an enemy of God.

How awful the thought! Oh beloved reader, do pause and consider, we beseech you. Give this solemn question your undivided attention. Do not put it aside. We appeal to you with all earnestness, as in the presence of Almighty God, of His Son Jesus Christ and of the Eternal Spirit. We adjure you by the value of your immortal soul, by the dread reality of the judgment seat of Christ, by all the horrors of that lake which burns with fire and brimstone, by the worm that never dies, by the awful fact of eternity – an eternity in the gloomy shades of hell – by the unutterable agony of being separated forever from God, from Christ and from all that is pure and lovely. By the combined force of all these arguments, we earnestly and affectionately beseech you to flee, this moment, to the Savior who stands with open arms and loving heart to receive you. Come to Jesus! Come now, just as you are! Only trust Him and you are safe – safe forever – safe as He.

We also would call the attention of our readers to the important distinction between *atonement* and *reconciliation*. They are often confounded through lack of attention to the precise terms of Holy Scripture. The fact is, they are distinct, though intimately connected – distinct as the foundation is from the building – connected as the building is with the foundation. Atonement is the foundation on which reconciliation rests. Without atonement, there could not possibly be any reconciliation, but reconciliation is not atonement. The reader will do well to weigh this matter thoroughly in the light of inspiration. It is most needful for all Christians to be clear and sound in their thoughts on divine subjects, and accurate in their way of stating them. It will invariably be found that the more spiritual anyone is, the closer he will keep to the language of Scripture in putting forth foundation truth. Unfortunately, our most excellent Authorized Version [KJV] is not accurate in this matter, inasmuch as we find in Romans 5:11 the word "atonement" where it ought to be "reconciliation." On the other hand, we have in Hebrews 2:17, the word "reconciliation" where it ought to be "atonement" or "propitiation." However, the two things are distinct and it is important that the distinction should be understood and maintained.

Furthermore, we would remind the reader that *there is no foundation whatsoever in the Word of God for the idea that God needed to be reconciled to us.* There is no such thought to be found within the covers of the Bible. It was man that needed to be reconciled to God, not God to man. Man was the enemy of God. He was not only "without strength," "ungodly," and "a sinner," but actually "an enemy."

Now it is the enemy – the alienated one, the estranged one – that needs to be brought back, to be reconciled. This is plain. But God, blessed be His name, was not man's enemy. He was man's friend, the Friend of sinners. Such was the blessed Lord Jesus Christ when on earth. "He went about doing good and healing all that were oppressed of the devil, for God was with Him" (Acts 10). It was His delight to do good unto all. He spent His life in doing good to those who preferred a robber and a mur-

140

derer to Him, and nailed Him to a cross between two thieves. Thus, whether we look at the life or at the death of Christ, we see in the clearest and most forcible manner the enmity of man, but the friendship, the kindness, the love of God.

How is man to be reconciled to God? Momentous question! Let us look well to the answer. The passage of Scripture which forms the theme of this article declares in the most distinct manner, that "We are reconciled to God *by the death* of his Son" (Rom. 5:10). Nothing else could do it. The death of the cross – the atoning death – the vicarious sacrifice – the precious priceless blood of Jesus – is the absolutely essential basis of our reconciliation to a sin-hating God. We must state this great truth in the most emphatic and unequivocal manner. Scripture is as clear and definite as possible. For us to be reconciled to God, sin must be put away, and "without shedding of blood, there is no remission" (Heb. 9:22).

Thus the matter stands if we are to be taught simply by Scripture. No blood-shedding, no remission; no remission, no reconciliation. Such is the divine order. Let men beware how they tamper with it. It is a very serious thing to touch the truth of God. We may rest assured that all who do so will meddle to their own hurt.

We are reconciled to God by the death of His Son. It is not by his incarnation, that is, His taking human nature upon Him. Incarnation could not reconcile us to God inasmuch as it could not blot out our sins. Incarnation is not atonement. It is well to note this. There is a subtle way of playing upon the word *atonement* which consists of a false division of the syllables – as though the word were *"at-one-ment."* This "atonement" is referred to the incarnation as though, in that mysterious act, our Lord took our fallen human nature into union with Himself. Against this we solemnly warn the reader. *It is fatally false doctrine.* It is an effort of the enemy to displace or set aside altogether the atoning death of Christ, with all those grand foundation truths which cluster round that most precious mystery.

We hold as a cardinal truth the incarnation of the eternal Son! It forms the foundation of that great mystery of godliness of which the topstone is a glorified Man on the throne of God. "And without controversy, great is the mystery of godliness: God was manifest in the flesh, justified in the Spirit, seen of angels, preached unto the Gentiles, believed on in the world, received up into glory" (1 Tim. 3:16).

We hold incarnation to be an integral part of the faith of a true Christian, nor could we own as a Christian anyone who denied it. But it is one thing to hold a truth and another thing altogether to displace it. It is a constant effort of Satan, if he cannot get men to reject a truth, to displace it. In this way he gains some of his greatest apparent triumphs. Thus it is with the essential doctrine of incarnation. Assuredly, the Son of God had to become a Man to die, but becoming Man is one thing and dying upon the cross is another. He might have become a Man; He might have lived and labored for 33 years on this earth; He might have been baptized in Jordan and tempted in the wilderness; He might have ascended from the mount of transfiguration to that glory from which He had come and which He had with the Father from before all worlds. At any moment during His blessed life, He might, so far as He was personally concerned, have returned to that heaven from where He had descended. What could hinder Him? There was no necessity laid on Him to die except the necessity of infinite and everlasting love. Death had no claim on Him inasmuch as He was the sinless, spotless, holy One of God. He had not come under the federal headship of the first man. Had He done so, He would have been under the curse and wrath of God all His days, and that not vicariously, but in virtue of His connection with the first Adam. This would be an open and positive blasphemy against His Person. He was the Second Man, the Lord from heaven, the only untainted grain of human wheat on which the eye of God could rest. As such, we repeat, He could at any point between the manger and the cross, have returned to the bosom of the Father – that dwelling-place of inexpressible love.

Let the reader seize with clearness and power this great truth. Let him dwell upon it. It is a truth of very great importance. Jesus stood alone in this world. He was alone in the manger, alone in the Jordan, alone in the wilderness, alone on the mount, alone in the garden. All this is in perfect keeping with His own memorable words in John 12, "Except a corn of wheat fall into the ground and die, it abideth alone; but if it die, it bringeth forth much fruit." Here is the grand point – "If it die." Unless He was to return to glory alone, He must die. If He was to have us with Him, He must die. If sins were to be forgiven, He must die. If sinners were to be saved, He must die. If a new and living way was to be opened for us into the presence of God, He must die. If the veil was to be rent, He must die. That mysterious curtain remained intact when the blessed One lay in the manger of Bethlehem – and when He was baptized and when He was anointed and when He was tempted and when He was transfigured and when He was bowed in Gethsemane, sweating great drops of blood, and when He was scourged before Pontius Pilate. Through all these stages of His marvelous life, the veil was unrent. There and thus it stood to bar the sinner's approach to God. Man was shut out from God and God shut in from man. Nor could all the living labors of the eternal Son – His miracles, His precious ministry, His tears, His sighs, His groans, His prayers, His sore testings and His untold living sorrows – have rent the veil. But the very moment death was accomplished, "The veil of the temple was rent in twain from the top to the bottom."

Such is the distinct teaching of Scripture on this vital question. The death of Christ is the foundation of everything. Is it a question of life? He has given His flesh for the life of the world. Is it a question of pardon? "Without shedding of blood is no remission." Is it a question of peace? "He made peace by the blood of His cross." Is it a question of reconciliation? "We are reconciled to God by the death of His Son." In short, it is through death we get everything; without death we get nothing. It is on the ground of death, the atoning death of Christ, that we are reconciled to God and united by the Holy Spirit to the risen and glorified Head in heaven. All rests on the solid groundwork of accomplished redemption. Sin is put away, the enmity is slain, all barriers are removed, God is glorified, the law magnified, and all this by the death of Christ. "He passed through death's dark raging flood" to settle everything for us, and to lay the imperishable foundation of all the counsels and purposes of the Holy Trinity.

Now a few words as to the life of Christ in heaven for us. "If while we were enemies, we were reconciled to God by the death of His Son, much more, being reconciled, we shall be saved by His life." Be it carefully noted that this refers to His life after death – His life in resurrection, His life in heaven. Some would teach us that it is His life on earth – His fulfillment of the law in our place. This is flatly contradicted by the very structure of the passage and by the entire teaching of the New Testament. It is not life before death, but life *after* death that the apostle speaks of. It is the priestly life of our blessed and adorable Lord, who ever lives to make intercession for us. It is by this we are saved through all the difficulties and dangers, the snares and temptations of this wilderness world.

We, though reconciled to God by the death of Christ, are nevertheless in ourselves, poor, feeble, helpless, erring creatures. We are prone to wander, ever liable to failure and sin, totally unable to get on for a single moment, if not kept by our great High Priest, our blessed Advocate, our Comforter. He keeps us day and night. He never slumbers nor sleeps. He maintains us continually before God in all the integrity of the position in which His death has placed us. It is impossible that our cause can ever fail in such hands. His intercession is all prevailing. "We have an Advocate with the Father, Jesus Christ the righteous." The One who bore our sins in His own body on the tree, now bears our sorrows on His heart upon the throne. And He will come again to bear the government upon His shoulder.

What a Savior! What a Victim! What a Priest! How blessed to have all our affairs in His hand and to be sustained by such a ministry! How precious to know that the One who has reconciled us to God by His death is now alive for us on the throne. Because He lives we shall live also! All praise to His peerless name!

"ACCEPTED" AND "ACCEPTABLE"

"He hath made us accepted in the Beloved" (Eph. 1:6). "Wherefore we labor, that whether present or absent, we may be acceptable to Him" (2 Cor. 5:9).

The two words which form the heading of this paper, though rendered by the same word in our Authorized Version, are not at all the same. The former has respect to the *person* of the believer, the later to his *practical ways*. The first refers to his standing, the second to his state. It is one thing to be accepted; it is quite another to be acceptable. The former is the fruit of God's free grace to us as sinners; the latter is the fruit of our earnest labor as saints, though most surely, it is only by grace we can do anything.

It is well that the Christian reader should thoroughly understand the distinction between these two things. It will preserve him effectively from legality on the one hand, and laxity on the other. It remains unalterably true of all believers, that God has made them accepted in the Beloved. Nothing can ever touch this. The very feeblest lamb in all the flock stands accepted in a risen Christ. There is no difference. The grace of God has placed them all on this high and blessed ground. We do not labor to be accepted. It is all the fruit of God's free grace. He found us all dead in trespasses and sins. We were morally dead, far off from God, hopeless, Godless, Christless, children of wrath, whether Jews or Gentiles. But Christ died for us, and God has co-quickened, co-raised and co-seated us in Christ, and made us accepted in Him.

This is the inalienable, eternal standing of all without exception, who believe in the name of the Son of God. Christ in His infinite grace placed Himself judicially where we were morally, and having put away our sins and perfectly satisfied on our behalf the claims of divine righteousness, God entered the scene and raised Him from the dead, and with Him all His members as seen in His own eternal purpose, and to be called in due time and brought into the actual possession and enjoyment of the marvelous place of blessing and privilege, by the effective operation of the Holy Spirit.

Well may we take up the opening words of the Epistle to the Ephesians and say, "Blessed be the God and Father of our Lord Jesus Christ, who hath blessed us with all spiritual blessings in the heavenlies in Christ. According as He hath chosen us in Him before the foundation of the world, that we should be holy and without blame before Him in love; having predestinated us unto the adoption of children by Jesus Christ to Himself, according to the good pleasure of His will, to the praise of the glory of His grace, wherein He hath made us accepted in the Beloved." All praise to His name throughout the everlasting ages!

All believers, then, are accepted – perfectly and forever accepted – in the Beloved. God sees them in Christ and as Christ. He thinks of them as He thinks of Him; loves them as He loves Him. They are ever before Him in perfect acceptance in the blessed Son of His love, nor can anything or anyone ever interfere with this their high and glorious position which rests on the eternal stability of the grace of God, the accomplished work of His Son, and attested by the Holy Spirit sent down from heaven.

But are all believers *acceptable* in their practical ways? Are all so conducting themselves that their dealings and doings will bear the light of the judgment-seat of Christ? Are all laboring to be agreeable to Him?

Christian reader, these are serious questions. Let us solemnly weigh them. Let us not turn away from the sharp edge of plain practical truth. The blessed apostle knew he was accepted. Did that make him lax, careless or indolent? Far from it. "We labor," he says, "to be *acceptable* to Him." The sweet assurance that we are *accepted* in Him is the ground of our labor to be acceptable to Him. "The love of Christ constraineth us; because we thus judge, that if One died for all, then were all dead. And He died for all, that they which live should not henceforth live unto themselves, but unto Him who died for them and rose again" (2 Cor. 5:14-15).

All this is preeminently practical. We are called upon, by every argument which can bear sway over the heart and conscience, to labor diligently to be acceptable to our blessed and adorable Lord. Is there anything of legality in this? Not the slightest tinge. The very reverse. It is the holy superstructure of a devoted life, erected on the solid foundation of our eternal election and perfect acceptance in a risen and glorified Christ at God's right hand. How could there be the very smallest atom of legality here? Utterly impossible! It is all the pure fruit of God's free and sovereign grace from first to last.

But ought we not, beloved Christian reader, to arouse ourselves to attend to the claims of Christ as to practical righteousness? Should we not zealously and lovingly aim at giving Him pleasure? Are we to content ourselves with simply talking about our acceptance in Christ, while at the same time having no real earnest care as to the acceptability of our ways?

Cod forbid! Yes, let us so dwell upon the rich grace that shines in the acceptance of our persons, that we may be led out in diligent and fervent effort to be found acceptable in our ways.

It is greatly to be feared that there is an appalling amount of unhallowed traffic in the doctrines of grace without any godly care as to the application of those doctrines to our practical conduct. How all this is to end, it would be hard to say, but most assuredly, there is an urgent call upon all who profess to be accepted in Christ to labor fervently to be acceptable to Him.

RELIEF FOR A BURDENED HEART
(A REPLY TO AN ANXIOUS ENQUIRER)

Your letter has interested us exceedingly. Few things lie nearer to the heart than the case of anxious and burdened spirits. The work of emancipating and soothing such is becoming more and more charming to us. Words cannot convey how intensely we long to be used as God's instruments in this most delightful work. We are fully persuaded that it is a work which lies very near the heart of Christ. How could we question this while hearkening to such words as these, "The Spirit of the Lord is upon Me because He hath anointed Me to preach the gospel to the poor; He hath sent Me to heal the broken-hearted, to preach deliverance to the captives and recovering of sight to the blind, to set at liberty them that are bruised" (Lk. 4:18). And again "Come unto Me all ye that labor and are heavy-laden, and I will give you rest" (Mt. 11:28). How precious is the thought of God sending His Son and anointing Him with the Holy Spirit, to preach glad tidings to the poor, to bring healing to the brokenhearted, sight to the blind, deliverance to the captive, liberty for the oppressed, rest for the weary! What unspeakable comfort for one who may find himself in any of these conditions!

Now dear friend, it seems very plain that you are a weary, heavy laden one, and as such, you are the very object for the gracious ministry of the Lord Jesus Christ. You are one of those for whom He was sent and for whom He was anointed by the Holy Spirit. We have not the slightest doubt but that the root of the matter is in you. The very anxieties to which you give expression are, in our judgment, the evidence of a spiritual work in your soul. Not that we want you to build your peace upon this. God forbid! If all the angels in heaven and all the men upon earth were to give expression to their confidence in your Christianity, it might be a comfort and an encouragement to you, but could never form the ground of your peace in the presence of a holy, sin-hating God. It matters little, comparatively, what men think about you: the question is, what does God think about you? He has found you out. He knows the worst about you; yet He loves you and gave His Son to die for you. Here is the only ground of a sinner's peace. God Himself has met your case. He has been glorified about your sins in the death of His Son. It does not matter the least what you are. You say you are sometimes at a loss to know in what light to regard yourself, whether as wholly unconverted or a backslider. The fact is, what you really want is to get to the end of yourself altogether. When you get there, you will find God in all the fullness of His grace as manifested in Christ. Surely to get to the end of oneself and find Christ, is the true way to find peace.

It seems to us that one special malady from which you are suffering is intense self-occupation. This is the case with thousands. It is quite true that the Spirit of God will exercise us about our condition and cause us to judge it, but then it is only for the purpose of leading us to the very bottom of it all, so we may find settled repose in the fullness and sufficiency of Christ. This kind of exercise is very good. We delight in seeing a soul under deep spiritual work – the deeper the better. We are of opinion that in spiritual farming, the deeper the furrow the stronger the root. We do not attach much value to a superficial work in the conscience. Although it is quite true that we are not saved by a process of exercise of heart or conscience, still we have frequently found that persons who easily and rapidly glided into a certain feeling of peace, were in danger of gliding as rapidly out of it and becoming as miserable as they had once been happy. Sin must be seen in its sinfulness, and the sooner it is thus seen the better, so that having it really judged in the conscience, we may lay hold of a full and precious Christ as God's answer to it all. When this is the case, the heart enjoys a more solid, abiding peace and is not subject to those variations of which so many complain.

But there is a kind of self-occupation into which Satan leads the awakened sinner for the purpose of keeping him from Christ. This must be carefully guarded against. We apprehend he has entangled your feet in this snare. The style and tone of your letter lead us to this conclusion. We most fully enter into your case. Indeed you possess our entire sympathy. We deeply respect the feeling which leads you to absent yourself from the Lord's Table in your present state of soul. We consider it vastly superior to the lightness, flippancy and heartless formality with which so many approach that sacred institution. Far be it from us to pen a single line which would have the effect of emboldening you to approach the Lord's Supper in an unhappy and untruthful condition of heart and conscience. But then we want you so to apprehend the gospel of the grace of God – the full forgiveness of your sins however magnified and multiplied, your complete justification through the death and resurrection of Christ. We want you so to see the application of all this to your own soul that you may be able, like the poor man in Acts 3, to rise from your crippled condition and enter into the temple, leaping and walking and praising God. Be assured of it, dearly beloved, this is your privilege. There is nothing to hinder your enjoyment

149

this moment, except the unbelief and legality of your own spirit. The enemy would keep you occupied with yourself to keep you from Christ. Watch against this. It is the most hopeless, gloomy labor to be seeking for anything in yourself. Look off unto Jesus. You will find all you want in Him. May the power of the Holy Spirit fill your whole soul with the fullness and preciousness of Christ so you may get into and continue in that holy and happy liberty which is the proper portion of every child of God.

You will further bear with us when we tell you that we discern in your letter a great deal of the legal element. This is an evil which is hateful to the Spirit of God and subversive of your own peace and comfort. You want to get into and breathe the genial atmosphere of free grace – that grace which reigns through righteousness unto eternal life by Jesus Christ our Lord. You have very unworthy thoughts of God's perfect, eternal and unchangeable love. You seem to measure God by the standard of your own thoughts. You are reasoning from what you are to God, instead of believing what God is to you. This is a serious mistake, the mistake of many. We are all, more or less, prone to this grievous error. Very few live in the actual enjoyment of salvation by grace. There is the continual weighing of self in a legal balance. The principle of law is so deeply embedded in the heart, that nothing but the mighty power of the Spirit of God can deliver us from it and lead us into the practical understanding of that brief but most comprehensive statement of the apostle: "Ye are not under law, but under grace" (Rom. 6).

We hold it to be utterly impossible for a soul to enjoy settled peace so long as it is in any measure under the influence of this law-principle. There may be occasional gleams of sunshine, such as you describe in your own experience, but there never can be abiding gospel-peace as long as a single trace of the legal element is allowed to hold sway over the conscience. Abiding peace can only flow from a deep, thorough, practical sense of free grace, and that free grace acts towards the sinner on the settled ground of accomplished atonement.

Legality will always direct the eye inward upon self – yes, ever and only upon self. It will lead us to measure our standing before God by our own progress in personal holiness, our efforts, our services, our doings, our ways, our feelings, our something or other. All this produces spiritual darkness, gloomy uncertainty, mental bondage, intense soul-torture, depression, irritability, sourness of temper. And these things again react most prejudicially upon our whole moral being. They fling back their demoralizing influence upon the life and character. The hymn of joyous praise can only be occasionally sung. The supper feast – that most precious memorial of accomplished redemption – is abandoned, or if not abandoned, is gone through without freshness, anointing, power, elevation, or depth of spiritual tone. In this way, Christ is dishonored, the Holy Spirit is grieved, the testimony is marred, and the standard of practical Christianity greatly lowered. Moreover, the enemy, finding us in this condition of soul, cuts out ample work for us by acting in various ways upon our lusts and passions, which only gather strength from the very fact of our being under law, for as the apostle says, "The strength of sin is the law." Thus the soul's history is summed up in two words, namely "lust and law," and one is tossed like a ball from one to the other until free grace comes in and gives full deliverance from both. Grace gives you power over sin, but law gives sin power over you. Grace keeps you in the place of continual victory; law keeps you in the place of continual defeat.

May the Lord lead you and all His people into a clearer apprehension of grace, so that your peace may flow as a river, and the fruits of righteousness abound to the praise of His name!

We are not yet done with your letter, dear friend. We think we discern another feature in your case which tends to produce the spiritual depression of which you complain. If we mistake not, you are afflicted with an unhealthy, gloomy conscience. This is a sore evil, a heavy burden, a very great trial. We deeply feel for anyone laboring under this grievous malady, for it not only affects oneself, but all with whom one comes in contact. There is a wide difference indeed between a scrupulous or exacting conscience and a tender conscience. The former is governed by its own fears; the latter by the Word of God. The former induces feebleness and uncertainty in all one's ways; the later, a holy stability and consistency. We can hardly conceive a more troublesome companion than a morbid, gloomy conscience. It is always creating difficulties for its possessor and placing stumbling-blocks in his way. But a tender conscience is invaluable. It resents only what ought to be resented. Its action is true and healthy. It does not morbidly seek out the cause of trouble and defilement, but being duly acted upon by the Word of God as applied by the Holy Spirit, it yields a true response and thus discharges with vigor its divinely appointed functions.

Think beloved, of all these things and seek to watch against them, and above all, believe against them. Get done with self-occupation, rise above your legal fears and cast away from you the workings of a morbid conscience. Be assured of it, these are three features in your case. They also

151

are features of many a case – a self-occupied heart, a legal mind, a morbid conscience. Terrible evils! May the power of the Holy Spirit give you full deliverance from these three efficient agents of the devil! May He break every chain and give you to taste the true sweetness of spiritual liberty and communion of heart with a reconciled God and Father.

Do not any longer harass yourself with the questions, "Am I a converted person or am I a backslider?" You are in yourself a poor lost, unworthy, good-for-nothing creature. Yet God commends His love toward you in that He gave His only begotten Son to bear your curse and burden on the tree. Cast yourself on His boundless love, "a sea where none can sink." See that all is done. The debt is paid. Satan is silenced. The law is magnified. Sin is put away. God is satisfied, yea, glorified. What more would you have? For what are you waiting? You may say to us, "I know all this." You do say in your letter that you "can hardly expect to hear anything more than you have already read." Well, we want you to make all this your own by simple, childlike faith. We want to drive you out of every legal lurking place into the full blaze of divine and everlasting love. Cast away from you, we beseech you, dear friend, all your legal reasonings and seek to exercise a believing mind that just takes God at His word and takes possession, without a question, of all that He gives. We do not want to heal your wound slightly; to cry "peace, peace, when there is no peace." This would be cruelty rather than kindness. But we desire that you should "know the things which are freely given to you of God," and which are as clearly revealed in the Word as they are freely given through grace. We long to see you as happy as the gospel of the grace of God is fitted to make you. Then you will be able to sing hymns of praise and take your seat at the table of the Lord in happy, holy, elevated communion and worship.

May the good Lord meet you in your present need! May He disperse, by the bright and blessed beams of His love, the dark cloud that has settled down upon your spirit, and fill you with all joy and peace in believing. To Him we do most affectionately commend you, praying Him to make use of what we have written in blessing to your precious soul, and His name shall have all the praise throughout the everlasting ages.

THREE PRECIOUS GIFTS

"I give unto My sheep eternal life and they shall never perish" (Jn. 10).

"The gift of God is eternal life through Jesus Christ our Lord" (Rom. 6).

"He that followeth Me shall not walk in darkness, but shall have the light of life" (Jn. 8).

"Christ shall give thee light" (Eph. 5).

"Ye shall know the truth, and the truth shall make you free" (Jn. 8:6).

"Stand fast therefore in the liberty wherewith Christ hath made us free" (Gal. 5:1).

The scriptures quoted above – and they are only a few of the many that might be used – teach us that there are three things bestowed upon every soul that, through grace, simply and truly and heartily believes in Jesus. These are "Life" "Light" and "Liberty" – three most precious gifts, gifts in comparison with which all earthly riches, pleasures and distinctions are but as dust.

But there are many who ought to be in the full and settled enjoyment of these immense privileges who actually do not know they possess them at all. They consider it the height of presumption for any soul to think of possessing them. There are many sincere and earnest souls – truly converted children of God – who, through bad teaching, self-occupation or legality, are thoroughly in the dark as to the very elements of Christianity, the simplest truths of the gospel. The dark atmosphere which enwraps Christendom so obscures the light of divine truth that they really do not know where they are or what they have got. In place of life, light and liberty, they are practically in the shadow of death, in darkness and bondage. They are robbed of those three precious gifts which God, in the fullness and riches of His grace, liberally bestows upon all who believe on the name of His only begotten Son.

It is for the special purpose of helping that large and interesting class of persons who are thus robbed and spoiled, that we have penned the few inspired sentences at the head of this paper. We affectionately entreat these souls to give earnest heed to them. We are not going to expound them nor enter upon a full statement of the doctrines indicated in them. Our object is rather to exhort than to expound. We long to see all the dear children of God in the full enjoyment of the things which are freely given them of God in Christ.

Let all such hear what our Lord Christ says, "I give unto My sheep eternal life." "Ah! yes," some exercised soul may say: "I quite see that all Christ's sheep have eternal life, but my soul-crushing difficulty is to know that I am a sheep of Christ. If only I knew that, I should count myself happy indeed."

Now this is a mistake. It is beginning at the wrong end. It is putting self and its feelings before Christ and His Word. Most surely, as long as one is doing this, he must be in doubt and darkness. It is utterly impossible to be otherwise. If it is something about myself I am called to feel or believe in order to be saved, then I never can have the settled knowledge or assurance of salvation. I must have something entirely outside and independent of myself, something divinely solid, something eternally stable, some settled and absolute truth, something true in itself apart from all my thoughts and feelings respecting it. In short, I must have God's own revelation to rest upon, or I never can know what abiding peace really is. It is the eternal truth of God, and that alone, which forms the real basis of the soul's peace – a basis which not all the powers of earth and hell, men and demons can ever disturb. It is by believing in Christ, and not by feeling or believing something about myself, that I get eternal life. He that believeth on the Son of God *has* eternal life.

Anxious reader, do ponder this. It is of the very deepest importance. It concerns the peace and rest of your soul. We would call your earnest attention to the weighty fact that what you are called upon to believe is not something about yourself, but something about Christ. "Verily, verily, I say unto you, He that believeth on Me hath everlasting life" (Jn. 6:47). Do you simply and heartily believe in Jesus? Do you confide in Him? Are you thoroughly satisfied with Him? If so, you have eternal life, and you should from this moment, know it and rejoice in it. Our Lord does not say, "He that *feeleth* he is one of My sheep shall have eternal life." Nothing of the kind, nothing like it, nothing approaching to it. "He that believeth on Me." So also in that well-known passage in John 5. "Verily, verily, I say unto you. He that heareth My word and believeth on Him that sent Me *hath* everlasting life and shall not come into judgment, but is passed from death unto life."

Can anything be plainer than this? Every one who hears the word of Jesus and believes in the One who sent Him, is the happy possessor of eternal life, and shall never come into judgment. Hence it follows that if we don't have eternal life, we do not believe on the Son of God, we have not heard His Word, we do not believe in God at all. Thus it stands if we are to be governed by the veritable teaching and authority of our Lord Christ. Every true believer in Jesus has eternal life, and everyone who does not have eternal life is an unbeliever. So speaks the Word of the living God.

But the believer should know what he possesses. Of what use or value could it be for anyone to be left a large fortune in Canada if he did not know anything about it? God would have us *know* what He has freely given us in Christ. The life is in Christ, so he that has Christ has the life, and he who has not life has not Christ. "God hath given to us eternal life, and this life is in His Son." Precious, all important word

Nor is it otherwise with respect to the second of our "three precious gifts." As we get "life" so we get "light" in Christ. "He that followeth Me shall not walk in darkness, but shall have the light of life." God would not give us life and leave us in the dark. This would not be like Him. He has given us His Son; and believing in Him, we get life. Then following Him, we get light – the light of life. Beautiful words! Words full of divine power! Liberating words for the soul that has been groping in darkness and the shadow of death! "The darkness is past, and the true light now shineth." And the proper sphere for the life which we now possess is the light in which we are called and privileged to walk.

The darkness is past, the shadows are gone, the clouds are rolled away, the dim twilight has given place to the full light of life streaming down into our souls and upon our path, enabling us to judge ourselves and our surroundings. We now can judge everything according to the true light that now shines within, upon and around us – shines from the Father, shines in the Son, shines in the power of the Holy Spirit, shines on the page of inspiration. Finally, it follows of blessed necessity that as we get "life" and "light," so we get "liberty." It is all in Christ. He quickens, He enlightens, He emancipates, He is our life, our light, our liberty. Blessed throughout all ages be His peerless name! "If the Son shall make you free, ye shall be free indeed." Surely it must be so. He would not give us life and leave us in the dark. He would not give us life and leave us in bondage or slavery. No, such is not His way. He sets us divinely and eternally free – free from guilt and condemnation, free from the dread of wrath and judgment to come, free from the fear of death, free from the present power of sin and from its future consequences. May the reader lay hold of these things in simple childlike faith, and join us in a note of fervent praise to the Giver of these "Three precious gifts."

RESURRECTION

A correspondent requests special notice of Philippians 3:11, "If by any means I might attain unto the resurrection from among the dead." The point toward which the desires of the true Christian ever tend is resurrection-glory. It matters not to him by what way he is to reach that point. He longs to reach the glory "by any means."

It may be that our friend finds difficulty in the word "if," as though it implied a doubt in the mind of the apostle as to his reaching the end in safety. The apostle did not have any such thought in his mind. The idea is simply that he had the goal before him and he was eagerly pressing toward it. His vision was filled with it, his heart was set on it, and as to the "means" by which he was to reach it, he was quite indifferent.

It may be interesting to observe that the word which is rendered "resurrection" only occurs in this one passage and properly signifies "resurrection from among." The Greek word *anastasis* (resurrection) occurs about 42 times in the New Testament and is applied to the broad fact of resurrection. But the word used in verse 11 is morally linked with the expression in Mark 9:10, "Questioning one with another what rising from *among* the dead should mean." The disciples would have found no difficulty in the thought of resurrection as such, seeing that every orthodox Jew believed in it. But a "rising from *among* the dead" was something strange to them. Hence their "questioning."

Now, the proper hope of the Christian is not merely "resurrection of the dead," but "resurrection from *among* the dead." This makes a substantial difference. It completely sets aside the idea of a general simultaneous resurrection. To speak of a resurrection from *among* the dead, obviously implies that all shall not rise together. Revelation 20:5 teaches us that there will be a thousand years between the two resurrections, but it is important to see that the very word used by the apostle to express that resurrection for which he was looking, is quite different from that usually employed to set forth the general thought of resurrection. Why is this? Simply because he meant a special thing and he therefore used a special word – a word which occurs only in this one place.

It is deeply solemn to remember that the Lord's people will rise from their graves and leave behind them the ashes of the wicked dead for a thousand years longer. This thought may seem to be foolishness to the natural man, but Scripture teaches it and that is quite enough for the Christian. The resurrection of the Church will be upon the same principle and partake of the same character as the resurrection of Christ; it will be "a resurrection from among the dead." May our hearts be set upon that glorious goal!

THE JUDGMENT SEAT OF CHRIST

We have received earnest requests for help as to the solemn subject of the judgment seat of Christ. One dear friend writes thus: "I am in a difficulty. A dear friend is very unhappy in the thought that, at the judgment seat of Christ, every secret thought and every motive of the heart will be made manifest to all there. She has no fears or doubts as to her eternal salvation or the forgiveness of her sins, but she shrinks with horror from the thought of having the secrets of her heart manifested to all there."

Another writes as follows: "Remembering those blessed and eternally-important truths in John 5:24; 1 John 1:7-9, 2:12 and Hebrews 10:1-17, I wish to know how you understand the following texts which I shall transcribe in full, to point out the particular words to which I refer.

"For we must all appear before the judgment seat of Christ that every one may receive the things done in his body, according to that he hath done, whether it be good or bad" (2 Cor. 5:10). "So then every one of us shall give account of himself to God" (Rom. 14:12). "But he that doeth wrong shall receive for the wrong he hath done: and there is no respect of persons" (Col. 3:24-25).

"It is on the above texts that I am anxious to be correct as to interpretation and application. I have thought it probable that you would not regard it as trespassing on your time if I were to ask your opinion on the subject."

We have been much interested in looking into the various reasons for the perplexity which seems to prevail in reference to the solemn subject of "the judgment seat of Christ." The very passages which our correspondent quotes are so plain, so pointed and so definite on the question, that we have only just to take them as they stand and allow them to have their due weight upon the heart and conscience. "We must all be manifested before the judgment seat of Christ." "Every one of us must give account of himself to God." "He that doeth wrong shall receive for the wrong he hath done."

These are plain statements. Should we desire to weaken their force, to blunt their edge, to turn away their point? God forbid! We should rather seek to make a holy use of them by keeping a pressure upon nature in all its vanities, lusts and tempers. The Lord intended we should use these verses thus. He never intended that we should use them in a legal way to shake our confidence in Christ and His full salvation. We shall never come into judgment as to our sins. John 5:24, Romans 8:1 and 1 John 4:17 are conclusive as to that point. But our *services* must come under the Master's eye. Every man's *work* shall be tried of what sort it is. The day will make everything manifest. All this is very solemn and should lead to great watchfulness and carefulness as to our works, ways, thoughts, words, motives and desires. The deepest sense of grace and the clearest apprehension of our perfect justification as sinners, will never weaken our sense of the deep solemnity of the judgment seat of Christ or lessen our desire so to walk that we may be acceptable to Him.

It is well to see this. The apostle labored that he might be accepted. He kept his body under lest he should be disapproved. Every saint should do the same. We are already accepted in Christ, and as such, we labor to be accepted of Him. We should seek to give every truth its proper place. The way to do this is to be much in the presence of God and to view each truth in immediate connection with Christ. There is always a danger of making such a use of one truth as, practically, to displace some other truth. This should be carefully guarded against. We believe there will be a full manifestation of everyone and everything before the judgment seat of Christ. Everything will come out there. Things that looked very brilliant and praiseworthy, and that made a great noise among men down here, will all be burned up as so much "wood, hay and stubble." Things that were blazed abroad and made use of to surround the names of men with a halo of human applause, will all be submitted to the searching action of "the fire" and much of them reduced to ashes.

The counsels of all hearts will be made manifest. Every motive, every purpose, every design will be weighed in the balances of the sanctuary. The fire will try every man's work, and nothing will be stamped as genuine except that which has been the fruit of divine grace in our hearts. All mixed motives will be judged, condemned and burnt up. All prejudices, all erroneous judgments, all evil surmisings concerning others – all these and such like things will be exposed and cast into the fire. We shall see things then as Christ sees them, judge them as He judges them. No one will be better pleased than myself to see all my stubble consumed. Even now, as we grow in light, knowledge and spirituality, as we get nearer and more like Christ, we heartily condemn many things which we once deemed all right. How much more shall we do so when we stand in the full blaze of the light of the judgment seat of Christ?

Now, what should be the practical effect of all this upon the believer? To make him doubt his salvation? To leave him in a state of uncertainty as to whether he is accepted or not? To make him question his relationship to God in Christ? Surely not. What then? To lead him to walk in holy carefulness from day to day, as under the eye of his Lord and Master – to produce watchfulness, sobriety and self-judgment, to induce faithfulness, diligence and integrity in all his services and all his ways.

Take a simple illustration. A father leaves home for a time. When taking leave of his children, he appoints a certain work to be done and a certain line of conduct to be adopted during his absence. When he returns, he may have to praise some for their faithfulness and diligence, while he blames others for the very reverse. But does he disown the latter? Does he break the relationship? By no means. They are just as much his children as the others, though he faithfully points out their failure and censures them for it. If they have been biting and devouring one another instead of doing his will; if one has been judging another's work instead of attending to his own; if there has been envy and jealousy instead of an earnest-hearted carrying out of the father's intentions, all these things will meet with well-deserved censure. How could it be otherwise?

But then some 'shrink with horror from the thought of having the secrets of the heart manifested to all there.' Well, the Holy Spirit declares that "the Lord will bring to light the hidden things of darkness and make manifest the counsels of the heart: and then shall every man have praise of God" (1 Cor. 3:9). He does not say *to whom* they shall be manifested; nor does this in the least affect the question, because every true-hearted person will be far more deeply concerned about the judgment of the Master than about the judgment of a fellow-servant. Provided I please Christ, I need not trouble myself much about man's judgment. If I am more troubled about the idea of having all my motives exposed to the view of man than I am about their being exposed to the view of Christ, it is plain there must be something wrong. It proves I am occupied about myself. I shrink from the exposure of "*my* secret motives." Then it is very plain that my secret motives are not right, and the sooner they are judged the better.

What difference would it make if all our sins and failures were made manifest to everybody? Are Peter and David any less happy because untold millions have read the account of their shameful fall? Surely not. They know that the record of their sins only magnifies the grace of God and illustrates the value of the blood of Christ, and hence they rejoice in it. Thus it is in every case. If we were more emptied of self and occupied with Christ, we should have more simple and correct thoughts about the judgment seat as well as about everything else.

May the Lord keep our hearts true to Himself in this the time of His absence, so that when He appears we may not be ashamed before Him! May all our works be so begun, continued and ended in Him, that the thought of having them duly weighed and estimated in the presence of His glory may not disturb our hearts! May we be constrained by the "*love* of Christ," not by the fear of judgment, to live unto Him who died for us and rose again! We may safely and happily leave everything in His hands, seeing He has borne our sins in His own body on the tree. We have no reason to fear, inasmuch as we know that when He shall appear, we shall be like Him, for we shall see Him as He is. The moment Christ appears we shall be changed into His image, pass into the presence of His glory, and there review the past. We shall look back from that high and holy elevation upon our course down here. We shall see things in a different light altogether. It may be we shall be astonished to find that many things of which we thought a great deal down here, will be found defective up there. On the other hand, many little things which were done in self-forgetfulness and love to Jesus, will be diligently recorded and abundantly rewarded. We shall also be able to see in the clear light of the Master's presence, many mistakes and failures which had never before come within the range of our vision. What will be the effect of all this? Just to evoke from our hearts loud and rapturous hosannas to the praise of Him who has brought us through all our toils and dangers, borne with all our mistakes and failures, and assigned us a place in His own everlasting kingdom, there to bask in the bright beams of His glory and shine in His image forever.

We shall not dwell further on this subject, but we trust sufficient has been said to relieve the minds of those dear friends who have consulted us on the point. We always regard it as a happy service to communicate on any question which may present difficulty to people's minds. We can truly say, our desire is to be a help and blessing to the souls of His people everywhere, and that the name of the Lord Jesus may be magnified.

WHAT IS A CASTAWAY?

"But I keep under my body, and bring it into subjection; lest that, by any means, when I have preached to others, I myself be a castaway" (1 Cor. 9:27).

This passage has perplexed and troubled many an earnest heart. Many have argued thus, while pondering the above solemn scripture, "If such an one as Paul was uncertain as to the direction of his course, who then can be sure?" But was Paul uncertain as to the issue? By no means. The verse immediately preceding teaches us the very opposite: "I therefore so run, not as uncertainly; so fight I, not as one that beateth the air." Paul knew quite well how the whole matter was to end, so far as he was concerned. He could say, "I know whom (not merely what) I have believed and am persuaded that He is able to keep that which I have committed unto Him against that day" (2 Tim. 2:12). And again, "I am persuaded that neither death, nor life, nor angels, nor principalities, nor powers, nor things present, nor things to come, nor height, nor depth, nor any other creature shall be able to separate us from the love of God which is in Christ Jesus our Lord" (Rom. 8:38-39).

These scriptures are amply sufficient to prove that Paul had not so much as a shadow of a doubt as to his eternal security. "I *know*," "I *am persuaded*." There is no doubt or uncertainty in such utterances. Paul knew better. His foundation was as stable as the throne of God. Whatever certainty Christ could give, that Paul possessed. We are fully convinced that, so far as Paul was concerned, from the moment the scales dropped from his eyes in the city of Damascus until he was offered up in the city of Rome, his heart never once harbored a single doubt, a single fear, a single misgiving. "He was troubled on every side, yet not distressed; perplexed but not in despair; persecuted, but not forsaken; cast down, but not destroyed." Yes, in the midst of all his conflict and trouble, he could say, "Our light affliction, which is but for a moment, worketh for us a far more exceeding and eternal weight of glory" (2 Cor. 4:17).

Paul had no doubts or fears as to the final issue. Neither should anyone who has truly come to Christ, inasmuch as He Himself has said, "Him that cometh to Me, I will in no wise cast out" (John 6:37). No one who is really cast upon Christ, will ever be cast away from Him. This is a divine axiom, a fundamental truth, an eternal reality. Christ is responsible for every lamb in the flock. The counsels of God have made Him so; the love of His own heart has made Him so; the Holy Scriptures declare

Him to be so. Not one of Christ's blood-bought lambs can ever be lost, not one can ever be cast away. They are all as safe as He can make them – as safe as Himself.

What then does Paul mean when he says, "Lest I myself should be a castaway?" If he does not mean to convey the idea of uncertainty as to his personal security in Christ, what then does he mean? I believe the expression applies not to his future, but his present service – not to his heavenly home, but his earthly path – not to his eternal privileges, but his present responsibilities. Paul was a servant as well as a son, so he exercised himself and kept his body in subjection, "lest that by any means he might be *disapproved of*," the better translation of *castaway*. The body is a good servant, but a bad master. If not kept down, it will altogether disqualify the servant of Christ for the discharge of his high and holy responsibilities. A person may be a child of God and yet be "disapproved" as a servant of Christ. To be an efficient servant of Christ involves self-denial, self-judgment, self-emptiness, self control. *I do not become a child of God by these exercises, but most assuredly, I shall never be a successful servant of Christ without them.*

This distinction is very plain and very important. We are too prone to think that the question of our personal security is the only one of any importance to us. This is a mistake. God has secured that, and He tells us so, that with free hearts we may run the race, carry on the warfare, fulfill the service. We do not run, fight or work for life; we *have* life-eternal before we take a single step in the Christian race, strike a blow in the Christian warfare, or perform a single act of Christian service. A dead man could not run a race, but a living man must run "lawfully," else he cannot be crowned. So also in reference to the servant of Christ. He must deny himself; he must keep nature down; he must keep his body in subjection, lest he be disapproved of and set aside as a servant unfit for the Master's work, a vessel not "meet for the Master's use." A true believer can *never* lose his relationship to Christ or the eternal dignities and privileges connected therewith, but he can lose his present fitness for service. He may so act as to be disapproved of as a workman. Solemn thought!

We have in the person of John Mark an illustration of the principle laid down in 1 Corinthians 9:27. In Acts 13:5 John Mark was counted worthy to be associated with Paul in the ministry. In Acts 15:38 he was disapproved, but in 2 Timothy 4:11 he was again acknowledged as a profitable servant. Now, Mark was as truly a child of God, a saved person, a believer in Christ, when Paul rejected him as a co-worker, as when he at first acknowledged him and finally restored him to confidence. In no case was the question of John Mark's personal salvation raised. It was altogether a matter of fitness for service. It is evident that the influence of natural affection had been allowed to act on Mark's heart to unfit him in Paul's judgment for that great work which he, as the steward of Christ, was carrying on.

If my reader will turn to Judges 7 he will find another example which strikingly illustrates our principle. What was the great question raised with respect to Gideon's company? Was it as to whether a man was an Israelite, a son of Abraham, a circumcised member of the congregation? By no means. What then? Simply as to whether he was a fit vessel for the service at hand. And what was it that rendered a man fit for such service? Confidence in God and self-denial! See verses 3 and 6. Those who were fearful were rejected (v.3). And those who consulted their own ease were rejected (v.7). Now, the 31700 who were rejected were as truly Israelites as were the 300 who were approved, but the former were not fit servants; the latter were.

All this is easily understood. There is no difficulty if the heart does not make difficulties for itself. Many passages of the Word, which are designed to act on the conscience of the *servant*, are used to alarm the heart of the *child*; many that are only intended to admonish us in reference to our irresponsibility, are used to make us question our relationship.

May the Lord increase in us the grace of a discerning mind and enable us to distinguish between things that differ, so that while our hearts enter into the sweetness and tranquilizing power of those words, "Him that cometh to Me, I will in no wise cast out," our conscience may also feel the solemnity of our position as servants and recoil from everything that might cause us to be set aside as an unclean vessel which the Master cannot take up and use.

May we ever remember that, while as children of God, we are eternally safe, yet as servants of Christ, we may be disapproved of and set aside.

SELF-DENIAL

"If only we exercise a little self denial every day, we shall get on to heaven very comfortably." What a volume of wholesome practical truth in this brief utterance! The path of self-denial is the Christian's true path. "If any man," says Christ, "will come after Me, let him deny himself and take up his cross daily, and follow Me" (Lk. 9:23). It is not, "let him deny certain things belonging to himself." No, he must "deny himself," and this is a "daily" thing. Each morning, as we rise and enter afresh upon the pathway of daily life, we have the same grand and all-important work before us, namely, to deny self.

This hateful self will meet us at every step, for, although we know through grace that "our old man is crucified" – is dead and buried out of God's sight – still this is only as regards our standing in Christ, according to God's view of us. We know that self has to be denied, judged and subjugated every day, every hour, every moment. The principle of our standing must be worked out in practice. God sees us perfect in Christ. We are not in the flesh, but the flesh is in us, and it must be denied and kept by the power of the Spirit.

Be it remembered, it is not merely in its grossness that self must be denied, but in its refinement – not merely in its low habits, but in its cultivated tastes – not merely in its roughness and rudeness, but in its most polished and elegant forms. This is not always seen. It too often happens that, like Saul, we spare that which we consider "the best" and bring the edge of the sword to bear only upon "the vile and refuse." This will never do. It is self that must be denied. Yes, self in all its length and breadth – not merely some branches, but the great parent stem – not merely some accessories of nature, but nature itself. It is a comparatively easy matter to deny certain things pertaining to self, while self is pampered and gratified all the time. I may deny my appetite to feed my religious pride. I may starve myself to minister to my love of money. I may wear shabby clothes while I pride myself in sumptuous furniture and splendid equipment. Hence, the need of being reminded that we must deny self.

Who can sum up all that is contained in this weighty word, self-denial? Self acts everywhere. In the closet, in the family, in the shop, in the railway car, in the street – everywhere, at all times and under all circumstances. It has its tastes and its habits, its prejudices, its likes and dislikes. It must be denied in all these. We may frequently detect ourselves liking our own image. This must be denied with uncommon decision.

Then again in matters of religion, we like those who suit us, who agree and sympathize with us, who admire our opinions or mode of propounding them. All this must be brought under the sharp edge of the knife of self-denial. If not, we may find ourselves despising some dear and honored Christian simply because of something which does not suit us. On the other hand, we may praise to the skies some hollow, worthless character, just because of some feature which we like. Indeed, of all the ten thousand shapes which self assumes, there is not one more hateful than that of religion. Clad in this garb it will make itself the center of a clique, confine its affections within that narrow enclosure, and call that Christian communion. From this contracted circle, it will diligently expel everyone who happens to have a single disagreeable point or angle. It will obstinately refuse to accommodate itself to the scruples and infirmities of others. As to these it will not yield a single hair's breadth, while at the same time, it will surrender any amount of truth to hold fellowship with its own image. All this is terrible and should be most diligently guarded against.

If my reader will study carefully 1 Corinthians 8:10, he will find a most precious lesson on the subject of self-denial. The heading of this entire section might be thus worded, *"Any length in self-denial; not an inch in surrendering truth."* This should ever be the Christian's motto. If it be merely a question of self, surrender all; if it be a question of truth, surrender nothing. "If meat make my brother to offend, I will eat no flesh while the world standeth, lest I make my brother to offend" (chap. 8:13). Noble resolution! May we have grace to carry it out!

Again, "Though I be free from all, yet have I made myself servant unto all, that I might gain the more.... I am made all things to all, that I might by all means save some" (chap. 9:19-22). "Let no man seek his own" – the very thing we are so ready to seek. "But every man another's wealth" – the very last thing we feel disposed to do.

It is important and very needful to observe that when the apostle declares that he was "made all things to all," it was entirely a matter of self-denial and not of self-indulgence. He neither indulged himself nor surrendered a single iota of the truth of God, but made himself servant to all for their good and God's glory. This is our model. May the Lord endow us with grace to imitate it! We are called to surrender not only our points and angles, prejudices and preferences, but also our personal rights for the profit of others. This is the Christian's daily business, and it is as he is enabled to discharge it that he will walk in the footsteps of Jesus and "get on comfortably to heaven."

SELF-JUDGMENT

There are few exercises more valuable or healthful for the Christian than self-judgment. I do not mean by this the unhappy practice of looking in upon oneself for evidences of life and security in Christ. This is terrible work to be at. To be looking at a worthless self instead of at a risen Christ, is as deplorable an occupation as we can conceive. The idea which many Christians seem to entertain in reference to what is called self-examination, is truly depressing. They look upon it as an exercise which may end in their discovering that they are not Christians at all. This, I repeat, is most terrible work.

No doubt it is well for those who have been building upon a sandy foundation, to have their eyes opened to see the dangerous delusion. It is well for such as have been complacently wrapping themselves up in pharisaic robes, to have those robes stripped off. It is well for those who have been sleeping in a house on fire, to be roused from their slumbers. It is well for such as have been walking blindfold to the brink of some frightful precipice, to have the bandage removed from their eyes so they may see their danger, and retreat. No intelligent and well-regulated mind would think of calling in question the rightness of all this. But fully admitting the above, the question of true self-judgment remains wholly untouched. The Christian is never once taught in the Word of God to examine himself with the idea of finding out that he is not a Christian. The very reverse is the case, as I shall endeavor to show.

There are two passages in the New Testament which are sadly misinterpreted. The first is in reference to the celebration of the Lord's supper: "Let a man examine himself and so let him eat of this bread and drink of this cup; for he that eateth and drinketh unworthily, eateth and drinketh judgment to himself, not discerning the Lord's body" (1 Cor. 11:28-29). It is usual to apply the term "unworthily" in this passage, to *persons* doing the act, whereas, it really refers to the *manner* of doing it. The apostle never thought of calling in question the Christianity of the Corinthians. In fact, in the opening address of his epistle he looks at them as "the church of God which is in Corinth, sanctified in Christ Jesus, called saints" (or saints by calling). How could he use this language in chapter 1, and in chapter 11 call in question the worthiness of these saints to take their seat at the Lord's supper? Impossible. He looked upon them as saints, and as such, he exhorted them to celebrate the Lord's supper in a worthy manner. The question of any but true Christians being there is never raised, so it is utterly impossible that the word "unworthily" could apply to persons. Its application is entirely to the manner. The persons were worthy, but their manner was not. Therefore, they were called *as saints* to judge themselves as to their ways, else the Lord might judge them in their persons, as was already the case. In a word, it was as true Christians they were called to judge themselves. If they were in doubt as to that, they were utterly unable to judge anything. I never think of setting my child to judge as to whether he is my child or not, but I expect him to judge himself as to his habits. If he does not, I may have to do *by chastening*, what he ought to do by self-judgment. It is because I look upon him as my child that I will not allow him to sit at my table with soiled garments and disorderly manners.

The second passage occurs in 2 Corinthians 13:3-5. "Since ye seek a proof of Christ speaking in me... examine yourselves." The rest of the passage is parenthetic. The real point is this. The apostle appeals to the Corinthians themselves as the clear proof that his apostleship was divine – that Christ had spoken in him, that his commission was from heaven. He looked upon them as true Christians, notwithstanding all their confusion. Inasmuch as they were seals to his ministry, that ministry must be divine. Hence, they ought not to listen to the false apostles who were speaking against him. Their Christianity and his apostleship were so intimately connected, that to question the one was to question the other. It is, therefore, plain that the apostle did not call upon the Corinthians to examine themselves with any such idea as the examination might show they were not Christians at all. Quite the reverse. In truth, it is as I were to show an expensive watch to a person and say, "Since you seek proof that the man who made this is a watchmaker, examine it."

Thus it is plain that neither of the above passages affords any warrant for that kind of self-examination for which some contend, which is really based upon a system of doubts and fears, and has no warrant whatever in the Word of God. The self-judgment to which I would call the reader's attention is a totally different thing. It is a sacred Christian exercise of the most salutary character. It is based upon the most unclouded confidence as to our salvation and acceptance in Christ. The Christian is called to judge self because he is – not to see if he be – a Christian. This makes all the difference. Were I to examine self for a thousand years, I should never find it to be anything else than a worthless, ruined, vile thing – a thing which God has set aside and which I am called to reckon as "dead." How could I ever expect to get any comforting evidences by such an examination? Impossible.

168

The Christian's evidences are not to be found in his ruined self, but in God's risen Christ. The more he can get done with the former and occupied with the latter, the happier and holier he will be. The Christian judges himself, judges his habits, judges his thoughts, words and actions, because he believes he is a Christian, not because he doubts it. If he doubts, he is not fit to judge anything. It is as knowing and enjoying the eternal stability of God's grace, the divine effectiveness of the blood of Jesus, the all-prevailing power of His advocacy, the unalterable authority of the Word, the divine security of the very feeblest of Christ's sheep. It is as entering by the teaching of God the Holy Spirit into these priceless realities, that the true believer judges himself. The human idea of self-examination is founded upon unbelief. The divine idea of self-judgment is founded upon confidence.

But, let us never forget that we are called to judge ourselves. If we lose sight of this, nature will soon get ahead of us and we shall make sorry work of it. The most devoted Christians have a mass of things which need to be judged, and if those things are not habitually judged, they will assuredly result in abundance of bitter work. If there be irritability or levity, pride or vanity, natural indolence or natural impulsiveness – whatever there be that belongs to our fallen nature, we must as Christians judge and subdue that thing. That which is abidingly judged will never get upon the conscience. Self-judgment keeps all our matters right and square, but if nature be not judged, there is no knowing how, when or where it may break out and produce keen anguish of soul and bring gross dishonor upon the Lord's name. The most grievous cases of failure and declension may be traced to the neglect of self-judgment in little things.

There are three distinct stages of judgment, namely self-judgment, church judgment and divine judgment. If a man judges himself, the assembly is kept clear. If he fail to do so, evil will break out in some shape or form and then the assembly is involved. If the assembly fail to judge the evil, then God must deal with the assembly. If Achan had judged the covetous thought, the assembly of Israel would not have become involved (Josh. 7). If the Corinthians had judged themselves in secret, the Lord would not to have had to judge the assembly in public (1 Cor. 11).

All this is deeply practical and soul-subduing. May all the Lord's people learn to walk in the cloudless sunshine of His favor, in the holy enjoyment of their relationship and in the habitual exercise of a spirit of self-judgment!

SELF-EMPTINESS

The fullness of God ever waits upon an empty vessel. This is a grand practical truth, very easily stated, but involving a great deal more than one might imagine. The entire Book of God illustrates this truth. The history of the people of God illustrates it; the experience of each believer illustrates it. Whether we study the Book of God or the ways of God – His ways with all and His ways with each – we have this most precious truth that "the fullness of God ever waits on an empty vessel."

This holds good with respect to the sinner in his first coming to Christ, and it holds good with respect to the believer at every stage of his career, from the starting post to the goal.

In the first place, as regards the sinner in his first coming to Christ, what is this but the fullness of God in redeeming love and pardoning mercy, waiting upon an empty vessel? The real matter is to get the sinner to take the place of an empty vessel. Once there, the whole question is settled. But what exercise, what struggling, what toil, what conflict, what fruitless efforts, what ups and downs, what vows and resolutions in thousands of cases before the sinner is really brought to take the place of an empty vessel and be filled with God's salvation! How marvelously difficult it is to get the poor legal heart emptied of its legality, that it may be filled with Christ! It will have something of its own to lean upon and cling to. Here lies the root of the difficulty. We can never "draw water from the wells of salvation" until we come there with empty vessels.

This is difficult work. Many spend years of legal effort before they reach the grand moral point of self-emptiness, even in its reference to the simple question of righteousness before God. When once they have reached that point, the matter is found to be so simple that the wonder is how they could have spent so long in getting hold of it and why they had never got hold of it before. There is never any difficulty found when the sinner really takes the ground of self-emptiness. The question, "Who shall deliver me?" is sure to be followed by the reply, "I thank God through Jesus Christ our Lord" (Rom. 7).

Now, it will always be found that the more completely the sinner gets emptied of himself, the more settled his peace will be. If self and its doings, its feelings and its reasonings, be not emptied out, there will assuredly be doubts and fears, ups and downs, wavering and fluctuation, seasons of darkness and cloudiness afterwards. Hence the vital importance of seeking to make a clean riddance of self so that Christ, "the fullness of the Godhead bodily," may be known and enjoyed. It is the one who can most truthfully and experimentally say,

"I'm a poor sinner and nothing at all,"

who can also adopt as his own that additional line,

"But Jesus Christ is my all in all."

It is ever thus. A full Christ is for an empty sinner, and an empty sinner for a full Christ. They are morally fitted to each other. The more I experience the emptiness, the more I shall enjoy the fullness. So long as I am full of self-confidence, so long as I am full of trust in my morality, my benevolence, my amiability, my religiousness, my righteousness, I have no room for Christ. All these things must be thrown overboard before a full Christ can be apprehended. It cannot be partly self and partly Christ. It must be either one or the other. One reason why so many are tossed up and down "in dark uncertainty" is because they still cling to some little bit of self. It may be a very little bit. They may not be trusting in any works of righteousness they have done, but still there is something of self retained and trusted in. It may be the very smallest possible atom of the creature – its state, its feelings, its mode of appropriating, its experiences, something or other of the creature kept in which keeps Christ out. It *must* be so, for if a full Christ were received, a full peace would be enjoyed. If a full peace be not enjoyed, it is only because a full Christ has not been received. This makes the matter as simple as possible.

Reader, do you fully understand this? Have you, as an empty sinner, come to Christ to be filled with His fullness, to be satisfied with His all-sufficiency, to find the solid rest of your heart and conscience in Him alone? Are you fully satisfied with Christ? I earnestly pray you to get this point settled! Is Christ enough for your heart, enough for your conscience, enough for your whole moral being? See that you make earnest, real, hearty work of it now. Are you resting wholly in Christ? Which is it, Christ alone or Christ and something else? Are you, in some secret chamber of your heart, hiding a little fragment of legality – some little atom of creature-confidence or element of self-righteousness? If so, you cannot enjoy true gospel-peace. It cannot be. Gospel-peace is the result of receiving a full Christ into a heart that has learned its own emptiness. Christ is our peace. True peace is not a mere feeling in the mind. It is found in a divine, living, real Person, even Christ Himself, who having made peace by the blood of His cross, has become our peace in the presence of God. This peace can never be disturbed, inasmuch as He who is our peace, is "the same, yesterday, today and forever" (Heb. 13). Were it a mere feeling in the mind, it would prove as variable as the mercury in a barometer. If I am occupied with my feelings, I am not self-emptied. As a consequence, I cannot know the joy and peace which flow from being occupied only with Christ, for the fullness of God ever waits upon an empty vessel.

Thus much as to the application of our thesis to the case of a sinner in his first coming to Christ.

Secondly, let us see how it applies to a believer at every stage of his career. This is a deeply practical branch of our subject. We have very little idea at times of how full we are of self and the world. Hence, in one way or another, we have to be emptied from vessel to vessel. Like Jacob of old, we struggle hard and hold fast our confidence in the flesh, until at length the source of our strength is dried up and the ground of our confidence swept from under us. Then we are constrained to cry out,

"Other refuge have I none,
Clings my helpless soul to Thee."

There can be no greater barrier to our peace and habitual enjoyment of God than our being filled with self-confidence. We must be emptied and humbled. God cannot divide the house with the creature. It is vain to expect it. Jacob had the hollow of his thigh touched so he might learn to lean upon God. The halting Jacob found his sure resource in Jehovah who only empties us of nature that we may be filled with Himself. He knows that just in so far as we are filled with self-confidence or creature-confidence, we are robbed of the deep blessedness of being filled with His fullness. Hence, in His great grace and mercy, He empties us out, that we may learn to cling in child-like confidence to Him. This is our only place of strength, victory and repose.

Someone has said, "I never was truly happy until I ceased to wish to be great." This is a fine moral truth. When we cease to wish to be anything, when we are content to be nothing, then it is we taste what true greatness, true elevation, true happiness, true peace really is. The restless desire to be something or somebody is destructive of the soul's tranquillity. The proud heart and ambitious spirit may pronounce this a poor, low, mean, contemptible sentiment, but when we have taken our place on the forms of the school of Christ and begun to learn of Him who was meek and lowly in heart – when we have drunk in any measure into the spirit of Him who made

Himself of no reputation – we then see things quite differently. "He that humbleth himself shall be exalted." The way to get up is to go down. This is the doctrine of Christ, the doctrine which He stated and is inscribed on His life. "And Jesus called a little child unto Him and set him in the midst of them, and said, Verily, I say unto you, except ye be converted and become as little children, ye shall not enter into the kingdom of heaven. Whosoever, therefore, shall humble himself as this little child, the same is greatest in the kingdom of heaven" (Mt. 18:2-4). This is the doctrine of heaven – the doctrine of self-emptiness. How unlike all that prevails down here in this scene of self-seeking and self-exaltation!

We have in the person of John the Baptist a true example of one who entered in some degree into the real meaning of self-emptiness. The Jews sent priests and Levites from Jerusalem to ask him, "Who art thou? What sayest thou of thyself?" What was his reply? A self-emptied one! He said he was just "a voice." This was taking his true place. "A voice" had not much to glory in. He did not say, "I am one crying in the wilderness." No; he was merely "the voice of One." He had no ambition to be anything more. This was self-emptiness. Observe the result. He found his engrossing object in Christ. "Again the next day after John stood, and two of his disciples; and looking upon Jesus as he walked, he saith, Behold the Lamb of God!" What was all this but the fullness of God waiting on an empty vessel! John was nothing, Christ was all. Hence, when John's disciples left his side to follow Jesus, we may feel assured that no murmuring word, no accent of disappointed ambition or wounded pride escaped his lips. There is no envy or jealousy in a self-emptied heart. There is nothing touchy, nothing tenacious about one who has learned to take his true place. Had John been seeking his own things, he might have complained when he saw himself abandoned. But, my reader, when a man has found his satisfying object in "the Lamb of God," he does not care much about losing a few disciples.

We have a further exhibition of the Baptist's self-emptied spirit in John 3. "And they came unto John and said unto him, Rabbi, He that was with thee beyond Jordan, to whom thou barest witness, behold, the same baptizeth and all come to Him." Here was a communication calculated to draw out the envy and jealousy of the poor human heart. But mark the noble reply of the Baptist: "A man can receive *nothing* except it be given him from heaven.... He must increase, but I must decrease. He that cometh from above is above all; he that is of the earth is earthly and speaketh of the earth: He that cometh from heaven is *above all*."

Precious testimony – a testimony to his own utter nothingness and to Christ's fullness, glory and peerless excellence! "A voice" was "nothing." Christ was high above all.

Oh! for a self-emptied spirit, "a heart free from itself," a mind delivered from all anxiety about one's own things! May we be more thoroughly delivered from self in all its detestable workings! Then could the Master use us, own us and bless us. Hearken to His testimony to John – the one who said of himself that he was nothing but a voice. "Verily I say unto you, among them that are born of women there hath not risen a greater than John the Baptist" (Mt. 11:11). How much better to hear this from the Master than from the servant! John said, "I am a voice." Christ said he was the greatest of prophets. Simon Magus "gave out that himself was some great one." Such is the way of the world – the manner of man. John the Baptist, the greatest of prophets, gave out that he was nothing and that Christ was "above all." What a contrast!

May we be kept lowly and self-emptied so we may be continually filled with Christ. This is true rest, true blessedness. May the language of our hearts and the distinct utterance of our lives ever be, "Behold the Lamb of God."

SELF-CONTROL

The word "temperance" in 2 Peter 1:6 means a great deal more than what is usually understood by that term. It is customary to apply the word "temperance" to a habit of moderation in reference to eating and drinking. No doubt it fully involves this, but it involves much more. Indeed, the Greek word used by the inspired apostle may be rendered "self-control." It gives the idea of one who has *self* habitually well reined in.

This is a rare and admirable grace, diffusing its hallowed influence over one's entire course, character and conduct. It not only bears directly upon one or two or twenty selfish habits, but upon self in all the length and breadth of that comprehensive and most odious term. Many a one who would look with proud disdain upon a glutton or a drunkard, may himself fail every hour in exhibiting the grace of self-control. True it is that gluttony and drunkenness should be ranked with the very vilest and most demoralizing forms of selfishness. They must be regarded as among the most bitter clusters that grow on that widespread tree. But self is a tree and not a mere branch of a tree or a cluster on a branch, and we should not only judge self when it works, but control it that it may not work.

Some may ask, "How can we control self?" The answer is blessedly simple: "I can do all things through Christ that strengtheneth me" (Phil. 4). Have we not gotten salvation in Christ? Yes, blessed be God, we have. And what does this wondrous word include? Is it mere deliverance from the wrath to come? Is it merely the pardon of our sins and the assurance of exemption from the lake that burns with fire and brimstone? It is far more than these, precious and priceless though they be. In a word, "salvation" implies a full and hearty acceptance of Christ as my "wisdom" to guide me out of folly's dark and devious paths, into paths of heavenly light and peace; as my "righteousness" to justify me in the sight of a holy God; as my "sanctification" to make me practically holy in all my ways; and as my "redemption" to give me final deliverance from all the power of death, and entrance upon the eternal fields of glory.

Hence, it is evident that "self-control" is included in the salvation which we have in Christ. It is a result of that practical sanctification with which divine grace has endowed us. We should carefully guard against the habit of taking a narrow view of salvation. We should seek to enter into all its fullness. It is a word which stretches from everlasting to everlasting and takes in, in its mighty sweep, all the practical details of daily

175

life. I have no right to talk of salvation of my soul in the future while I refuse to know and exhibit its practical bearing upon my conduct in the present. We are saved, not only from the guilt and condemnation of sin, but as fully from the power, the practice and the love of it. These things should never be separated, nor will they be by anyone who has been divinely taught the meaning, the extent and the power of that precious word "salvation."

Now, in presenting to my reader a few practical sentences on the subject of self-control, I shall contemplate it under the three following divisions, namely the thoughts, the tongue and the temper. I take it for granted that I am addressing a saved person. If my reader be not that, I can only direct him to the one true and living way, "Believe on the Lord Jesus Christ, and thou shalt be saved, and thy house" (Acts 16). Put your whole trust in Him and you shall be as safe as He is Himself. Now I shall proceed to deal with the practical and much-needed subject of self-control.

First, as to our thoughts and the habitual government thereof. I suppose there are few Christians who have not suffered from evil thoughts – those troublesome intruders upon our most profound privacy, those constant disturbers of our mental repose that so frequently darken the atmosphere around us and prevent us from getting a full, clear view upward into the bright heaven above. The Psalmist could say, "I hate vain thoughts." No wonder. They are truly hateful and should be judged, condemned and expelled. Someone, in speaking of the subject of evil thoughts, has said, "I cannot prevent birds from flying over me, but I can prevent their alighting upon me. In like manner, I cannot prevent evil thoughts being suggested to my mind, but I can refuse them a lodging therein."

But how can we control our thoughts? No more than we could blot out our sins or create a world. What are we to do? Look to Christ. This is the true secret of self-control. He can keep us, not only from the lodging, but also from the *suggestion* of the evil thoughts. We could no more prevent the one than the other. He can prevent both. He can keep the vile intruders, not only from getting in, but even from knocking at the door. When the divine life is in energy – when the current of spiritual thought and feeling is deep and rapid, when the heart's affections are intensely occupied with the Person of Christ – vain thoughts do not trouble us. It is only when spiritual indolence creeps over us that evil thoughts – vile and horrible issue – come in upon us. Then our only resource is to look straight to Jesus. We might as well attempt to cope with the marshalled hosts of hell, as with a horde of evil thoughts. Our refuge is in Christ. He is made unto us sanctification. We can do all things through Him. We have just to bring the name of Jesus to bear upon the flood of evil thoughts, and He will most assuredly give full and immediate deliverance.

However, the more excellent way is to be preserved from the suggestions of evil by the power of pre-occupation with good. When the channel of thought is decidedly upward, when it is deep and well formed, free from all curves and indentations, then the current of imagination and feeling, as it gushes up from the deep fountains of the soul, will naturally flow onward in the bed of that channel. This is unquestionably the more excellent way. May we prove it in our own experience. "Finally, brethren, whatsoever things are true, whatsoever things are honest, whatsoever things are just, whatsoever things are lovely, whatsoever things are of good report, if there be any virtue, and if there be any praise, think on these things. Those things which ye have both learned and received and heard and seen in me, do; and the God of peace shall be with you" (Phil. 4:8-9). When the heart is fully engrossed with Christ, the living embodiment of all those things enumerated in verse 8, we enjoy profound peace, unruffled by evil thoughts. This is true self-control.

Secondly, as to the tongue, that influential member so fruitful in good, so fruitful in evil – the instrument whereby we can either give forth accents of soft and soothing sympathy or words of bitter sarcasm and burning indignation. How deeply important is the grace of self-control in its application to such a member! Mischief, which years cannot repair, may be done by the tongue in a moment. Words which we would give the world to recall, may be uttered by the tongue in an unguarded moment. Hear what the inspired apostle says on this subject: "If any man offend not in word, the same is a perfect man and able also to bridle the whole body. Behold, we put bits in the horses' mouths, that they may obey us; and we turn about their whole body. Behold also the ships, which though they be so great and are driven of fierce winds, yet are they turned about with a very small helm, whithersoever the governor listeth. Even so the tongue is a little member and boasteth great things. Behold, how great a matter a little fire kindleth! And the tongue is a fire, a world of iniquity: so is the tongue among our members, that it defileth the whole body and setteth on fire the course of nature; and it is set on fire of hell. For every kind of beasts, and of birds, and of serpents, and of things in the sea is tamed, and hath been tamed of mankind. But the tongue can no man tame; it is an unruly evil, full of deadly poison" (Jas. 3:2-8).

Who then can control the tongue? "No man" can do it, but Christ can, and we have only to look to Him in simple faith. This implies both the sense of our own utter helplessness and His all-sufficiency. It is utterly impossible that we could control the tongue. As well might we attempt to stem the ocean's tide, the mountain torrent or the Alpine avalanche. How often, when suffering under the effects of some blunder of the tongue, have we resolved to command that unruly member somewhat better next time, but our resolution proved to be like the morning cloud that passes away, and we had only to retire and weep over our lamentable failure in the matter of self-control. Why was this? Simply because we undertook the matter in our own strength or at least without a sufficiently deep consciousness of our own weakness. This is the cause of constant failure. We must cling to Christ as a babe clings to its mother. Not that our clinging is of any value; still we must cling. Thus alone can we successfully bridle the tongue. Let us remember at all times the solemn searching words of the same apostle James, "If any one (man, woman or child) among you seem to be religious and bridleth not his tongue, but deceiveth his own heart, this man's religion is vain" (chap. 1:26). These are wholesome words for a day like the present when there are so many unruly tongues abroad. May we have grace to attend to these words! May their holy influence appear in our ways!

The third point to be considered is the temper, which is intimately connected with both the tongue and the thoughts. Indeed, all three are very closely linked. When the spring of thought is spiritual and the current heavenly, the tongue is only the active agent for good, and the temper is calm and unruffled. Christ dwelling in the heart by faith regulates everything. Without Him, all is worse than worthless. I may possess and exhibit the self-command of a Socrates and all the while be wholly ignorant of the "self-control" of 2 Peter 1:6. The latter is founded on "faith;" the former on philosophy – two totally different things. We must remember that the word is "Add to your faith." This puts faith first as the only link to connect the heart with Christ, the living source of all power. Having Christ and abiding in Him, we are enabled to add "courage, knowledge, self-control, patience, godliness, brotherly kindness, love." Such are the precious fruits that flow from abiding in Christ. But I can no more control my temper than my tongue or my thoughts, and if I set about it, I shall be sure to break down every hour. A mere philosopher without Christ may exhibit more self-control as to tongue and temper than a Christian, if he abides not in Christ. This ought not to be and would not be if the Christian simply looked to Jesus. It is when he fails in this that the enemy gains the advantage. The philosopher without Christ seems to succeed in the great business of self-control only that he may be the more effectively blinded as to the truth of his condition and carried headlong to eternal ruin. But Satan delights to make a Christian stumble and fall, only that he may thereby blaspheme the precious name of Christ.

Christian reader, let us remember these things. Let us look to Christ to control our thoughts, our tongue and our temper. Let us "give all diligence." Let us think how much is involved. "If these things be in you and abound, they make you that ye shall neither be barren nor unfruitful in the knowledge of our Lord Jesus Christ. But he that lacketh these things is blind and cannot see afar off, and hath forgotten that he was purged from his old sins." This is deeply solemn. How easy it is to drop into a state of spiritual blindness and forgetfulness! No amount of knowledge, either of doctrine or the letter of Scripture, will preserve the soul from this awful condition. Nothing but "the knowledge of our Lord Jesus Christ" will avail. This knowledge is increased in the soul by "giving all diligence to add to our faith" the various graces to which the apostle refers in the above eminently practical and soul-stirring passage. "Wherefore the rather, brethren, give diligence to make your calling and election sure: for if ye do these things ye shall never fall: for so an entrance shall be ministered unto you abundantly into the everlasting kingdom of our Lord and Savior Jesus Christ."

PROVISION FOR PERILOUS TIMES
(READ 2 TIMOTHY)

It is of the greatest importance for the servant of Christ in all ages to have a clear, deep, abiding, influential sense of his position, his path, his portion and his prospects – a divinely wrought apprehension of the ground which he is called to occupy, the sphere of action which is thrown open to him, the divine provision made for his comfort and encouragement and strength and guidance, and the brilliant hopes held out to him. There is considerable danger of our being allured into a mere region of theory and speculation, of opinion and sentiment, of dogmas and principles. The freshness of first love is frequently lost by contact with the men and things of what may be called "the religious world." The lovely freshness of early personal Christianity is often destroyed by a wrong use of the machinery of religion, if we may be allowed to use such a term.

In the kingdom of nature, it frequently happens that some stray seed has dropped into the ground, taken root and sprung up into a tender plant. The hand of man had nothing to do with it. God planted it, watered it and made it grow. He assigned it its position, gave it its strength and covered it with beautiful freshness. By and by, man intruded upon its solitude and transplanted it to his own artificial enclosure, there to wither and droop. Thus it is too often with the plants of God's spiritual kingdom. They are often injured by man's rude hand. They would be far better if left to the sole management of the Hand that planted them. Young Christians frequently suffer immensely from not being left to the exclusive training of the Holy Spirit and the exclusive teaching of Holy Scripture. Human management is almost sure to stunt the growth of God's spiritual plants. It is not that God may not use men as His instruments in watering, culturing and caring for His precious plants. He assuredly may and does, but then, it is *God's* culture and care, not man's. This makes all the difference. The Christian is God's plant. The seed which produced him was divine. It was directed and planted by God's own hand, and that same hand must be allowed to train it.

Now, what is true of the individual believer is equally true of the Church as a whole. In 1 Timothy, the Church is looked at in its original order and glory. It is there viewed as "the House of God," "the Church of the living God," "the pillar and ground of the truth." Its officebearers, its functions and its responsibilities are there minutely and formally described. The servant of Christ is instructed as to the mode in which he is to conduct himself in the midst of such a hallowed and dignified sphere. Such is the character, such the scope and object of Paul's First Epistle to Timothy.

But in the Second Epistle, we have something quite different. The scene is entirely changed. The house which in the first epistle was looked at in its rule, is here contemplated in its ruin. The Church as an economy set up on the earth, had like every other economy, utterly failed. Man fails in everything. He failed amid the beauty and order of Paradise. He failed in that favored land "that flowed with milk and honey, the glory of all lands." He failed amid the rare privileges of the gospel dispensation, and he will fail amid the bright beams of millennial glory. Compare Genesis 3; Judges 2; Acts 20:29; 3 John 9; Revelation 1:2 and 20:7-9.

The remembrance of this will help us in understanding 2 Timothy. It may very properly be termed "a divine provision for perilous times." The apostle seems to be weeping over the ruins of that once beautiful structure. Like the weeping prophet, he beholds "the stones of the sanctuary poured out in the top of every street." He calls to remembrance the tears of his beloved Timothy. He is glad to have even one sympathizing bosom into which to pour his sorrows. All who were in Asia had turned away from him. He was left to stand alone before Caesar's judgment seat. Demas forsook him. Alexander the coppersmith did him much evil. All around him, so far as man was concerned, looked gloomy and dark. He begs of his beloved Timothy to bring him his cloak, his books and his parchments. All is strongly marked. "Perilous times" are anticipated. "A form of godliness without the power" – the mantle of profession thrown over the grossest abominations of the human heart – men not able to endure sound doctrine, heaping to themselves teachers after their own lusts, having itching ears which must needs be tickled by the fabulous and baseless absurdities of the human mind. Such are the features of 2 Timothy. Who can fail to notice them? Who can fail to see that our lot is cast in the very midst of the evils and dangers here contemplated? Is it not well to have a clear perception of these things? Why should we desire to blind our eyes to the truth? Why deceive ourselves with vain dreams of increasing light and spiritual prosperity? Is it not far better to look the true condition of things straight in the face? Assuredly; and so much the more when the selfsame epistle which so faithfully points out "the perilous times," fully unfolds the divine provision.

Why should we imagine that man under the Christian dispensation would prove any better than man under all the dispensations which have gone before, or under the millennial dispensation which is yet to follow? Would not analogy, even in the absence of direct and positive proof, lead us to expect failure under this present economy as well as under all the others? If we, without exception, find judgment at the close of all the other dispensations, why should we look for anything else at the close of this? Let my reader ponder these things and then accompany me while I seek by the grace of God to unfold some of the divine provisions for "perilous times."

I do not attempt to expound this most touching and interesting epistle in detail. This would be impossible in this short article. I shall merely single out one point from each of the four chapters into which the epistle has been divided. These are, first, "unfeigned faith" (ch. 1:5); secondly, "the sure foundation" (chap. 2:19); thirdly, "the Holy Scriptures" (chap. 3:15); and fourthly, "the crown of righteousness" (chap. 4:8). The man who knows anything of the power of these things, is divinely provided for "perilous times."

First, as to "the unfeigned faith" – that priceless possession. The apostle says, "I thank God, whom I serve from my forefathers with pure conscience, that without ceasing I have remembrance of thee in my prayers night and day; greatly desiring to see thee, being mindful of thy tears, that I may be filled with joy; when I call to remembrance the unfeigned faith that is in thee, which dwelt first in thy grandmother Lois and thy mother Eunice; and I am persuaded that in thee also." Here we have something above and beyond everything ecclesiastical – something which one must have before he is introduced to the Church, and which will stand good though the Church were in ruins around him. This unfeigned faith connects the soul immediately with Christ in the power of a link which must of necessity be prior to all ecclesiastical associations, however important they may be – a link which shall endure when all earthly associations shall have been dissolved forever. We do not get to Christ through the Church. We get to Christ first, and then to the Church. Christ is our life, not the Church. No doubt, church fellowship is most valuable, but there is something above and beyond it, and it is of that something that "unfeigned faith" takes possession. Timothy had this faith dwelling in him before ever he entered the house of God. He was connected with the God of the house previous to his manifested association with the house of God.

It is well to be clear as to this. We must never surrender the intense individuality which characterizes "unfeigned faith." We must carry it with us through all the scenes and circumstances, the links and associations of our Christian life and service. We must not traffic in mere church position or build upon religious machinery or be borne up by a routine of duty, or cling to the worthless props of sectarian sympathy or denominational preference. Let us cultivate those fresh, vivid and powerful affections which were created in our heart when first we knew the Lord. Let the beautiful blossom of our spring-time be succeeded, not by barrenness and sterility, but by those mellow clusters which spring from realized connection with the root.

Too often it is otherwise. Too often the earnest, zealous, simple-hearted young Christian is lost in the bigoted, narrow-minded member of a sect, or the intolerant defender of some peculiar opinion. The freshness, softness, simplicity, tenderness and earnest affection of our young days are rarely carried forward into the advanced stages of vigorous manhood and mature old age. Very frequently, one finds a depth of tone, a richness of experience, of moral elevation in the early stages of the Christian life which too soon gives place to a chilling formalism in one's personal ways, or a mere energy in the defense of some barren system of theology. How rarely are those words of the Psalmist realized, "They shall bring forth fruit in old age; they shall be fat and flourishing" (Ps. 42:14).

The truth is, we all want to cultivate more diligently an "unfeigned faith." We want to enter with more spiritual vigor, into the power of the link which binds us, individually, to Christ. This would render us "fat and flourishing," even in old age. "The righteous shall flourish like the palm tree; he shall grow like a cedar in Lebanon. Those that be planted in the house of the Lord shall flourish in the courts of our God." We suffer materially by allowing what is called Christian fellowship to interfere with our personal connection and communion with Christ. We are far too prone to substitute fellowship with man for fellowship with God – to walk in the footsteps of our fellow, rather than in the footsteps of Christ – to look around rather than upward for sympathy, support and encouragement.

These are not the fruits of "unfeigned faith." Quite the opposite. That faith is as blooming and vigorous amid the solitudes of a desert as in the bosom of an assembly. Its immediate, all-engrossing business is with God Himself. "It endures as seeing Him who is invisible." It fixes its earnest gaze upon things unseen and eternal. "It enters into that within the veil." It lives amid the unseen realities of an eternal world. Having conducted the soul to the feet of Jesus, there to get a full and final forgiveness of all its sins through His most precious blood, it bears it majestically onward through all the windings and labyrinths of desert life, and enables it to bask in the bright beams of millennial glory.

Thus much as to this first precious item in the divine provision for "perilous times" – this "unfeigned faith." No one can ever get on without it, let the times be peaceful or perilous, easy or difficult, rough or smooth, dark or bright. If a man be destitute of this faith, deeply implanted and diligently cultivated in him, he must sooner or later break down. He may be urged on for a time by the impulses of surrounding circumstances and their influence. He may be propped up and borne along by his co-religionists. He may float down along the stream of religious profession. But most assuredly, if he be not possessed of "unfeigned faith," the time is rapidly approaching when it will be all over with him forever. The "perilous times" will soon rise to a head. Then will come the awful crisis of judgment, from which none can escape except the happy possessors of "unfeigned faith." God grant my reader may be one of these! If so, all is eternally safe.

Secondly, we shall now consider "the sure foundation." "Nevertheless the foundation of God standeth sure, having this seal, the Lord knoweth them that are his. And let everyone that nameth the name of Christ depart from iniquity" (Chap. 2:9). In the midst of all the "trouble," the "hardness," the "striving about words," the "profane and vain babblings," the errors of "Hymenaeus and Philetus" – in the midst of all these varied features of the "perilous times," how precious to fall back upon God's sure foundation. The soul that is built upon this, in the divine energy of "unfeigned faith," is able to resist the rapidly rising tide of evil – is divinely furnished for the most appalling times. There is a fine moral link between the unfeigned faith in the heart of man and the sure foundation laid by the hand of God. All may go to ruin. The Church may go to pieces and all who love the Church may have to sit down and weep over its ruins, but there stands that imperishable foundation laid by God's own hand, against which the surging tide of error and evil may roll with all its fury and have no effect, except to prove the eternal stability of that Rock and of all who are built thereon.

"The Lord knoweth them that are His." There is abundance of false profession, but the eye of Jehovah rests on all those who belong to Him. Not one of them is, or ever can be forgotten by Him. Their names are engraven on His heart. They are as precious to Him as the price He paid for them, and that is nothing less than the "precious blood" of His own dear Son. No evil can befall them. No weapon formed against them can prosper. "The eternal God is their refuge, and underneath are the everlasting arms." What rich, what ample provision for "perilous times!" Why should we fear? Why should we be anxious? Having "unfeigned faith within and God's foundation beneath, it is our happy privilege to pursue, with tranquilized hearts, our upward and onward way in the assurance that all is and shall be well.

> "I know My sheep," He cries,
> "My soul approves them well:
> Vain is the treacherous world's disguise,
> And vain the rage of hell."

It has been well said that the seal on God's foundation has two sides. One bears the inscription, "The Lord knoweth them that are His"; the other, "Let every one that nameth the name of Christ depart from iniquity." The former is as peace-giving as the latter is practical. Let the strife and confusion be ever so great, let the storm rage and the billow arise, let the darkness thicken, let all the powers of earth and hell combine, "the Lord knoweth them that are His." He has sealed them for Himself. The assurance of this is calculated to maintain the heart in profound repose, let the "times" be ever so "perilous."

But, let us never forget that each one who "names the name of Christ" is solemnly responsible to "depart from iniquity" wherever he finds it. This is applicable to all true Christians. The moment I see anything that deserves the epithet of "iniquity," be it what or where it may, I am called upon to "depart from" that thing. I am not to wait till others see with me, for what may seem to be "iniquity" to one, may not seem to be so to another. Hence, it is entirely a personal question. "Let every one." The language used in this epistle is very personal, very strong, very intense. "If a man purge himself." "Flee also youthful lusts." "From such turn away." "Continue thou." "I charge thee." "Watch thou in all things, endure afflictions." "Of whom be thou aware also." These are solemn, earnest, weighty words – words which distinctly prove that our lot is cast in times when we must not lean upon the arm or gaze upon the countenance of our fellow.

We must be sustained by the energy of an "unfeigned faith" and by our personal connection with the "sure foundation." Thus shall we be able, let others do or think as they will, to "depart from iniquity," to "flee youthful lusts." We shall be able to "turn away" from the adherents of a powerless "form of godliness," wherever we find them, and to "beware" of every "Alexander the coppersmith."* If we permit our feet to be moved from the rock, if we surrender ourselves to the impulse of surrounding circumstances and influences, we shall never be able to make headway against the special forms of evil and error in these "perilous times."

Our third point is "the Holy Scriptures" – that precious portion of every "man of God." "But continue thou in the things which thou hast learned and hast been assured of, knowing of whom thou hast learned them; and that from a child thou hast known the Holy Scriptures which are able to make thee wise unto salvation through faith which is in Christ Jesus. All Scripture is given by inspiration of God and is profitable for doctrine, for reproof, for correction, for instruction in righteousness; that the man of God may be perfect, *thoroughly* furnished unto *all* good works" (chap. 3:14-17). Here we have rich provision for "perilous times." We need a thorough knowledge of the One from "whom we have learned" an accurate, personal, experimental acquaintance with "Holy Scripture," that pure fountain of divine authority, that changeless source of heavenly wisdom which even a child may possess, and without which a wise man must err.

If a man be not able to refer all his thoughts, all his convictions, all his principles to God as their living source, to Christ as their living center, and to "the Holy Scriptures" as their divine authority, he will never be able to get on through "perilous times." A second-hand faith will never do. We must hold truth directly from God, through the medium and on the authority of "the Holy Scriptures." God may use a man to show me certain things in the Word, but I do not hold them from man but from God. It is "knowing of *whom* thou hast learned." When this is the case I am able, through grace, to get on through the thickest darkness and through all the devious paths of this wilderness world. Inspiration's heavenly lamp emits a light so clear, so full, so steady, that its brightness is only made the more manifest by the surrounding gloom. "The man of God" is not left to drink of the muddy streams that flow along the channel of human tradition. With the vessel of "unfeigned faith," he sits beside the ever-gushing fountain of "Holy Scripture" to drink of its refreshing waters to the full satisfaction of his thirsty soul.

It is worthy of remark that, although the inspired apostle was fully aware when writing his first epistle, of Timothy's "unfeigned faith" and

---

* I suppose there has never been a "Nehemiah" without a "Sanballat," or an "Ezra" without a "Rehum;" or a "Paul" without an "Alexander."

of his knowledge from childhood's earliest dawn of "the Holy Scriptures," yet he does not allude to these things until, in his second epistle, he contemplates the appalling features of the "perilous times." The reason is obvious. It is in the very midst of the perils of "the last days" that one has the most urgent need of "unfeigned faith" and "the Holy Scriptures." We cannot get on without them. When all around is fresh and vigorous – when all are borne onward as by one common impulse of genuine devotedness – when every heart is full to overflowing of deep and earnest attachment to the Person and cause of Christ – when every countenance beams with heavenly joy – then it is comparatively easy to get on.

But the condition of things contemplated in 2 Timothy is the very reverse of all this. It is such, that unless one is walking closely with God in the habitual exercise of "unfeigned faith" – in the abiding realization of the link which connects him indissolubly with "the foundation of God" – and in clear, unquestionable, accurate knowledge of "the Holy Scriptures," he must make shipwreck. This is a deeply solemn consideration, well worth my reader's undivided, prayerful attention. The time has arrived when each one must follow the Lord according to his measure. "What is that to thee? Follow thou Me." These words fall on the ear with unique power as one seeks to make his way amid the ruins of everything ecclesiastical.

Let me not be misunderstood. It is not that I would detract in the smallest degree from the value of true church fellowship or from the divine institution of the Assembly and all the privileges and responsibilities attaching thereto. Far be the thought. I most fully believe that Christians are called to seek the maintenance of the very highest principles of communion. Moreover, we are warranted from the epistle which now lies open before us, to expect that, in the darkest times, the "purged vessel" will be able to "follow righteousness, faith, love, peace, with them that call on the Lord out of a pure heart" (2 Tim. 2:22).

All this is plain and has its due place and value, but it in no wise interferes with the fact that each one is responsible to pursue a path of holy independence, without waiting for the approval, sympathy, support, or company of his fellow. True, we are to be deeply thankful for brotherly fellowship when we can get it on true ground. Of such fellowship no words can tell the worth. Would that we knew more of it! The Lord increase it to us a hundred fold! But let us never stoop to purchase fellowship at the heavy price of giving up all that is "lovely and of good report." May the name of Jesus be more precious to our hearts than all beside. And may our happy lot be cast on earth with all those who *truly* love His name, as it shall be throughout eternity in the regions of unfading light and purity, above.

Fourthly, a closing word as to "the crown of righteousness." "For I am now ready to be offered, and the time of my departure is at hand. I have fought a good fight, I have finished my course, I have kept the faith. Henceforth there is laid up for me a crown of righteousness which the Lord, the righteous Judge, shall give me at that day; and not to me only, but unto all them also who love His appearing" (chap. 4:6-8). Here, the venerable pilgrim takes his stand on the summit of the spiritual Mount Pisgah and with undimmed eye, surveys the bright plains of glory. He sees the crown of righteousness glittering in the Master's hand. He looks back over the course which he had run, and over the battlefield whereon he had fought. He stands on the confines of earth and in the very midst of the ruins of that Church whose rise and progress he had watched with such intense eagerness, and over whose decline and fall he had poured forth the tears of tender though disappointed affection, and he fixes his eye on the goal of immortality which no power of the enemy can prevent his reaching in triumph. Whether it were by Caesar's axe that he was to reach that goal or by any other means, it mattered not to one who was able to say, "*I am ready.*" What true greatness! What moral grandeur! What noble elevation is here!

Yet there was nothing of the ascetic in this incomparable servant, for though his vision was filled with the crown of righteousness, though he is ready to step like a conqueror into his triumphal chariot, he nevertheless feels it perfectly right to give detailed directions about his cloak and books. This is divinely perfect. It teaches us that the more vividly we enter into the glories of heaven, the more faithfully shall we discharge the functions of earth. The more we realize the nearness of eternity, the more effectively shall we order the things of time.

Such, beloved reader, is the ample provision made by the grace of God for "the perilous times" through which you and I are now passing. "Unfeigned faith" – "The sure foundation" – "The Holy Scriptures" – and "The crown of righteousness." May the Holy Spirit lead us into a deep sense of the importance and value of these things! May we love the appearing of Jesus and earnestly look out for that cloudless morning when "the righteous Judge" shall place a diadem of glory upon the brow of each one who really loves His appearing!

THE CLOSING SCENES OF
MALACHI AND JUDE

In comparing these two inspired writings, we find many points of similarity and many points of contrast. Both the prophet and apostle portray scenes of ruin, corruption and apostasy. The former is occupied with the ruin of Judaism, the latter with the ruin of Christendom. The prophet Malachi, in his opening sentences, gives with uncommon vividness the source of Israel's blessing and the secret of their fall. "I have loved you, saith the Lord." Here was the grand source of all their blessedness, all their glory, all their dignity. Jehovah's love accounts for all the brighter glories of Israel's past and all the brighter glories of Israel's future. On the other hand, their bold and infidel challenge, "Wherein hast Thou loved us?" accounts for the deepest depths of Israel's present degradation.

To put such a question, after all that Jehovah had done for them from the days of Moses to the days of Solomon, proved a condition of heart insensible to the very last degree. Those who, with the marvelous history of Jehovah's actings before their eyes, could say, "Wherein hast Thou loved us?" were beyond the reach of all moral appeal. Therefore, we need not be surprised at the prophet's burning words. We are prepared for such sentences as the following: "If then I be a father, where is My honor? and if I be a master, where is My fear? saith the Lord of hosts unto you, O priests that despise My name. And ye say, Wherein have we despised Thy name?" There was the most thorough insensibility both as to the Lord's love and as to their own evil ways. There was the hardness of heart that could say, "Wherein hast Thou loved us?" and "Wherein have we wronged Thee?" And all this with the history of a thousand years before their eyes – a history overlapped by the unexampled grace, mercy and patience of God, a history stained from first to last with the record of their unfaithfulness, folly and sin.

But let us hearken to the touching remonstrances of the grieved and offended God of Israel. "Ye offer polluted bread upon Mine altar; and ye say, Wherein have we polluted Thee? In that ye say, The table of the Lord is contemptible. And if ye offer the blind sacrifice, is it not evil? and if ye offer the lame and sick, is it not evil? Offer it now unto thy governor; will he be pleased with thee or accept thy person? saith the Lord of hosts... who is there even among you that would shut the doors for nought? Neither do ye kindle fire on Mine altar for nought. I have no pleasure in you, saith the Lord of hosts, neither will I accept an offering at your hand.

For from the rising of the sun even unto the going down of the same, My name shall be great among the Gentiles; and in every place incense shall be offered unto My name, and a pure offering; for My name shall be great among the heathen, saith the Lord of hosts. But ye have profaned it, in that ye say, The table of the Lord is polluted; and the fruit thereof, even His meat is contemptible. Ye said also, Behold, what a weariness is it! and ye have snuffed at it, saith the Lord of hosts; and ye brought that which was torn, and the lame and the sick; thus ye brought an offering; should I accept this of your hand? saith the Lord."

Here then we have a sad and dreary picture of Israel's moral condition. The public worship of God had fallen into utter contempt. His altar was insulted, His service despised. As to the priests, it was a mere question of money. As to the people, the whole thing had become a weariness, an empty formality, a dull and heartless routine. There was no heart for God. There was plenty of heart for gain. Any sacrifice, however maimed and torn, was deemed good enough for the altar of God. The lame, the blind and the sick, the very worst that could be had, such as they would not dare to offer to a human governor, was laid on the altar of God. And if a door was to be opened or a fire kindled, it must be paid for. No pay, no work. Such was the lamentable condition of things in the days of Malachi. It makes the heart sick to contemplate it.

But, thanks and praise be to God, there is another side of the picture. There were some rare and lovely exceptions to the gloomy rule – some striking and beautiful forms standing out in relief from the dark background. It is truly refreshing in the midst of all this venality and corruption, coldness and hollowness, barrenness and heartlessness, pride and stoutness of heart, to read such words as these: "Then they that feared the Lord spake often one to another; and the Lord hearkened and heard it, and a book of remembrance was written before Him for them that feared the Lord, and that thought upon His name."

How precious is this brief record! How delightful to contemplate this remnant in the midst of the moral ruin! There is no pretension or assumption, no attempt to set up anything, no effort to reconstruct the fallen economy, no affected display of power. Here is felt-weakness and a looking to Jehovah. This is the true secret of all real power. We need never be afraid of conscious weakness. It is impressive strength that we have to dread and shrink from. "When I am weak, then am I strong" is ever the rule for the people of God – a blessed rule, most surely. God is to be counted upon always. We may lay it down as a great root principle that, no matter what may be the actual state of the professing body, individual faith can enjoy communion with God according to the very highest truth of the dispensation.

This is a grand principle to grasp and hold fast. Let the professing people of God be ever individuals who judge and humble themselves before God, who can enjoy His presence and blessing without hindrance or limit. Witness the Daniels, the Mordecais, the Ezras, the Nehemiahs, the Josiahs, the Hezekiahs, and scores of others who walked with God, carried out the highest principles and enjoyed the rarest privileges of the dispensation, when all lay in hopeless ruin around them. There was a passover celebrated in the days of Josiah such as had not been known from the days of Samuel the prophet (2 Chron. 35:18). The feeble remnant, on their return from Babylon, celebrated the feast of tabernacles, a privilege which had not been tasted since the days of Joshua the son of Nun (Neh.8:17). Mordecai, without ever striking a blow, gained as splendid a victory over Amalek as that achieved by Joshua in the days of Exodus 17 (Esther 6:11-12). In the book of Daniel we see earth's proudest monarch prostrate at the feet of a captive Jew.

What do all these cases teach us? What lesson do they tell out in our ears? Simply that the humble, believing and obedient soul is permitted to enjoy the very deepest and richest communion with God, in spite of the failure and ruin of God's professing people and the departed glory of the dispensation in which his lot is cast.

Thus it was in the closing scenes of Malachi. All was in hopeless ruin, but that did not hinder those who loved and feared the Lord from getting together to speak about Him and to muse upon His precious name. True, that feeble remnant was not like the great congregation which assembled in the days of Solomon, from Dan to Beersheba, but it had a glory unique to itself. It had the divine presence in a way no less marvelous though not so striking. We are not told of any "book of remembrance" in the days of Solomon. We are not told of Jehovah's hearkening and hearing. Perhaps it may be said, there was no need. Be it so, but that does not dim the luster of the grace that shone upon the little band in the days of Malachi. We may boldly affirm that Jehovah's heart was as refreshed by the loving breathings of that little band as by the splendid sacrifice in the days of Solomon's dedication. Their love shines out all the brighter in contrast with the heartless formalism of the professing body, and the corruption of the priests.

"And they shall be Mine, saith the Lord of hosts, in that day when I make up My jewels; and I will spare them as a man spareth his own son that serveth him. Then shall ye return and discern between the righteous and the wicked, between him that serveth God and him that serveth Him not. For behold, the day cometh that shall burn as an oven; and all the proud, yea, and all that do wickedly, shall be stubble; and the day that cometh shall burn them up, saith the Lord of hosts, that it shall leave them neither root nor branch. But unto you that fear My name shall the Sun of Righteousness arise with healing in His wings; and ye shall go forth and grow up as calves of the stall. And ye shall tread down the wicked; for they shall be ashes under the soles of your feet in the day that I shall do this, saith the Lord of hosts."

We shall now briefly glance at the epistle of Jude. Here we have a still more appalling picture of apostasy and corruption. It is a familiar saying among us, that the corruption of the best thing is the worst corruption. Hence it is that the Apostle Jude spreads before us a page so very much darker and more awful than that presented by the prophet Malachi. It is the record of man's utter failure and ruin under the very highest and richest privileges which could be conferred upon him.

In the opening of his solemn address, the apostle lets us know that it was laid upon his heart "to write unto us of the common salvation." This would have been his far more delightful task. It would have been his joy and his refreshment to expand upon the present privileges and future glories wrapped up in the comprehensive folds of that precious word "salvation." But he felt it "needful" to turn from this more congenial work to fortify our souls against the rising tide of error and evil which threatened the very foundations of Christianity. "Beloved, when I gave all diligence to write unto you of the common salvation, it was needful for me to write unto you and exhort you that ye should *earnestly contend for the faith* which was once delivered unto the saints." All that was vital and fundamental was at stake. It was a question of earnestly contending for the faith itself. "For there are certain men crept in unawares who were before of old ordained to this condemnation; ungodly men, turning the grace of our God into lasciviousness and denying the only Lord God, and our Lord Jesus Christ."

This is far worse than anything we have in Malachi. There it was a question of the law, as we read, "Remember ye the law of Moses My servant, which I commanded unto him in Horeb for all Israel, with the statutes and judgments." But in Jude it is not a question of forgetting the law, but of actually turning into sensualness the pure and precious grace of God, and denying the Lordship of Christ. Therefore, instead of dwelling upon the salvation of God, the apostle seeks to fortify us against the wickedness and lawlessness of men. "I will therefore," he says, "put you in remembrance, though ye once knew this, how that the Lord, having saved the people out of the land of Egypt, afterward destroyed them that believed not. And the angels which kept not their first estate, but left their own habitation, He hath reserved in everlasting chains under darkness unto the judgment of the great day."

All this is most solemn, but we cannot dwell upon the dark features of this scene: space does not allow it. Besides, we rather desire to present to the Christian reader the charming picture of the Christian remnant given in the closing lines of this most searching scripture. As in Malachi we have amid the helpless ruin of Judaism, a devoted band of Jewish worshipers who loved and feared the Lord and took sweet counsel together, so in Jude, amid the more appalling ruins of Christian profession, the Holy Spirit introduces a company whom He addresses as "Beloved." These are "sanctified by God the Father and preserved in Jesus Christ, and called." These He solemnly warns against the varied forms of error and evil which were already beginning to make their appearance, but have since assumed such formidable proportions. To these He turns, with the most exquisite grace, and addresses the following exhortation, "But ye, beloved, building up yourselves on your most holy faith, praying in the Holy Spirit, keep yourselves in the love of God, looking for the mercy of our Lord Jesus Christ unto eternal life."

Here we have divine security against all the dark and terrible forms of apostasy – "the way of Cain, the error of Baalam, the gainsaying of Core, the murmurers and complainers, the great swelling words, the raging waves, the wandering stars, having men's persons in admiration because of advantage." The "beloved" are to "build themselves up on their most holy faith."

Let the reader note this. There is not a syllable here about an order of men to succeed the apostles, not a word about gifted men of any sort. It is well to see this and to bear it ever in mind. We hear a great deal of our lack of gift and power, of our not having pastors and teachers. How could we expect to have much gift or power? Do we deserve them? Regretfully we have failed and sinned and come short. Let us own this and cast ourselves upon the living God who never fails a trusting heart.

Look at Paul's touching address to the elders of Ephesus in Acts 20. To whom does he there commend us in view of the passing away of apostolic ministry? Is there a word about successors to the apostles? Not one, unless indeed it be the "grievous wolves" of which he speaks or those men who were to arise in the very bosom of the Church, speaking perverse things to draw away disciples after them. What then is the resource of the faithful? "I commend you *to God and to the Word of His grace,* which is able to build you up and to give you an inheritance among all them which are sanctified."

What a precious resource! Not a word about gifted men, valuable as such may be in their right place. God forbid we should in any way depreciate the gifts which, in spite of all the failure and sin, our gracious Lord may see fit to bestow upon His Church. But still it holds good that the blessed apostle, in taking leave of the Church, commends us not to gifted men, but to God Himself and the Word of His grace. Hence it follows that, let our weakness be ever so great, we have God to look to and to lean upon. He never fails those who trust Him. There is no limit whatsoever to the blessing which our souls may taste, if only we look to God in humility of mind and childlike confidence.

Here lies the secret of all true blessedness and spiritual power – humility of mind and simple confidence. There must on the one hand be no assumption of power, and on the other, we must not, in the unbelief of our hearts, limit the goodness and faithfulness of our God. He can and does bestow gifts for the building up of His people. He would bestow much more if we were not so ready to manage for ourselves. If the Church would but look more to Christ her living Head and loving Lord, instead of to the arrangements of men and the methods of this world, she would have a very different tale to tell. But if we, by our unbelieving plans and our restless efforts to provide a machinery for ourselves, quench, hinder and grieve the Holy Spirit, need we marvel if we are left to prove the barrenness and emptiness, the desolation and confusion of all such things? Christ is sufficient, but He must be proved, He must be trusted, He must be allowed to act. The platform must be left perfectly clear for the Holy Spirit to display thereon the preciousness, the fullness, the all-sufficiency of Christ.

But it is precisely in this very thing we so remarkably fail. We try to hide our weakness instead of owning it. We seek to cover our nakedness by a drapery of our own providing, instead of confiding simply and entirely in Christ for all we need. We grow weary of the attitude of humble patient waiting. We are in haste to put on an appearance of strength. This is our folly and our grievous loss. If we could only be induced to believe it, our real strength is to know our weakness and cling to Christ in absolute faith from day to day.

It is to this most excellent way that the apostle Jude exhorts the Christian remnant in his closing lines. "Ye, beloved, building up yourselves in your most holy faith." These words set forth the responsibility of all true Christians to be found together instead of being divided and scattered. We are to help one another in love, according to the measure of grace bestowed and the nature of the gift communicated. It is a mutual thing – "building up yourselves." It is not looking to an order of men, nor is it complaining of our lack of gifts, but simply each doing what he can to promote the common blessing and profit of all.

The reader will notice the four things which we are exhorted to do, namely "Building," "Praying," "Keeping," "Looking." What blessed work is here! Yes, and it is work for all. There is not one true Christian on the face of the earth who cannot fulfill any or all of these branches of ministry. Indeed every person is responsible so to do. We can build ourselves up on our most holy faith, we can pray in the Holy Spirit, we can keep ourselves in the love of God, and while doing these things we can look out for the mercy of our Lord Jesus Christ.

It may be asked, "Who are the beloved? To whom does the term apply?" Our answer is, "To whomsoever it may concern." Let us see to it that we are on the ground of those to whom the precious title applies. It is not *assuming* the title, but *occupying* the true moral ground. It is not empty profession, but real possession. It is not claiming the name, but being the thing.

Nor does the responsibility of the Christian remnant end here. It is not merely of themselves they have to think. They are to cast a loving look and stretch forth a helping hand beyond the circumference of their own circle. "And of some have compassion, making a difference: and others save with fear, pulling them out of the fire; hating even the garment spotted by the flesh." Who are the "some?" and who are the "others?" Is there not the same beautiful undefinedness about these as there is about the "Beloved?" These latter will be at no loss to find out the former. There are precious souls scattered up and down amid the appalling ruins of Christendom, "some" of them to be looked upon with tender compassion, "others" to be saved with godly fear, lest the "beloved" should become involved in the defilement.

It is a fatal mistake to suppose that, in order to pluck people out of the fire, we must go into the fire ourselves. This would never do. The best way to deliver people from an evil position *is to be thoroughly out of that position myself.* How can I best pull a man out of a morass? Surely not by going into the morass, but by standing on firm ground and from there lending him a helping hand. I cannot pull a man out of anything unless I am out myself. If we want to help the people of God who are mixed up with the surrounding ruin, the first thing for ourselves is to be in thorough and decided separation. The next thing is to have our hearts brimful and flowing over with tender and fervent love to all who bear the precious name of Jesus.

Here we must close, and in doing so we shall quote for the reader that blessed doxology with which the apostle sums up his solemn and weighty address. "Now unto Him that is able to keep you from falling, and to present you faultless before the presence of His glory with exceeding joy, to the only wise God our Savior, be glory and majesty, dominion and power, both now and ever. Amen." We have a great deal about "falling" in this epistle –Israel falling, angels falling, cities falling, but blessed be God, there is One who is able to keep us from falling, and it is to His holy keeping we are committed.

THE SYMPATHY AND GRACE OF JESUS

(READ CAREFULLY MATTHEW 14:1-21
AND MARK 6:30-44)

In these two parallel scriptures we are presented with two distinct conditions of heart which both find their answer in the sympathy and grace of Jesus. Let us look closely at them and may the Holy Spirit enable us to gather up and bear away their precious teaching!

It was a moment of deep sorrow to John's disciples when their master fell by the sword of Herod, when the one on whom they had been accustomed to lean and from whose lips they had been accustomed to drink instruction, was taken from them after such a fashion. This was indeed a moment of gloom and desolation to the followers of the Baptist.

But there was One to whom they could come in their sorrow and into whose ear they could pour their tale of grief – the One of whom their master had spoken, to whom he had pointed and of whom he had said, "He must increase, but I must decrease." To Him the bereaved disciples betook themselves. We read, "They came and took up the body and buried it, and went and told Jesus" (Mt. 14:12). This was the very best thing they could have done. There was not another heart on earth in which they could have found such a response as in the tender, loving heart of Jesus. His sympathy was perfect. He knew all about their sorrow. He knew their loss and how they would be feeling it. They therefore acted wisely when "they went and told Jesus." His ear was ever open and His heart ever prepared to soothe and sympathize. He perfectly exemplified the precept afterwards embodied in the words of the Holy Spirit, "Rejoice with them that do rejoice, and weep with them that weep" (Rom. 12:15).

Who can tell the value of genuine sympathy? Who can declare the value of having one who can really make your joys and sorrows his own? Thank God! we have such an one in the blessed Lord Jesus Christ. Although we cannot see Him with the bodily eye, yet can faith use Him in all the preciousness and power of His perfect sympathy. We can, if only our faith is simple and childlike, come from the tomb where we have just deposited the remains of some fondly-cherished person, to the feet of Jesus and there pour out the anguish of a bereaved and desolate heart. We shall there meet no rude repulse, no heartless reproof for our folly and weakness in feeling so deeply. Nor any clumsy effort to say something suitable, an awkward effort to put on some expression of condolence. Ah!

197

no; Jesus knows how to sympathize with a heart that is crushed and bowed down beneath the heavy weight of sorrow. His is a perfect human heart. What a thought! What a privilege to have access at all times, in all places and under all circumstances, to a perfect human heart! We may look in vain for this down here. In many cases, there is a real desire to sympathize, but a total lack of capacity. I may find myself, in moments of sorrow, in company with one who knows nothing about my sorrow or the source thereof. How could he sympathize? And even though I should tell him, his heart might be so occupied with other things as to have no room and no time for me.

Not so with the perfect Man, Christ Jesus. He has both room and time for each and all. No matter when, how or with what you come, the heart of Jesus is always open. He will never repulse, never fail, never disappoint. If we are in sorrow, what should we do? We should just do as the disciples of the Baptist did, "go and tell Jesus." This is the right thing to do. Let us go straight from the tomb to the feet of Jesus. He will dry up our tears, soothe our sorrows, heal our wounds and fill up our blanks. In this way we shall be able to enter into the truth of Rutherford's words when he says, "I try to lay up all my good things in Christ and then a little of the creature goes a great way with me." This is an experience which we may well covet. May the blessed Spirit lead us more into it!

We may now contemplate another condition of heart as furnished by the twelve apostles on their return from a successful mission. "And the apostles gathered themselves together unto Jesus and told Him all things, both what they had done and what they had taught" (Mk. 6:30). Here we have not a case of sorrow and bereavement, but one of rejoicing and encouragement. The twelve made their way to Jesus to tell Him of their success, just as the disciples of the Baptist made their way to Him in the moment of their loss. Jesus was equal to both. He could meet the heart that was crushed with sorrow and He could meet the heart that was flushed with success. He knew how to control, to moderate and to direct both the one and the other. Blessings forever be upon His honored name!

"And He said unto them, Come ye yourselves apart into a desert place and rest a while: for there were many coming and going, and they had no leisure so much as to eat" (Mk.6:31). Here we are conducted to a point at which the moral glories of Christ shine out with uncommon luster and correct the selfishness of our poor narrow hearts. Here we are taught with unmistakable clearness that to make Jesus the depository of our thoughts and feelings will never produce in us a spirit of haughty self-sufficiency and independence, or a feeling of contempt for others. Quite the reverse. The more we have to do with Jesus, the more will our hearts be opened to meet the varied forms of human need which may present themselves to our view from day to day. It is when we come to Jesus and empty our whole hearts to Him, tell Him of our sorrows and our joys, and cast our whole burden at His feet, that we really learn how to feel for others.

There is great beauty and power in the words, "come ye yourselves apart." He does not say, "Go ye." This would never do. There is no use in going apart into a desert place if Jesus is not there to go to. To go into solitude without Jesus is but to make our cold, narrow hearts, colder and narrower still. I may retire from the scene around me in chagrin and disappointment, only to wrap myself up in an impenetrable selfishness. I may fancy that my fellows have not made enough of me and I may retire to make much of myself. I may make myself the center of my whole being and thus become a coldhearted, contracted, miserable creature. But when Jesus says "come," the case is totally different. Our finest moral lessons are learned alone with Jesus. We cannot breathe the atmosphere of His presence without having our hearts expanded. If the apostles had gone into the desert without Jesus, they would have eaten the loaves and fishes themselves, but having gone with Jesus they learned differently. He knew how to meet the need of a hungry multitude, as well as that of a company of sorrowing or rejoicing disciples. The sympathy and grace of Jesus are perfect. He can meet all. If one is sorrowful, he can go to Jesus; if he is happy, he can go to Jesus; if he is hungry, he can go to Jesus. We can bring everything to Jesus, for in Him all fullness dwells, and, blessed be His name, He never sends anyone away empty.

Not so, regretfully, with His poor disciples. How forbidding is their selfishness when viewed in the light of His magnificent grace! "And Jesus, when He came out, saw much people, and was moved with compassion toward them, because they were as sheep not having a shepherd; and He began to teach them many things." He had gone to a desert place to give His disciples rest, but no sooner does human need present itself than the deep flowing tide of compassion rolls forth from His tender heart.

"And when the day was now far spent, His disciples came unto Him and said, This is a desert place, and now the time is far past: send them away." What words from men who had just returned from preaching the gospel! "Send them away." Ah! it is one thing to preach grace and another thing to act it. It is well to preach, but it is also well to act. Indeed, the preaching will be worth little if not combined with acting. It is well to instruct the ignorant, but it is also well to feed the hungry. The latter may involve more self-denial than the former. It may cost us nothing to preach, but it may cost us something to feed, and we do not like to have our private store intruded upon. The heart is ready to put forth its ten thousand objections, "What shall I do for myself? What will become of my family? We must act judiciously. We cannot do impossibilities." These and similar arguments the selfish heart can urge when a needy object presents itself.

"Send them away." What made the disciples say this? What was the real source of this selfish request? Simply unbelief. Had they only remembered that they had in their midst the One who of old had fed "600,000 footmen" for forty years in the wilderness, they would have known that He would not send a hungry multitude away. Surely the same hand that had nourished such a host for so long a time could easily furnish a single meal for five thousand. Thus faith would reason, but unbelief darkens the understanding and contracts the heart. There is nothing so absurd as unbelief and nothing which so shuts up the bowels of compassion. Faith and love always go together, and in proportion to the growth of the one is the growth of the other. Faith opens the floodgates of the heart and lets the tide of love flow forth. Thus the apostle could say to the Thessalonians, "Your faith groweth exceedingly, and the love of every one of you all toward each other aboundeth." This is the divine rule. A heart full of faith can afford to be charitable; an unbelieving heart can afford nothing.

Faith places the heart in immediate contact with God's exhaustless treasury and fills it with the most benevolent affections. Unbelief throws the heart in upon itself and fills it with all manner of selfish fears. Faith conducts us into the soul-expanding atmosphere of heaven. Unbelief leaves us enwrapped in the withering atmosphere of this heartless world. Faith enables us to hearken to Christ's gracious words, "Give ye them to eat." Unbelief makes us utter our own heartless words, "Send the multitude away." In a word, there is nothing which enlarges the heart like simple faith, and nothing so contracting as unbelief. Oh! that our faith may grow exceedingly so that our love may abound more and more! May we reap much permanent profit from the contemplation of the sympathy and grace of Jesus!

What a striking contrast between "Send the multitude away" and "Give ye them to eat." Thus it is ever. God's ways are not as our ways. It is by looking at His ways that we learn to judge our ways – by looking at Him that we learn to judge ourselves. In this lovely scene Jesus corrects the selfishness of the disciples, first by making them the channels through which His grace may flow to the multitude, and secondly, by making them gather up "twelve baskets full of the fragments" for themselves.

Nor is this all. Not merely is selfishness rebuked, but the heart is most blessedly instructed. Nature might say, "What need is there of the five loaves and two fishes at all? Surely, the One who can feed such a multitude with the loaves and fishes, can as easily feed them without such an instrumentality." Nature might argue thus, but Jesus teaches us that we are not to despise God's creatures. We are to use what we have with God's blessing. This is a fine moral lesson for the heart. "What hast thou in the house?" is the question. It is just that and nothing else that God will use. It is easy to be liberal with what we have not, but the thing is to bring out what we have and with God's blessing, apply it to the present need.

So also in the gathering up of the fragments. The foolish here might say, "What need of gathering up those scattered crumbs? Surely the One who has wrought such a miracle can have no need of fragments." Yes, but we are not to waste God's creatures. If in the using of the loaves and fishes we are taught not to despise any creature of God, in the gathering up of the fragments we are taught not to waste it. Let human need be liberally met, but let not a single crumb be wasted. How divinely perfect! How unlike us! Sometimes we are stingy, at other times extravagant. Jesus was never either the one or the other. "Give ye them to eat." But, "Let nothing be lost." Perfect grace! Perfect wisdom! May we adore it and learn from it! May we rejoice in the assurance that the blessed One who manifested all this wisdom and grace *is our life*. Christ is our life, and it is the manifestation of this life that constitutes practical Christianity. It is not living by rules and regulations, but simply having Christ dwelling in the heart by faith – Christ the source of perfect sympathy and perfect grace.

"LOOPS OF BLUE"
(EXODUS 26:4)

In contemplating the structure of the tabernacle in the wilderness, we may observe what an important place was assigned to the "loops of blue." By means of them and the "taches of gold," the curtains were joined together and the manifested unity of the whole structure preserved. These loops and taches might seem to be very insignificant and unimportant, but without them, there could have been no unity. The curtains, however beautiful in themselves, would have hung apart from each other, and thus one grand feature of the manifestation would have been lost.

Looking at the tabernacle as a figure of Christ, as surely we may, we can easily trace the beauty and significance of those "loops of blue and taches of gold." They typified that perfect unity and consistency in the character and ways of "the Man Christ Jesus" which were the result of His heavenly grace and divine energy. In the life of the blessed Lord Jesus, and in all the scenes and circumstances of that life, we not only see each distinct phase and feature perfect in itself, but also a perfect combination of all those phases and features by the power of that which was heavenly and divine in Him. The curtains of the true Tabernacle were not only beautiful in themselves, but they were beautifully combined – exquisitely linked together by means of those "loops of blue and taches of gold" which can only be discerned and appreciated by those who are in some measure instructed in the holy mysteries of the sanctuary.

And let me add that what is true of the divine Living Word is equally true of the divine written Word. The spiritual student of Holy Scripture will readily discern the "loops of blue and taches of gold." This is only what we might expect. The Living Word is the divine embodiment of the written Word, and the written Word is the divine transcript of the Living Word. Hence, we may look for the same heavenly unity, the same divine consistency, the same rare and exquisite combination in both the one and the other. It would be pleasant and profitable to trace the various illustrations of the loops and taches through the Word of God, but I have merely time and space for a brief fragment. I will give an example or two from the written Word which may lead my reader to study the subject for himself.

In 1 Corinthians 16 we have a lovely and practical illustration of our subject. Verse 13 says, "Quit you like men, be strong." Here we have one fine feature of the Christian character – that manly strength which is so desirable. But this, if taken by itself, might easily degenerate into a rough, rude, high-handed way of dealing with others, the very opposite of what we find in our divine Exemplar. Hence the Spirit in the apostle forms a loop of blue, and by means of a golden tach links on to this manly strength another feature which is so needful – love. "Let all your things be done with love." Most precious combination! Strength and love. Love and strength. If you untie this heavenly loop you will either have a high, haughty, inconsiderate style, or a soft, pliable, enfeebled mode of acting which will sacrifice everything for peace and quietness.

Again, look at that noble definition of pure religion given at the close of James 2. There the apostle uses the loop and tach to connect together the two phases of divine religion. "To visit the fatherless and the widow in their affliction" is looped with unspotted separation from the world. In other words, active benevolence and personal holiness are inseparably linked together. Untie the loop and what have you got? Either a sort of benevolence which can go hand-in-hand with the most intense spirit of worldliness, or a rigid pharisaic separation without a single generous emotion. It is only the presence of that which is heavenly and divine that can secure true unity and consistency of character. Let it never be forgotten that true Christianity is simply Christ reproduced by the Holy Spirit in the life of the Christian. Dry rules will never do. It must be Christ in all.

CHRIST AND HIS YOKE
(MATTHEW 11:28-30)

"Come unto Me all ye that labor and are heavy laden, and I will give you rest. Take My yoke upon you and learn of Me; for I am meek and lowly in heart: and ye shall find rest unto your souls. For My yoke is easy and My burden is light."

In this precious and well-known passage we have two points which are very distinct and yet intimately connected – Christ and His yoke. First, we have *coming to Christ* and its results. Secondly, taking His yoke and its results. "Come unto Me and I will give you rest." "Take My yoke and ye shall find rest." These things, being distinct, should never be confounded, and being intimately connected, they should never be separated. To confound them is to dim the luster of divine grace; to separate them is to infringe upon the claims of divine holiness. Both these evils should be carefully guarded against.

Many there are who hold up before the eye of the "heavy laden" sinner, the yoke of Christ as something which he must "take on" before his burdened heart can taste of that blessed rest which Christ *gives* to "all" who simply "come unto Him" just as they are. The passage before us does not teach this. It puts Christ first and His yoke afterwards. It does not hide Christ behind His yoke, but rather places Him, in all His attractive grace, before the heart as the One who can meet every need, remove every weight, hush every guilty fear, fill up every blank, satisfy longing desire. He is able to do as He says He will, even to "give rest." There are no conditions proposed, no demands made, no barriers erected. The simple, touching, melting, subduing, inviting, winning word is "Come." It is not "Go," "Do," "Give," "Bring," "Feel," or "Realize." No, it is, "Come." And how are we to "Come?" Just as we are. To whom are we to "Come?" To Jesus. When are we to "Come?" Now.

Observe, we are to come just as we are. We are not to wait to alter a single jot or tittle of our state, condition or character. To do this would be to "come" to some alteration or improvement in ourselves, whereas Christ distinctly and emphatically says "Come unto Me." Many souls err on this point. They think they must amend their ways, alter their course or improve their moral condition before they come to Christ. In point of fact, until they really do come to Christ they *cannot* amend or alter or improve anything. There is no warrant whatever for anyone to believe that he will be any better an hour, a day, a month or a year hence, than he is this moment. Even were he better, it would not on that account be worth the wait. The word is, *"Today,* if ye will hear His voice, harden not your hearts"* (Heb. 3:15). "Behold *now* is the accepted time; behold, now is the day of salvation" (2 Cor. 6:2).

There is nothing more certain than that all who have ever tried the self-improvement plan have found it an utter failure. They have begun in darkness, continued in misery and ended in despair. Yet, strange to say, in view of the numberless beacons which are ranged before us to warn us of the folly and danger of traveling that road, we are sure at the first to adopt it. In some way or another, self is looked to and worked upon to procure a warrant to come to Christ. "They, being ignorant of God's righteousness, and going about to establish their own righteousness, have not submitted themselves unto the righteousness of God" (Rom. 10:3). Nothing can possibly be a more dreary, depressing, hopeless task than "going about to establish one's own righteousness." Indeed, the dreariness of the task must always be commensurate with the earnestness and sincerity of the soul that undertakes it. Such an one will sooner or later have to give utterance to the cry, "O wretched man that I am!" and also to ask the question, "Who shall deliver me?" (Rom. 7:24). There can be no exception. All with whom the Spirit of God has ever worked, have in one way or another been constrained to own the hopelessness of seeking to work out a righteousness for themselves. Christ must be all; self nothing. This doctrine is easily stated, but oh, the experience!

The same is true in reference to the grand reality of sanctification. Many who have come to Christ for righteousness have not practically and experimentally laid hold of Him as their sanctification. But He is made of God, unto us, the one as well as the other. "But of Him are ye in Christ Jesus, who of God is made unto us wisdom and righteousness and sanctification and redemption: that according as it is written, He that glorieth, *let him glory in the Lord*" (1 Cor. 1:30-31). The believer is just as powerless in the work of sanctification as in the work of righteousness. If it were not so, some flesh might glory in the divine presence. I could no more subdue a single lust or trample under foot a single passion or gain the mastery over a single temper, than I could open the kingdom of heaven or establish my own righteousness before God. This is not sufficiently understood. Hence, many true Christians constantly suffer the most humiliating defeats in their practical career. They know that Christ is their righteousness, that their sins are forgiven, that they are children of God, but they are sorely put about by their constant failure in personal holiness, in practical sanctification. Again and again they experience some unhallowed desire or unsanctified temper. Again and again they are compelled to retire with shame and confusion of face. A person or a circumstance crossed their path yesterday and caused them to lose their temper. Having to meet the same today, they resolve to do better, but sorrowfully, they are again forced to retreat in disappointment and humiliation.

It is not that such persons may not pray earnestly for the grace of the Holy Spirit to enable them to conquer both themselves and the influences which surround them. This is not the point. They have not yet learned *practically* – how worthless the mere theory – that they are as completely "without strength" in the matter of "sanctification" as they are in the matter of "righteousness," and that as regards both the one and the other, Christ must be all; self nothing. They have not yet entered into the meaning of the words, "Come unto Me and I will give you rest." Here lies the source of their failure. They are as thoroughly powerless in the most trivial matter connected with practical sanctification as they are in the entire question of their standing before God. And they must be brought to believe this before they can know the fullness of the "rest" which Christ gives. It is impossible that I can enjoy rest amid incessant defeats in my practical, daily life.

True, I can come over and over again and pour into my heavenly Father's ear the humiliating tale of my failure and overthrow. I can confess my sins and find Him ever "faithful and just to forgive me my sins, and to cleanse me from all unrighteousness" (1 Jn. 1:9). *But we must learn Christ as the Lord our sanctification* as well as "The Lord our righteousness." Moreover, it is by faith and not by effort that we enter into both the one and the other. We look to Christ for righteousness because we have none of our own, and we look to Christ for practical sanctification because we have none of our own. It needed no personal effort on our part to get righteousness because Christ is our righteousness, and it needs no personal effort on our part to get sanctification because Christ is our sanctification.

It seems strange that, while the inspired apostle distinctly tells us that Christ is "made of God unto us wisdom, righteousness, sanctification and redemption," we nevertheless should attach the idea of personal effort to one out of the four things which he enumerates. Can we guide ourselves in the ten thousand difficulties and details of our Christian course by our own wisdom or discernment? Surely not. Should we make an effort? By no means. Why not? Because God has made Christ to be our "wisdom." Therefore it is our precious privilege, having been brought to our wits' end, to look to

Christ for wisdom. In other words, when Christ says, "Come unto Me," He means that we are to come unto Him for wisdom as well as for all else, and we cannot come to Christ and to our own efforts at the same time. No, so long as we are making efforts, we must be strangers to "rest."

The same holds good with respect to "righteousness." Can we work out a righteousness for ourselves? Surely not. Should we make an effort? By no means. Why not? Because God has made Christ to be unto us "righteousness," and that righteousness is "to him that worketh not" (Rom.5:5).

So also in the matter of "redemption," which is put last in 1 Corinthians 1:30 because it includes the final deliverance of the body of the believer from under the power of death. Could we by personal effort deliver our bodies from the dominion of mortality? Surely not. Should we try? The thought is impious. Why? Because God has made Christ to be unto us "redemption" as regards both soul and body, and He who has already applied by the power of His Spirit that glorious redemption to our souls, will before long apply it to our bodies.

Why then should "sanctification" be singled out from the precious list and be saddled with the legal and depressing idea of personal effort? If we cannot by our own efforts get "wisdom, righteousness and redemption," are we any more likely to succeed in getting "sanctification?" Clearly not. Have we not proved this times without number? Have not our closet-walls witnessed our tears and groans evoked by the painful sense of failure after failure in our own efforts to tread with steady step and erect carriage, the lofty walks of personal sanctity? Will the reader deny this? I trust not. I would certainly hope he has responded to the call of Jesus, "Come unto Me all ye that labor and are heavy laden, and I will give you rest." It is vain to "labor" in our own strength after sanctification. We must come to Jesus for *that* as well as for everything else. And having come to Jesus, we shall find that there is no lust which He cannot slay, no temper that He cannot subdue, no passion that He cannot overcome. The self-same hand that has cancelled our sins, that guides us in our difficulties and that will soon deliver our bodies from the power of death, can give us complete victory over all our personal infirmities and besetments, and fill our hearts with His sacred rest.

It is immensely important to have a clear understanding of the question of sanctification. Many have gone on "laboring and heavy laden" for years, endeavoring to work out in one way or another, their sanctification, and not succeeded to their satisfaction, for who ever did or ever could? They have even been tempted to question if they were ever converted at all. Many, were they to tell "all the truth," could adopt as their own, the mournful lines of the poet,

> "Tis a point I long to know,
> Oft it causeth anxious thought,
> Do I love the Lord or no?
> Am I His or am I not?"

Such persons have clear views of gospel truth. They could with Scriptural accuracy tell an inquirer after righteousness how, where and when he could get it. And yet, if that self-same inquirer were to ask them about their own state of heart before God, they could give but a sorry answer. Why is this? Simply because they have not laid hold of Christ as their sanctification as well as their righteousness. They have been endeavoring, partly in their own strength and partly by praying for the influences of the Holy Spirit, to stumble along the path of sanctification. They would deem a person very ignorant of "the plan of salvation" if they found him "going about to establish his own righteousness," but they do not see that they themselves exhibit ignorance of that "plan" by going about to establish their own sanctification. Truly if in the one case it is a sorry righteousness which is worked out, so in the other case it is a lame sanctification. For if it be true that "all our righteousnesses are as filthy rags," it is equally true that all our sanctifications are as filthy rags.

Whatever has the word "our" attached to it must be altogether imperfect. Christ is God's righteousness and Christ is God's sanctification. Both the one and the other are obtained by simply coming, looking, clinging, trusting to Christ. I need hardly say, it is by the power of the Spirit and through the Holy Scriptures that Christ is applied to us, both as our righteousness and our sanctification. But all this only takes the matter more and more out of our hands and leaves us nothing to glory in. If we could conquer an evil temper, we might indeed think ourselves clever, but since we are not asked to pick up a feather to add to our righteousness or our wisdom or our redemption, so neither are we asked to pick up a feather in order to add to our sanctification. In this as in those, Christ is all, self nothing. This doctrine is easily stated, but oh, the experience!

Will anyone say that the writer is doing away with sanctification? If so, he may just as well say that he is doing away with "righteousness," "wisdom" or "redemption." Who will contend for self-righteousness, self-wisdom or self-redemption? Who but the man that contends for self-sanctification? Who is likely to attain and exhibit the more elevated standard of personal sanctity? Is it the man who is perpetually floundering amid his own imperfect struggles and cobweb-resolutions, or he who is daily, hourly and momentarily clinging to Christ as his sanctification? The answer is simple. The sanctification which we get in Christ is as perfect as the righteousness, the wisdom and the redemption. Am I doing away with "wisdom" because I say I am foolish? Am I doing away with "righteousness" because I say I am guilty? Am I doing away with "redemption" because I say I am mortal? Am I doing away with "sanctification" because I say I am vile? Yes, I am doing away with all these things so far as "*I*" am concerned, so I may find them all in Christ. This is the point. All – all in Christ!

Oh! when shall we learn to get to the end of self and cling simply to Christ? When shall we enter into the depth and power of those words "Come unto Me?" He does not say, "Come unto My yoke." No; but "come unto Me." We must cease from our own works in every shape and form, and come to Christ, come just as we are, come now. We come to Christ and get rest from and in Him before ever we hear a word about the "yoke." To put the yoke first is to displace everything. If a "heavy laden" sinner thinks of the yoke, he must be overwhelmed by the thought of his own total inability to take it upon him or carry it. But when he comes to Jesus and enters into His precious rest, he finds the "yoke is easy and the burden light."

This conducts us to the second point in our subject – "the yoke." We must keep the two things distinct. To confound them is to tarnish the heavenly luster of the grace of Christ and to put a yoke upon the sinner's neck and a burden upon his shoulder which he, being "without strength," is wholly unable to bear. But they are morally connected. All who come to Christ must take His yoke upon them and learn of Him, if they would "find rest unto their souls."

To come to Christ is one thing; to walk with Him or learn of Him is quite another. Christ was "meek and lowly in heart." He could meet the most adverse and discouraging circumstances with an "even so, Father." The Baptist's heart might fail amid the heavy clouds which gathered around him in Herod's dungeon; the men of that generation might refuse the double testimony of righteousness and grace as furnished by the ministry of John and of our Lord Himself; Bethsaida, Chorazin and Capernaum might refuse the testimony of His mighty works – a torrent of evidence which one might suppose would sweep away every opposing barrier. All these things and many more might cross the path of the divine Workman, but being "meek and lowly in heart," He could say, "I thank Thee, O Father – even so, Father, for so it seemed good in Thy sight." His "rest" in the Father's counsels was profound and perfect, and He invites us to take His yoke, to learn of Him, to drink into His spirit, to know the practical results of a subject mind, that we may "find rest unto our souls."

A broken will is the real ground of the rest which we are to "find" after we have come to Christ. If God wills one thing and we will another, we cannot find rest in that. It matters not what the scene or circumstance may be. We may expand a list of things to any imaginable extent, in which our will may run counter to the will of God, but in whatever it is, we cannot find rest so long as our will is unbroken. We must get to the end of self in the matter of will as well as in the matter of "wisdom, righteousness, sanctification or redemption," else we shall not "find rest."

This, my beloved reader, is deep, real, earnest, personal work. Moreover, it is a daily thing. It is a continual taking of Christ's yoke upon us and learning of Him. It is not that we take the yoke in order to come to Christ. No. We come to Christ first, and when His love fills and satisfies our souls, when His rest refreshes our spirits, when we can gaze by faith upon His gracious countenance and see Him stooping down to confer upon us the high and holy privilege of wearing His yoke and learning His lesson, we find that His yoke is indeed easy and His burden light. Unsubdued, unjudged, unmortified nature could never wear that yoke or bear that burden. The first thing is, "Come unto Me and I will give you rest." The second thing is, "Take My yoke upon you and ye shall find rest."

We must never reverse these things, never confound them, never displace them, never separate them. To call upon a sinner to take Christ's yoke before he has gotten Christ's rest, is to place Christ on the top of Mount Sinai, the sinner at the foot of that Mount and a dark impenetrable gulf between. This must not be done. Christ stands in all His matchless grace before the sinner's eye and pours forth His touching invitation, "Come," and adds His heart-assuring promise, "I will give." There is no condition, no demand, "no servile work." All is the purest, freest, richest grace. Just, "come and I will give you rest." And what then? Is it bondage, doubt and fear? Ah! no. "Take My yoke upon you." How marvelously near this brings us to the One who has already given us rest! What a high honor to wear the same yoke with Him! It is not that He puts a grievous yoke upon our neck and a heavy burden upon our shoulder which we have to carry up the rugged sides of yon fiery Mount. This is not Christ's way. It is not thus He deals with the weary and heavy laden who come unto Him. He gives them rest. He gives them part of His yoke and a share of His burden. In other words, He calls them into fellowship with

Himself, and in proportion as they enter into this fellowship they find still deeper rest in Him and in His blessed ways. And at the close, He will conduct them into that eternal rest which remains for the people of God.

May the Lord enable us to enter more fully into the power of all these divine realities, so that His joy remain in us and our joy may be full. There is an urgent need of a full, unreserved surrender of the heart to Christ and a full, unreserved acceptance of Him in all His precious adaptation to our every need. We want the whole heart, the single eye, the mortified mind, the broken will. Where these exist, there will be little complaining of doubts and fears, ups and downs, heavy days, vacant hours, restless moments, dullness and stupor, wandering and barrenness. When one has got to the end of himself regarding wisdom, righteousness, holiness and all beside, and when he has really found Christ as God's provision for *all*, then, but not until then, he will know the depth and power of that word "*rest.*"

> "Now, then, my Lord, my Way, my Life,
> Henceforth, let trouble, doubt, and strife,
>   Drop off as Autumn leaves:
> Henceforth, as privileged by Thee,
> Simple and undistracted be,
>   My soul which to Thy scepter cleaves.
>
> At all times, to my spirit bear
> An inward witness, soft and clear,
>   Of Thy redeeming power:
> This will instruct Thy child, and fit,
> Will sparkle forth what'ere is meet,
>   For exigence of every hour.
>
> Thus, all the sequel is well weighed;
> I cast myself upon Thine aid,
>   A sea where none can sink,
> Yea, in that sphere I stand, poor worm,
> Where Thou wilt for Thy Name perform
> Above what'er I ask or think."

THE DIVINE ANATHEMA

"If any man love not the Lord Jesus Christ, let him be Anathema Maranatha" (1 Cor. 16:22).

The position which this solemn anathema occupies is truly remarkable. In the course of his lengthened epistle, the apostle had to rebuke and correct many practical evils and doctrinal errors. There were divisions among the Corinthians. They were puffed up one against another. There was fornication among them. They went to law one with another. There was gross disorder at the Lord's Supper. Some of them called in question the grand foundation truth of the resurrection of the dead.

These were grave errors and formidable evils – errors and evils which called forth the sharp and stern reproof of the inspired apostle. But when at the close he pronounces his solemn "Anathema Maranatha," it is not directed against those who had introduced the errors or practiced the evils, but against "any man" who loves not the Lord Jesus Christ.* This is well worthy of serious thought. The only security against all manner of error and evil is genuine love to the Lord Jesus Christ. A man may be so strictly moral that no one could put his finger upon a single blot in his character or a single stain in his reputation. Yet underneath that strict morality, there may be a heart as cold as ice, so far as the Lord Jesus is concerned. Again, a man may be so marked by a spirit of noble benevolence that his influence is felt throughout the entire sphere in which he moves, and all the while, his heart may not have a single pulsation of love to Christ. Finally, a man may possess in his understanding, a perfectly orthodox creed and he may be devotedly attached to the ordinances and observances of traditional religion, and be wholly without affection for the adorable Person of the Lord Jesus Christ. It may even happen that all these things – lofty morality, noble benevolence, sound orthodoxy and devoted attachment to religious forms, exist in one and the same individual, and that individual be wholly void of a single spark of genuine affection for the Lord Jesus Christ, and as a solemn and startling consequence, stand exposed to the burning Anathema of God the Holy Spirit. I may be moral through love to self. I may be benevolent through love to my fellow. I may be orthodox through a love of dogmas. I may be religious through a love of a sect. But none of these things can shield me from the

---

* The word "Anathema" signifies anything devoted to death; and "Maranatha" signifies the Lord comes to judgment.

merited judgment which is denounced by the Holy Spirit against "any man," no matter who or what, who "loves not the Lord Jesus Christ."

This is a deeply solemn and most seasonable word for the present moment. Let the reader deeply ponder it. Let him remember that the only basis for true morality, the only basis for divine orthodoxy, the only basis for "pure religion," is love to the Lord Jesus Christ. Where this love does not exist, all is cold, sterile and worthless, all exposed to death and judgment by the "Anathema Maranatha" of the Holy Spirit. If the heart be really touched with the vital spark of love to Jesus, then every effort after pure morality, every struggle against our hateful lusts, passions and tempers, every opening of the hand of genuine benevolence, every sound and truthful principle, every act of devotion, every pious aspiration, every fervent breathing, every outgoing of the soul, is precious to the Father, to the Son and to the Holy Spirit. All is fragrant with the perfume of that dear Name which is the theme of heaven's wonder, the center of heaven's joy, the object of heaven's worship.

My beloved reader, should we not "love the Lord Jesus Christ?" Should we not hold Him dearer to our heart than all beside? Should we not be ready to surrender all for Him? Should not our bosoms swell with emotions of sincere attachment to His Person in heaven and His cause on earth? How could we trace Him from the bosom of the Father to the manager of Bethlehem, from the manger of Bethlehem to the cross of Calvary, and from the cross of Calvary to the throne of the majesty in the heavens – how could we "consider" Him as "the Apostle and High Priest of our profession" – and not have our whole moral being brought under the mighty constraining influence of His love?

May the Holy Spirit so unfold to our souls His matchless glories and peerless excellencies, that we may "count all things but loss for the excellency of the knowledge of Christ Jesus our Lord."

> "Jesus, I love Thy charming name;
>   'Tis music to mine ear,
> Fain would I sound it out so loud,
>   That earth and heaven should hear.
>
> Yes, Thou are precious to my soul
>   My transport and my trust:
> Jewels to Thee are gaudy toys,
>   And gold is sordid dust.

All my capacious powers can wish,
  In Thee doth richly meet:
Nor, to mine eyes, is light so dear,
  Nor friendship half so sweet.

Thy grace still dwells upon my heart,
  And sheds its fragrance there;
The noblest balm of all its wounds,
  The cordial of its care."

THE TWO ALTARS
(EXODUS 20:24-26)

"An altar of earth thou shalt make unto Me, and shalt sacrifice thereon thy burnt offerings and thy peace offerings, thy sheep and thine oxen: in all places where I record My name I will come unto thee, and I will bless thee."

If anything could enhance the value or add to the interest of this passage of Scripture, it is the context in which it stands. To find such words at the close of Exodus 20 is something which must strike the thoughtful reader. In the opening of this chapter we find God speaking from the top of Mount Sinai and laying down the law as to man's duty toward God and his duty toward his neighbor. This law is published amid thunderings, blackness, darkness and tempest. "Thou shalt do this" and "Thou shalt not do that." Such are the terms in which God speaks from the top of the fiery mount. Thus is He compelled to erect around Himself and around His rights, certain barriers to keep man off. And in the same way, has man to be kept from infringing the rights of his fellow.

Thus much as to the opening of Exodus 20. There are no such words here as, "I will come unto thee." Quite the reverse. The word was, "Beware lest thou come unto Me." See Exodus 19:12, 24. It was impossible for man to get to God by way of law. The barriers that were placed around that mount were insurmountable to man. "By works of law shall no man living be justified." Under the law there is no possible way of access to God. "Keep off" is the stern utterance of the entire legal system – the expression of the very spirit and character of the whole Mosaic economy. Nearness and liberty are unknown under the law, and cannot possibly be enjoyed by anyone on legal ground.

Hence we may safely say with reverence that Jehovah was not at home on the top of Mount Sinai. It was not natural to Him to surround Himself with barriers. He was forced into that position by the legality of the human heart. Israel had taken upon them to say, "All that the Lord hath spoken we will do" (Ex. 19:8). It was this that caused Jehovah to place Himself at a distance so that man might be tested and the offense might abound. He had just said to the people, "Ye have seen what I did unto the Egyptians and how I bore you on eagles' wings, and brought you unto Myself. Now, therefore, if ye will obey My voice indeed and keep My covenant, then ye shall be a peculiar treasure unto Me above all people: for all the earth is Mine."

To what "covenant" does He here refer? To the covenant made with Abraham – the covenant of grace. There was nothing of man's doing in this covenant. It set forth what God would do for Abraham and his seed, what He would give them and what He would be to them. It was on the ground of this covenant that Jehovah could say to Israel, "I have brought you unto Myself." But the very moment Israel undertook to say, "All that the Lord hath spoken we will do," we hear the command issued to "set bounds about the mount" that the people might be put at a distance.

However, this was not according to the loving heart of the God of Israel. It did not suit His nature and character to place Himself at a distance from His people. They had compelled Him to retire within the narrow enclosures of mount Sinai and to surround Himself with clouds and darkness, thunderings, lightnings and tempest. Man had undertaken to *do*, and he must be put to the test. "The law entered that the offense might abound." Again, "By the law is the knowledge of sin."

It is not our intention in this short article to dwell upon the subject of "the law." We have merely referred to it to bring out the striking contrast between the opening and the close of Exodus 20. It would seem as though God were in haste to come down from the top of that dreadful mountain in order to meet man at "an altar of earth" – the place of grace – the place where man's doings are displaced by God's. "An altar of earth thou shalt make unto Me, and shalt sacrifice thereon thy burnt offerings and thy peace offerings, thy sheep and thine oxen: in all places where I record My name, I will come unto thee and I will bless thee."

What a contrast! It is as though He had said to them, "You cannot come to Me if I remain on the top of this mountain, but I will come unto you. If I remain here I must curse you, but I will meet you at an altar of earth and bless you." Blessed be His Name, He delights not in cursing. Hence He would not record His Name on Mount Sinai, the place of distance and darkness where He could not come unto His people and bless them.

How blessedly all this tells out what God is! This teaching about the altar is like a ray of divine light piercing through the gloom which surrounded Mount Sinai, and shining on the spot where God would record His Name, where He could meet His people in all the fullness of blessing.

And let the reader note the character of the offerings referred to in verse 24. We have "burnt offerings and peace offerings." Not a word about sin offerings and trespass offerings. Why is this? Surely this is the very place in which we should expect to find these latter introduced. But no. We have the burnt offering – the type of Christ surrendering Himself in life and in death to do the will of God. And we have the peace offering – the type of Christ as the Object on which the worshipper feeds in communion with God. And not a word about the sin offering or trespass offering. Why? Is it that these are not needed? Far be the thought! They lie at the very foundation of that altar where God and the worshipper meet. The sin offering is the type of Christ bearing the judgment of God against sin. The trespass offering is the type of Christ bearing our sins in His own body on the tree. *These form the foundation of all worship.* But they are omitted in Exodus 20:24 because we have here the nature and character of the worship in which God delights, a worship in which the soul is occupied with Christ in the very highest aspect of His Person and work. This is what we have in the burnt offering, wherein Christ is seen making atonement, not merely according to our need, but according to the claims of God – not merely according to the measure of the hatefulness of sin, but according to the measure of the preciousness of Christ to the heart of God.

What a striking contrast between the opening and closing lines of Exodus 20! What lessons are here for our hearts! What a rebuke to all our legal tendencies! We are all prone to be occupied with our doings in some shape or form. Legality is natural to our hearts. And let us remember, it was this that forced Jehovah (to speak after the manner of men) to take up the position in which we find Him in Exodus 19 and 20. Abraham did not know God in such a position. It was not as a lawgiver that God revealed Himself to the father of the faithful, but as a God of grace, as a God of promise. There were no thunderings and lightnings, no blackness, darkness and tempest surrounding the Blessed One when He appeared unto Abraham in Ur of the Chaldees, or when He partook of his hospitality in the plains of Mamre. It was always God's delight to have His people near Him, enjoying the precious fruits of His grace, rather than afar off, reaping the bitter fruits of their works. This latter was simply the result of man's legal utterance, "All that the Lord hath spoken we will do." Up to the fatal moment in the which these words were spoken, God had been speaking and acting in the same unqualified grace toward the seed of Abraham as He had toward that favored patriarch himself. But when Israel undertook to *do,* it was needful to put them thoroughly to the test. This was done by the law.

But, it may be asked, was it not always God's purpose to give the law? Was it not necessary? Is it not designed to be the abiding rule of man's conduct – the statement of his duty to God and man, the divine summary and embodiment of his righteousness? To all this we reply, Most surely God knew from the beginning what He would do. Moreover, in His infinite wisdom He overruled man's legal folly and made use of the law to raise the great question of righteousness and prove whether it was possible for man to work out a righteousness which could be accepted. But what was the result? Did man ever get righteousness by keeping the ten commandments? Never. "By the deeds of the law shall no flesh be justified in His sight, for by law is the knowledge of sin" (Rom. 3:20). Again, "For as many as are of the works of the law are under the curse: for it is written, Cursed is every one that continueth not in all things which are written in the book of the law to do them. But that no man is justified by the law in the sight of God, it is evident: for the just shall live by faith" (Gal. 3:10-11).

What, then, was the object of the law? Why was it given? What was its effect? "The law entered that the offense might abound" (Rom. 5:20). "Wherefore then serveth the law? It was added because of transgressions" (Gal. 3:19). "The law worketh wrath" (Rom. 4:15).

Thus Scripture answers our three questions in the plainest possible manner. Not only so, it settles the entire law question in such a way as to remove every difficulty and every cloud from the mind that will submit absolutely to the authority of the Word.

When we sat down to pen this brief article, we had no thought whatever of entering on the domain of theology. It was merely our purpose to present to the heart and mind of the reader the striking lesson taught by the two altars in Exodus 20 – the altar of earth and the altar of hewn stone. In the former we have the very spirit of the dispensation of grace; in the latter the spirit of the dispensation of law. God wanted man to be near Him. Therefore He would have an altar of earth. In other words, man was to approach God without any efforts or doings of his own. "If thou wilt make Me an altar of stone, thou shalt not build it of hewn stone (or, as the margin reads, "build them with hewing"): for if thou lift up thy tool upon it, thou hast polluted it. Neither shalt thou go up by steps unto Mine altar, that thy nakedness be not discovered thereon."

Oh! that men would only consider these things! How little are they understood! Man will be doing. He will lift up his tool in the building of his altar; the result is pollution. He will ascend by steps; the result is discovered nakedness. Thus it must be because man is a sinner and his very best works can only issue in pollution and nakedness.

One thing is certain. *God does not record His Name in any place where man's doings are set up as the basis of worship.* This truth shines with heavenly luster on every page of the sacred Volume, and it shines where we should least of all have expected to find it – at the close of Exodus 20. It is something perfectly wonderful, amid the thunderings of Mount Sinai, to catch such heavenly words as these, "In all places where I record My name I will come unto thee, and I will bless thee." These are words of purest grace, words flowing from the very heart of God, words expressing the very nature and character of God. "I will come unto thee." Precious words! May they sink down into our hearts and there abide! May it be our aim and object ever to be found worshipping in that place where God records His Name, and where, instead of the nakedness and pollution which ever mark the efforts of man, we have the infinite preciousness of the grace of God and the fullness and excellency of Christ in His Person and work!

CLOVEN TONGUES
(ACTS 2:1-11)

It will greatly enhance the grace of this lovely passage of Scripture to bear in mind what it was that rendered the cloven tongues necessary. In Genesis 11 we have the inspired record of the first grand effort of the children of men to establish themselves in the earth, to form a great association and make themselves a name. And all this, be it remembered, without God. His name is never mentioned. He was not to form any part of this proud and popular scheme. He was entirely shut out. It was not a dwelling place for God that was to be erected on the plain of Shinar. It was a city for man, a center round which men were to gather.

Such was the object of the children of men as they stood together on the plain of Shinar. It was not, as some have imagined, to escape another flood. There is not a shadow of foundation in the passage for any such idea. Here are their words, "And they said, Go to, let us build us a city and a tower whose top may reach unto heaven; and let us make us a name, lest we be scattered abroad upon the face of the whole earth." There is no thought here of escaping another flood. It is sheer imagination without any Scripture basis. The object is as plain as possible. It is precisely similar to all those great confederacies, associations or masses of flesh that have been formed on the earth from that day to this. The Shinar Association could compete with any association of modern times, both in its principle and object.

But it proved to be a Babel. Jehovah wrote *confusion* upon it. He divided their tongues and scattered them abroad. In a word, divided tongues were sent as the expression of divine judgment upon this first great human association. This is a solemn and weighty fact. An association without God, no matter what its object, is really nothing but a mass of flesh, based on pride and ending in hopeless confusion. "Associate yourselves, O ye people, and ye shall be broken in pieces" (Isa. 8:9). So much for all human associations. May we learn to keep clear of them! May we adhere to that one divine association – the Church of the living God, of which a risen Christ in glory is the living Head, the Holy Spirit the living Guide, and the Word of God the living Charter!

It was to gather this blessed Assembly that the cloven tongues were sent in grace on the day of Pentecost. No sooner had the Lord Jesus Christ taken His seat at the right hand of power, amid the brightness of heaven's majesty, than He sent down the Holy Spirit to publish the glad tidings of salvation in the ears of His very murderers. Inasmuch as that message of pardon and peace was intended for men of various tongues, so the divine messenger came down prepared to address each "in his own tongue wherein he was born." The God of all grace made it plain – so plain that it cannot be mistaken – that He desired to make His way to each heart with the sweet story of grace. Man, on the plain of Shinar, did not want God, but God on the day of Pentecost proved that He wanted man. Blessed forever be His holy Name! God had sent His Son and man had just murdered Him. Now He sends the Holy Spirit to tell man there is pardon through that very blood which He had shed, for his guilt in shedding it. Matchless, marvelous, overwhelming grace! Oh! that it may subdue our hearts and bind us to Him who is its source, its channel and the power of enjoyment! The grace of God has far surpassed all the enmity of man. It has proved itself victorious over all the opposition of the human heart and all the rage of hell.

In Genesis 11 divided tongues were sent in judgment. In Acts 2 divided tongues were sent in grace. The blessed God of all grace would cause each one to hear of full salvation, and hear of it in those very words in which his infant ears had hearkened to the earliest whisperings of a mother's love – in "his own tongue wherein he was born." It mattered not whether the language were soft or harsh, refined or barbarous, the Holy Spirit would use it as the vehicle for conveying the precious message of salvation right home to the poor heart. If divided tongues had once been given to *scatter* in judgment, they were again given to *gather* in grace – not now around an earthly tower, but around a heavenly Christ – not for the exaltation of man, but for the glory of God.

It is worthy of notice that when God was giving the law from Mount Sinai, He spoke only in one tongue and to one people. The law was carefully wrapped up in one language and deposited in the midst of one nation. Not so the gospel. When that was the burden, God the Holy Spirit Himself descended from heaven in cloven tongues to send the soul-stirring tidings far and wide over the whole world and convey them "to every creature under heaven" in the very dialect wherein he was born. This is a great moral fact. It comes down upon the heart with uncommon weight and power. When God was speaking in terms of requirement and prohibition, He confined Himself to one language, but when He was publishing the message of life and salvation, pardon and peace through the blood of the Lamb, He spoke in every language under heaven. When *man's duty* was to be declared, God spoke in one dialect, but when *God's salvation* was to be published, He spoke in every dialect under heaven.

This surely tells a tale. It declares plainly which is more in harmony with the divine mind, law or grace. Blessed be His Name, He delights in grace. Law and judgment are His strange work. He has pronounced the feet of those who publish the gospel to be beautiful. Of those who desired to be teachers of the law, He said, "I would they were even cut off that trouble you." Thus His acts and His words show the bent of His loving heart towards poor unworthy sinners. He has left nothing undone, nothing unsaid, to prove His perfect willingness to save and bless. Therefore all who die in their sins will perish without excuse, and those awful words will echo through the regions of eternal gloom forever and ever, "I would, but ye would not!" Reader, think of this! Are you yet in your sins? If so, we earnestly beseech you to flee *now* from the wrath to come. Accept the message of pardon now sent to you in your own language wherein you were born, and go on your way rejoicing.

In conclusion, we might add that Genesis 11, Acts 2 and Revelation 7:9-17 form a very lovely group of scriptures. In the first, we see divided tongues sent in judgment; in the second, divided tongues are given in grace; and in the third, divided tongues are seen gathered in glory. Well may we say, "Thy testimonies are wonderful, therefore doth my soul love them."

ISRAEL AND THE NATIONS
(READ PSALM 67)

It would help to give clearness and definiteness to missionary effort to keep fully before our minds God's original purpose in sending the gospel to the Gentiles, or the nations. This we have stated in the most distinct manner in Acts 15, "Simeon hath declared," says James, "how God at the first did visit the Gentiles to take out of them a people for His name."

Nothing can be simpler than this. It affords no warrant whatsoever for the idea so persistently held by the professing church that the whole world is to be converted by the preaching of the gospel. Simeon knew that such was not God's object in visiting the Gentiles, but simply to take out of them a people for His name. The two things are as distinct as any two things can be. Indeed, they stand in direct opposition. To convert all the nations is one thing; to take out of the nations a people is quite another.

The latter, not the former, is God's present object. It is what He has been doing since the day that Simon Peter opened the kingdom of heaven to the Gentile in Acts 10. And it is what He will continue to do until the moment so rapidly approaching in which the last elect one is gathered out and our Lord shall come to receive His people unto Himself.

Let all missionaries remember this. They may rest assured it will not clip their wings or cripple their energies. It will only guide their movements by giving them a divine aim and object. Of what possible use can it be for a man to propose as the end of his labors something wholly different from that which is before the mind of God? Ought not a servant seek to do his master's will? Can he expect to please his master by running directly counter to his clearly expressed object?

Now, clearly, it is not God's purpose to convert the world by the preaching of the gospel. He only means "to take out a people." True it is, blessedly true, that all the earth shall yet be filled with the knowledge of the Lord as the waters cover the sea. There is no question as to this. All Scripture bears witness to it. To quote the passages would literally fill a volume.

But the question is, how is this grand and glorious result to be brought about? Is it the purpose of God to use the professing Church as His agent or a preached gospel as His instrument in the conversion of the world? Scripture says No! with all emphasis and a clearness which ought to sweep away every doubt and difficulty.

Let it be distinctly understood that we delight in all true missionary effort. We heartily wish God's speed to every true missionary – to everyone who has left home and kindred and friends and all the comforts and privileges of civilized life to carry the glad tidings of salvation into the dark places of the earth. Further, we desire to render hearty thanks to God for all that has been accomplished in the fields of foreign mission, though we cannot approve the mode by which the work is carried on, or the great root-principle of missionary societies. We consider there is a lack of simple faith in God and of subjection to the authority of Christ and the guidance of the Holy Spirit. There is too much of mere human machinery and looking to the world for aid.

But all this is beside our present mark. We are not now discussing the principle of missionary organization or the various methods adopted for carrying on of missionary operation. The point with which we are occupied in this brief paper is this: will God make use of the professing Church to convert the nations? We don't ask whether He has done so? Were we to put the question thus, we should receive an unqualified negative from the ends of the earth. What! Christendom convert the world! Impossible! She is herself the darkest moral blot in the universe of God and a grievous stumbling-block in the pathway of both Jew and Gentile. The professing Church has been at work for nearly 2000 years and what is the result? Let the reader take a glance at a missionary map and he will see. Look at those patches of black which set forth the dismal regions over which heathenism bears sway. Look at the red, the green, the yellow, setting forth popery, the Greek church, Islam. And where is – we say not true Christianity – but even mere nominal Protestantism? That is indicated by those tiny spots of blue which, if all put together, would make but a very small fraction indeed. And as to what this Protestantism is in its best condition, we need not now stop to inquire.

But is it the revealed purpose of God to make use of the professing Church in any way to convert the nations? If it be so, we admit at once that, in spite of the most discouraging appearances, we must believe and hope. We freely grant that the true way in which to test any principle is not by results, but simply by the Word of God.

What say the Scriptures on the great question of the conversation of the nations? Take the lovely psalm that stands at the head of this paper. It is but one proof, but it is a most striking and beautiful one, and it perfectly harmonizes with the testimony of all Scripture from Genesis to Revelation. We cannot refrain from giving it at full length to the reader.

"God be merciful unto us and bless us; and cause His face to shine upon us. That Thy way may be known upon earth; Thy saving health among the nations. Let the people praise Thee, O God; let all the people praise Thee. O let the nations be glad and sing for joy: for Thou shalt judge the people righteously, and govern the nations upon earth. Let the people praise Thee, O God, let all the people praise Thee. Then shall the earth yield her increase; and God, even our own God, shall bless us. God shall bless us, and all the ends of the earth shall fear Him."

Here, the simple truth shines before us with remarkable force and beauty. It is when God shall have mercy upon Israel, when He shall cause His light to shine upon Zion – then and not until then – will His way be known upon earth, His saving health among all nations. It is through Israel and not through the professing Church that God will yet bless the nations.

That the "us" of the foregoing psalm refers to Israel, no intelligent reader of Scripture needs be told. Indeed, the great burden of the Psalms, the prophets and the entire Old Testament, is Israel. There is not a syllable about the Church from cover to cover of the Old Testament. Types and shadows there are in which – ,now that we have the light of the New Testament – we can see the truth of the Church prefigured. But without that light no one could find the truth of the Church in Old Testament Scripture. That great mystery was, as the inspired apostle tells us, "hid" – not in the Scriptures, for whatever is contained in the Scriptures in no longer hid but revealed – but "hid in God." It was not and could not be revealed until Christ, King rejected by Israel, was crucified and raised from the dead. So long as the testimony to Israel was pending, the *doctrine* of the Church could not be unfolded.

Hence, although at the day of Pentecost we have the *fact* of the Church, yet it was not until Israel had rejected the testimony of the Holy Spirit in Stephen that a special witness was called out in the person of Saul, to whom the doctrine of the Church was committed. We must distinguish between the *fact* and the *doctrine*; indeed it is not until we reach the last chapter of the Acts that the curtain finally drops upon Israel and Paul the prisoner at Rome, fully unfolds the grand mystery of the Church which from ages and generations had been hid in God, but was now made manifest. Let the reader ponder Romans 16:25-26; Ephesians 3:l-11; and Colossians 1:24-27.

We cannot attempt to go fully into this glorious subject here; indeed, to refer to it at all is a digression from our present line. But we deem it needful just to say thus much so the reader may fully see that Psalm 67 refers to Israel; and seeing this, the whole truth will flow into his soul that the conversion of the nations stands connected with Israel and not with the Church. It is through Israel and not through the Church that God will yet bless the nations. It is His eternal purpose that the seed of Abraham, His friend, shall yet be preeminent in the earth and that all nations shall be blessed in and through them. "Thus saith the Lord of hosts, In those days it shall come to pass that ten men shall take hold, out of all languages of the nations, even shall take hold of the skirt of him that is a Jew, saying, We will go with you, for we have heard that God is with you" (Zech. 8:23).

There is no need to multiply proofs. All Scripture bears witness to the truth that God's present object is not to convert the nations, but to take out of them a people for His name, and further, that when these nations shall be brought in – as they most assuredly shall be – it will not be by the instrumentality of the Church at all, but by that of the restored nation of Israel.

It would be an easy and a delightful task to prove from the New Testament that, previous to the restoration and blessing of Israel and therefore previous to the conversion of the nations, the true Church of God, the body of Christ, shall have been taken up to be forever with the Lord in the full and wonderful communion of the Father's house. So the Church will not be God's agency in the conversion of the Jews as a nation, any more than in the conversion of the Gentiles. But we do not desire at this time to do more than establish the two points above stated, which we deem of much interest and importance in reference to the grand object of missionary operations. When missionary societies propose for their object the conversion of the world, they propose a great mistake. And when Christendom imagines that she is to be God's instrument in converting the nations, it is simply a delusion and an empty conceit. Hence, let all who go forth as missionaries see that they are ruled in their blessed work by a divine object and that they are pursuing that object in a divinely-appointed way.

A HEART FOR CHRIST
(READ MATTHEW 26)

In this solemn chapter we have a great many hearts revealed. The heart of the chief priests, the heart of the elders, the heart of the scribes, the heart of Peter, the heart of Judas. But there is one heart in particular, unlike all the others, and that is the heart of the woman who brought the alabaster box of very precious ointment to anoint the body of Jesus. This woman had a heart for Christ. She may have been a very great sinner, a very ignorant sinner, but her eyes had been opened to see a beauty in Jesus which led her to judge that nothing was too costly to be spent on Him. In a word, she had a heart for Christ.

Passing over the chief priests, the elders and the scribes, let us look at the heart of this woman in contrast with the heart of Judas and the heart of Peter.

Judas was a covetous man. He loved money – a very common love in every age. He had preached the gospel. He had walked in company with the Lord Jesus during the days of His public ministry. He had heard His words, seen His ways, experienced His kindness. But, sadly, though an apostle, though a companion of Jesus, though a preacher of the gospel, he had no heart for Christ. He had a heart for money. His heart was ever moved by the thought of gain. When money was in question, he was all alive. The deepest depths of his being were stirred by money. "The bag" was his nearest and dearest object. Satan knew this. He knew the special lust of Judas. He was fully aware of the price at which he could be bought. He understood his man, how to tempt him and how to use him. Solemn thought!

Be it observed that the very position of Judas made him all the more fit for Satan. His acquaintance with the ways of Christ made him a fit person to betray Him into the hands of His enemies. Head knowledge of sacred things, if the heart be not touched, renders a man more awfully callous, profane and wicked. The chief priests and scribes in Matthew 2 had a head knowledge of the letter of Scripture, but no heart for Christ. They could at once hand down the prophetic roll and find the place where it was written, "Thou Bethlehem in the land of Judah, art not the least among the princes of Judas; for out of thee shall come a Governor that shall rule My people Israel" (v. 6). All this was very well, very true and very beautiful, but they had no heart for this "Governor," no eyes to see

Him. They did not want Him. They had Scripture at their fingertips. They would have felt ashamed, no doubt, had they not been able to answer Herod's question. It would have been a disgrace to men in their position to exhibit ignorance, but they had no heart for Christ. Hence they laid their Scriptural knowledge at the feet of an ungodly king who was about to use it, if he could, for the purpose of slaying the true Heir to the throne. So much for head-knowledge without heart-love.

It is not that we would make little of Scriptural knowledge. Far from it. The true knowledge of Scripture must lead the heart to Jesus. But there is such a thing as knowing the letter of Scripture so as to be able to repeat chapter after chapter, verse after verse, yes, so as to be a sort of walking concordance, and, all the while the heart be cold and callous toward Christ. This knowledge will only throw one more into the hands of Satan, as in the case of the chief priests and scribes. Herod would not have asked ignorant men for information. The devil never takes up ignorant or stupid men to act against the truth of God. No; he finds fitter agents to do his work. The learned, the intellectual, the deep-thinking are used, provided they have no heart for Christ.

What saved "the wise men from the east?" Why could not Herod – why could not Satan – enlist them into his service? Oh! reader mark the reply. *They had a heart for Christ.* Blessed safeguard! Doubtless, they were ignorant of Scripture. They would have made but a poor hand of searching for a passage in the prophets, but they were looking for Jesus – earnestly, honestly, diligently looking for Jesus! Herod would eagerly have made use of them if he could, but they were not to be used by him. They found their way to Jesus. They did not know much about the prophet who had spoken of the "Governor," but they found their way to the "Governor" Himself. They found Him in the Person of the Babe in the manger at Bethlehem. Instead of being tools in the hands of Herod, they were worshippers at the feet of Jesus.

Now, it is not that we would commend ignorance of Scripture. By no means! People are sure to err greatly who know not the Scriptures. It was to the praise of Timothy that the apostle could say to him, "From a child thou hast known the Holy Scriptures which are able to make thee wise unto salvation," but then he adds, "Through faith which is in Christ Jesus" (2 Tim. 3:15). The true knowledge of Scripture will always conduct us to the feet of Jesus, but mere head-knowledge of Scripture, without heart-love for Christ, will only render us the more effective agents in the hands of Satan.

228

Thus it was in the case of the hard-hearted, money-loving Judas. He had knowledge without a spark of affection for Christ, and his very familiarity with that blessed One made him a suitable instrument for the devil. His nearness to Jesus enabled him to be a traitor. The devil knew that thirty pieces of silver could purchase his service in the horrible work of betraying his Master.

Reader, think of this! Here was an apostle – a preacher of the gospel, a high professor. Yet underneath the cloak of profession lay "a heart exercised in covetous practices" – a heart which had a wide place for "thirty pieces of silver," but not a corner for Jesus. What a case! What a picture! What a warning! Oh! all you heartless professors, think of Judas! Think of his course! Think of his character! Think of his end! He preached the gospel, but he never knew it, never believed it, never felt it. He had painted sunbeams on canvas, but he never felt their influence. He had plenty of heart for money, but no heart for Christ. As "the son of perdition" "he hanged himself" and "went to his own place." Professing Christians, beware of head-knowledge, lip profession, official piety, mechanical religion. Beware of these things and seek to have a heart for Christ.

In Peter we have another warning, though of a different kind. He really loved Jesus, but he feared the cross. He shrank from confessing His name in the midst of the enemy's ranks. He boasted of what he would do when he should have been self-emptied. He was fast asleep when he ought to have been on his knees. Instead of praying he was sleeping. Then, instead of being still, he was drawing his sword. "He followed Jesus afar off" and then "warmed himself at the high priest's fire." Finally, he cursed and swore that he did not know this gracious Master. All this was terrible! Who could suppose that the Peter of Matthew 16:16 is the Peter of Matthew 26? Yet so it is. Man in his best estate is only like an autumn leaf. "There is none abiding." The highest position, the loudest profession, may all end in following Jesus afar off, and in basely denying His name.

It is almost certain that Peter would have spurned the thought of selling Jesus for thirty pieces of silver. Yet he was afraid to confess Him before a servant girl. He might not have betrayed Him to His enemies, but he denied Him before them. He may not have loved money, but he failed to manifest a heart for Christ.

Christian reader, remember Peter's fall and beware of self-confidence. Cultivate a prayerful spirit. Keep close to Jesus. Keep away from the influence of this world's favor. "Keep thyself pure." Beware of dropping into a sleepy, tepid condition of soul. Be earnest and watchful. Be occupied with Christ. This is the true safeguard. Do not be satisfied with the mere avoidance of open sin. Do not rest in mere blamelessness of conduct and character. Cherish lively, warm affections toward Christ. One who "follows Jesus afar off" may deny Him before long. Let us think of this. Let us profit by the case of Peter. He himself afterwards tells us to "be sober, be vigilant, because your adversary the devil, as a roaring lion, walketh about, seeking whom he may devour: whom resist, steadfast in the faith" (1 Pet. 5:8-9). These are weighty words, coming as they do, from the Holy Spirit through the pen of one who had suffered so from lack of "vigilance."

Blessed be the grace that could say to Peter before his fall, "I have prayed for thee that thy faith fail not." Mark, the Lord did not say, "I have prayed for thee that thou mayest not fall." No; but "that thy faith fail not" when you have fallen. Precious, matchless grace! This was Peter's resource. He was a debtor to grace from first to last. As a lost sinner, he was a debtor to "the precious blood of Christ"; as a stumbling saint, he was a debtor to the all-prevailing advocacy of Christ. Thus it was with Peter. The advocacy of Christ was the basis of his happy restoration. Of this advocacy Judas knew nothing. It is only those who are washed in the blood that partake of the advocacy. Judas knew nothing of either. Hence "he went and hanged himself," whereas Peter went forth as a restored soul to "strengthen his brethren." *There is no one so fit to strengthen his brethren as one who has himself experienced the restoring grace of Christ.* Peter was able to stand before the congregation of Israel and say, "Ye denied the Holy One and the Just," the very thing he had done himself. This shows how entirely his conscience was purged by the blood and his heart restored by the advocacy of Christ.

Now, one word as to the woman with the alabaster box. She stands forth in bright and beautiful contrast with all. While the chief priests, elders and scribes were plotting against Christ "in the palace of the high priest who was called Caiaphas," she was anointing His body "in the house of Simon the leper." While Judas was covenanting with the chief priests to sell Jesus for thirty pieces of silver, she was pouring the precious contents of her alabaster box upon His Person. Touching contrast! She was wholly absorbed with her object, and her object was Christ. Those who knew not His worth and beauty might pronounce her sacrifice a waste. Those who could sell Him for thirty pieces of silver might talk of "giving to the poor," but she heeded them not. Their surmisings and murmurings were nothing to her. She had found her all in Christ. They might murmur, but she could worship and adore. Jesus was more to her than all the poor in the world. She felt that nothing was "waste" that was spent on Him. He might only be worth thirty pieces of silver to one who had a heart for money. He was worth ten thousand words to her, because she had a heart for Christ. Happy woman! May we imitate her! May we ever find our place at the feet of Jesus, loving, adoring, admiring and worshipping His blessed Person. May we spend and be spent in His service, even though heartless professors should deem our service a foolish "waste."

The time is rapidly approaching when we shall not repent of anything done for His name's sake. If there could be room for a single regret, it will be that we so faintly and feebly served His cause in the world. If, on "the morning without clouds," a single blush could mantle the cheek, it will be that we did not, when down here, dedicate ourselves more undividely to His service.

Reader, let us ponder these things. And may the Lord grant us *a heart for Christ!*

STEPHEN
(Acts 7:55-60)

There are two grand facts which characterize Christianity and mark it off from all that had gone before. These are, first, Man glorified in heaven, and secondly, God dwelling in man on the earth. These are stupendous facts, divinely glorious and fitted to produce the most powerful effect upon the heart and life of the Christian.

They are unique to Christianity. They were never known until redemption was fully accomplished and the Redeemer took His seat at the right hand of the Majesty in the heavens. Then was seen for the first time in the annals of eternity, a Man on the throne of God. Wondrous sight! Magnificent result of accomplished redemption! The enemy seemed to have triumphed when the first man was expelled from Eden, but the Second Man has made His victorious way into heaven and taken His seat on the eternal throne of God.

This, we repeat, is a fact of transcendent glory. The counterpart, the companion fact is God the Holy Spirit dwelling with and in man on earth. These things were unknown in Old Testament times. What did Abraham know of a glorified Man in heaven? What did any of the ancient worthies know of it? Nothing; how could they? There was no man on the throne of heaven until Jesus took His seat there. Until He was glorified in heaven, the Holy Spirit could not take up His abode in man on earth. "He that believeth on Me, as the Scripture hath said, out of his belly shall flow rivers of living water. But this spake He of the Spirit, which they that believe on Him should receive: *for the Holy Spirit was not yet; because that Jesus was not yet glorified*" (Jn. 7:38-39). "Nevertheless I tell you the truth; it is expedient for you that I go away: *for if I go not away, the Comforter will not come unto you; but if I depart, I will send Him unto you*" (Jn. 16:7).

Here we have our two facts linked together in the most direct and positive manner: Christ glorified above and the Holy Spirit dwelling in man below. The two are inseparably connected; the latter is entirely dependent upon the former, and both together form the two great distinguishing features of that glorious Christianity revealed in the gospel of God.

It is not our purpose to enter upon any elaborate proof of these truths. We assume them as established. Moreover, we assume that the Christian reader cordially receives and holds them as *eternal* truths and that he is prepared to appreciate the illustration of their practical power and formative influence presented in the history of Stephen as recorded in Acts 7:55-60. Let us draw near and gaze on the marvelous picture – the picture of a true Christian.

The principal part of Acts 7 is occupied with a most powerful unfolding of the history of the nation of Israel — a history stretching from the call of Abraham to the death of Christ. At the close of his address, Stephen made a painful application to the consciences of his hearers, which drew forth their most bitter animosity and deadly rage. "When they heard these things they were cut to the heart and they gnashed on him with their teeth." Here we see the effect of religiousness without Christ. These men were the professed guardians of religion and the guides of the people, but it proved to be religion versus Christianity. In them we have the terrible exponent of a godless, Christless religion; in Stephen we have the lovely exhibition of true Christianity. They were full of religious animosity and rage: he was full of the Holy Spirit. They gnashed their teeth: his face was like that of an angel. What a contrast!

We must quote the passage for the reader. "But he, being full of the Holy Spirit, looked up steadfastly into heaven and saw the glory of God and Jesus standing on the right hand of God, and said, Behold, I see the heavens opened and the Son of man standing on the right hand of God."

Here are our two great facts again displayed in a man of like passions with ourselves. Stephen was full of the Holy Spirit and his earnest gaze was fixed on a glorified Man in heaven. This is Christianity. This is the true, the normal idea of a Christian. He is a man full of the Holy Spirit, looking with the steady gaze of faith into heaven and occupied with a glorified Christ. We cannot accept any lower standard than this, short as we may come of it practically. It is very high and very holy. Moreover, we have to confess how very little we are up to it. Still it is the divine standard, and every devoted heart will aspire to it and nothing less. It is the happy privilege of every Christian to be full of the Holy Spirit and to have the eye of faith fixed on the glorified Man in heaven. There is no divine reason why it should not be so. Redemption is accomplished, sin is put away, grace reigns through righteousness, there is a Man on the throne of God, the Holy Spirit has come down to this earth and taken up His abode in the believer individually and in the Church corporately.

Thus it stands. Be it carefully noted that these things are not mere speculations or cold theories. Alas! they may be held as such, but in themselves they are not. On the contrary they are immensely practical, divinely formative, powerfully influential, as we can distinctly see in the case of the blessed martyr Stephen. It is impossible to read the closing verses of Acts 7 and not see the powerful effect produced upon Stephen by the Object which filled the vision of his soul. There we behold a man surrounded by the most terrible circumstances, enemies rushing upon him, death staring him in the face. But instead of being in any wise affected or governed by those circumstances, he is entirely governed by heavenly objects. He looked up steadfastly into heaven and saw Jesus. Earth was rejecting him, as it already rejected his Lord, but heaven was opened to him, and looking up into that open heaven he caught some of the rays of glory shining in the face of his risen Lord. He not only caught them but reflected them back upon the moral gloom which surrounded him.

Is not all this most deeply practical? Assuredly it is! Stephen was not only lifted above his surroundings in the most wonderful manner, but he was enabled to exhibit to his persecutors the meekness and grace of Christ. In him we see a most striking illustration of 2 Corinthians 3:18 – a passage of great depth and fullness. "But we all, with open face beholding as in a glass the glory of the Lord, are changed into the same image from glory to glory, as by the Lord the Spirit."*

Only see how all this is livingly unfolded in the scene before us. The very highest expression of heavenly Christianity is met by the deepest, darkest and most deadly display of religious resentment. We can see the two culminating in the death of the first Christian martyr. "Then they cried out with a loud voice and stopped their ears, and ran upon him with one accord and cast him out of the city, and stoned him: and the witnesses laid down their clothes at a young man's feet whose name was Saul. And they stoned Stephen, calling upon God and saying, Lord Jesus, receive my spirit! And he kneeled down and cried with a loud voice, Lord, lay not this sin to their charge. And when he had said this he fell asleep."

Here is genuine practical Christianity – living conformity to the image of Christ. Here we see a man so lifted above circumstances, so lifted out

---

* "Beholding as in a glass" hardly conveys the force, fullness and beauty of the original word. The English reader should be informed that the entire clause is expressed by the one Greek word which conveys the double idea of beholding and reflecting. The passage might be rendered thus: "We all, with open face mirroring the glory, are changed ..." The real idea is that the Christian reflects, like a mirror, the glory on which he gazes and thus becomes conformed to the image of his Lord by the powerful ministry of the Lord the Spirit. The whole verse is one of the most condensed, yet comprehensive and magnificent statements of practical Christianity anywhere to be found in the sacred canon. It furnishes a concise commentary on the facts, of which Stephen is a vivid illustration. Would that we all more fully entered into and more faithfully exhibited the power of these things!

of himself as to be able – after the pattern of his Lord – to pray for his murderers. Instead of being occupied with himself or thinking of his own sufferings, he thinks of others and pleads for them. So far as he was concerned all was settled. His eye was fixed on the glory – so fixed as to catch its concentrated beams and reflect them back upon the very faces of his murderers. His countenance was radiant with the light of that glory into which he was about to enter, and he was enabled by the power of the Holy Spirit to imitate his blessed Master and to spend his last breath in praying for his murderers: "Lord, lay not this sin to their charge." And what then? He had nothing more to do but fall asleep – to close his eyes upon a scene of death and open them upon a scene of deathless glory, or rather to enter upon that scene which already filled the vision of his enraptured soul.

Reader, let us remember that this is true Christianity. It is the happy privilege of a Christian to be full of the Holy Spirit, looking off from himself and up from his surroundings, whatever they may be, gazing steadfastly into heaven and occupied with the glorified Man Christ Jesus. The necessary result of being thus occupied is practical living conformity to that blessed One on whom the eye is fixed. We become like Him in spirit, in ways and in our entire character. It must be so. "We all, with open face mirroring the glory, are changed into the same image."

It is of very great importance to see and know that nothing short of this is up to the mark of the Christianity presented in the New Testament. This is the divine standard. We should not be satisfied with anything less. We see in Stephen a man reflecting the glory of Christ in a very positive practical way. He was not merely talking about glory, but actually reflecting it. We may talk about heavenly glory while our practical ways are anything but heavenly. It was not so with Stephen. He was a living mirror in which men could see the glory reflected. And should it not be so with us? Unquestionably. But is it so? Are we so absorbed with our risen Lord, so fixed on Him, so centered in Him that our fellow men – those with whom we meet from day to day – can see the traits, the features of His image reflected in our character, our habits, our spirit, our style? Regretfully we cannot say much on this score. But then, dearly beloved Christian reader, can we not at least say, "Is it our heart's deep and earnest *desire* to be so occupied and filled with Christ that His lovely grace may shine out in us to the praise of His name?" God, in His rich mercy, grant that our eye may be so fixed on Jesus that we too may, in some degree, mirror the glory and thus shed some tiny ray of that glory upon the darkness around!

When the pangs of trial seize us,
When the waves of sorrow roll,
I will lay my head on Jesus –
Pillow of the troubled soul:
Surely none can feel like Thee,
Weeping One of Bethany!

"Jesus wept!" – that tear of sorrow
Is a legacy of love.
Yesterday, today, tomorrow,
He the same doth ever prove.
Thou art all in all to me,
Living One of Bethany!

PETER ON THE WATER
(READ MATTHEW 14:22-33)

There are two ways in which we may view the interesting portion of Scripture given above. We may read it from a dispensational standpoint as bearing upon the subject of God's dealings with Israel. Also, we may read it as a portion directly bearing on the subject of our own practical walk with God from day to day.

Our Lord, having fed the multitude and dismissed them, "went up into a mountain apart to pray, and when the evening was come, He was there alone." This answers precisely to His present position with reference to the nation of Israel. He has left them and gone on high to enter upon the blessed work of intercession. Meanwhile, the disciples – a type of the pious remnant – were tossed on the stormy sea during the dark watches of the night, deeply tried and exercised in the absence of their Lord. But He never for a moment lost sight of them, never withdrew His eyes from them. And when they were brought, as it were, to their wits' end, He appears for their relief, hushes the wind, calms the sea and brings them to their desired haven.

Thus much as to the dispensational bearing of this passage of Scripture, inasmuch as our object is to present to the heart of the reader the precious truth unfolded in the narrative of Peter on the water – truth bearing directly upon our own individual path, whatever the nature of that path may be.

It demands no stretch of imagination to see in the case of Peter, a striking figure of the Church of God collectively or of the individual Christian. Peter left the ship at the call of Christ. He abandoned all that the heart would so fondly cling to, and came forth to walk on the stormy water – a path of faith, a path in which nothing but simple faith could live for a single hour. To all who are called to tread that path, it must be either Christ or nothing. Our only source of power is in keeping the eye of faith firmly fixed on Jesus, "Looking off unto Jesus, the author and finisher of faith" (Heb. 12). The moment we take the eye off Him, we begin to sink.

It is not a question of salvation – of reaching the shore in safety. By no means! We are speaking now of the walk of the Christian in this world, of the practical career of one who is called to abandon this world, to give up all that mere nature would lean upon and trust in, to relinquish earthly things and human resources to walk with Jesus above the power and influence of things seen and temporal.

Such is the high calling of the Christian and of the whole Church of God, in contrast with Israel, God's earthly people. We are called to live by faith, to walk in calm confidence above the circumstances of this world altogether, to move in holy companionship with Jesus. It was after this that Peter's soul was seeking when he uttered those words, "Lord, if it be Thou, bid me come unto Thee on the water." Here was the point: "If it be Thou." If it were not He, the wildest mistake that Peter could possibly make would be to leave the ship. But if indeed it was Jesus – that blessed One, that most glorious, most gracious One who Peter saw moving peacefully over the surface of the troubled deep – then, assuredly, the very highest, the very happiest, the very best thing he could do was to abandon every earthly and natural resource to come forth to Him and taste the wonderful blessedness of companionship with Him.

There is immense force, depth and significance in these clauses – "If it be Thou" – "Bid me come unto Thee" – "On the water." Mark, it is "unto Thee *on the water.*" It was not Jesus coming to Peter *in the ship*, blessed and precious as that is, but Peter coming to Jesus on the water. It is one thing to have Jesus coming into the midst of our circumstances, hushing our fears, allaying our anxieties, tranquilizing our hearts, but it is quite another thing for us to push out from the shore of circumstances or from the ship of nature's devices, to walk in calm victory over the circumstances simply to be with Jesus where He is. The former reminds us somewhat of the Sareptan in 1 Kings 17. The latter, of the Shunammite in 2 Kings 4.

Is it that we do not appreciate the excellent grace that breathes in those words, "Be of good cheer; it is I; be not afraid?" Far be the thought! These words are most precious. Moreover, Peter might have tasted, yes reveled in their sweetness, even though he had never left the ship at all. It is well to distinguish between these two things. They are very often confounded. We are all prone to rest in the *thought* of having the Lord with us and His mercies around us in our daily path. We linger amid the relationships of nature, the joys of earth, such as they are, and the blessings which our gracious God pours so liberally upon us. We cling to circumstances instead of breathing after more intimate companionship with a rejected Christ. In this way we suffer immense loss.

Yes, we say it advisedly, *"immense loss."* It is not that we should prize God's blessings and mercies less, but we should prize *Him* more. We believe that Peter would have been a loser had he remained in the ship. Some may deem it restlessness and forwardness; we believe it was the fruit of earnest longing after his much loved Lord – an intense desire to be near Him, cost what it might. He beheld his Lord walking on the water and he longed to walk with Him, and his longing was right. It was pleasing to the heart of Jesus.

Besides, he had the authority of his Lord for leaving the ship. That word "come" – a word of mighty moral force – fell on his heart and drew him forth from the ship to go to Jesus. Christ's word was the authority for entering on that strange mysterious path, and Christ's realized presence was the power to pursue it. Without that word he dare not start; without that presence he could not proceed. It was strange, it was unearthly, it was above and beyond nature to walk on the sea, but Jesus was walking there and faith could walk with Him. So Peter thought, and therefore "he came down out of the ship, and walked on the water to go to Jesus."

Now this is a striking figure of the true path of a Christian, the path of faith. The warrant for that path is Christ's Word. The power to pursue it is to keep the eye fixed on Him. It is not a question of right or wrong. There was nothing wrong in remaining in the ship. But the question is, "At what do we aim?" Is it the fixed purpose of the soul to get as near as we can to Jesus? Do we desire to taste a deeper, closer, fuller communion with Him? Is He enough for us? Can we give up all that mere nature clings to, and lean on Jesus only? He beckons us forth to Himself in His infinite love. He says, "Come." Shall we refuse? Shall we hesitate and hang back? Shall we cling to the ship while the voice of Jesus bids us "come"?

It may be said that Peter broke down and therefore it is better, safer and wiser to remain in the ship than to sink in the water. It is better not to take a prominent place, than having taken it, to fail therein. Well, it is quite true that Peter failed, but why? Was it because he left the ship? No, but because he ceased to look to Jesus. "When he saw the wind boisterous, he was afraid; and beginning to sink, he cried, saying, Lord, save me." Thus it was with poor Peter. His mistake was not in leaving the ship, but in looking at the waves and the winds – looking at his surroundings in place of looking off unto Jesus. He had entered upon a path which could only be trodden by faith – a path in which, if he had not Jesus, he had nothing at all – no ship, not a spar or a plank to cling to. In a word, it was either Christ or nothing. It was either walking with Jesus on the water or sinking beneath it without Him. Nothing but faith could sustain the heart in such a course. But faith could sustain, for faith can live amid the roughest waves and the stormiest skies. Faith can walk on the roughest waters; unbelief cannot walk on the smoothest.

But Peter failed. Yes; and what then? Does that prove he was wrong in obeying the call of his Lord? Did Jesus reprove him for leaving the ship? Ah! no; that would not have been like Him. He could not tell His poor servant to come, and then rebuke him for coming. He knew and could feel for Peter's weakness. Hence we read that "Immediately Jesus stretched forth His hand and caught him, and said unto him, O thou of little faith, wherefore didst thou doubt?" He does not say, "O you restless forward one, why did you leave the ship?" No; but "wherefore didst thou doubt?" Such was the tender reproof. And where was Peter when he heard it? *In the arms of his Lord!* What a place! What an experience! Was it not well worth leaving the ship to taste such blessedness? Assuredly it was! Peter was right in leaving the ship, and although he broke down in that lofty path on which he had entered, it only led him into a deeper sense of his own weakness and nothingness, and of the grace and love of his Lord.

Christian reader, what is the moral of all this to us? Simply this. Jesus calls us forth from the things of time and sense to walk with Him. He summons us to abandon all our earthly hopes and creature confidences – the props and resources on which our poor hearts lean. His voice may be heard far above the din of waves and storms, and that voice says "Come!" Oh! let us obey. Let us heartily yield ourselves to His call. "Let us go forth unto Him without the camp, bearing His reproach." He wants to have us near Himself, walking with and leaning on Him, not looking at circumstances, but looking only and always unto Him.

ALONE WITH JESUS
(READ JOHN 8:1-11)

The more closely and prayerfully we study the four Gospels, the more clearly do we see the distinct design of the Holy Spirit in each, and the perfect way in which He has pursued and carried out that design even in the most minute details. The grand theme of each is Christ, but in no two of the Gospels is He presented in the same way. In Matthew we have Him as the Messiah, Son of Abraham, Son of David, a Jew, heir of the promises made to the fathers, heir of the throne of David, fulfiller of the prophecies, presented to Israel according to their own Scriptures and deliberately rejected.

Such is the distinct object of the Holy Spirit in Matthew – such is His marked design. This He pursues throughout with unswerving faithfulness. To this end everything is made subservient. With a view to this He culls, groups and arranges His materials. For this, chronological order is set aside without hesitation and without apology. Scenes and circumstances, separated by many months, are grouped together by the skillful hand of the Holy Spirit for the specific purpose of presenting His subject in perfect keeping with the scope and design of the entire Gospel, from which He never diverges the breadth of a hair. In a word, Matthew groups *for dispensational ends* what we may call the great dispensational Gospel.

In Mark we have our blessed Lord as the Servant, the perfect Workman, the divine Minister, the diligent Preacher and Teacher whose days were given to work and His nights to prayer. He could hardly find time to eat or sleep – the most laborious Worker who ever worked in God's great harvest field. Mark tells us by the Holy Spirit what the Savior did and how He did it. His gospel is a marvelous record of *work* from first to last. We have no record of our Lord's birth – no genealogical chain stretching back to David, to Abraham or to Adam. There was no need to trace the pedigree of One who came to serve, to work, to toil night and day. The question in Mark is not so much who He was as *what He did.* We are simply told He was "Jesus Christ the Son of God." Then the inspired penman plunges into his subject and gives a rapid survey of a life of unparalleled labor – a path of service pursued with unflinching decision from the manger of Bethlehem to the cross of Calvary, and resumed in resurrection and carried on from the right hand of the Majesty in the heavens. See Mark 16:19-20.

Thus much as to Mark who observes throughout the strict historical order. It is important for the reader to note this, as it will enable him to see the instances in which both Matthew and Luke depart from strict chronological sequence.

Luke gives us "The *Man* Christ Jesus." Such is preeminently his theme. Hence he gives us the pedigree traced up, not merely to David and Abraham, but to Adam and to God. It is not the Messiah nor the Jew nor the worker, but the Man. All that which is exquisitely human we have in Luke, just as we have all that is purely Jewish in Matthew and all that is directly ministerial in Mark. Luke groups for *moral ends* as Matthew for *dispensational purposes.* Mark does not group; he simply records *in historic order* the facts of our Lord's marvelous ministry.

Now, before turning to that gospel from which the subject of this paper is selected, we would request the reader's earnest attention to what we have stated in reference to the three *synoptical Gospels* as they have been called. We would ask him to study the Gospels for himself, to compare the passages diligently, to seek to understand why Matthew or Luke departs in any given case from the exact order of time, to ask God to teach him by His Holy Spirit the true reason for every such departure. In this way we feel persuaded he will reap a rich harvest of blessing. He will obtain a deeper insight into the infinite wisdom that dictated those peerless documents. He will rise from his study with a more profound faith in the complete inspiration of these wonderful narratives.

Furthermore, he will see that those very passages in which the rationalist, the skeptic or the infidel has sought to find flaws and discrepancies, present the most striking and exquisite proofs of divine wisdom and marked design. He will be convinced that there is no standing-ground between these two conclusions, that the evangelists were either divinely inspired or they were the most senseless narrators that ever put pen to paper. That they were divinely inspired is proved in every page, in every paragraph, in every line. The internal evidence is irresistible. Hence it follows that these inspired writers could no more clash one with another than two heavenly bodies while pursuing their divinely appointed orbits, could come into collision. If there seems to be a discrepancy, it is simply because of our ignorance. Let us devoutly own this and wait for further light.

We shall now proceed with our immediate theme.

The Gospel of John has a character uniquely its own. In it the Holy Spirit unfolds to our view the Person of the Son of God, the Word, the

Eternal Life, the true God. It is not the Messiah as in Matthew – not the Minister as in Mark – not the social Man as in Luke, but *the Son* – what He was in Himself from all eternity; what He was though rejected by Israel and the world at large; what He was to any poor way-worn, heavy laden, sin-burdened creature who crossed His blessed path.

Such is the lofty theme of the divinely inspired John. And what is so uniquely touching is that while John gives us the very highest possible view of the Blessed One – the most glorious revelation of the Person of the Son – he nevertheless continually shows Him to us alone with the sinner. This surely is a fact full of sweetness, comfort and divine power for us.

Let us look at the opening paragraph of John 8, a paragraph that bears upon its every clause the stamp of divine inspiration. Our blessed Lord, having spent His night on the lonely mountain top, is found early in the morning at His post, teaching the people in the temple. Into His holy and gracious presence, the scribes and Pharisees bring a poor convicted sinner – one respecting whom there could be no possible mistake, one who had openly and flagrantly broken the law of Moses. They quote the law against her. "Moses in the law commanded us that such should be stoned, but what sayest Thou?"

Here then was a case. These men, no doubt, thought to involve our Lord in a dilemma. They wanted to bring Him into collision with Moses – to make it appear that He was throwing the law overboard. This might seem very clever, but what is cleverness in the presence of God? Still their purpose was obvious. If He had said, "Stone her," they might pronounce Him no better than Moses. If He had said, "You must not stone her," then He was making void the law. But He said neither. "The law was given by Moses," and the Lord allows it to stand in all its majesty, in all its stringency, in all its force. He came not to destroy the law, but to magnify it in the very highest possible manner, both in His life and in His death.

It is a very grave error indeed to suppose the law is set aside. So far from this, the apostle in 1 Timothy declares that "The law is good if a man use it lawfully." If the law were dead or set aside, it could not be said to be good for anything, for that which is dead is good for nothing. What then is the law good for? Not for justification, but for conviction – not as a rule of life, but as a rule of death.

It is thus our Lord uses it in the scene now before us. He turns the sharp edge of the law right back against the men who had quoted it against a poor fellow sinner. With those men He could have no sympathy whatever. They had conducted this woman into His presence to have judgment pronounced and executed upon her. But He had not come to judge, but to save. Yet, as He says at verse 16, if He judged, His judgment was true: oh! how true in the case of the scribes and Pharisees! They had accused the sinner and were eager to accuse the Savior, but He makes them accuse themselves. "Jesus stooped down and with his finger wrote on the ground." There was the great Lawgiver Himself, the very One whose finger wrote on the ground. There was the great Lawgiver Himself, the very One whose finger had written the first set of tables. How little they knew this! They were quoting the law against a fellow sinner to find occasion against the Lawgiver. What a position for men to find themselves in! In the presence of the Lawgiver, quoting the law, themselves guilty before Him!

There is something very interesting here. Indeed there is not such a scene anywhere else in the sacred canon. It is unique! Little did these men know what they were doing for the poor convicted one and for untold millions besides, when they led her into the presence of Jesus. Her very best friends could not have done better for her. Let us pursue the marvelous narrative.

"So, when they continued asking Him, He lifted up Himself and said unto them, He that is without sin among you, let him first cast a stone at her." They were determined to have an answer, and truly He let them have one. If they would place Him, before the time, in the judgment seat, He must judge all. He could not give a partial judgment. He could not judge one and let another pass. In point of fact, He judged no man. The object of His blessed mission to a world of sinners was not judgment but salvation. He came not to cast a stone at a poor guilty sinner. They could never get Him to engage in such work, blessed forever be His glorious name. How could a divine Savior cast the stone of judgment at a lost convicted sinner? Impossible. If there was a sinless one among them, let him proceed to do the work of judgment. No doubt the sinner was guilty and the sentence of Moses was as distinct as possible, but where was the executioner? This was the puzzling question. Who would dare to lift the first stone?

What a complete turning of the tables! What becomes of all the cleverness! What an intensely interesting moment! What principle was at stake? There is the sinner; there is the law; there too is the Lawgiver; but who will presume in His presence to execute the sentence? This is the point. "And again He stopped down and wrote on the ground." Does this remind us of the writing of the second set of tables that were enclosed in the ark and covered with the mercy seat? Is there anything significant, anything suggestive in these two writings on the ground? One thing is clear – conscience was set to work. "They which heard it, being convicted by their own conscience, went out one by one, beginning at the eldest, unto the last: and Jesus was left alone and the woman standing in the midst."

Nothing can exceed the moral power of all this. These scribes and Pharisees are driven out by the intense power of the light that was shining upon them. They could not stand it. Neither human cleverness nor human righteousness can stand the test of the divine presence. These men were wrapped up in the cloak of their own fancied sanctity. Hence they could not endure the light. To be able to abide in the presence of God, we must take our true place as utterly lost, guilty and undone – no cloak, no righteousness, no holiness, no wisdom, not one jot or tittle of anything good in ourselves. But the scribes and Pharisees were not on this ground at all. They were men of character, men of weight, men of reputation in the world. But the light of what God is – God in Christ – was shining in full blaze upon them, and they dare not say they were without sin. All that remained was for them to make their escape as speedily as possible from the action of a light that was reading them through and through.

Why did they begin with the eldest? Why was he the first to retreat? Because he had the greatest reputation to maintain, the character of highest standing to support! No one who has a reputation to maintain – a name or a character to keep up among his fellows – can stand for a moment in the light of the presence of God. Such an one can do well enough in the presence of his fellows. He can get on in the world inasmuch as *there*, such are highly esteemed. A man of character is respected among men. But let us remember these solemn and salutary words, "That which is highly esteemed among men is abomination in the sight of God." God values a broken heart, a contrite spirit, a lowly mind. "To this man will *I* look, even to him who is of a broken and contrite spirit, and trembleth at My word." Now the scribes and Pharisees were the direct opposite of all this. Hence they could find no place in the presence of Jesus.

"They went out," not in a crowd, but "one by one." Conscience is an individual thing. Had they remained, they must strip off their cloaks and cry out, "Just as I am without one plea." For this they were not prepared. They were thoroughly confounded and went about their business. The Light of the world was shining in the full luster of His heavenly beams, and these muffled men could not endure His brightness. So they went out and left the poor sinner alone with Jesus.

Blessed moment for her! The whole scene cleared. No answer, no sentence, no executioner – not a single stone of judgment. How was this? Was she not a sinner? Yes, a flagrant one. Was not the law against her? No doubt. How was it then? Jesus was there – the divine embodiment of "grace and truth," and He was not going to stone a poor convicted sinner. It was not for such an object that He had left that bright and blessed world above. Had it been only a question of stoning the sinner, Moses could have managed that. There was no need for Moses' Master to come down into this world to do that.

But oh! there was grace in the heart of Jesus – yes, grace and truth and truth and grace. Both shine out with unique luster in this truly unequaled scene. "Truth" in its mighty moral force had driven the accusers from the scene. Now "grace" in all its sweetness and soothing power, rises with healing in its wings upon the soul of the poor trembling sinner and sounds in her ears these precious words, "Neither do I condemn thee." Precious words! sweet, wonderfully sweet to a broken heart and contrite spirit! They are gladdening beyond expression to one who had, a moment before, been expecting the stones of judgment to fall thick upon her guilty head. Mercy rejoices over judgment and grace reigns through righteousness unto eternal life by Jesus Christ our Lord.

Yes, that blessed One knew what it would cost Him to speak such words in the ear of a sinner. It was to cost Him His life. That woman deserved to die. There was no question about that. "The soul that sinneth shall die" was the stern sentence of God's law, the solemn enactment of His government. Was Jesus going to reverse this sentence? No, but He was going to bear it in the sinner's stead. He, the sinless One who alone had the right to cast the stone at the sinner, was to expose Himself to the stroke of justice and have the stone cast at Him.

Such is the solid basis on which the glorious ministry of reconciliation rests – the atoning death of Christ, His giving Himself the Just for the unjust. It will perhaps be said that there is nothing about *atonement* in John 8. True. The great subject of the entire Gospel of John is the *Person*, not the atoning work of the Son. But it is essential for us to know the ground on which our blessed Lord could speak those words of balm and consolation in a sinner's ear, "Neither do I condemn thee." That ground is His sacrificial atoning death. In no other way, on no other ground, could sin be passed, remitted or blotted out. "Without shedding of blood is no remission." Solemn yet glorious words! Solemn, as letting us know what sin is; glorious, as letting us know what remission is.

246

But let us carefully mark the authority on which the woman knew she was not condemned. What was it? Simply the word of Jesus. She knew it because He said it. Blessed authority – nothing like it, none other but it. Christ's work is the basis, His word the authority. How simple! How solid! How satisfactory! Nothing can touch it. All the powers of earth and hell, of men and demons, cannot shake this foundation – the foundation of a divine work, a divine word – a foundation on which the reader who needs and desires it, may rest this moment and forever.

The scribes and Pharisees knew nothing of this ground or this authority. If they had met the woman on her way out from the Lord's presence and questioned her as to the outcome of her interview, how they would have scorned the idea of "no condemnation!" They would have sent her to a reformatory or a penitentiary, and after some years of moral reform they might begin to admit that there was some faint hope for such a wretched creature. But ah! what a sorry basis is moral reform! What a poor authority is a human certificate! No, reader, it will never do, never stand, never suit either for God or for your precious soul. It must be all divine. And so it is, blessed be God! Christ did the work, God speaks the word, faith believes and fills the heart with peace, and gives power over sin in all its workings. For let it never be forgotten that an indissoluble link binds together these two utterances, "No condemnation" and "Sin nor more." Grace shines in the one, holiness breathes in the other.

A SLEEPLESS NIGHT
(READ ESTHER 6)

"On that night could not the king sleep." How was this? What was it that drove sleep from the monarch's eyes and slumber from his eyelids? Why could not the mighty Ahasuerus enjoy a mercy which was the portion of the very least of his subjects? Some may say, "The heavy cares of royalty robbed him of that which 'a laboring man' enjoys." This might be so on other nights, but "on that night" we must account for his restlessness in quite another way. The finger of the Almighty was in that sleepless night. "The Lord God of the Hebrews" had a mighty work to accomplish on behalf of His beloved people and in order to bring that about, He drove "balmy sleep" from the luxurious couch of the monarch of 127 provinces.

This brings out in a marked way the character of the Book of Esther. The reader will observe that, throughout this interesting section of inspiration, the name of God is never heard. Yet His finger is visibly stamped upon everything. The most trivial circumstances displays His "wonderful counsel and excellent working." Nature's vision cannot trace the movement of the wheels of Jehovah's chariot, but faith not only traces it, but knows the direction in which it moves. The enemy plots, but God is above him. Satan's every movement is seen to be but a link in the marvelous chain of events by which the God of Israel was bringing about His purpose of grace respecting His people. Thus it has been, thus it is and thus it shall ever be. Satan's malice, man's pride, the most hostile influences, are all but so many instruments in the hand of God for the accomplishment of His gracious purposes. This gives the sweetest rest to the heart amid the ceaseless tossings and fluctuations of human affairs. "The end of the Lord" shall assuredly be seen. "His counsel shall stand, and He will do all His pleasure." Blessed be His name for this soul-sustaining assurance! It quiets the heart at all times. Jehovah is behind the scenes. Every wheel, every screw, every pivot in the vast machine of human affairs is under His control. Though His name be not known or acknowledged by the children of earth, His finger is seen, His word is trusted and His end expected by the children of faith.

How clearly is all this seen in the Book of Esther. Vashti's beauty, the king's pride therein, his unseemly command, her indignant refusal, the advice of the king's counselors, are all but the unfolding of Jehovah's ripening purposes. Of "all the fair young virgins gathered at Shushan the

248

palace," not one must be allowed to win the king's heart except Esther, the daughter of an obscure Jewish house, a desolate orphan. Again, of all the officers, ministers and attendants about the palace, not one must be allowed to discover the conspiracy against the king's life except "a certain Jew whose name was Mordecai." And on that sleepless night, nothing must be brought to while away the monarch's weary hours except "the book of the records of the chronicles." Strange recreation for a sensuous king! But God was behind all this. There was a certain record in that book about "a certain Jew" which must be brought immediately under the eye of the restless monarch. Mordecai must come into notice. He must be rewarded for his fidelity, and so rewarded as to cover with overwhelming confusion the face of the proud Amalekite. At the very moment that this record was passing under review, none other than the haughty and wicked Haman must be seen in the court of the king's house. He had come to ensure the death of Mordecai, but is forced by the providence of God to plan for Mordecai's triumph and dignity. He had come to get him hanged on a gallows, but, he is made to clothe him with the king's robe, to set him on the king's horse and like a footman, to conduct him through the streets of the city, and like a mere herald, to announce his triumph.

"Oh! scenes surpassing fable, and yet true."

Who could have imagined that the noblest lord in all the dominions of Ahasuerus – a descendant of the house of Agag – should be compelled thus to wait upon a poor Jew, and such a Jew, at such a moment? Surely the finger of the Almighty was in all this. Who but an infidel, an atheist or a skeptic could question a truth so obvious?

Thus much as to the providence of God. Let us now look at the pride of Haman. Despite all his dignity, wealth and splendor, his wretched heart was wounded by one little matter, not worth a thought in the judgment of a really great mind or a well-regulated heart. He was rendered miserable by the simple fact that Mordecai would not bow to him! Although he occupied the nearest place to the throne and was entrusted with the king's ring – although possessed of princely wealth and placed in a princely station, "yet" he says, "all this availeth me nothing so long as I see Mordecai the Jew sitting at the king's gate" (Esth. 5:13). Miserable man! The highest position, the greatest wealth, the most extensive influence, the most flattering tokens of royal favor all "availed nothing" just because a poor Jew refused to bow to him! Such is the human heart! Such is man! Such is the world!

But "pride cometh before destruction, and a haughty spirit before a fall." Haman proved this. At the very moment when he seemed to be about to plant his foot on the loftiest summit of his ambition, a just and retributive providence so brought it about that he was obliged to wait upon Mordecai, and the very gallows which he had ordered to be prepared for his intended victim was used for his own execution!

Let us ask why Mordecai refused to bow to Haman? Did it not seem like a blind obstinacy to refuse the customary honor to the king's noblest lord – his highest officer? Assuredly not! Haman was the highest officer of Ahasuerus, but he was the greatest "enemy of Jehovah," being the greatest "enemy of the Jews." He was an Amalekite, and Jehovah had sworn that He would "have war with Amalek from generation to generation" (Ex. 17:16). How then could a true son of Abraham bow to one with whom Jehovah was at war? Impossible! Mordecai could save the life of an Ahasuerus, but he never could bow to an Amalekite. As a faithful Jew, he walked too closely with the God of his fathers to pay attention to one of the seed of Amalek.

Hence Mordecai's stern refusal to bow to Haman was not the fruit of a blind obstinacy and senseless pride, but of lovely faith *in* and high communion *with* the God of Abraham, Isaac and Jacob. He could never relinquish the dignity which belonged to the Israel of God. He would abide by faith under Jehovah's banner, and while so abiding he could never do obeisance to an Amalekite. What though His people were "scattered and peeled" – "though their beautiful house" was in ruins – though Jerusalem's ancient glory was departed – was faith therefore to abandon the high position assigned by God's counsels to His people? By no means. Faith would recognize the ruin and walk softly. At the same time, faith laid hold of God's promise and occupied in holy dignity the platform which that promise had opened up for all who believed it. Mordecai was made to feel deeply the ruin. He clothed himself in sackcloth, but he would never bow to an Amalekite.

What was the result? His sackcloth was exchanged for royal apparel. His place at the king's gate was exchanged for a place next to the throne. He realized in his own happy experience the truth of that ancient promise that Israel should be "the head and not the tail." Thus it was with this faithful Jew of old. He took his stand on that elevated ground where faith ever places the soul. He shaped his way, not according to nature's view of things around, but according to faith's view of the Word of God. Nature might say, "Why not lower your standard of action to the level of your circumstances?

Why not suit yourself to your outward condition? Had you not better acknowledge the Amalekite, seeing that the Amalekite is in the place of power?" Nature might speak thus, but faith's answer was simple: "Jehovah hath sworn that He will have war with Amalek from generation to generation." Thus it is ever. Faith lays hold of *the living God and His eternal Word*, and abides in peace and walks in holy elevation.

Christian reader, may the hallowed instruction of the Book of Esther be brought home to our souls in the power of the Holy Spirit. In it, we see the providence of God, the pride of man, the power of faith. Moreover we are furnished with a striking picture of the actings of Jehovah on behalf of His people Israel – the sudden overthrow of their last proud oppressor, their restoration and their everlasting blessedness, rest and glory.

"HAVE FAITH IN GOD"

How prone we are in moments of pressure and difficulty to turn the eye to some creature resource! Our hearts are full of creature confidence, human hopes and earthly expectations. We know comparatively little of the deep blessedness of looking simply to God. We are ready to look anywhere and everywhere rather than unto Him. We run to any broken cistern and lean on any broken reed, although we have an exhaustless Fountain and the Rock of Ages ever near.

And yet we have proved times without number that "creature streams are dry." Man is sure to disappoint us when we look to him. "Cease ye from man whose breath is in his nostrils; for wherein is he to be accounted of?" And again, "Cursed is the man that trusteth in man and maketh flesh his arm, and whose heart departeth from the Lord. For he shall be like the shrub in the desert and shall not see when good cometh; but shall inhabit the parched places in the wilderness, in a salt land and not inhabited" (Jer. 17:5-6).

Such is the sad result of leaning upon the creature – barrenness, desolation, disappointment. Like the shrub in the desert. No refreshing showers, no dew from heaven, nothing but drought and sterility. How can it be otherwise when the heart is turned away from the Lord, the only source of blessing? It lies not within the range of the creature to satisfy the heart. God alone can do this. He can meet our every need and satisfy our every desire. He never fails a trusting heart.

But He must be trusted in reality. "What doth it profit, my brethren, though a man *say*" he trusts God, if he does not really do so? A sham faith will not do. It will not do to trust in word, neither in tongue. It must be in deed and in truth. Of what use is a faith with one eye on the Creator and another on the creature? Can God and the creature occupy the same platform? Impossible. It must be God *or* the creature, and the curse that ever follows creature-confidence.

Mark the contrast. "Blessed is the man that trusteth in the Lord, and whose hope the Lord is. For he shall be as a tree planted by the waters and that spreadeth out her roots by the river, and shall not see when heat cometh, but her leaf shall be green; and shall not be careful in the year of drought, neither shall cease from yielding fruit."

How blessed! How bright! How beautiful! Who would not put his trust in such a God? How delightful to find oneself wholly and absolutely cast upon Him! To be shut up to Him. To have Him filling the entire range of the soul's vision. To find all our springs in Him. To be able to say, "My soul, wait thou only upon God, for my expectation is from Him. He only is my rock and my salvation; He is my defense; I shall not be moved."

Note the little word "only." It is very searching. It will not do to say we are trusting in God while the eye is all the while upon the creature. It is much to be feared that we frequently *talk* about looking to the Lord while in reality, we are expecting our fellow-man to help us. "The heart is deceitful above all things and desperately wicked; who can know it? I the Lord search the heart. I try the reins, even to give every man according to his ways, and according to the fruit of his doings."

How needful to have the heart's deepest motive-springs judged in the presence of God! We are so apt to deceive ourselves by the use of certain phrases which, so far as we are concerned, have no force, no value, no truth whatever. The language of faith is on our lips, but the heart is full of creature confidence. We talk to men about our faith in God so they may help us out of our difficulties.

Let us be honest. Let us walk in the clear light of God's presence where everything is seen as it really is. Let us not rob God of His glory and our souls of abundant blessing by an empty profession of dependence upon Him, while the heart is secretly going out after some creature stream. Let us not miss the deep joy, peace and blessing, the strength, stability and victory that faith ever finds in the living God, in the living Christ of God and in the living Word of God. Oh! Let us "have faith in God."

"WHAT WAIT I FOR?"
(PSALM 39:7)

This is a searching question for the heart, but it is oftentimes a most necessary one, inasmuch as we may constantly detect ourselves in an attitude of waiting for things which, when they come, prove not to be worth waiting for.

The human heart is very much like the poor lame man at the gate of the temple in Acts 3. He was looking at every passerby "expecting to receive something." And the heart will ever be looking out for some relief, some comfort or some enjoyment in passing circumstances. It may be found sitting by the side of some creature-stream, vainly expecting some refreshment to flow along its channel.

It is amazing to think of the trifles on which nature will fix its expectant gaze – a change of circumstances, change of scene, a journey, a visit, a letter, a book. Anything is sufficient to raise expectations in a poor heart which is not finding its center, its spring, its all, in Christ.

Hence the practical importance of frequently turning sharp round upon the heart with the question, "What wait I for?" Doubtless, the true answer to this enquiry would at times furnish the most advanced Christian with matter for deep humiliation and self-judgment before the Lord.

In Psalm 39:6 we have three great types of character as set forth in the "vain show," "vain disquietude" and "heaping up." These types may sometimes be found combined, but very often they have a distinct development.

There are many whose whole life is one "vain show," whether in their personal character, their commercial position, their political or religious profession. There is nothing solid about them, nothing real, nothing true. The glitter is the most shallow gilding possible. There is nothing deep, nothing intrinsic. All is surface work – all the merest flash and smoke.

Then we find another class whose life is one continued scene of "vain disquietude." You will never find them at ease – never satisfied, never happy. There is always some terrible thing coming – some catastrophe in the distance, the mere anticipation of which keeps them in a constant fever of anxiety. They are troubled about property, about friends, about trade, about children, about servants. Though placed in circumstances which thousands of their fellow-creatures would deem most enviable, they seem to be in a perpetual fret. They harass themselves in reference to troubles

254

that may never come, difficulties they may never encounter, sorrows they may never live to see. Instead of remembering the blessings of the past and rejoicing in the mercies of the present, they are anticipating the trials and sorrows of the future. In a word, *"they are disquieted in vain."*

Finally, you will meet another class, quite different from either of the preceding – keen, shrewd, industrious, money-making people who would live where others would starve. There is not much "vain show" about them. They are too solid, and life is too practical a reality for anything of that sort. Neither can you say there is much disquietude about them. Theirs is an easy-going, quiet, plodding spirit, or an active, enterprising, speculating turn of mind. "They heap up, and know not who shall gather."

But remember, on all three alike the Spirit has stamped *"vanity."* Yes, "all" without any exception, "under the sun," has been pronounced by one who knew it by experience and wrote it by inspiration, *"vanity and vexation of spirit."* Turn where you will "under the sun" and you will not find anything on which the heart can rest. You must rise on the steady and vigorous pinion of faith to regions "above the sun," to find "a better and an enduring substance." The One who sits at the right hand of God has said, "I lead in the way of righteousness, in the midst of the paths of judgment: that I may cause them that love Me to inherit substance, and I will fill their treasures" (Prov. 8:20-21). None but Jesus can give "substance." None but He can "fill." None but He can "satisfy." There is that in Christ's perfect work which meets the deepest need of conscience. There is that in His glorious Person which can satisfy the most earnest longings of the heart. The one who has found Christ on the cross and Christ on the throne, has found all he can possibly need for time or eternity.

Well might the psalmist, having challenged his heart with the question, "What wait I for?" reply, "My hope is in Thee." No "vain show," no "vain disquietude," no "heaping up" for him. He had found an object in God worth waiting for. Therefore, turning away his eye from all beside, he says, "My hope is in Thee."

This, my beloved reader, is the only true, peaceful and happy position. The soul that leans on, looks to, and waits for Jesus will never be disappointed. Such an one possesses an exhaustless fund of present enjoyment in fellowship with Christ. At the same time he is cheered by "that blessed hope" that when this present scene, with all its "vain show," its "vain disquietude" and its vain resources shall have passed away, he shall be with Jesus where He is, to behold His glory, to bask in the light of His countenance and to be conformed to His image forever.

May we, then, be much in the habit of challenging our earth-bound, creatures-seeking hearts with the searching enquiry, "What wait I for?" Am I waiting for some change of circumstances or "for the Son from heaven?" Can I look up to Jesus and with a full and an honest heart, say, "Lord, my hope is in Thee?"

May we be more thoroughly separated from this present evil world and all that pertains thereto, by the power of communion with those things that are unseen and eternal.

"From various cares my heart retires,
Though deep and boundless its desires,
I'm now to please but One;
He before whom the elders bow,
With Him is all my business now,
And with the souls that are His own.

"With these my happy lot is cast,
Through the world's deserts rude and waste,
Or through its gardens fair;
Whether the storms of trouble sweep,
Or all in dead supineness sleep,
Still to go on be my whole care."

AN EARNEST APPEAL

Christian reader, I feel constrained to make an earnest appeal to your heart and conscience in the presence of Him to whom you and I are responsible and to whom our hearts and ways are fully known. I do not mean to judge you or speak ill to you. Neither do I wish to write in a bitter or complaining spirit. I only desire to stir up your pure mind – to wake up the energies of your new nature – to exhort and encourage you to a more earnest zeal and whole-hearted devotedness in the service of Christ.

The present is a deeply solemn moment. The day of God's long-suffering is rapidly drawing to a close. The day of wrath is at hand. The wheels of divine government are moving onward with a rapidity truly soul-subduing. Human affairs are working to a point. There is an awful crisis approaching. Immortal souls are rushing forward along the surface of the stream of time into the boundless ocean of eternity. The end of all things is at hand. "The days are at hand, and the effect of every vision."

Now, my reader, seeing these things are so, let us ask each other how are we affected thereby? What are we doing in the midst of the scene which surrounds us? How are we discharging our fourfold responsibility – our responsibility to God, our responsibility to the Church, our responsibility to perishing sinners, and our responsibility to our own souls? This is a weighty question. Let us take it into the presence of God and there survey it in all its magnitude. Are we really doing all we might do for the advancement of the cause of Christ, the prosperity of His Church, the progress of His gospel? I candidly confess to you, my friend, that I very much fear we are not making a right use of all the grace, the light and the knowledge which our God has graciously imparted to us. I fear we are not faithfully and diligently trading with our talents or occupying till the Master returns. It often occurs to me that people with far less knowledge, far less profession, are far more practical, more fruitful in good works, more honored in the conversion of precious souls, more generally used of God. How is this? Are you and I sufficiently self-emptied, sufficiently prayerful, sufficiently single-eyed?

You may reply, "It is a poor thing to be occupied with ourselves, our ways or our works." Yes; but if our ways and our works are not what they ought to be, we *must* be occupied with them. *We must judge them.* The Lord, by His prophet Haggai, called upon the Jews of old to "consider their ways." The Lord Jesus said to each of the seven churches, "I know thy works." There is a great danger of resting satisfied with our knowledge, our principles, our position, while at the same time we are walking in a carnal, worldly, self-indulgent, careless spirit. The end of this will be terrible. Let us consider these things. May the apostolic admonition fall with divine power on our hearts. "Look to yourselves, that we lose not those things which we have wrought, but that we receive a full reward" (2 Jn. 8).

"LET US GO AGAIN"
(ACTS 15:36)

"Let us go again and visit our brethren in every city where we have preached the Word of the Lord and see how they do."

A motto for the evangelist is the expression, "to preach the gospel in the regions beyond." This is the grand object of the evangelist, let his talents or sphere of action be what they may.

But the pastor has his work as well as the evangelist, and we desire to also furnish a motto for him. Such a motto we have in the words, "let us go again." We are not merely to regard this expression as the narrative of what was done, but a model of what *ought* to be done. If the evangelist is responsible to preach the gospel in the regions beyond, so long as there are regions to be evangelized, the pastor is responsible to "go again and visit his brethren," so long as there are brethren to be visited. The evangelist forms the vital connection; the pastor maintains and strengthens that connection. The one is the instrument of creating the beautiful link, the other of perpetuating it. It is quite possible that the two gifts may exist in the same person, as in Paul's case, but whether this be so or not, each gift has its own specific sphere and object. The business of the evangelist is to call out the brethren; the business of the pastor is to look after them. The evangelist goes first and preaches the Word of the Lord; the pastor goes again and visits those upon whom that Word has taken effect. The former calls out the sheep, the latter feeds and takes care of them.

The order of these things is divinely beautiful. The Lord will not gather out His sheep and leave them to wander uncared for and unfed. This would be wholly unlike His gracious, tender, thoughtful way. Hence, He not only imparts the gift whereby His sheep are to be called into existence, but also that gift whereby they are to be fed and maintained. He has His own interest in them and in every stage of their history. He watches over them with intense care from the moment in which they hear the first quickening words until they are safely in the mansions above.

His desire to gather the sheep tells itself forth in the large-heartedness of the expression, "the regions beyond." His desire for their well-being is seen in the words, "let us go again." The two things are intimately connected. Wherever the Word of the Lord has been preached and received, there you have the formation of mysterious but real and most precious links between heaven and earth. The eye of faith can discern the most beautiful link of divine sympathy between the heart of Christ in heaven and "every city" where "the Word of the Lord" has been preached and received. This is as true now as it was then. There may be many things to hinder our spiritual perception of this link, but it is there. God sees it and faith sees it likewise. Christ has His eye – an eye beaming with intense interest and radiant with tender love – upon every city, every town, every village, every street, every house in which His Word has been received.

The assurance of this is most comforting to every one who feels that he has truly received the Word of the Lord. Were we called upon to prove from Scripture the truth of our assertion, we should do so by the following quotation: "And there was a certain disciple at Damascus, named Ananias; and to him said the Lord in a vision, Ananias. And he said, Behold, I am here, Lord. And the Lord said unto him, Arise and go into the street which is called Straight and enquire in the house of Judas for one called Saul of Tarsus: for behold he prayeth" (Acts 9:10-11). Can anything be more touching than to hear the Lord of glory giving, with such minuteness, the address of His newly-found sheep? He gives the street, the number (so to speak) and Saul's very occupation at the moment. His gracious eye takes in everything connected with each one of those for whom He gave His precious life. There is not a circumstance, however trivial, in the path of the very feeblest of His members in which the blessed Lord Jesus is not interested. His name be praised for such a comforting assurance! May we be enabled to enter more fully into the reality and power of such a truth!

Now, our gracious Shepherd would fill the heart of each one acting under Him with His own tender care for the sheep. It was He who animated the heart of Paul to express and carry out the design embodied in the words, "let us go again." It was the grace of Christ flowing down into the heart of Paul and giving character and direction to the zealous service of that most devoted and laboring apostle.

Observe the force of the words "go again." It does not matter how often you may have been there before. It may be once or twice or thrice. This is not the question. "Let us go again" is the motto for the pastoral heart, for there is always a demand for the pastoral gift. Matters are always springing up in the various places in which "the Word of the Lord" has been preached and received, demanding the labors of the divinely-qualified pastor. This is especially true in this day of spiritual poverty. There is immense demand on the pastor to "go again and visit his brethren in every city" where "the Word of the Lord" has been preached, "and see how they do."

Reader, do you possess anything of a pastoral gift? If so, think of those comprehensive words, "let us go again." Have you been acting on them? Have you been thinking of your "brethren" – of those "who have obtained like precious faith" – those who, by receiving "the Word of the Lord," have become spiritual brethren? Are your interests and sympathies engaged on behalf of "every city" in which a spiritual link has been formed with the Head above? Oh! how the heart longs for a greater exhibition of holy zeal and energy, of individual and independent devotedness – independent, I mean, not of the sacred fellowship of the truly spiritual, but of every influence which would tend to clog and hinder that elevated service to which each one is distinctly called in responsibility to the Master alone.

Let us beware of the restraints of cumbrous religious machinery, of religious routine, of false order. Let us beware, too, of indolence, of love of personal ease, of a false economy which would lead us to attach an undue importance to the matter of expense. The silver and the gold are the Lord's and His sheep are far more precious to Him than silver and gold. His own words are, "Lovest thou Me? feed My sheep." And if only there is the heart to do this, the means will never be wanting. How often may we detect ourselves spending sums of money unnecessarily on the table, the wardrobe and the library, which would be amply sufficient to carry us to "the regions beyond" to preach the gospel, or to "every city" to "visit our brethren"!

May the Lord grant unto us an earnest self-denying spirit, a devoted heart to Him and to His most holy service, a true desire for the spread of His gospel and the prosperity of His people. May the time passed of our lives be sufficient for us to have lived and labored for self and its interests, and may the time to come be given to Christ and His interests. Let us not allow our treacherous hearts to deceive us by plausible reasonings about domestic, commercial or other claims. All such should be strictly attended to, no doubt. A well-regulated mind will never offer to God a sacrifice arising out of the neglect of any just claim. If I am at the head of a family, the claims of that family *must* be duly responded to. If I am at the head of a business, the claims of that business must be duly met. If I am a hired servant, I must attend to my work. To fail in any of these would be to dishonor the Lord instead of serving Him.

But, allowing the widest possible margin for all righteous claims, let us ask, are we doing all we can for "the regions beyond" and for "our brethren in every city where we have preached the Word of the Lord?" Has there not been a blameworthy abandonment both of evangelistic and pastoral work? Have we not allowed domestic and commercial ties to act *unduly* upon us? And what has been the result? What have we gained? Have our children turned out well and our commercial interests prospered? Has it not often happened that, where the Lord's work has been neglected, the children have grown up in carelessness and worldliness? And as to the business, have we not often toiled all the night and gazed on an empty net in the morning? On the other hand, where the family and the circumstances have been left with absolute confidence in the hand of Jehovah-Jireh (the Lord will provide), have they not been far better cared for?

Let these things be deeply pondered with an honest heart and a single eye, and we shall be sure to arrive at just conclusions.

I cannot lay down the pen without calling the reader's attention to the fullness of the expression, "see how they do." How very much is involved in these words! "How they do" publicly, socially, privately. "How they do" in doctrine, in association, in walk. "How they do" spiritually, morally, relatively – "how they do" in every way. Be it well remembered that this seeing how our brethren do must *never* resolve itself into a curious, prying, gossiping, busybody spirit – a spirit that wounds and heals not, that meddles and mends not. To all who would visit us in such a spirit as this we should assuredly say, "be yet far from here." But to all who would carry out Acts 15:36, we desire to say, "our hands, our hearts, our houses are wide open; come in, ye blessed of the Lord. 'If ye have judged me to be faithful to the Lord, come into my house and abide.' "

O Lord, be pleased to raise up evangelists to visit "the regions beyond" and pastors to visit, again and again, "the brethren in every city."

JOHN THE BAPTIST

It is not our object in the following pages to dwell upon the ministry of the Baptist, nor yet upon the place which he filled in the history of God's dealings with Israel, deeply interesting as all this might be and profitable too, inasmuch as his ministry was solemn and powerful, and his dispensational position full of the very deepest interest. But we must confine ourselves to two or three of his utterances as recorded by the Holy Spirit in the Gospel of John, in which we shall find two things very strikingly presented to our view – his estimate of himself and his estimate of his Lord.

These are points worthy of our attention. John the Baptist was, according to the testimony of his blessed Master, the greatest "among them that are born of women." This is the very highest testimony that could be borne to anyone, whether we consider the source from which it came or the terms in which it is stated. He was not only a prophet, but the greatest of prophets – the forerunner of the Messiah, the harbinger of the King, the great preacher of righteousness.

Such was John, officially. Hence it must be of the deepest interest to know what such an one thought of himself and what he thought of Christ – to hearken to his fervent utterances on both these points as given on the page of inspiration. Indeed we shall find herein a mine of most precious practical instruction.

Let us turn to John 1:19. "And this is the record of John, when the Jews sent priests and Levites from Jerusalem to ask him, Who art thou? And he confessed and denied not, but confessed, I am not the Christ. And they asked him, What then? Art thou Elias? And he saith, I am not. Art thou that prophet? And he answered, No. Then said they unto him, Who art thou? that we may give an answer to them that sent us. What sayest thou of thyself? He said, I am *the voice* of one crying in the wilderness."

They were determined to have an answer, and he gives them one. They would compel him to speak of himself, and he does so. But mark his answer! Who or what was he? Nobody. He was only "a voice." This is morally lovely. The self-emptiness of this most honored servant is beautiful. It does the heart good to be brought in contact with such practical grace as this. Here was a man of real power and dignity, one of Christ's most illustrious servants, occupying the very highest position, whose preaching had stirred the hearts of thousands, whose birth had been announced by angels, whose ministry had been foretold by prophets, the herald of the kingdom, the friend of the King. Yet this remarkable man, when forced to speak of himself, can merely be induced to say, "I am a voice." Not even a man, but only a voice.

What a lesson is here for us! What a wholesome "corrective" for our lamentable self-occupation, self-complacency and self-exaltation. It is truly wonderful to think of the Baptist's brilliant career, of his powerful ministry, of his widespread influence, extending even to the heart of Herod the king, of the place he occupied and the work he did. Yet, notwithstanding all this, when forced to give out what he had to say of himself, he sums it all up in that one self-emptied word, "A voice."

This contains a volume of deep practical instruction for the heart. It is precisely what is needed in this day of busy self-importance – needed by each – needed by all; for have we not, each and all, to judge ourselves on the ground of our inordinate tendency to think of ourselves more highly than we ought to think? Are we not all prone to attach importance to any little work with which we ourselves happen to stand connected? Alas! it is even so. Hence it is that we so deeply need the wholesome teaching furnished by the lovely self-emptiness of John the Baptist, who when challenged to speak of himself, could retire into the shade and say, "I am only a voice."

Now this was a very remarkable answer to fall on the ears of the Pharisees who were the messengers sent to question the Baptist, as we read, "They which were sent were of the Pharisees." Surely it is not without meaning that this fact is stated. Pharisees know very little of self-hiding or self-emptiness. Such rare and exquisite fruits do not thrive beneath the withering atmosphere of Pharisaism. They only grow in the new creation and there is no Pharisaism there. Pharisaism, in all its phases and in all its grades, is the moral direct opposite of self-denial. Therefore, John's reply must have sounded strange in the ears of the questioners.

"And they asked him and said unto him, Why baptizest thou then, if thou be not the Christ nor Elias, neither that prophet? John answered them, saying, I baptize with water, but there standeth one among you, whom ye know not; He it is, who coming after me is preferred before me, whose shoe's latchet I am not worthy to unloose."

Thus, the more this dear servant of Christ is forced to speak of himself or of his work, the more he retires into the shade. When asked about himself, he says "I am a voice." Then asked about his work, he says, "I am not worthy to unloose my Master's shoe-latchet." There is no puffing up or exalting of self, no making much ado of his service, no parading of his work. The greatest of prophets was, in his own eyes, merely a voice. The most honored of servants deemed himself unworthy to touch his Master's shoe.

All this is truly refreshing and edifying. It is most healthful for the soul to breathe such an atmosphere as this in a day like the present of so much contemptible egotism and empty pretension. John was a man of *real* power, *real* worth, *real* gift and grace. Therefore he was a lowly unpretending man. It is generally thus. Really great men are fond of the shade. If they must speak of themselves, they make short work of it. David never spoke of his wonderful feat with the lion and the bear until compelled to do so by Saul's unbelief. Paul never spoke of his rapture to paradise till it was drawn forth by the folly of the Corinthians; and when forced to speak of himself or his work, he apologizes and says again and again, "I speak as a fool."

Thus it is ever. True worth is modest and retiring. The Davids, the Johns and the Pauls have delighted to retire behind their Master and lose sight of themselves in the blaze of His moral glory. This was their joy. Here they found and ever shall find their deepest, fullest, richest blessing. The very highest and purest enjoyment which the creature can taste is to lose sight of self in the immediate presence of God. Oh! to know more of it! It is what we want. It would effectively deliver us from the tendency to be occupied with and influenced by the thoughts and opinions of men. It would impart a moral elevation to the character and a holy stability to the course which is for the glory of God and for our souls' true peace and blessing.

But we must gather up further instruction from the history of John the Baptist. Let the reader turn to John 3:25: "Then there arose a question between some of John's disciples and the Jews about purifying." There were questions then as there are questions now, for our hearts are full of questions. "And they came unto John and said unto him, Rabbi, He that was with thee beyond Jordan, to whom thou barest witness, behold, the same baptizeth and all men come to Him."

Here was something calculated to test the heart of the Baptist. Could he bear to lose all his disciples? Was he prepared for desertion? Was he really up to the height of his own words? Was he merely a voice, a nothing and a nobody? These were pertinent questions, for we all know it is one thing to talk humbly and another thing to *be* humble. It is one thing to speak about self-emptiness and quite another to *be* self-emptied.

Was the Baptist, then, up to the mark? Was he prepared to be superceded and set aside? Was it of any importance to him *who* did the work, provided the work was done? Hearken to his reply: "John answered and said, A man can receive nothing except it be given him from heaven." This is a great practical truth. Let us seize it and hold it fast. It is an effective remedy for self-confidence and self-exaltation.

If a man can "take unto himself" nothing, if he can do nothing, if he is nothing, it ill becomes him to be boastful, pretentious or self-occupied. The abiding sense of our own nothingness would ever keep us humble. The abiding sense of God's goodness would ever keep up happy. "Every good gift and every perfect gift is from above, and cometh down from the Father of lights." The remembrance of this would ever keep us looking up. Whatever good there is in us or around us, comes from heaven, comes from God – the living and ever flowing Source of all goodness and blessedness. To be near Him, to have Him before the heart, to serve in His holy presence is the true secret of peace, the unfailing safeguard against envy and jealousy.

The Baptist knew something of this. Hence he had an answer ready for his disciples. "A man can receive nothing except it be given him from heaven. Ye yourselves bear me witness that I said, I am not the Christ, but that I am sent before Him. He that hath the bride is the bridegroom, but the friend of the bridegroom, which standeth and heareth him, rejoiceth greatly because of the bridegroom's voice. This my joy therefore is fulfilled. *He must increase, but I must decrease.*"

Here lay the deep and precious secret of John's happiness and peace. His joy was not in his own work, not in gathering a number of disciples round himself, not in his personal influence or popularity, not in any or all of these things put together. His pure and holy joy was to stand and hear the voice of the Bridegroom and to see others including his own disciples, flocking to that blessed One and finding all their springs in Him.

> "This is my joy, which ne'er can fail,
> To see my Savior's arm prevail.
> And mark His steps of grace;
> Now new-born souls convinced of sin,
> His blood revealed to them within,
> Extol the Lamb in every place."

Such was the Baptist's estimate of himself and of his Lord. As to himself, he was but a voice and must decrease. As to his Lord, He was the

Bridegroom, He was from heaven, He was above all, the center of all, whose glory must increase and fill with its blessed beams the whole universe of God when all other glory shall have faded away forever.

But we have further testimony from the lips of this beloved and honored servant of God. This testimony is drawn forth, not by any "question" about purifying or any appeal to his personal feelings on the subject of his ministry, but simply by his intense admiration of Christ as an Object for his own heart. "The next day John seeth Jesus coming unto him and saith, Behold the Lamb of God which taketh away the sin of the world. This is He of whom I said, After me cometh a Man which is preferred before me: for He was before me. And I knew Him not, but that He should be made manifest to Israel, therefore am I come baptizing with water. And John bare record, saying, I saw the Spirit descending from heaven like a dove, and it abode upon Him. And I knew Him not: but He that sent me to baptize with water, the same said unto me, Upon whom thou shalt see the Spirit descending and remaining on Him, the same is He which baptizeth with the Holy Spirit. And I saw, and bare record that this is the Son of God. Again the next day after John stood, and two of his disciples; and looking upon Jesus as He walked, he saith, Behold the Lamb of God" (Jn. 1:29-36).

Here was what occupied John's heart. *The Lamb of God.* Peerless, precious Object! Satisfying portion! Christ Himself – His work, His Person. In verse 29 we have one great branch of His work – "He taketh away the *sin* of the world." His atoning death is the foundation of everything. It is the propitiation for His people's sins and for the whole world. In virtue of this precious sacrifice, every stain is removed from the believer's conscience, and in virtue thereof every stain shall yet be obliterated from the whole creation. The cross is the divine pedestal on which the glory of God and the blessedness of man shall rest forever.

Then in verse 33 we have another branch of Christ's work. "He baptizeth with the Holy Spirit." This was made good on the day of Pentecost when the Holy Spirit came down from the risen and glorified Head to baptize believers into one body. We do not attempt to enter upon these weighty subjects here, inasmuch as our object is to present to the heart of the reader the great practical effect of occupation with Christ Himself, the only true object of all believers. This effect comes very strikingly out in the following verses. "Again the next day after John stood, and two of his disciples; and looking upon Jesus as He walked, he saith, Behold the Lamb of God" (vv. 35-36).

Here the Baptist is wholly engrossed with the *Person* of his Lord. Hence we have no reference to His work. This is a point of the deepest possible interest and importance. "John stood" – fixed – riveted – gazing upon the most glorious Object that had ever fixed the gaze of men and angels – the Object of the Father's delight and of heaven's adoration, *"the Lamb of God."* Mark the effect. "The two disciples heard Him speak and they followed Jesus." They felt there must be something uniquely attractive in One who could so command their master's heart. Therefore, leaving him, they attached themselves to that glorious Person of whom he spoke.

This is full of instruction for us. There is immense moral power in true occupation of heart with Christ and in the testimony which flows from thence. The positive enjoyment of Christ – feeding upon and delighting in Him, the heart going out in holy adoration after Him, the affections centered in Him – these are the things that tell powerfully upon the hearts of others because they tell upon our own hearts and ways. A man who is finding his delight in Christ is lifted out of himself and lifted above the circumstances and influences which surround him. Such an one is morally elevated above the thoughts and opinions of men. He enjoys a holy calmness and independence. He is not thinking about himself or seeking a name or a place for himself. He has found a satisfying portion and is therefore able to tell the world that he is wholly independent of it.

Was John troubled by the loss of his disciples? No, it was the joy of his heart to see them finding their center and their object where he had found his own. He had not sought to make a party or to gather disciples around himself. He had borne witness to another, and that other was "the Lamb of God" in whom he himself delighted, not only because of His work, but because of His worth – His moral glory, His intrinsic, peerless, divine excellence. He heard the Bridegroom's voice and saw His face, and his joy was full.

Now we may well inquire, What can the world offer to a man whose joy is full? What can circumstances, what can the creature do for him? If men slight and desert him, if they wound and insult him, what then? Why, he can say, "My joy is full. I have found all I want in that blessed One who not only has taken away my sins and filled me with the Holy Spirit, but who has drawn me to Himself and filled me with His own divine preciousness and eternal excellency."

Reader, let us earnestly seek to know more of this deep blessedness. Rest assured we shall find therein an effective cure for the thousand and one ills that afflict us in the scene through which we are passing. How is it that *professors* so often exhibit a gloomy and unlovely temper? Why are they peevish, fretful and irritable in the domestic life? Why so ruffled and put about by the petty annoyances of their daily history? Why so easily upset by the most contemptible trifles? Why put out of temper if the dinner be not properly and punctually served up? Why so touchy and tenacious? Why so ready to take offense if self be touched or its interests intruded upon? Ah! the answer is easily given. The poor heart is not finding its center, its satisfying portion in "the Lamb of God." Here lies the secret of our failure. The moment we take our eye off Christ, the moment we cease to abide in Him by a living faith, that moment we get under the power of every passing current of circumstances and influences. We become feeble and lose our balance; self and its surroundings rise into prominence and fill the heart's vision. Thus, instead of exhibiting the beautiful features of the image of Christ, we exhibit the very reverse, even the odious and humiliating tempers and dispositions of unsubdued nature.

May God enable us to lay these things seriously to heart, for we may depend upon it that serious damage is done to the cause of Christ, and grievous dishonor brought upon His holy name by the uncomely manners, tempers and ways of those who profess to belong to Him.

269

WHAT SHOULD I READ?
A QUESTION FOR THE TIMES

The question which forms the heading of this paper is one of real weight and practical importance. There is much more involved in it than we might want to admit. It is a common saying, "Show me your company and I will tell you *what* you are." It may, with equal truth, be said, "Show me your library and I will tell *where* you are." Our reading may be taken as the great indicator of our moral, intellectual and spiritual condition. Our books are our mental and spiritual food, the material on which the inner man feeds. Hence the seriousness of the entire question of Christian reading. Indeed we may freely own to our readers that this subject has engrossed us much of late. Therefore, we feel constrained in faithfulness to the Lord and to the souls of our readers, to offer a few words of admonition in reference to what we regard as a matter of real importance to all Christians.

We observe with deep concern a growing distaste for solid reading, specially among young Christians, although it is not confined to them. Newspapers, religious novels, sensational tales, all sorts of poisonous and trashy literature are eagerly devoured, while volumes of most weighty and precious truth lie neglected on the bookshelf.

All this we consider most deplorable. We look upon it as a most alarming indication of a low spiritual condition. Indeed it is difficult to conceive how anyone possessing a single spark of divine life can find pleasure in such defiling rubbish as one sees now-a-days in the hands of many who occupy the high ground of Christian profession. The inspired apostle exhorts all Christians, "As newborn babes, to desire the sincere milk *of the Word* that ye may grow thereby." How can we grow if we neglect the Word of God and yet devour newspapers and light, worthless books? How is it possible for any Christian to be in a healthy condition of soul who can barely find a few hasty moments to run his eye over a verse or two of Scripture, but can give hours to light and useless reading? We may depend upon it: our reading proves beyond question what we are and where we are. If our reading is light and frivolous, our state is the same. If our Christianity is of a solid and earnest type, it will be distinctly evidenced by our habitual and voluntary reading – the reading to which we turn for our recreation and refreshment.

Some may say, "We cannot be always reading the Bible and good books." We reply plainly that *the new nature would never care to read anything else.* Now the question is, whether we wish to minister to the old nature or the new? If the latter, we may rest assured that newspapers and light literature are not the means to be used. It is impossible that a truly spiritual, earnest Christian can find enjoyment in such reading. It may be that a Christian engaged in business or in public official life will have occasion, in connection with his business or his official duty, to refer to a newspaper, but this is another thing altogether from finding his actual enjoyment and recreation in such reading. He will not find the hidden manna or the old corn of the land of Canaan in the newspaper. He will not find Christ in the sensational novel.

It is a poor, low thing to hear a Christian say, "How can we be always reading the Bible?" or "What harm is there in reading a story book?" All such questions evidence the fact that the soul has got far away from Christ. This is what makes it so very serious. Spiritual decline must have set in and made alarming progress before a Christian could think of asking such questions. Hence there is little use in arguing about the right or the wrong of things. There is no ability to argue aright, no capacity to weigh evidence. The whole spiritual and moral condition is wrong. "There is death in the pot." What is needed is thorough restoration of soul. You must "bring meal," or in other words, apply a divine remedy to meet the diseased state of the constitution.

We feel pressed in spirit to call the serious attention of the Christian reader to this great practical question. We deem it to be one of deepest seriousness. The extremely low spiritual tone of Christianity among us is owing, in many cases, to the reading of light and worthless literature. The moral effect of all such is most harmful. How can a soul prosper, how can there be growth in the divine life where there is no real love for the Bible or for books which unfold the precious contents of the Bible to our souls? Is it possible that a Christian can be in a healthy condition of soul who really prefers some light work to a volume designed for true spiritual edification? We cannot believe it. We are persuaded that all true-hearted, earnest Christians – all who truly desire to get on in divine things, all who really love Christ and desire heaven and heavenly things – all such will be found diligently reading the Holy Scriptures and thankfully availing themselves of all good, helpful books which come within their reach. They will have neither time nor taste for newspapers or light literature. With them it will not be a question as to the right or the wrong of such reading: they simply have no desire for it, do not want it, would not have it. They have something far better. "With ashes who would grudge to part, when called on angels' bread to feast?"

We trust our readers will bear with us in writing thus plainly and pointedly. We feel constrained in view of the judgment-seat of Christ to do so. Would that we could write as earnestly as we feel on the subject. We consider it one of the weightiest and most practical questions which can engage our attention. We entreat the Christian reader to shun and discontinue all light reading. Let us each ask the question, when about to take up a book or a paper, "Should I like my Lord to come and find this in my hand? or can I take this into the presence of God and ask His blessing upon the reading of it? Can I read it to the glory of the name of Jesus?" If we cannot say "Yes" to these questions, then by the grace of God, let us fling the paper or the book away and devote our spare moments to the blessed Word of God or to some spiritual volume written thereon. Then shall our souls be nourished and strengthened; we shall grow in grace and in the knowledge and love of our Lord and Savior Jesus Christ, and the fruits of righteousness shall abound in our practical life, to the glory of God.

It may be that some of our friends would repudiate altogether the habit of reading human writings. Some there are who take the ground of reading nothing but the Bible. They tell us they find all they want in that peerless volume and that human writings are a hindrance rather than a help.

Well, as to this, each one must judge for himself. No one can be a rule for another. But we certainly cannot take this high ground. We bless the Lord each day more and more for all the gracious helps given us by means of the writings of His beloved servants. We look upon them as a most precious stream of refreshment and spiritual blessing flowing down from our glorified Head in the heavens, for which we can never praise Him enough. We should just as soon think of refusing to hear a brother speak in the assembly as of refusing to read his writings, for what is either but a branch of ministry given of God for our profit and edification?

We do need to exercise care lest we make too much of ministry, whether oral or written, but the possible *abuse* of a thing is no valid argument against the *use* of it. There is danger on every side, and most surely it is a very dangerous thing to despise ministry. None of us are self-sufficient. It is the divine purpose that we should be helpful one to another. We cannot do without "that which every joint supplieth." How many will have to praise God throughout eternity for blessing received through books and tracts! How many there are who never get an atom of spiritual ministry except what the Lord sends them through the press. It will be said, "They have the Bible." True, but all have not the same ability to fathom the living depths or seize the moral glories of the Bible. No doubt, if we cannot have either oral or written ministry, the Spirit of God can feed us directly in the green pastures of Holy Scripture. But who will deny that the writings of God's servants are used by the Holy Spirit as a most powerful agency in building up the Lord's people in their most holy faith? It is our firm conviction that God has made more use of such agency during the last forty years than ever before in the entire history of the Church.

Cannot we praise Him for it? Truly so. We should praise Him with full and glowing hearts. And we should earnestly pray Him to grant still further blessing on the writings of His servants – to deepen their tone, increase their power and widen their sphere. Human writings, if not clothed with the power of the Holy Spirit, are just so much waste paper. In like manner the voice of the public preacher or teacher, if not the living vehicle of the Holy Spirit, is but a sounding brass or a tinkling cymbal. But the Holy Spirit *does* make use of both agencies for the blessing of souls and the spread of the truth, and we deem it a serious mistake for anyone to despise an agency which God is pleased to adopt. Indeed we have rarely met anyone who refused the help of human writings who did not prove exceedingly narrow, crude and one-sided. This is only what we might expect, inasmuch as it is the divine method to make us mutually helpful one to another. Hence, if anyone claims to be independent or self-sufficient, he must sooner or later find out his mistake.

THE WORK OF GOD IN THE SOUL

We have from time to time written about the work of God for us. This work lies at the very foundation of all true practical Christianity and personal religion. The knowledge of what has been accomplished by the atoning death of Christ is essential to the soul's peace and liberty. We cannot too frequently reiterate or too strongly insist upon the fundamental truth that it is the work wrought *for* us and not the work wrought *in* us that saves us. Nor should we ever forget that faith is the soul's outward, not its inward look.

All this is of the deepest importance and the reader may rest assured that nothing is further from our thoughts than to pen a single line which might tend to lessen its importance. But this grand and interesting line of truth has been largely unfolded. Therefore, we feel the more free to enter in this article upon a subject which ought ever to hold a prominent place in our minds – the work of God *in* us. May God's Spirit guide our thoughts as we dwell upon this theme!

In tracing the work of the Holy Spirit in the soul of a sinner, there are three distinct things to be noticed. First, *He creates a need.* Secondly, He reveals an Object to meet that need. And thirdly, He enables the soul to lay hold on that Object. These are the three stages of the Spirit's work in the soul and nothing can be more interesting than to trace them. There are various other branches of the work of the Holy Spirit, but we now confine ourselves to that special branch which bears upon the individual soul in its passage from darkness to light and from the power of Satan to God.

This need may develop itself in several ways. In some cases it takes the form of a deep sense of guilt; in others, a sense of the utter vanity and emptiness of all beneath the sun. Doubtless, in many instances, we may find all ways operating.

Let us take an example or two from the pages of inspiration. Look at Peter by the lake of Gennesaret (Lk. 5). No sooner had a ray of divine light entered his soul in convicting power, than he exclaims, "Depart from me, for I am a sinful man, O Lord." Here we have a sense of guilt – a deep, keen sense of personal sinfulness and unworthiness, the result of a divine operation in the soul of Peter. This is very important. It is well to remember that the question of sin must be raised and settled in the human conscience. Sin is a serious thing in God's judgment and it must be felt as such in the soul of the sinner. Peter felt he had no right or title to be in the presence of that blessed One whose glory had just shone upon him. He felt himself utterly unfit to be there. He felt that sin and holiness could not be together, any more than light and darkness.

This was a right feeling in Peter; it is a right feeling in every case. It is always a good thing to begin with a profound sense of personal guilt. It is well to have the arrow of conviction piercing to the very center of the soul. It is well to have the plough-share breaking up the fallow ground and making a deep furrow in the heart. We invariably find that the steadiest and most solid Christians are those who have, at the first, gone through the deepest waters and endured the keenest exercises.

We do not mean to say that the soul's exercises have anything to do with the ground of the soul's salvation, anymore than the feelings of a man in a house on fire have to do with the fire escape by which he descends from the burning building. But still we believe it is a good thing for the soul to begin with a very clear and full sense of its guilt and ruin – *a just apprehension of the judgment of God against sin.* The more keenly one has felt his awful position in the burning house, the more thoroughly will he appreciate the fire escape, the mind that planned it and the hand that provided it. And so in the case of the sinner; the more he feels his guilt and unworthiness, the more will he prize the precious blood that cancels his guilt and brings him without spot into the presence of a holy, sin-hating God.

It is to be feared that, in many cases, the work of conviction or repentance is very superficial. It strikes us, too, that at times, in our great anxiety to bring the soul into peace, we interfere with the work of conviction. We go before, in stead of following after the Holy Spirit. This is very serious. It is a perilous thing to tamper with God's work in the soul. It is most marvelous grace that deigns to use us, but let us beware not to run before the Holy Spirit. It is our place to mark His operations, not to mar them.

If, for example, we meet a soul under conviction of sin, it may be that the work is not yet complete; it may be only in progress. What should we do? Seek to hasten the individual into a confession of faith in Christ, to extract from him an acknowledgment of peace with God? By no means; to do so would be to damage the precious work of God in the soul. What then should we do? Seek to follow in the wake of the Holy Spirit, to be His instrument in carrying on the work which He has in hand. He will assuredly perfect His own work. If we are waiting on Him, He will teach us what to do and how to do it, what to say and when to say it. If Ananias had gone to Saul one hour before the close of the "three days," he would have gone too soon. Those days were serious days – days which left their imprint on the whole of the apostle's history – days never to be forgotten. They were days during which his eyes, closed upon the external world, were turned inward upon himself and backward upon his ways. And are we not warranted in asserting that it would have been an injudicious if not an unhallowed intrusion, had Ananias gone to interfere with the deep and holy work which was going on in the soul of that remarkable man? Unquestionably; and so it is in every case. We may depend upon it, that we only injure souls if we attempt to urge them by our work, one hair's breadth beyond the actual point to which the work of God has conducted them.

All true spiritual ministry will tend to deepen in the soul that special character of work which the Holy Spirit is carrying on at the moment. Hence, if we come in contact with one in whom the work of conviction or repentance is in progress, we should not seek too hastily to urge the soul into a confession of having found peace. If we aim at being co-workers with God, it will be our place to watch, with earnest prayer and holy diligence, the progress of the divine work – to wait much on God that He may be pleased to use us as His instruments in carrying out the purposes of His grace. This is most blessed work, but it is most solemn and demands much spirituality, much nearness to Christ, much self-denial. The most serious mistakes are committed by unskillful hands undertaking to deal with cases in which the work of God's Spirit is going on. We must remember that God's work is sometimes very slow, but it is always very sure. We, on the contrary, are often impetuous. In our desire to reach speedy results, we may often unduly hasten on the soul to a professed position far beyond its actual practical state. We may often urge from the lips more than the Holy Spirit has worked in the heart. This is very serious for all who have to deal with souls.

But the grace of God is all-sufficient for every case. Nothing can be more interesting than to watch the unfoldings of the Spirit's work in the soul – to mark the stages of God's new creation, the establishment and progress of His kingdom in the heart. Far be it from us to urge or encourage cold heartless indifference as to precious souls in their deep and varied spiritual exercises – a species of most miserable fatalism which, under the plea of leaving souls entirely in the hands of the Holy Spirit, in reality throws off all sense of responsibility. God forbid that we should lend any approval to anything of this kind. We deeply feel ourselves responsible to care for souls. We believe all Christians are responsible. Hence arises the need of skill and spiritual tact in dealing with souls so we may not in any way retard, but by all means further the blessed work of God's Spirit in them.

But we have been rather digressing from our immediate line, to which we shall now return.

We have stated that the Spirit of God sometimes produces in the soul a sense of danger. He presses upon the heart and conscience the awful reality of the Lake of Fire and the worm that never dies. He at times sees fit to draw aside the curtain and reveal what awaits all those who die in their sins. The sense of guilt and the sense of danger frequently go together, but they are distinct exercises, and in many cases the latter is the more prominent of the two. The soul is filled with horror at the thought of burning forever and ever in the flames of hell. The Holy Spirit uses this horror to make the heart feel its need of Christ.

Many object to the preaching of everlasting punishment as a means of leading souls to Christ. Not that they deny the truth on this subject, but they question the propriety or usefulness of it. They deem it wiser to dwell only upon the love of God in giving His Son, and the love of Christ in giving Himself. They judge it better and more effective to dwell upon the joys and glories of heaven than the woes and horrors of hell. Well, we do not mean for a moment to compare the two themes; no intelligent person could think of so doing. But we must bear in mind that our blessed Lord again and again addressed His hearers on the awful subject of hell fire. Read Matthew 5:22-30. Three times in this brief passage He warns His hearers against the danger of hell.

So also in that most solemn passage at the close of Luke 16. Who can read this without feeling pressed with the weight and seriousness of the parable? What a presentation of the past, the present and the future! "Son, remember." Here memory is flung back upon the past. And what a past! Memory will be terribly active in hell. "But now thou art tormented." Here the lost soul is called to contemplate the present. And what a present! Tormented in the flames of hell! But is there no end, no faint hope of cessation? None whatever. "There is a great gulf *fixed.*" Here is the future. And what a future! Hell is an eternal reality. If hell fire is not everlasting, what would be the force of the word "fixed"?

Are not the above Scriptures quite sufficient to prove that the Holy Spirit uses the truth of everlasting punishment to create a need in the immortal soul? Most surely. And if He does so, should not we? Did not the Apostle Paul reason before Felix on the subject of judgment to come, and in such a manner as to make that sensuous man tremble on his throne? Ah! yes; it is a wholesome thing for the soul of a sinner to be impressed with a deep sense of his danger of hell. And when we find a soul so impressed, what should we do? Should we not seek to deepen the impression? Would it not be our wisdom to follow up what the Holy Spirit is manifestly doing? Truly so. To act otherwise would be to hinder instead of furthering the work of God in the soul. The blessed Spirit will teach us the proper moment to present the divine Object to meet the need of the exercised soul. The Master will at the right moment issue the command, "Loose him and let him go." God will do His work and use us therein, if we wait on Him. All we desire is to press upon the reader the reality of God's work in the soul and the necessity of guarding against anything like undue haste in urging souls beyond the measure of the Spirit's operation. We should beware of healing the wound slightly and of crying Peace, where there is no peace, yes, where there is not even true preparedness for that blessed peace which Jesus has made by the blood of His cross, which God proclaims in His Word and which the heart enjoys by faith through the power of the Holy Spirit.

Having glanced at two of those modes in which the Spirit of God works in the soul to produce a sense of need – by convincing the conscience of guilt and by pressing upon the spirit the just dread of danger – it remains for us to consider a third method which is by making the heart to feel the utter vanity and dissatisfaction of all that this poor world can offer in the way of pleasure or enjoyment.

This is by no means uncommon. We frequently meet with very matured Christians who say they were brought to Christ, not so much by a sense of guilt or a dread of danger, as by an intense longing after a certain undefinable something – a painful void in the heart, a sense of weariness, loneliness and desolation. They felt an emptiness which nothing in this world could fill. They were heartsick and disappointed. No doubt they felt and acknowledged the broad truth that they were sinners. Moreover, when they looked in the direction of the future they felt there was nothing for them but eternal misery and torment. But then the great prominent feature of the divine work in them was not so much conviction of sin or a fear of punishment as a feeling of utter desolation and dissatisfaction. They found themselves in that condition of soul in which the study of the book of Ecclesiastes shows. They had tried the world in every shape and form, and like the royal Preacher had found it to be "vanity and vexation of spirit."

Now we must be prepared for this variety in the ways of the Spirit of God. We are not to suppose that He will confine Himself in His blessed operations to any one particular type. Sometimes He produces in the soul the most overwhelming sense of guilt so the heart is crushed to the earth, and nothing is felt, seen or thought of but the vileness, the heinousness, the blackness of sin. The dark catalog of sins rises like a great mountain before the vision of the soul and nearly sinks it into despair. The soul refuses to be comforted. Shame and confusion, sackcloth and ashes, are felt to be the only suited portion of the guilty one.

At other times God sees fit to bring before the soul the terrors of hell and the awful reality of spending an eternity in that region of unutterable gloom and misery. The dark shadow of the future is made to fall upon the brightest scenes of the present. The thought of the wrath to come so presses upon the heart that nothing seems to yield the smallest relief or comfort. All is deep, deep gloom and horror.

Finally, in other cases, the divine Worker is pleased to awaken the soul to the painful discovery and consciousness that it is not within the boundaries of earth to furnish a satisfying portion for an immortal spirit, that all under the sun wears the stamp of death upon it, that human life is but a vapor that speedily vanishes away, that if a man were to live a thousand years and possess the wealth of the universe and concentrate in his own person all the honors and all the dignities which this world could bestow – were he at the very highest pinnacle of power and be renowned throughout the world for genius, intellect and moral worth, if he had all that earth could yield or mortal man possess – the heart would still want something. There would still be a painful void. There would still be the cry, "Oh! for an object."

Thus varied are the operations of the Spirit of God in the souls of men. No doubt, there may be a sense of guilt, a fear of danger and a painful consciousness of the emptiness and vanity of all earthly possessions and enjoyments, altogether apart from any divine work in the soul, but we are now occupied only with this latter, and we feel the deep importance of being able to discern and appreciate the work of God's Spirit in the human heart, as also of seeking to help it on. We greatly dread anything like human interference with the progress of the kingdom of God in the soul. There is danger on all sides. There is danger of casting a damper on converts and there is danger of mistaking the mere workings of nature for the action of the Spirit of God. Nor is this all. We are frequently in danger of running directly counter to the object which the Lord has in view in His dealings with the soul. We may, for example, be seeking to extract the arrow which He is sending home to the very center of the soul. We may be seeking to cover up a wound which He would have probed to the very bottom.

All these things demand the utmost vigilance and care on the part of those who take an interest in souls. We are, all of us, liable to make the most serious mistakes either in the way of discouraging and repulsing souls that ought rather to be fostered and cheered, or of recognizing and accrediting as of God what is merely the fruit of religious nature working. In short, it is a serious thing to seek to do the work of God in any way. He alone can give the needed wisdom and grace in each case as it arises. And He will, blessed be His name, give abundantly to all who simply wait on Him. "He giveth more grace." Precious word! There is absolutely no limit to it. It shines as an exhaustless motto on our Father's treasury door, assuring us of the most ample supply "for the urgent need of every hour."

Let us not, therefore, be discouraged by the magnitude and seriousness of the work, or the danger attending it. God is sufficient. The work is His. If He deigns in His marvelous grace to use us, as He surely does, as His co-workers, He will liberally furnish us with all that is needed for each case as it arises. But we must wait patiently, humbly and trustfully on Him. We must seek to lay self aside with its bustling self-importance and excitement. We must seek through grace to get rid of that spirit which would be continually thrusting forward that wretched "I, I, I." In a word, nature must be kept in the shade and Christ alone exalted. Then, assuredly, the Spirit of God will use us in the glorious work which He is carrying on in souls. He will give us the needed skill and ability for each specific case. He will lead us along that path in which He is moving and in which, too, He is displaying the precious mysteries of His new creation.

Nothing can be more wonderful, nothing more intensely interesting, than to mark the progress of the work of God in the soul. A poet has given expression to this when he says

> "This is my joy that ne'er can fail,
> To see my Savior's arm prevail,
> To mark the steps of grace:
> Now new born souls convinced of sin,
> His blood revealed to them within,
> Extol the Lamb in every place."

But in order to discern and appreciate – to say nothing of cooperating in – this most precious and sacred work, there must be the anointed eye, the circumcised heart, the unshod foot, the clean hands. The Spirit of God is very sensitive, very easily grieved, quenched and hindered. He does not like to have a noise made about His work. We have seen the work of the Holy Spirit interrupted altogether by reason of the unhallowed excitement of those who were engaged in it.

It is well to remember this. Unbelief hinders the commencing of the Spirit's work. Undue interference also hinders its progress. The slightest mark of the human finger is apt to soil the mysterious and beautiful work of God. True it is, the Lord will use us if we really look to Him in humility of mind and self-emptiness. Indeed, we constantly find that, in carrying on His work, He allows us to do just as much as we can do, while He Himself, adored be His holy Name, only does what we cannot. This is strikingly illustrated in the scene at the tomb of Lazarus in John 11. There, the Lord commands those around Him to "take away the stone" because it was something they could do. But it is He who cries, "Lazarus, come forth," because this was something which only He could do. Then again He says, "Loose him and let him go," thus allowing them to cooperate so far as they were able.

It strikes us that we have in all this a sample of the Lord's gracious way with His servants. In every little thing in which He can use them He does. But oh! let us be careful not to meddle with His work. Let it be ours to gaze and worship, to mark the marvelous unfoldings of that new creation in which "all things are of God." His work shall endure throughout all generations. All which bears the stamp of His hand shall abide forever. Hence it is our wisdom as well as our blessing, just to mark His hand and follow where He leads.

> Carry on Thy new creation –
> Faithful, holy, may we be,
> Joyful in Thy full salvation,
> More and more conformed to Thee.
> Changed from glory into glory,
> Till in heaven we take our place,
> Then to worship and adore Thee,
> Lost in wonder, love and praise!

Before entering upon the second division of our subject, we feel constrained to put a pointed question or two to the reader. We trust he will bear with us in so doing. We are aware that some persons do not like close, personal dealing. They prefer the simple unfolding of truth and leaving it to do its own work. Well, we also value the unfolding of truth in saving or edifying power to the heart and conscience of the reader or the hearer.

But we believe it to be the absolute duty of the writer or speaker to do his very utmost in the way of appeal, exhortation and pointed enquiry to affect the heart, reach the conscience and enlighten the understanding of his reader or hearer. We must remember we have a double duty to perform. We have to unfold truth and we have to deal with the soul. All preachers, teachers and writers should remember this. If a man occupies himself only with abstract truth, his ministry is apt to prove unpractical and unfruitful. If he occupies himself only with souls, his ministry will prove unfurnished and uninteresting. If he occupies himself duly with both, he will prove "a good minister of Jesus Christ."

Hence, beloved reader, we feel we should be leaving one half of our work undone, did we not from time to time turn from our subject to make an earnest appeal to you; and we would now earnestly entreat of you, as in the immediate presence of Him with whom we have to do, to give your undivided attention to the following question. Be honest with yourself, be earnest, be real, and rest assured that God will bless you.

Have you, dear friend, been led to feel your need? Has the Spirit of God worked in your heart to produce a sense of guilt, a dread of judgment or a consciousness of the utter vanity of all under the sun? Can you say from your very heart, "Woe is me! for I am undone," "Behold, I am vile," "I am a sinful man?" All these are distinct utterances of men like yourself – men of like passions – but of men under the quickening visitation of the Holy Spirit and the convicting action of the truth of God. Be assured of it, they are good words, the fruit of most precious exercises in the soul, such exercises as we delight to see.

It is a grand thing to see the soul thoroughly broken down before God, thoroughly sensible of its lost and ruined condition, of its deep guilt, and of its exposure to the just judgment and wrath of a holy, sin-hating God. It was no mere surface work with Job, Isaiah or Peter when they said the words we have just transcribed. The ploughshare had entered the very depths of the soul. The whole moral being was permeated by the light of divine holiness. The arrow of conviction had pierced to the very center of the heart. It was real work. Not one of those beloved saints of God could have rested in the flippant wordy confession of the fact that "we are *all* sinners." No mere empty generalities would do for them. All was deep, real and personal. They were in the presence of God, and this is always a real and a solemn matter.

Now we would here distinctly state, once for all, that the exercises of the soul have nothing to do with the ground of salvation or peace. We cannot possibly be too simple and clear as to this. Job did not rest in his own words, "Behold, I am vile," but in God's declaration, "I have found a ransom." Isaiah did not build upon a "Woe is me!" but upon "This hath touched thy lips." Peter did not find relief in his own exclamation, "I am a sinful man," but upon those two sweet and soothing words of Jesus, "Fear not."

All this is most true. Far from us be the thought of leading any soul to build upon its exercises, however deep, real and spiritual they may be. No, we must build only and altogether on Christ. "Thus saith the Lord God, Behold, I lay in Zion for a foundation a stone, a tried stone, a precious corner stone, a sure foundation: he that believeth shall not make haste" (Isa. 28:16). This "stone" is not an exercise of any sort. It is not even the work of the Holy Spirit, essential as that is. It is not even the Holy Spirit Himself. It is the One to whom the Holy Spirit ever delights to bear witness, even Christ who is the "tried," the "precious," the "sure foundation" who died for our sins according to the Scriptures, and rose again for our justification, according to the Scriptures.

Still, while we not only fully admit, but earnestly and constantly insist upon all this, we must be allowed to give expression to our deep and ever deepening sense of the value of a profound work of the Spirit of God in the soul. We fear there is an appalling amount of unbroken material to be found in the ranks of Christian profession, a quantity of truth floating about as so much unpractical and uninfluential theory in the region of the intellect, a large amount of mental traffic in unfelt truth, a great deal of what is unreal. We question if, in many cases, the head is not far in advance of the heart – the mind more at work than the conscience. This is the secret of much of the unreality, the hollowness and the inconsistency so grievous to contemplate. We are convinced of this. Hence it is that we so earnestly desire to deal faithfully with the heart and conscience of the reader. He need not be the least afraid to look this weighty matter straight in the face. Let him not be afraid of the knife. Let him beware of mere intellectualism which is bringing about the temporary reign of superstition and infidelity.

We shall now proceed to consider

THE OBJECT UNFOLDED

Inasmuch as pointed reference has already been made to Isaiah and Peter – a prophet of the Old Testament times and an apostle of the New

– we can hardly do better than to look at the mode in which our thesis is illustrated in the history of these two remarkable men. First, let us contemplate the case of Isaiah the prophet. We have seen in his case how the need was created; let us now consider how the object was revealed.

No sooner had the convicted soul given utterance to the cry, "Woe is me! for I am undone," than the angelic messenger was dispatched with all the earnestness and energy of divine love from the very throne of the eternal thrice holy Jehovah. "Then flew one of the seraphims unto me, having a live coal in his hand, which he had taken with the tongs from off the altar: and he laid it upon my mouth and said, Lo, this hath touched thy lips and thine iniquity is taken away, and thy sin purged" (Isa. 6:6-7).

There are two things in the foregoing quotation demanding our attention. First, the substance; secondly, the style of the action recorded. The substance is the thing that was done; the style is the way of doing it. The prophet had been led to see himself in the light which came from the throne of God. This was a serious moment. It could not possibly be otherwise. It is deeply solemn to be brought to the discovery of what we are in the presence of God. When so brought, nothing but divine provision can meet our need, nothing but a divine object can satisfy the heart. Had Isaiah seen only the throne, his condition would have been hopeless. But there was the altar as well, and here lay the secret of life and salvation for him as for every other convicted and self-destroyed sinner. If the throne had its claims, the altar had its provision. The one stood over against the other – two prominent figures in this most sublime vision, two grand realities in the glorious economy of divine grace. The light of the throne revealed the sinner's guilt; the grace of the altar removed it.

Most assuredly, nothing else could have done for Isaiah, nothing else for the reader. It must be this in every case. The measure may vary, but the great fact is always the same. "Woe is me!" and "This hath touched thy lips" must go together. The former is the effect of the throne; the latter, the fruit of the altar. The former is the need created; the latter is the object revealed. Nothing can be more simple, nothing more blessed. It is only the One who creates the need who can unfold the object to meet it; the former He does by the action of truth; the latter by the provision of grace.

"This hath touched thy lips." Mark the words, reader! Note them carefully. See that you understand their force, their meaning and their application to yourself. "This" – what is it? It is the provision – the rich, ample, perfect provision of divine grace. It has wrapped up in its comprehensive folds all a poor guilty, hell-deserving, broken-hearted sinner can need to meet his guilt and ruin. It is not anything from within, but something from without. It is not a process, it is not an exercise, it is not a feeling; it is a divine provision to meet the sinner's deepest need, to remove his guilt, to hush his fears, to save his soul. All was contained in that mysterious "live coal from off the altar."

We may have occasion to return to this scene again in connection with the last point in our subject – the soul's taking hold of the object. We shall here just refer to the *style* of that wonderful action which spoke peace to the troubled soul of Isaiah. There is no one who is not conscious of the immense power of style over the heart. Indeed, we may almost say that the style of an action is more influential than the substance. And is it not most blessed to know that our God has His own unique style? Truly so. Adored forever be His holy Name, He not only meets our need, but He does it in such a way as to let us know without a shadow of a doubt, that "His whole heart and his whole soul" are in the act. He not only pardons our sins, but does it after such a fashion as to convince our souls that it is His own richest joy to do it.

The style of the divine action in Isaiah 6 shines forth in that little word "flew." It is as though God was in haste to apply the divine balm to a wounded spirit. Not a moment was to be lost. That bitter cry, "Woe is me!" coming forth as it did from the very depths of a sinner's broken heart, had gone straight to the ear and heart of God, and with the intense rapidity of a seraph's wing, must a divine response be sent from the sanctuary of God to purge the convicted conscience and tranquilize the troubled heart.

Such is the way of our God. Such is the manner of His love. Such is the style of His grace. He not only saves us, but He does it in such a way as to assure us that it makes Him far happier to save us than it makes us to be saved. The poor legal, doubting, reasoning heart may often be full of fear as to how God will deal with us. In spite of all the precious assurances of His love, all the proofs of His mercy and goodness, all the pledges of His readiness to save and bless, still the heart doubts and hangs back. It still refuses to listen to that voice of love speaking in ten thousand touching and eloquent strains. It still proves its readiness to lend a willing ear to the dark suggestions of the arch enemy – to its own wretched reasonings, to anything and everything but the whispers of divine love. In vain does a Savior God stand before the sinner, beseeching him to come; in vain does He open His very heart to the sinner's view, "showing His thoughts how kind they be"; in vain He points to the sacrifice of His own providing – the Lamb of His free giving, the son of His bosom. Still the heart will harbor its dark and depressing suspicions. It will not give God credit for love so full so free. It will not admit that God delights to save, delights to bless, delights to make us happy.

Oh! beloved reader, are you a doubter? Do you still hang back? Do you still continue to wrong and wound that deep, tender, marvelous love of God that stopped not short of giving His only begotten Son from His bosom and bruising Him on Calvary's cursed tree? Why, oh why, do you hesitate? What are you waiting for? What more do you want? Say not, we beseech you, "I cannot believe; I would if I could, but I cannot. I am waiting for power." Hear these words. "If we receive the testimony of man, the testimony of God is greater." Have you not, many a time, received the testimony, the record, the witness of man? If you were to tell a fellow man that you could not believe him, what would he say to you? Would he not tell you that you were calling him a liar? Will you make *God* a liar? You have done it long enough. Do it no longer, we beseech you, but come now, just as you are, and behold the manner of the love of God – its substance and its style. Come now with all your guilt, all your wretchedness, all your misery, all your need, and you will find in that object which God unfolds in His Word, all you can need for time and eternity. Not only so, but you will receive a welcome as hearty as the God of all grace can give. Do come!

For further illustration of our theme, look to the case of Peter at the Lake of Gennesaret as recorded in the opening paragraph of Luke 5. He, too, like the prophet Isaiah, was made to feel his need – his deep, deep need. The same convicting light which had entered the soul of the prophet, here penetrates the heart of the future apostle and elicits those earnest words, "Depart from me; for I am a sinful man, O Lord."

Here we have the need created, the sense of guilt produced. But mark in passing the strange yet lovely inconsistency! Peter has not the least idea of making his escape from the light which had shone upon him; no, he actually draws nearer and nearer to it. He felt he had no right to be there and yet he would not be anywhere else. And why? Because mingled with that powerful convicting light, there was the equally powerful converting grace which irresistibly drew the heart of the "sinful man" toward it. "Grace and truth came by Jesus Christ." "And we beheld His glory, the glory as of the only begotten of the Father, full of grace and truth" (John 1). What could be more suited to a man full of sin than a Savior full of grace? Surely nothing and no one. Though that blessed Savior was full of truth likewise, and truth puts everything and everyone in the right place, yet the grace was amply sufficient to meet all the need which the truth revealed. Hence, although the poor convicted sinner cries out, "Depart from me, for I am a sinful man, O Lord," he nevertheless feels that the only place for him is "at Jesus' knees."

It is ever thus in cases of true conviction. In every instance in which the genuine work of God's Spirit is worked in the soul, we notice more or less of what we have called this strange yet lovely inconsistency, this seeming contradiction, the striking phenomenon of a sinner confessing his utter unfitness to be in the presence of a holy God and yet having a certain inward consciousness that it is the only place he can be in.

This is very beautiful and touchingly interesting. It is the sure evidence of the work of God in the soul. There is the profound sense of sinfulness and guilt and yet that marvelous and mysterious clinging of the heart to the One whose moral glory has humbled us in the dust. "Depart from me, for I am a sinful man, O Lord." But where were these glowing words said? At the knees of a Savior-God. Blessed place! Did Peter imagine that Jesus was going to depart from him? Did he really think that the gracious One who had deigned to make use of his ship and then given him such a miraculous draught of fish, would leave him in the depth of his misery? We do not and cannot believe it. Ah! no; the Spirit of God, in His most precious operations in the soul, always combines these two elements – the consciousness of utter unworthiness and an earnest clinging to and breathing after Christ. The former is conviction; the latter conversion. By the former, the furrow is made; by the latter, the seed deposited. In short, it is the need created and the object revealed. The two things go together. As in the case of Isaiah, "Woe is me!" is instantly followed by "This hath touched thy lips". So in the case of Peter, "Depart from me" is followed by the gracious words, "Fear not."

This is divine. The object revealed is perfectly adequate to meet the need created. It must be so because the creation of the need and the unfolding of the object are both operations of one and the selfsame Spirit. And not only so, but the object so unfolded is found to be adequate to meet all the claims of God Himself. Therefore it must be adequate to meet all the claims of the convicted and exercised soul. If God is satisfied with the Person and work of Christ, we may well be so likewise. How did Isaiah learn that he was undone? By light from on high. How did he learn that his sin was purged? By grace from on high. He rested upon the testimony of God and not upon his own feelings or notions. If at the close of the beautiful scene recorded in chapter 6, anyone had asked Isaiah, "How do you know your sin is purged?" what would have been his reply? Would he have said, "I *feel* it is so?" We believe not. We are persuaded that this man of God rested upon something far better, far deeper, far more solid than any mere feeling of his own mind. Doubtless he did feel. But why? Just because he did not make feeling the ground of his faith, but faith the ground of his feeling, and divine revelation the ground of his faith.

Such is the divine order, an order so constantly reversed to the serious damage of souls, the subversion of their peace and the dishonor of their Lord. When we turn to Scripture, when we examine the various cases which it records for our learning, we invariably find the order to be, first, the Word; secondly, faith; thirdly, feeling. On the other hand, when we turn to the history of souls today and examine their exercises and experiences, we constantly find they *begin* with their feelings. As a consequence, they rarely enjoy a right sense of the nature and foundation of true Christian faith.

All this is greatly to be deplored. It claims the earnest attention of those who take an interest in souls and are called to watch the progress of the work of God therein. It is of the greatest importance to lead all exercised souls to the sure foundation of Holy Scripture and to teach them that faith is simply taking God at His word. It is believing what He says, not because we feel it, but because He says it. To believe because we feel, would not be faith in God's Word at all, but faith in our own feelings, which is a worthless faith that will not stand for a moment in the presence of the enemy. The Word of God is settled forever in heaven. "He has magnified His Word above all His name." This is the solid foundation of Christian faith.

True, it is by the Holy Spirit that the soul is led to rest on this foundation, but the foundation is Scripture and Scripture alone. It is not feelings or experiences, but the plain testimony of Holy Scripture. "Christ died for our sins according to the Scriptures; He was buried and rose again the third day, according to the Scriptures." Here lies the true foundation of Christian faith, yea, of faith in all ages. Abraham believed God and thus found rest for his soul. So with Isaiah, so with Peter, so with all. Patriarchs, prophets, apostles and saints of every age, every condition and every clime rested upon the stable rock of divine revelation, and if the reader will only do the same, he will possess a peace which no power of earth or hell can ever disturb.

But we must draw this paper to a close, and this we shall do by a very brief reference in the third and last place, to

THE OBJECT LAID HOLD OF

We may be brief on this point as a good deal has already been said which bears upon it. But we would specially call attention to the practical results which are sure to follow in every case in which the soul lays hold of Christ. Our two examples, Isaiah and Peter, will serve us here as well as in the other branches of our subject.

No sooner was Isaiah's need met, his guilt purged, than we see in him a whole-hearted consecration of himself to God and His service which may well stir the very depth of the soul and humble us, too, at the thought of how little we imitate him therein. No sooner does he hear that Jehovah wants a messenger, than the ready response comes forth from his heart and expresses itself in those ardent words, "Here am I; send me." He was ready now to go forth in service to the One who had made him see his own ruin and revealed also the divine remedy. The order is beautiful. We have, first, "Woe is me;" secondly, "This hath touched thy lips"; and thirdly, "Here am I."

So also in Peter's case, we have precisely the same lovely moral order. His "Depart from me" is followed by Christ's "Fear not." And then the practical result follows, "He forsook all and followed Him." This truly was a laying hold of the Object. Peter evidently felt at this moment that Christ was worthy of all he was and all he had. In the early bloom of divine life in his soul, all was readily let go. Secular occupations, however right in themselves; natural ties, however important, are all surrendered for the one absorbing Object which had been revealed to, and laid hold of by his new-born and emancipated soul. Christ was more to Peter than boats and nets, father and mother, sisters and brothers.

He forsook all. Nor was it difficult in the freshness of first love to let go those natural ties and occupations. The difficulty at such a moment would be to retain them or cling to them. Regretfully that we should ever have been called to hear from Peter's lips such words as these, "I go a fishing," and that too after three years of marvelous companionship with that blessed One who had once commanded his whole moral being and drawn him off from all earthly cares and natural relationships.

But we shall not dwell upon this painful and humbling theme. We shall think of Peter at the Lake of Gennesaret; we shall dwell upon the moments of his first love – those charming moments when Peter could, without reserve, say, "Jesus, my all in all Thou art." This is what we all want to look to. We want to understand the real secret, the mighty moral power, the true motive spring of all genuine devotedness and personal consecration. We want to bend our whole attention to the question, "How can I be most effectively drawn off from all those things which so readily and powerfully attract this wandering heart of mine?" What is the answer? Simply this: "Keep the heart fixed on Christ, filled with Christ, dedicated to Christ. Nothing else will do. Rules and regulations will not do, vows and resolutions will not avail. It must be "The expulsive power of a new affection.' "

This is the grand requirement, the special lack of our souls, but the only effective preservative against the ten thousand fascinations and allurements of the scene through which we are passing. The moment we begin to ask, "What harm is there in this or that?" it is all over with personal devotedness. Decline has set in, our hearts have gotten away from Christ. Peter, at the Lake of Gennesaret, never thought of asking "What harm is there in fishing? What sin is there in boats and nets? Why should I not tarry with my father and friends? There was no harm in fishing, nothing sinful in boats and nets, looked at in themselves. But why did Peter give them up? Because he was called to something better. He abandoned the inferior because he had laid hold of the superior. And we may rest assured of this, if Peter returned to the inferior again, it was only because the superior had, for the moment, lost its power over his heart.

Here we must stop. We had no intention of dwelling at such length upon the subject of "The work of God in the soul," but we have found it intensely interesting and we fondly hope it has been profitable to the reader.

"FIVE WORDS"
(1 CORINTHIANS 14:19)

It is often wonderful to mark the way in which the words of Scripture seize upon the heart. They are "as goads and as nails fastened by the masters of assemblies." At times some brief sentence or clause of a sentence will lay hold upon the heart, penetrate the conscience or occupy the mind in such a way as to prove beyond all question the divinity of the book in which it is found. What force of reasoning, what fullness of meaning, what power of application, what an unfolding of the springs of nature, what an unveiling of the heart, what point and pungency, what condensing energy we meet with throughout the sacred pages! One delights to dwell upon these things at all times, but more especially at a moment like the present when the enemy of God and man is seeking in such varied ways to cast a slur upon the inspired volume.

The foregoing train of thought has been suggested to the mind by the expression which forms the title of this article. "I had rather," says the self-emptied and devoted apostle, "speak five words with my understanding, that I might teach others also, than ten thousand words in an unknown tongue." How important for all speakers to remember this! We know that tongues had their value. They were for a sign to the unbelieving. But in the assembly they were useless unless there was an interpreter.

The grand end of speaking in the assembly is edification, and this end can only be reached by persons understanding what is said. It is impossible for a man to edify me if I cannot understand what he says. He must speak in an intelligible language and in an audible voice, else I cannot receive any edification. This surely is plain and worthy of the serious attention of all who speak in public.

Further, we would do well to bear in mind that our only warrant for standing up to speak in the assembly is that the Lord Himself has given us something to say. If it be but "five words," let us say the five and sit down. Nothing can be more unintelligent than for a man to attempt to speak "ten thousand words" when God has only given him "five." It is regretful that something like this should so often occur! What a mercy it would be if we could only keep within our measure! That measure may be small. It matters not; let us be simple, earnest and real. An earnest heart is better than a clever head. A fervent spirit is better than an eloquent tongue. Where there is a genuine, hearty desire to promote the real

291

good of souls, it will prove more effective with me and more acceptable to God than the most brilliant gifts without it. We should covet earnestly the best gifts, but we should also remember the "more excellent way," even the way of love that ever hides itself and seeks only the profit of others. It is not that we value gifts less, but we value love more.

Finally, it would greatly tend to raise the tone of public teaching and preaching to remember the following very simple rule, "Do not set about looking for something to say because you have *got* to speak, but speak because you have got something that ought to be said." This is very simple. It is a poor thing for a man to be merely collecting as much matter as will fill up a certain space of time. This should never be. Let the teacher or preacher attend diligently upon his ministry. Let him cultivate his gift; let him wait on God for guidance, power and blessing; let him live in the spirit of prayer and breathe the atmosphere of Scripture; then will he be always ready for the Master's use. Then his words, whether "five" or "ten thousand," will assuredly glorify Christ and do good to men. But in no case should a man rise to address his fellows without the conviction that God has given him something to say and the desire to say it to edification.

THE BOOK AND THE SOUL

In the formation of the character of a successful minister of the Word of God, two ingredients are essential – an accurate acquaintance with the Bible and a due sense of the value of the soul and of its necessities. The combination of these two qualities is of the utmost importance in the case of every person who is called to minister in the Word and doctrine. To possess only one of them will leave a man a thoroughly one-sided minister. I may be deeply read in Scripture; I may have a profound acquaintance with the contents of the Book and a most exquisite sense of its moral glories, but if I forget the soul and its deep and manifold necessities, my ministry will be lamentably defective. It will lack point, pungency and power. It will not meet the cravings of the heart or tell upon the conscience. It will be ministry from the Book, but not to the soul. True and beautiful, no doubt, but deficient in usefulness and practical power.

On the other hand I may have the soul and its need distinctly before me. I may long to be useful. It may be my heart's desire to minister to the heart and the conscience of my hearer or my reader, but if I am not acquainted with my Bible, if I am not a well-taught scribe, I shall have no material wherewith to be useful. I shall have nothing to give the soul, nothing to reach the heart, nothing to act on the conscience. My ministry will prove barren and tiresome. Instead of teaching souls, I shall tease them. Instead of edifying I shall irritate them. My exhortation, instead of urging souls on along the upward path of discipleship, will, from a lack of basis, have the effect of discouraging them.

These things are worthy of consideration. You may sometimes listen to a person ministering the Word who possesses a great deal of the first of the above-named qualities and very little of the second. It is evident he has the Book and its moral glories before his spiritual vision. He is occupied, yea, engrossed with them – *so engrossed as almost to forget that he has souls before him.* There is not pointed and powerful appeal to the heart, no fervent grappling with the conscience, no practical application of the contents of the Book to the souls of the hearers. It is very beautiful, but not as useful as it might be. The minister is deficient in the second quality. He is more a minister of the Book than a minister to the soul.

Then again you will find some who, in their ministry, seem to be wholly occupied with the soul. They appeal, they exhort, they urge. But from lack of acquaintance and regular occupation with Scripture, souls are absolutely exhausted and worn out under their ministry. True, they ostensibly make the Book the basis of their ministry, but their use of it so unskillful, their handling of it so awkward, their application of it so unintelligent, that their ministry proves as uninteresting as it is unprofitable.

Now, if we were asked which of the two characters of ministry should we prefer, without hesitation we should say the first. If the moral glories of the Book are unfolded, there is *something* to interest and affect the heart, and if one is at all earnest and conscientious, he may get on. Whereas, in the second case, there is nothing but tiresome appeal and scolding exhortation.

But we long to see an accurate acquaintance with the Bible and a due sense of the value of the soul, combined and healthfully adjusted in each one who stands up to minister to souls. The instruction will not do without the persuasion, or the persuasion without the instruction. Hence, let every minister study the Book and its glories and think of the soul and its needs. Let each one remember the link between the Book and the soul.

A LETTER TO A FRIEND ON THE
STUDY OF THE BOOK OF PSALMS

Dear Friend.

You desire a little light on the Book of Psalms and especially to know how they are divided. We can do little more in our brief space than give you a mere hint or two.

In the first place it is important in approaching the study of this most precious book, to remember that in its primary aspect, it is for God's earthly people Israel. This is very clear from Romans 3:18 where the apostle, after quoting from the Psalms, goes on to say, "Now we know that what things soever the law saith, it saith to them who are under the law." This marks the application of the Psalms with great distinctness. It is to those who are under the law. Hence, when you come to study them, you do not find in them the knowledge of full redemption. You do not hear the cry of "Abba." You do not trace the breathings of the spirit of adoption, the spirit of liberty. Sonship and an indwelling Spirit are unknown to souls under the law.

True, you get most precious piety in the Psalms – real confidence in and looking to God, an earnest thirsting after Him. All this we may well cultivate and long after. But you find the soul ofttimes in a state of bondage and fear, dreading the wrath of God and sighing for deliverance. Further, you continually listen to the cry for vengeance upon enemies, the calling upon God to judge them – things in agreement with a legal state and an earthly standing, but wholly unsuited to a people in the enjoyment of grace, knowing redemption and consciously standing in the relationship of children.

Hence, dear friend, it would be a great mistake for a Christian – a child of God, a heavenly man – to go back to the position of soul presented in the Psalms or make the language of those Psalms the measure of his godliness or his experience. No doubt such an one can richly enjoy the Psalms and adopt many of the expressions therein. Indeed, it is only when one knows his true standing in a risen and glorified Christ, as well as the true dispensational place of the Book of Psalms, that he can truly enjoy them. It is not to be supposed that a child of God in a low and legal state, who goes to the Psalms to find in their language the true vehicle in which to convey his own feelings and experience, can have proper enjoyment of them. Far from it. If you really want to understand and enjoy the Psalms, you must approach them in the full light of the New Testament – in the clear understanding that they belong to a state out of which you have been taken by the death and resurrection of Christ. Where do you get anything of life in a risen Christ in the Psalms? Nowhere!

But to aid you a little in seizing the true idea of the dispensational place of this profound and wondrous Book, let us call your attention to the mode in which the Holy Spirit quotes from it in the New Testament. Take the following: "The face of the Lord is against them that do evil, to cut off the remembrance of them from the earth" (Ps. 34:16). Now, part of this verse contains a dispensational truth and part of it contains an eternal truth, above and beyond all dispensations. It is always true that "The face of the Lord is against them that do evil," but it is not always true that He is cutting off the remembrance of them from the earth. Accordingly, when the Spirit in the apostle Peter quotes this verse, He leaves out the last clause (see 1 Peter 3:12). Why is this? Because God is now dealing in grace. He is reconciling sinners instead of cutting them off. Take another instance, though we do not refer to it as a quotation. "Trust in the Lord and do good." Here is an eternal principle. But mark what follows. "So shalt thou dwell in the land, and verily thou shalt be fed." Here you have a dispensational promise, applicable to an earthly people. The Christian is not promised any earthly blessings. Paul trusted in the Lord and did good, but in stead of dwelling in the land, he was beheaded at Rome. And even during his lifetime, he often suffered hunger and nakedness.

But enough. We must leave you to think and study for yourself. We merely add a word as to the division of this most delightful Book. It is divided into five distinct books as follows:

Book I contains Psalms 1-41

Book II contains Psalms 42-72

Book III contains Psalms 73-89

Book IV contains Psalms 90-106

Book V contains Psalms 107-150

Into the distinct principle running through these divisions, we cannot now enter. We merely add that while we have, scattered throughout the whole volume of Psalms, some of the most blessed, beautiful and fervent utterances of praise and thanksgiving to God – expressions of delight in Him and longing after Him which may be adopted by the saint of every age – still we must remember that the Psalms are not the expression of the

Church's worship, though they may well be the subject of the Church's prayerful study and adoring contemplation. God forbid we should pen a single line that might even seem to anyone to be a depreciation of a book which has proved an ever gushing fountain of refreshment to the saints of God in all ages. All we desire is to set before you, dear friend, what we consider to be the true dispensational place of the Psalms.

Many consider the Psalms to be the only vehicle of the Church's worship. The reason they so state is the Psalms are divinely inspired, whereas hymns are merely human compositions and even paraphrases more or less. But this argument will not stand. If we can produce a single expression throughout the entire 150 Psalms which a Christian could not intelligently and truthfully use, it entirely breaks down. Now we know that many of the Psalms contain utterances of the spirit of Christ – utterances given forth when He was making atonement for our sins, when He was enduring the wrath due to us, when He was forsaken of God, when He stood where we, thanks be to God, can never stand. Clearly, such utterances are not suited to us. Therefore the whole argument founded upon divine inspiration falls to the ground.

We believe in the divine inspiration of every line of the Psalms, but that no more proves them to be the suited utterance of the Church of God now, than the divine inspiration of Exodus 20 proves that we are under the law. It is not that the Church cannot adopt some of the expressions in the Psalms. Assuredly she can, but what we maintain is that, as a whole, they are not for the Church's worship, and it would be doing positive violence to dispensational integrity to confine the Church thereto. Only ask yourself this question, What must be the condition of a soul who, in the utterance of its worship, never once says the name of Jesus, never gives forth the cry of "Abba"? Yet neither of these precious words is to be found throughout the entire Book of Psalms.

Many other reasons might be brought out in connection with this deeply interesting subject, but we forbear and rest satisfied with commending what has been said to your prayerful consideration, and you, dear friend, to God's own teaching and blessing.

Affectionately yours,

C.H.M.

SUPERSTITION AND INFIDELITY

It is a common saying that "extremes meet," and certainly its truth is forcibly illustrated in the two things named at the head of this article, Superstition and Infidelity – things which, though so unlike, meet in one point, namely, positive opposition to the plain Word of God. They both alike rob the soul of the authority, preciousness and power of divine revelation. True, they do this by different routes, but they reach the same end. Hence it is that we link them together and lift a warning voice against both. The two elements are working around us in very subtle and dangerous forms, and the human mind is tossed like a ball from one to the other.

Now, it is not our purpose in this brief paper to analyze these two evil influences. We merely call the attention of our readers to the startling fact that wherever they operate, they are found in direct hostility to the truth of God. Superstition admits that there is a divine revelation, but it denies that anyone can understand it except by the interpretation of the clergy or the church. In other words, the Word of God is not sufficient without man's aid. God has spoken, but I cannot hear His voice or understand His Word without human intervention.

This is superstition. Infidelity, on the other hand, boldly denies a divine revelation. It does not believe in such a thing. It maintains that God could not give us a book-revelation of His mind and will. Infidels can write books and can tell us *their* mind and will, but God cannot.

So says infidelity, and in so saying it finds a point of contact in common with superstition. For wherein lies the difference between denying that God has spoken and maintaining that He cannot make us understand what He says? Would there be any appreciable difference between the man who denies that the sun shines and the man who maintains that, though it shines, you need a flashlight to enable you to enjoy its beams? We confess they both seem to us to stand on precisely the same moral ground. The infidelity that boldly and impiously denies that God can speak His mind to man is no worse than the superstition which denies that He can make man understand what He says. Both alike are dishonoring to God and by both alike is man deprived of the priceless treasure of the volume of divine inspiration.

We are extremely anxious that the reader should seize this fact. Indeed our one object in penning these lines is to put him in full possession of it.

We consider that we shall have done him good service if he rises from reading this paper with the clear and firm conviction worked in his soul that infidelity and superstition are the two great agencies by which the devil is seeking to remove from beneath our feet the solid rock of Holy Scripture. It is simply infidelity and superstition versus divine revelation.

And let the reader further note that both infidelity and superstition are alike impious and absurd. It is as impious and absurd to affirm that God could not write a book as to say that He could not make us understand the book that He has written. In either case it is reducing God below the level of the creature, which is simply blasphemy. It is not strange that a man who undertakes to give us a written revelation of his mind should deny that God could do the same? And is it not equally strange that a man should undertake to expound and interpret the Scriptures to his fellow and yet deny that God could do the same? Well, the former is infidelity; the latter, superstition; and both alike exalt the creature and blaspheme the Creator. Both alike shut out God and rob the soul of the unspeakable privilege of direct communion with God by means of His Word.

Thus it has been from the beginning and thus it is now. "There is nothing new under the sun." It has ever been the grand object of the enemy to quench the lamp of inspiration and plunge the soul into the thick darkness of infidelity and atheism. We believe there is an amount of rationalism in the professing Church appalling to contemplate. Divine revelation is being gradually lowered from its lofty position, and human reason exalted, and this is the very germ of infidelity. True, it clothes itself in very attractive robes. It adopts very high-sounding and imposing language. It talks of "freedom of thought" and "liberty of opinion," of "breadth of mind," "progress," "cultivated taste" and "dispassionate investigation." It adopts a most withering style and assumes an attitude of sovereign contempt when speaking of "old prejudices," "old school notions," "narrow-mindedness," "men of one idea," and such like.

But, we may depend upon it, the one aim of the enemy is to set aside the authority of the Word of God and he cares not by what agency he gains his end. This is very serious and we greatly fear that Christians are not fully alive to its seriousness. Whether we look at the religion or the education of the country, we observe a fixed purpose to set aside the Bible – a settled determination, not only to cast it down from its excellency, but to fling it completely into the shade.

Nor is it merely a question of the hostility of open and avowed infidels, which we can understand and account for. But we must confess our inability to understand the half-heartedness and indifference of many who occupy a high position in evangelical circles. The discussion of the great question of "education" has made manifest a most deplorable amount of weakness in quarters where we should least have looked for it. It is being made sadly apparent that the Word of God has a very slender hold of the minds of professing Christians. Only think of a suggestion recently offered, that the Bible might at least get in our schools the place of a Hebrew classic!

Reader, what say you to this? Are you prepared to see the divine Volume – God's inspired Book – degraded into a mere classic and placed alongside of Homer, Horace and Virgil? We fondly trust not. We would trust that every reader would shrink with horror from such a proposal. Nevertheless, we feel called upon to sound a note of alarm in the ears of our dear fellow Christians everywhere, and we entreat them not to disregard it. We want to see them thoroughly roused to a sense of the true state of the case – so aroused that they may be led to cry earnestly to the great Head of the Church that He would be graciously pleased to raise up and send forth men full of the Holy Spirit and of power, full of faith and holy zeal, men permeated by solid belief in the plenary inspiration of Holy Scripture. These, we are persuaded, are the men for the present crisis. May God supply them!

THE GRACE OF GOD
(READ TITUS 2:11-14)

This lovely and familiar passage of Holy Scripture occurs in the midst of a number of exhortations adapted to various classes of people in reference to their conduct and character. Aged men, aged women, young men, young women and servants are to be exhorted as to their proper conduct in their respective conditions.

But lest we should be tempted to place these exhortations upon a legal basis, the inspired apostle breaks forth in one of the most magnificent and comprehensive statements of the gospel which is anywhere to be found in the Sacred Volume. "The grace of God" and that alone, must be the foundation of all Christian conduct and character. Legality in all its forms and workings is most hateful to the Spirit of God. The robe of self-righteousness with which man attempts to cover his sins, is more unsightly in God's view than the very blackest sin that could be committed. Nothing can be accepted of God but that which flows from His own grace in our hearts.

Now in the Scripture before us, the reader will find three distinct points – the salvation which grace brings, the lessons which grace teaches, and the hope which grace presents. First, as to:

THE SALVATION WHICH GRACE BRINGS

This is a grand cardinal point. To be uncertain or obscure as to this, must involve uncertainty and obscurity in everything. "The grace of God that bringeth salvation unto all men hath appeared." (See the marginal reading.) This is clear and conclusive enough. The very first thing that grace does for the lost sinner is to save him unconditionally, perfectly and eternally. It does not ask him to be anything but what he is. It does not ask him to give anything. It brings him salvation on the ground of his being lost. It is only as a lost one that I need salvation, and the more I feel myself to be lost, the more clearly I see my title to that full and free salvation which the grace of God brings. Salvation is intended for the lost. If, therefore, I am lost, salvation applies itself to me, just as distinctly as though I were the only lost sinner in the whole world.

Observe the immense breadth of this word "lost." It takes in all. High and low, rich and poor, learned and unlearned, savage and civilized, moral and immoral, religious and irreligious – all are comprehended under this one title, "lost." It is well to see this clearly. Men make distinctions and necessarily so. Social life has its distinctions. Law and equity maintain their distinctions which must be duly recognized by every well regulated mind. Society awards to the chaste, the sober and the moral a respect which it justly withholds from the wicked, the drunkard and the unprincipled. But once we get into the presence of the grace of God, all these distinctions are swept away and all are looked at on one common ground as *lost*. The most respectable member of society and the vilest outcast are both in the same condition as regards themselves: they are both lost; they both need salvation; and the grace of God brings salvation to the one as well as the other.

Be it well remembered that the poor broken-hearted outcast is nearer to the salvation which grace brings, than is the cold hearted self-sufficient moralist. See Matthew 21:31. If the law of God could bring salvation, then the case would be quite the reverse. But the law never brought salvation to anyone because no one could keep it. But grace brings salvation to all because all need it. It is no longer confined to the Jews. The Sun has risen far above the Jewish horizon and poured His blessed beams over "all the world" so "every creature under heaven" may bask in the light thereof. Such is the wide aspect of "the grace of God" which leaves wholly untouched the grand question of God's eternal counsels and God's moral government. God has His counsels and God displays His mysterious wisdom in government. This must never be forgotten, nor does it interfere with the precious truth that "the grace of God bringeth salvation *unto* all" and "the righteousness of God is unto all." The inspired apostle is speaking of the *wide aspect* of these things, not of their final result – a great and important distinction.

It must be obvious to my reader that the term *"all"* necessarily includes him. It could not possibly be otherwise. If he be not included, then it follows that there is someone for whom the grace of God has not brought salvation, but the Holy Spirit expressly declares that it brings salvation unto all. This must satisfy the most anxious soul as to the question so often raised, "How am I to know that salvation is intended for me?" Is anyone excluded? Is not salvation brought to all? Does not this term comprehend every anxious inquirer? Unquestionably! The declaration of the inspired writer is that "The grace of God, which bringeth salvation unto all men hath appeared." This is as plain as a sunbeam.

Men may reject this salvation. Regretfully, they do reject it, but that can never touch the question of the wide aspect of that grace which shines with undimmed luster in the gospel and brings a full and free salvation *unto* all. Their guilt in rejecting it flows from the fact that it is freely offered. If they could not get it, where would be their guilt in not having it? Where the righteous judgment in punishing men for not receiving what was never intended for them? (2 Thes. 1:6-10). True it is that God is sovereign, but it is equally true that man is responsible. Are we called to reconcile these things? *No, they are reconciled already inasmuch as both are taught in the Word.* All we have to do is believe them.

But let us inquire what is included in the salvation which the grace of God brings? The answer is, Everything. Salvation is a precious box containing all I want for time and eternity. It includes salvation from the future consequence of sin and from its present power. To be a divinely-saved person – a person saved by the grace of God, saved by the blood of Christ as every believer is – involves entire deliverance from wrath, from hell, from Satan, from everything that could possibly be against me. A man whom God has saved is surely safe from all. There is nothing doubtful about God's salvation; it is all settled. There is no delay; it is all finished. We have neither to wait for it nor to add to it, but to receive it now and enjoy it forever. The mighty tide of grace rolls down from the very throne of God and bears upon its bosom a full salvation for me. I receive it as a free gift; I bow my head and worship, and go on my way rejoicing.

We shall now proceed to consider

THE LESSONS WHICH GRACE TEACHES

Grace is a teacher as well as a savior, but it never begins to teach me until it has saved me. It is well to see this. Before ever it asks me to hearken to its pure and holy lessons, it brings me a salvation as free as the air we breathe. It is as a divinely-saved person I enter the precincts of the school of grace. Grace teaches only the saved. All its pupils are saved. Grace as a savior seeks only the lost. Grace as a teacher instructs only the saved. This makes all plain and puts everything in its right place. We must never place unsaved persons in the school of grace. Such have no capacity to learn its holy lessons. There must be a proper material, a proper capacity. This capacity is included in the salvation which grace brings me. I am a debtor to grace both for the lesson which I learn and the capacity to learn it. I owe all to grace. Grace seeks me and finds me in my lost estate; it saves me with an everlasting salvation and introduces me as a saved person to the sphere in which its hallowed instructions are imparted. Grace does not teach those who are dead; it quickens them. It does not teach those who are guilty; it cleanses them. It does not teach those who

303

are condemned; it justifies them. It is as quickened, cleansed and justified that I become the pupil of grace. The very first thing that grace does for the lost sinner is to bring him salvation, and when he receives this salvation it teaches him to "deny ungodliness and worldly lusts, and to live soberly, righteously and godly in this present world."

I desire that my reader be clear as to this. If he be as yet in an unsaved state, let him understand that the grace of God brings him salvation as a present thing. Moreover, until he has accepted this free gift, he is wholly unable to understand or take in the lessons which grace teaches. If grace is to be his teacher, he must be saved to be a pupil. This simple fact gives the death-blow to all legality, to all human righteousness, to all man's pretensions. If none can comprehend the lessons which grace teaches except those who have accepted the salvation which grace brings, then, assuredly, our language must ever be, "Not unto us, O Lord, not unto us, but unto Thy name give glory."

Let us look particularly at the lessons which grace teaches. It teaches us to deny everything unlike God and all desire after this present world. It teaches us how we are to live. The law could never do this. Law tells us how we *ought* to live, but it does not teach us. It neither gives us the lesson to learn nor the capacity to learn it. It does not bring us salvation. The law could never have any saved pupils because it does not save the lost, but condemns them for being lost. No doubt men ought to keep the law, and if they were right they would, but they are not right. Quite the opposite, they are wrong, totally, irremediably wrong, hopelessly lost, and in this condition grace brings them salvation. Christ the Savior is our Teacher, not Moses the lawgiver. May we learn His lessons! May we sit at His feet in all quietness and drink in His hallowed instructions!

These instructions arrange themselves under three distinct heads as suggested by the words "soberly, righteously and godly."

Soberly refers to the inner circle of one's own heart. It simply means *with inward self-government* – a most comprehensive expression. The grace that saves me teaches me to exercise a holy government over self. I am to govern my thoughts, govern my tongue, govern my temper – govern them, not in order to be saved, but because I am saved. The One who teaches me to exercise this government has saved me before ever He commenced His course of instruction. It is as a saved person that I submit my whole moral being to the wholesome control of my heavenly Teacher. The law could not teach me to govern my nature. It condemns me, root and branch, throws me overboard and leaves me there. Grace follows me, saves me and endows me with a new nature, and seals me with the Holy Spirit so I can exercise myself in self-government.

And be it observed that this self-government is totally different from anything that human philosophy or the energy of an untamed will could ever produce. These things might enable me to subdue some of the accessories of "self" while the parent stem was left wholly untouched. But "the grace of God that bringeth salvation" gives me victory over self in all the length and breadth of that comprehensive term. Full victory over all the evil that dwells in me is as much a part of "salvation" as deliverance from hell. Regretfully, we fail to make use of this victory. Through spiritual indifference and unbelief we fail to possess ourselves practically of that full salvation which grace has brought us, but that in no wise alters the truth of the matter. If I am a saved man I should live as a saved man in every respect. And how is this to be done? By faith. "The just shall live by faith" (Hab. 2:4; Gal. 3:11; Heb. 10:38). I can only exercise inward self-government by faith.

The second grand lesson which grace teaches me as to my practical life is to live "*righteously.*" This contemplates me not merely in the inner circle of my own moral being, but in the midst of the circumstances and relationships of the scene around me – that outward world in which I am called to live and move from day to day. My divine Teacher not only instructs me as to the government of myself, but also as to the government of all my transactions with my fellow man. Here, too, I am to remember that my teacher is the grace that saved me. I must never forget this. If the resources of philosophy or the energy of a strong will might enable me to exercise a kind of inward self-government, so also the principles of a lofty morality or that pride which rejects a wrong action, might lead me to seek the maintenance of an unblemished reputation in all my transactions with my fellow men. But all this leaves me unsaved. Philosophy cannot save me and therefore it cannot teach me. Morality cannot save me and therefore it cannot teach me.

It is "the grace of God" that alone can save me, and it is that same grace which alone can teach me. Hence, if I see a person who professes to be saved, giving way to bad temper, indulging in passion or enslaved by a habit, I infer that that person has not learned practically the first great lesson of his divine Teacher. And if I see a person who professes to be saved, yet not guiding his affairs with discretion, but getting into debt and indulging in extravagance, I infer that he has not learned the second great lesson of his divine Teacher. Let us not be deceived with vain words. If the legalist is silenced by the *freeness* of the salvation which grace brings, the antinomian* is silenced by the *purity* of the lessons which grace teaches. "These things are good and profitable unto men." The gospel meets everything. It meets the lost sinner with a full salvation and it meets the saved sinner with the purest and most perfect lessons – lessons of holy self-government and practical righteousness.

But there is a third lesson which grace teaches its saved pupils. It teaches them to live "*godly*." This opens up our relations with the world above. There is great force, beauty and completeness in these words used by the inspired apostle. They present to us three great circles in which we are called to act: the world within, the world without and the world above. They must be all taken together to see their divine beauty. There is really nothing left out. All we can possibly want to learn is taught in the school of grace if we will only accept the lessons. Let us bear in mind that the surest proof of our having received the salvation which grace brings, is our learning the lessons which grace teaches – those hallowed lessons of inward self-government, practical righteousness and true godliness. May God the Holy Spirit make us to understand the fullness and freeness of the salvation, and the purity and elevation of the lessons so we may more distinctly apprehend, in the third and last place,

THE HOPE WHICH GRACE PRESENTS

The apostle speaks of it as "a blessed hope," and surely nothing can be more blessed than "The appearing of the glory of the great God and our Savior Jesus Christ." This is the proper hope of the believer. And he is taught to look for it by the selfsame grace that has brought him salvation and that teaches him how to carry himself in reference to the world within, the world without and the world above. "The Lord will give grace and glory, and no good thing will He withhold from them that walk uprightly" (Ps. 84).

Now there are three things in reference to this "blessed hope" which I desire that my reader clearly understand – title, capacity and moral condition. Our *title* is furnished by the blood of the cross; the *capacity* is furnished by the Holy Spirit; and the *moral condition* is founded upon our learning and exhibiting the holy lessons taught in the school of grace.

---

* One who holds that under the gospel dispensation, the moral law is no obligation because faith alone is necessary for salvation; one who rejects an established morality (Webster).

Reader, permit me to ask you if, when the subject of Christ's *appearing* is introduced, you ever feel a sort of difficulty or reserve in your mind? Would you be afraid to see Jesus? Would you rather put off the moment of His coming? Do you feel yourself not quite ready? If so, it may be you are not yet able to "read your title clear" or you are not cultivating a spiritual capacity, or your moral condition is not such as would naturally introduce you to that scene of glory for which we are privileged daily to look. These are points of immense importance – points to which my reader should give deep and prayerful attention. If there be cloudiness as to my title; if I am doubtful as to the salvation which grace brings, or if I am backward in learning the lessons which grace teaches; if there is defectiveness in spiritual capacity or if my general moral tone and character is not formed by the holy lessons of grace, I shall not be in an attitude of waiting for the glory before us. It is well to see this in all its clearness, point and power. If we are the recipients of grace and the expectants of glory, should not our lives exhibit the moral power of these things? Should they not have their proper effect in the formation of our character? Unquestionably. "He that hath this hope in him purifieth himself even as he is pure." If I expect to be with Jesus and like Jesus by and by, I shall seek to be as much with Him and as much like Him as possible.

May the Lord work in us that which is well pleasing in His sight and bring out in all our ways a more faithful exhibition of the divine life! The language with which our Scripture closes is eminently calculated to awaken in our souls the most intense desire after these things. Indeed, I cannot conclude this paper without quoting this noble passage at full length, praying the Holy Spirit to apply it in much power to the heart and conscience of both the writer and the reader.

"For the grace of God that bringeth salvation unto all men hath appeared, teaching us that, denying ungodliness and worldly lusts, we should live soberly, righteously, and godly in this present world; looking for that blessed hope and the glorious appearing of the great God and our Savior Jesus Christ; who gave Himself for us [what a price! what objects!] that He might redeem us from all iniquity and purify unto Himself a people of possession, zealous of good works."

> *"The day of glory bearing*
> *Its brightness far and near,*
> *The day of Christ's appearing*
> *We now no longer fear.*

He once a spotless victim
For us on Calv'ry bled;
Jehovah did afflict Him,
And bruised Him in our stead.

To Him by grace united,
We joy in Him alone;
And now by faith delighted,
Behold Him on the throne.

Then let Him come in glory,
Who comes His saints to raise,
To perfect all the story
Of wonder, love and praise."

CHRISTIAN LIFE: WHAT IS IT?

The question which we propose to consider in the following pages is one of the most interesting and important that could possibly engage our attention. It is this: What is the life which, as Christians, we possess? What is its source? What are its characteristics? What is its issue? These great questions have only to be named to secure the attention of every thoughtful reader.

The divine Word speaks of two distinct heads of sources. It speaks of a first man and it speaks of a second. In the opening of the book of Genesis we read these words, "And God said, Let Us make man in Our image, after Our likeness ... So God created man in His own image, in the image of God created He him; male and female created He them" (Gen. 1:26-27). This statement is repeated in Genesis 5: "In the day that God created man, in the likeness of God made He him." After this, we read, "And Adam lived an hundred and thirty years and begat a son in his own likeness, after *his* image."

But between Adam's creation in the image of God and the birth of a son in his own image, a great change took place. Sin entered. Innocence fled. Adam had become a fallen, ruined, outcast man. This fact must be seized and pondered by the reader. It is a weighty, influential fact. It lets us into the secret of the source of that life which, as sons of Adam, we possess. That source was a guilty, ruined, outcast head. It was not in innocence that Adam became the head of a race. It was not within the bounds of Paradise that Cain was brought forth, but outside in a ruined and cursed world. It was not in the image of God that Cain was begotten, but in the image of a fallen father.

We fully believe that, personally, Adam was the subject of divine grace and that he was saved by faith in the promised Seed of the woman. But looking at him *federally*, that is, as the head of a race, he was a fallen, ruined, outcast man, and everyone of his posterity is born into the same condition. As is the head, so are the members – all the members together, each member in particular. The son bears the image of his fallen father and inherits his nature. "That which is born of the flesh is flesh," and do what you will with "flesh" – educate, cultivate, sublimate it as you will, it will never yield "spirit." You may improve flesh according to human thinking, but improved "flesh" is not "spirit." The two things are totally opposite. The former expresses all we are as born into this world, as sprung from the first Adam. The latter expresses what we are as born again, as united to the Second Adam.

We frequently hear the expression, "Raising the masses." What does it mean? There are three questions which we should like to ask those who propose to elevate the masses. First, What is it you are going to elevate? Secondly, How are you going to elevate them? Thirdly, Where are you going to elevate them to? It is impossible for water to ever rise above its level. So it is impossible that you can ever raise the sons of fallen Adam above the level of their fallen father. Do what you will with them, you cannot possibly elevate them higher than their ruined outcast head. Man cannot grow out of the nature in which he was born. He can grow *in* it, but not out of it. Trace the river of fallen humanity up to its source and you find that source to be a fallen, ruined, outcast man.

This simple truth strikes at the root of all human pride – all pride of birth, all pride of ancestry. We are all, as men, sprung from one common stock, one head, one source. We are all begotten in one image and that is a ruined man. The head of the race and the race of which he is head, are all involved in one common ruin. Looked at from a legal or social standpoint, there may be differences, but looked at from a *divine* standpoint, there is none. If you want a true idea of the condition of each member of the human race, you must look at the condition of the head. You must go back to Genesis 3 and read these words, "He drove out the man." Here is the root of the whole matter. Here is the source of the river the streams whereof have made sad the millions of Adam's posterity for nearly 6000 thousand years. Sin has entered and snapped the link, defaced the image of God, corrupted the sources of life, brought in death and given Satan the power of death.

Thus it stands in reference to Adam's race – to the race as a whole and to each member of that race in particular. All are involved in guilt and ruin. All are exposed to death and judgment. There is no exception. "By one man sin entered into the world, and death by sin; and so death passed upon all men, for that all have sinned (Rom. 3:12). "In Adam all die" (1 Cor. 15:22). Here are the two sad and solemn realities linked together – "Sin and death."

But, thanks to God, a Second Man has entered the scene. This great fact, while it sets forth the marvelous grace of God towards the first man and his posterity, proves in the clearest and most unanswerable manner that the first man has been completely set aside. If the first had been found faultless, then should no place have been sought for the Second. If there had been a single ray of hope as to the first Adam, there would have been no need for the Second.

But God sent His Son into this world. He was "the Seed of the woman." Let this fact be seized and pondered. Jesus Christ did not come under the federal headship of Adam. He was *legally* descended from David and Abraham, as we read in Matthew. "He was of the seed of David according to the flesh" (2 Tim. 2:8). Moreover, His genealogy is traced to Adam by the inspired penman in Luke's gospel. But here is the angelic announcement as the mystery of His conception: "And the angel answered and said unto Mary, The Holy Spirit shall come upon thee, and the power of the Highest shall overshadow thee; therefore that holy thing which shall be born of thee shall be called the Son of God" (Luke 1:35).

Here we have a real Man, but One without a single taint of sin or a single seed of mortality. He was made of the woman, of the substance of the virgin, a Man in every particular, just as we are, but wholly without sin and entirely free from any association which could have given sin or death a claim upon Him. Had our blessed Lord come as to His human nature, under the headship of Adam, He could not have been called the Second Man since He would have been a member of the first, like any other man. Further, He would have been subject to death in His own person, which is blasphemy to assert or suppose.

But, adored forever be His peerless name, He was the pure, holy, spotless One of God. He was unique. He stood alone – the only pure untainted grain of human seed that earth had ever seen. He came into this world of sin and death, Himself sinless and lifegiving. In Him was life and nowhere else. All beside was death and darkness. There was not a single pulse of spiritual life, not one ray of divine light apart from Him. The entire race of the first man was involved in sin, under the power of death, and exposed to eternal judgment. He could say, "I am the light of the world." Apart from Him, all was moral darkness and spiritual death. "In Adam all die; in Christ shall all be made alive." Let us see how.

No sooner did the Second Man appear upon the scene than Satan appeared to dispute every inch of ground with Him. It was a grand reality. The Man Christ Jesus had undertaken the mighty work of glorifying God on this earth, of destroying the works of the devil and of redeeming His people. Stupendous work – work which none but the God-man could accomplish. But it was a real thing. *Jesus had to meet all the craft and power of Satan.* He had to meet him as the serpent and meet him as the lion. Hence, at the very opening of His blessed career, as the baptized and anointed Man, He stood in the wilderness to be tempted of the devil. See Matthew 4 and Luke 4. And note the contrast between the first man and the Second. The first man stood in the midst of a garden of delights, with everything that could possible plead for God against the tempter. The Second Man, on the contrary, stood in the midst of a wilderness of privations with everything, apparently, to plead against God and for the tempter. Satan tried with the Second Man precisely the same weapons which he had found so effective with the first – "the lust of the flesh, the lust of the eye, and the pride of life." Compare Genesis 3:6; Matthew 4:1-19; Luke 4:1-12; and 1 John 2:16.

But the Second Man vanquished the tempter with one simple weapon, the written Word. "*It is written*" was the one unvarying reply of the dependent and obedient Man. No reasoning, no questioning, no looking this way or that way. The Word of the living God was the commanding authority for the perfect Man. Blessed forever be His name! The homage of the universe be His throughout everlasting ages! Amen and amen.

Now we hasten on to unfold our special theme. We want the reader to see in the light of Holy Scripture how the Second Adam imparts life to His members.

By the victory in the wilderness, the strong man was "bound," not "destroyed." Hence, we find that, at the close, he is allowed once more to try his hand. Having "departed for a season," he returned again in another character, as the one who had the power of death by which to terrify the soul of man. Tremendous thought! This power was brought to bear in all its terrible intensity on the spirit of Christ in the garden of Gethsemane. We cannot possibly contemplate the scene in that garden and not feel that the spirit of our blessed Lord was passing through something which He had never experienced before. It is evident that Satan was permitted to come before Him in a very special manner and to put forth special power in order, if possible, to deter Him. Thus He says in John 16:30, "The prince of this world cometh, and hath nothing in Me." So also in Luke 22:53, we find Him saying to the chief priests and captains of the temple, "Be ye come out as against a thief with swords and staves? When I was daily with you in the temple, ye stretched forth no hands against Me, but this is your hour *and the power of darkness.*"

Evidently the period from the last supper to the cross was marked by features quite distinct from every previous stage of the marvelous history of our Lord. "This is your hour." And further, "The power of darkness." The prince of this world came against the Second Man, armed with all the power with which the first man's sin had invested him. He brought to bear upon the Lord's spirit all the power and all the terrors of death as the just judgment of God. Jesus met all this in its utmost force and in all its awful intensity. Hence, we hear such words as these, "My soul is exceeding sorrowful, even unto death." And again we read that, "Being in an agony He prayed more earnestly; and His sweat was as it were great drops of blood falling down to the ground."

In a word, then, the One who undertook to redeem His people, to give eternal life to His members, to accomplish the will and counsels of God, had to meet all the consequences of man's condition. There was no escaping them. He passed through them all, but He passed through them alone, for who but Himself could have done it? He, the true Ark, had to go over alone into the dark and dreadful river of death to make a way for His people to pass over on dry land. He was alone in the horrible pit and the miry clay, that we might be with Him on the rock. He earned the new song alone, that He might sing it in the midst of the Church.

But not only did our Lord meet all the power of Satan as the prince of this world, all the power of death as the just judgment of God, all the violence and bitter enmity of fallen man, there was something far beyond all this. When man and Satan, earth and hell, had done their very utmost, there remained a region of darkness and impenetrable gloom to be traversed by the spirit of the Blessed One, into which it is impossible for human thought to enter. We can only stand upon the confines and with our heads bowed in the deep hush of unutterable worship, hearken to the loud and bitter cry which issues from there, accompanied by those words, *"My God, My God, why hast Thou forsaken Me?"* – words which eternity itself will be insufficient to unfold.

Here we must pause and ascribe once more, eternal and universal praise, homage and adoration to the One who went through all this to procure life for us. May our hearts adore Him! May our lips praise Him! May our lives glorify Him! He alone is worthy. May His love constrain us to live not unto ourselves, but unto Him who died for us and rose again, and gave us life in resurrection.

It is not possible to over-estimate the interest and value of the great truth that the source of the life which we Christians possess is a risen and victorious Christ. It is as risen from the dead that the Second Man becomes the head of a race – Head of His body the Church. The life which the believer now possesses is a life which has been tested and tried in every possible way. Consequently, it can never come into judgment. It is a life which has passed through death and judgment. Therefore it can never die, never come into judgment. Christ our living Head has abolished death and brought life and incorruptibility to light through the gospel. He met death in all its reality that we might never meet it. He died that we might never die. He has so worked for us in His marvelous love and grace as to render death part of our property. See 1 Corinthians 3:22.

In the old creation, man belongs to death. Hence it has been truly said that the very moment man begins to live he begins to die. Solemn fact! Man cannot escape death. "It is appointed unto men once to die, and after this the judgment." There is not so much as a single thing which man possesses in the old creation that will not be wrenched from his grasp by the ruthless hand of death. Death takes everything from him, reduces his body to dust and sends his soul to judgment. Houses, lands, wealth and distinction, fame and influence, all go when the last grim foe approaches. The wealth of the universe, were it in a man's possession, could not purchase one moment's respite. Death strips man of all and bears him away to judgment. The king and the beggar, the peer and the peasant, the learned philosopher and the ignorant clown, the civilized and the savage, are all alike. Death seizes upon all within the limits of the old creation. The grave is the end of man's earthly history, and beyond that the throne of judgment and the Lake of Fire.

But in the new creation, death belongs to man. There is not so much as a single thing that the Christian possesses which he does not owe to death. He has life, pardon, righteousness, peace, acceptance, glory, all through death – the death of Christ. The entire aspect of death is changed. Satan can no longer bring it to bear upon the soul of the believer as the judgment of God against sin, although God can and does use it in His governmental dealings with His people in the way of discipline and chastening. See Acts 4; 1 Corinthians 11:30; and 1 John 5:16.

But as the one who had the power of death, Satan has been destroyed. Our Lord Christ has wrested his power from him and He now holds in His omnipotent hand the keys of death and the grave. Death has lost its sting, the grave its victory. Therefore, if death does come to the believer, it comes not as a master but as a servant. It comes, not like a policeman to drag the soul to its eternal prison house, but as a friendly hand to open the door of the cage and let the spirit fly to its native home in the skies.

All this makes a great difference. It tends, among other things, to take away the fear of death, which was perfectly consistent with the state of believers under the law, but is wholly incompatible with the standing and privileges of those who are united to Him who is alive from the dead. Nor is this all. The entire life and character of the Christian must take its tone from the source from where that life emanates. "If ye then be *risen with Christ*, seek those things which are above, where Christ sitteth on the right hand of God. Set your affection on things above, not on things on the earth. For ye are dead, and your life is hid with Christ in God. When Christ our life shall appear, then shall ye also appear with Him in glory" (Col. 3:1-4). Water always finds its own level. Likewise the life of the Christian, strengthened and guided by the Holy Spirit, always springs up toward its source.

Let no one imagine that all this for which we are contending is a mere question of human opinion or an unimportant point, an uninfluential notion. Far from it. It is a great practical truth constantly set forth and insisted upon by the apostle Paul – a truth which he preached as an evangelist, taught and unfolded as a teacher, and watched its effects as a faithful vigilant pastor. So prominent was the place which the great truth of resurrection held in the apostle's preaching, that it was said of him by some of the Athenian philosophers, "He seemeth to be a setter forth of strange gods because he preached unto them *Jesus and the resurrection*" (Acts 17:18).

Let the reader note this. *"Jesus and the resurrection."* Why was it not Jesus and the incarnation or Jesus and the crucifixion? Was it because these profound and priceless mysteries held no place in apostolic preaching and teaching? Read 1 Timothy 3:16 for the answer. "And without controversy, great is the mystery of godliness: God was manifest in the flesh, justified in the Spirit, seen of angels, preached unto the Gentiles, believed on in the world, received up into glory." Read also Galatians 4:4-5: "But when the fullness of the time was come, God sent forth His Son, made of a woman, made under the law, to redeem them that were under the law."

These passages settle the question as to the foundation doctrines of incarnation and crucifixion. But Paul preached and taught and jealousy insisted upon *resurrection*. He himself was converted to a risen and glorified Christ. The very first glimpse he caught of Jesus of Nazareth was as a risen Man in glory. It was only thus he knew Him, as he tells us in 2 Corinthians 5. "Wherefore henceforth know we no man after the flesh: yea, though we have known Christ after the flesh, yet now henceforth know we Him no more." Paul preached a resurrection gospel. He labored to present every man perfect in a risen, glorified Christ. He did not confine himself to the mere question of forgiveness of sin and salvation from hell, precious beyond all price as are these fruits of the atoning death of Christ. He aimed at the glorious end of planting the soul *in* Christ and of keeping it there. "As ye have therefore received Christ Jesus the Lord, so walk ye in Him, rooted and built up in Him and established in the faith, as ye have been taught, abounding therein with thanksgiving." "Ye are complete in Him." "Buried with Him in baptism, wherein also ye are risen with Him." "Quickened together with Him" (Col. 2).

Such was Paul's preaching and teaching. This was his gospel. This is true Christianity in contrast with all the forms of human religiousness and fleshy pietism under the sun. Life in a risen Christ was Paul's grand theme. It was not merely forgiveness and salvation by Christ, but *union with Him.* Paul's gospel planted the soul at once in a risen and glorified Christ, redemption and forgiveness of sins being the obvious and necessary consequence. This was the glorious gospel of the blessed God which was committed to Paul's trust (1 Tim. 1:2).

Most gladly would we dwell at greater length on the blessed theme of the source of Christian life, but we must hasten on to the remaining points of our subject. We shall therefore very briefly call the reader's attention to the characteristics or moral features of the life which as Christians we possess. To do anything like justice to this point we should seek to unfold the precious mystery of the life of Christ as a Man on this earth, to trace His ways, to mark the style and spirit with which He passed through all the scenes and circumstances of His course here below.

We should view Him as a Child subject to His parents, growing up beneath the eye of God, increasing from day to day in wisdom and stature, exhibiting all that was lovely in the sight of God and man. We should trace His path as a Servant, faithful in all things – a path marked by incessant labor and toil. We should ponder Him as the lowly, humble and obedient Man, subject and dependent in all things, emptying Himself and making Himself of no reputation, surrendering Himself perfectly for the glory of God and the good of man, never seeking His own interest in anything. We should mark Him as the gracious, loving, sympathizing friend and companion, ever ready with the cup of consolation for every child of sorrow, ever at hand to dry the widow's tear, to hear the cry of the distressed, to feed the hungry, to cleanse the leper, to heal all manner of disease. In a word, we should point out the countless rays of moral glory that shine forth in the precious and perfect life of Him who went about doing good.

But who is sufficient for these things? We can merely say to the Christian reader, Go study your great Exemplar. Gaze upon your Model. If a risen Christ is the source of your life, the Christ who lived down here in this world is your pattern. The features of your life are those selfsame features that shone in Him as a Man here below. Through death, He has made His life to be your life, the Christ who lived down here in this world is your pattern. He has linked you with Himself by a bond that can never be severed. And now you are privileged to go back and study the gospel narratives to see how He walked, that you may, through the grace of the Holy Spirit, walk even as He walked.

It is a very blessed though a very solemn truth that there is nothing of any value in God's thoughts except the outflow of the life of Christ from His members here. All that is not the direct fruit of that life is utterly valueless in God's thoughts. The activities of the old nature are not merely worthless but sinful. There are certain natural relationships in which we stand, which are sanctioned by God and in which Christ is our model. For example, "Husbands, love your wives as Christ loved the Church." We are recognized as parents and children, masters and servants, and instructed as to our deportment in these holy relationships, but all this is on the new ground of risen life in Christ. See Colossians 3 and Ephesians 5:6.

The old man is not recognized at all. It is viewed as crucified, dead and buried, and we are called upon to reckon it as dead and to count as dead our members which are on the earth, and to walk even as Christ walked. We are to live a life of self-surrender, to manifest the life of Christ, to reproduce Him. This is practical Christianity. May we understand it better! May we remember that nothing is of the smallest value in God's account except the life of Christ shown out in the believer from day to day by the power of the Holy Spirit. The feeblest expression of this life is a sweet odor to God. The mightiest efforts of mere religious flesh – the costliest sacrifices, the most imposing ordinances and ceremonies – are but "dead works" in the sight of God. Religiousness is one thing; Christianity is quite another.

And now one word as to the issue of the life which as Christians we possess. We may truly say "one word" and what is that? *Glory.* This is the only issue of Christian life. "When Christ our life shall appear, then shall ye also appear with him *in glory.*" Jesus is waiting for the moment of His manifestation in glory, and we wait in and with Him. He is seated and expecting likewise. "As He is so are we in this world" (1 John 4:17). Death and judgment are behind us, nothing but glory before. If we may so express it, our yesterday is the cross; our today is a risen Christ; our tomorrow, glory. Thus it stands with all true believers. It is with them as with their living and exalted Head. As is the Head so are the members. They cannot be separated for a single moment for any object whatsoever. They are inseparably joined together in the power of a union that no influence of earth or hell can ever dissolve. The Head and the members are eternally one. The Head has passed through death and judgment; so have the members. The Head is seated in the presence of God, so are the members – co-quickened, co-raised and co-seated with the Head in glory.

Reader, this is Christian life. Think of it. Think deeply. Look at it in the light of the New Testament. Its source, a risen Christ. Its characteristics, the very features of the life of Christ as seen in this world. Its issue, cloudless and eternal glory. Contrast with this the life which we possess as sons and daughters of Adam. Its source, a ruined, fallen, outcast man. Its characteristics, the ten thousand forms of selfishness in which fallen humanity clothes itself. Its issue, the Lake of Fire. This is the simple truth of the matter if we are to be guided by Scripture.

Let us just say in conclusion, in reference to the life which Christians possess, that there is no such thing as "a higher Christian life." It may be that persons who use this form of speech mean a right thing, but the form is incorrect. There is but the one life and that is Christ. No doubt there are varied measures in the *enjoyment and exhibition* of this life, but however the measure may vary, the life is one. There may be higher or lower stages in this life, but the life is one. The most advanced saint on earth and the feeblest babe possess the same life, for Christ is the life of each, the life of both, the life of all.

All this is most blessedly simple and we desire that the reader should carefully ponder it. We are fully persuaded that there is an urgent need for the clear unfolding and faithful proclamation of this resurrection gospel. Many stop at incarnation; others go on to the crucifixion. We want a gospel that gives all – incarnation, crucifixion and resurrection. This is the gospel which possesses the true moral power, the mighty leverage to lift the soul out of all earthly association and set it free to walk with God in the power of risen life in Christ. May this gospel be sent forth far and wide in living energy throughout the length and breadth of the professing Church. There are thousands of God's people who need to know it. They are afflicted with doubts and questions which would all be removed by the simple reception of the blessed truth of life in a risen Christ. There are no doubts or fears in Christianity. Christians sometimes have them, but such doubts and fears do not belong to Christianity at all. May the bright light of Paul's gospel stream in upon all the saints of God and disperse the fogs and mists which surround them, so they may really enter into that holy liberty wherewith Christ makes His people free!

DEVOTEDNESS: WHAT IS IT?
(READ GENESIS 22:1-12)

It has often been said, "There are two sides to every question." This saying is true and very important. It demands special attention in approaching the subject which stands at the head of this paper. The history of the professing Church affords many proofs of the fact that serious mischief has been done by devoted men who were not guided by sound principle. Indeed it will ever be found that, in proportion to the degree of the devotedness, will be the gravity of the mischief where the judgment is not wisely directed. We must confess we long for more true devotedness in ourselves and others. It does seem to us the special need today. There is abundance of profession, even of a very high character. Knowledge is greatly increased among us and we are thankful for knowledge, but knowledge is not energy and profession is not devotedness. It is not that we desire to set the one against the other; we want to combine the two. "God hath not given us the spirit of fear, but of power and of love, and of a sound mind."

Mark this lovely union, this exquisite entwining of a threefold cord – "Power, love and a sound mind." Were it *power* alone, it might lead one to carry himself with a high hand and to push aside or crush any who could not come up to one's own mark – to cherish and manifest a spirit of haughty independence, to be intolerant of any difference of thought or feeling. On the other hand, were it a spirit of *love* only, it might induce an easygoing temper, a total indifference to the claims of truth and holiness – a readiness to tolerate error for the sake of peace. But there is both love and power, the one to balance the other. Moreover, there is the *sound mind* to adjust the two and give to each its proper range and its just application. Such is the adjusting power of Holy Scripture for which we cannot be too thankful.

We are so apt to be one-sided – to run to wild extremes, to run one principle to seed while another, though equally important, is not even allowed to take root. One will be all for what he calls power, another for what he calls love. Again, one will extol energy; another will only speak of the value of principle. We want both, and our God most graciously supplies both. A man who is all for principle may do nothing through fear of doing wrong. A man who is all for power may do mischief through fear of doing nothing. But the man who is enabled by grace to combine the two, will do the right thing at the right time and in the right way. This is

319

what we want. And to meet in some feeble way this want is one special object of this paper to which may God most graciously attach the seal of His blessing.

In handling our theme it may help us in the way of clearness and precision to first consider the ground; secondly, the spirit; and thirdly, the object.

THE GROUND OF TRUE DEVOTEDNESS

If we answer this question from the ample materials furnished by the history of Abraham, we must say it is simple faith in the living God. This must be the solid ground of true, earnest, steady devotedness. If there is not the link of personal faith in God, we shall be driven here and there by every breath of human opinion and tossed about by every ripple of the tide of circumstances. If we are not conscious of this living link between our souls and God, we shall never be able to stand at all, much less to make any headway in the path of real devotedness. "Without faith it is impossible to please God: for he that cometh to God must believe that He is, and that He is a rewarder of them that diligently seek Him" (Heb. 11:6).

Here lies the secret. We must believe *that* He is and *what* He is. We must have to do with God in the secret of our own souls, apart from and independent of all beside. Our individual connection with God must be a grand reality, a living fact, a real and unmistakable experience, lying at the very root of our existence and forming the stay and prop of our souls at all times and under all circumstances. Mere opinions will not do; dogmas and creeds will not avail. It will not be sufficient to say, "I believe in God the Father Almighty." Neither this nor any other form of mere words will do. It must be a heart question, a matter between the soul and God Himself. Nothing short of this can sustain the soul at any time, but more particularly in a day like the present in which we find ourselves surrounded by so much that is hollow and superficial.

Few things tend more to sap the foundations of the soul's confidence than a large amount of unreal profession. One may gather this in some measure from the fact that the finger of the infidel is continually pointed at the gross inconsistencies exhibited in the lives of the teachers and professors of religion. And although it be true that such inconsistencies, even were they multiplied ten thousand fold, will never shelter the infidel from the just consequences of his unbelief inasmuch as each one must give account of himself and for himself before the judgment seat of Christ, yet it is a fact that unreal profession tends to shake confidence. Hence the urgent need of simple, earnest, personal faith in God – of unquestioning childlike confidence in His Word, of constant dependence upon His wisdom, goodness, power and faithfulness.

This is the anchor of the soul without which it will be impossible to ride securely in the midst of Christendom's troubled waters. If we are in any way propped up by our circumstances, if we are leaning upon an arm of flesh, if we are deriving support from the thoughts of a mortal, if our faith stands in the wisdom of man or the best of men, if our fear toward God is taught by the precept of men, we may rest assured that all this will be tested and fully manifested. Nothing will stand except the faith that endures as seeing Him who is invisible – that looks not at the things that are seen and temporal, but at the things that are unseen and eternal.

How vividly all this was illustrated in the life of the father of the faithful, we may easily learn from the marvelous history of his life given by the pen of inspiration. "Abraham believed God." Observe, it was not something *about* God that he believed – some doctrine or opinion respecting God, received by tradition from man. No; this would never have availed for Abraham. It was with God Himself he had to do in the profoundest depths of his own individual being. "The God of glory appeared unto our father Abraham when he was in Mesopotamia, before he dwelt in Charran, and said unto him, Get thee out of thy country and from thy kindred, and come into the land which I shall show thee" (Acts 7:2-3).

These opening sentences of Stephen's powerful address to the Council set forth the true secret of Abraham's entire career from Ur of the Chaldees to Mount Moriah. It is not our purpose to dwell upon the solemn and instructive interval at Charran. Our desire is rather to set before the reader, as plainly and pointedly as we can, the unspeakable value, the absolute necessity of faith in God, not only for life and salvation, but for anything like true devotedness of heart to Christ and His cause. True, that honored servant of God tarried at Charran, traveled down into Egypt, turned to Hagar, trembled at Gerar and denied his wife. All this appears upon the surface of his history, for he was but a man – even a man of like passions with ourselves. But "he believed God."

Yes, from first to last, this remarkable man exercised in the main an unshaken confidence in the living God. He believed in that great truth that lies at the bottom of all truth, namely, that God is; and he believed also that God is a rewarder of all those who diligently seek Him. It was this that drew Abraham forth from Ur of the Chaldees – from the midst of all those ties and associations in the which he had lived and moved and had his being. It was this that sustained him through all the changes of his pil-grim-course. Finally, it was this that enabled him to stand on Mount Moriah and there show himself ready to lay upon the altar that one who was not only the son of his bosom, but also the channel through which all the families of the earth were yet to be blessed.

Nothing but faith could have enabled Abraham to turn his back upon the land of his birth, to go forth not knowing where he went. To the men of his day he must have seemed to be a fool or a madman. But oh! he knew whom he believed. Here lay the source of his strength. He was not following cunningly devised fables. He was not propped up by the circumstances or the influences which surrounded him. He was not supported by the thoughts of man. Flesh and blood afforded him no aid in his wonderful career. God was his shield, his portion and his reward, and in leaning on Him he found the true secret of all his victory over the world and of that calm and holy elevation which characterized him from first to last.

Reader, have you faith in God? Do you know Him? Is there a link between your soul and Him? Can you trust Him for everything? Are you at this moment consciously leaning upon Him, upon His Word, upon His arm? Remember, if there is any darkness or hesitation as to this, devotedness is and must be out of the question. All steady devotedness rests upon the solid ground of personal faith in the living God. We cannot too strongly insist upon this in a day of profession as widespread as it is shallow. It will not do to *say* "we believe." There is far too much of this, far too much head knowledge and lip profession, far too much of mere surface work.

It is easy to *say* we believe, but as James puts it, "What doth it profit though a man *say* he have faith?" Faith is a divine reality and not a mere human effort. It is based upon divine revelation and not upon the working of human reason. It connects the soul with God with a living, mighty link which nothing can ever snap. It bears the soul above and carries it on in triumph, come what may. There may be failure and confusion, error and evil, coldness and deadness, strife and division, breaking down and turning aside, stumblings and inconsistencies – all manner of things to shake the confidence and stagger the soul – but faith holds on its peaceful, steady way, undaunted and undismayed. Faith leans on God alone and finds all its springs in Him. Nothing can touch the faithfulness of God and nothing can shake the confidence of the heart that simply takes God at His word.

And be it remembered that faith is simply taking God at His word. It is believing what God says because He says it. It is taking God's thoughts in place of our own. "He that believeth hath set to his seal that God is true." How simple! God has revealed Himself, faith walks in the light of that revelation. God has spoken, faith believes the Word. But, if it be asked, "How has God revealed Himself? Where is His voice to be heard?" He has revealed Himself in the face of Jesus Christ, and His voice may be heard in His Word. He has not, blessed be His name, left us in the darkness of night, nor even in the dimness of twilight. He has poured upon us the full flood-tide of His own eternal truth so we may possess all the certainty, all the clearness, all the authority which a divine revelation can give.

Is it asked, "How can we know that God has spoken?" We reply, "How can we know the sun is shining?" Surely by the gentle influence of its beams. How can we know the dew has fallen? Surely by its refreshing influence upon the earth and by the luster of its pearly drops. So of the precious Word of God. It speaks for itself. Do I want a philosopher to tell me the sun is shining or the dewdrops are falling? Assuredly not. I feel their influence. I recognize their power. No doubt a philosopher might explain to me the properties of light and a chemist might instruct me as to the component parts of the dew. They might do all this for me, even though I had been born and reared in a coal-mine and had never seen either the one or the other. But they could not make me feel their influence. So it is in a divine way as to the Word of God. It makes itself felt – felt in the heart, felt in the conscience, felt in the deep chambers of the soul. True, it is by the power of the Holy Spirit, but all the while, there is power in the Word.

Let us remember this. Let no one imagine that God cannot speak to the heart or that the heart cannot understand what He says and feel the power of His Word. Cannot a father speak to his child and cannot the child understand his father? Yes, surely, and our heavenly Father can speak to our very hearts and we can hear His voice and know His mind and lean upon His eternal Word. And this is faith – simple, living, saving faith. Such a definition of faith might not satisfy a profound theologian, but that makes no difference. The heart does not need learned theological definitions. It wants God and it has Him in His Word. God has spoken. He has revealed Himself. He has come forth from the thick darkness, chased away the shades of twilight, and shone upon us in the face of Jesus Christ and on the eternal pages of Holy Scripture.

Reader, have you found Him? Do you really know Him by the revelation which He has given and by the Word which He has spoken? Is His

Word a reality to you? Is it your stay and support? Is it the real ground on which you are resting for time and eternity? Do, we beseech you, make sure work of it at this moment. See to it that you have a living faith in God and such a sense of the value, the importance and the authority of His Word, that you would rather part with all else than surrender it. It is the only ground of devotedness. It is utterly impossible that a heart distracted and tossed about with unbelieving reasonings can ever be truly devoted to Christ or His service. "He that cometh to God must believe that He is." How simple! How plain! How could Abraham have left his country; how could he have run the race; how could he have given up everything and come forth as a stranger and a pilgrim, not having so much ground as to set his foot upon? How could he have stood upon Mount Moriah and stretched forth his hand for the knife to slay his son? How could he have done all or any of these things if he did not have simple faith in the one living and true God? Impossible.

And so in your case, beloved reader, unless you can trust God, unless you are sustained by the real power of simple faith in the Word of the living God, you will never be able to get on. In fact, you have no life in you. Truly we may say, "No faith, no life." There may be high profession. There may be the semblance of devotedness, but if there is not a living faith, there can be no spiritual life. And if there is no life there cannot be any true devotedness. "The just shall live by faith." They not only get life by faith, but live day by day and hour by hour *by faith*. It is the spring of life and power to the soul all the journey through. It connects the soul with God, and by so doing imparts steadiness, consistency, energy and holy decision to the servant of Christ. If there be not the constant exercise of faith in God, there will be fluctuation and uncertainty. Work will be taken up by fits and starts, instead of being the necessary result of calm abiding in Christ by faith. There will be an occasional rush at some line of service which is merely taken up for the time and then coldly abandoned. The course, instead of being a steady, upward and onward one, will be zigzag and most unsatisfactory. At times there will be a feverish excitement, and then again, deadness and indifference.

All this is the very reverse of true devotedness. It does serious damage to the cause of Christ. Better to never start on the course at all, than having started, to turn aside and give it up. "No man having put his hand to the plough, and looking back, is fit for the kingdom of God." True devotedness is based upon a profound and earnest faith in God. It has its root deep down in the heart. It is not fitful or whimsical, but calm, consistent, decided and steadily progressive. It may at times, when tried by the rule of a romantic and visionary enthusiasm, seem slow-paced, but if it is slow it is only because it will be sure. The end will prove the difference between the energy of nature and the acting of faith.

May God by His Spirit lead all His people into a truer and deeper sense of what devotedness really is. There is an energy abroad. The minds of men are active. Principles as well as passions are in action. Contending elements are at work underneath the surface of human life. Society is becoming more and more an unsettled thing. Men seem to be on the look-out for something. There is evidently a crisis at hand. Men are taking sides. The stage is being reared for some grand act of the drama. What is needed in view of all this? Unquestionably, a calm, deep, earnest faith in the Word of God. This is the only thing to keep the heart steady, come what may. Nothing will keep the soul in peace; nothing can give fixedness to the course; nothing can maintain us in the path of devotedness but the realization of that living link between the soul and God Himself, which, as being divine and eternal, must of necessity outlive all that is merely human and temporal.

Having sought to lay down what we consider to be the essential *ground* of all true devotedness – an earnest, personal faith in the living Cod – we shall now, in dependence upon divine guidance and teaching, proceed to consider:

THE SPIRIT OF DEVOTEDNESS

The two things are intimately connected inasmuch as it is impossible for anyone to have to do with God in the realities of a life of faith, without having his heart drawn out in true worship. And the spirit of worship is, in very deed, the spirit that must ever characterize true devotedness. It is faith alone that gives God His proper place and leaves the scene clear for Him to display Himself in His own proper glory. Hence it is that faith enjoys ten thousand occasions of realizing what God is to all who trust Him and diligently seek Him, and each fresh realization draws forth fresh strains of praise. Thus a living faith ministers to a spirit of worship, and a spirit of worship is the vehicle through which to convey the experiences of a living faith. The more we trust God the more we shall know Him, and the more we know Him the more we must praise Him.

We have little idea of how much we lose by our lack of simple confidence in God. Unbelief ever hinders the display of divine power and goodness. "He could there do not many mighty works because of their unbelief." This holds good in our individual history every day. God will not show Himself if our unbelief fills the field of vision with other objects. It is impossible that God and the creature can occupy the same platform or jointly form the ground of the soul's confidence. It must be God alone from first to last. "My soul, wait thou only upon God; for my expectation is from Him. He only is my rock and my salvation .... Trust in Him at all times." Such is the language of faith "only and at all times." This is the ground – the solid and unassailable ground of true devotedness – and the soul that really occupies this ground will ever be clothed with a spirit of worship. Faith counts on God; God reveals Himself to faith; and faith responds in words of praise and adoration. Nothing can be simpler and nothing on earth more blessed. Faith can ever address God in the following words, "Lord, You know me; we are on the same old terms." Blessed term! May we understand them better!

There is nothing in all this world like having to do with God in the secret of our own souls and in all the details of our personal history, day by day. It imparts a calmness not easily ruffled, a stability not easily moved, a holy independence of human thinkings and speakings, a moral elevation that lifts the soul above the reach of surrounding influences. There is an atmosphere enwrapping this world – an atmosphere so dense, so murky, so depressing, that nothing but the eye of faith can pierce it. Our own hearts also are full of unbelief, ever ready to depart from the living God, constantly sending up infidel reasonings from within or hearkening to infidel suggestions from without. Therefore we so greatly need to have the foundations of our personal confidence strengthened so our devotedness may be of a more decided type.

But in contemplating the spirit of devotedness as illustrated in the life of Abraham, we must look somewhat closely at the facts of his instructive history, especially at those facts which immediately precede his call to Mount Moriah. For example in Genesis 20 we find him called to apply the sharp knife of self-judgment to an old root of evil which had found lodging in his heart for many days. This self-same root may teach the writer and the reader a deeply solemn and an eminently practical lesson.

When Abraham started on his career, we may notice that he was clogged and hindered by a natural tie and that he was secretly influenced by a root of moral evil. The natural tie was snapped at Charran by the hand of death and Abraham was set free and enabled to get up to the place to which God had called him. (Compare carefully Genesis 11:31-32 and chapter 12 with Acts 7:2-4). He was told to get up out of his country and from his kindred and come into the land of Canaan, but he brought some of his kindred with him and stopped short at Charran. There his father died. Thereupon Abraham made his way to the true point of divine revelation.

The ties of nature, right enough and really of God in their proper place, are sure, if not kept in their place, to hinder true devotedness. It was all right and very beautiful in Elisha to love with the tenderness of a son, his father and mother, but when Elijah had flung around him the prophetic mantle, it was entirely below the mark of a deep-toned and genuine devotedness to say, "Let me, I pray thee, kiss my father and my mother and then I will follow thee." Natural ties are like honey: we must beware of how much we eat and when. Was ever a son's love so tender as that which glowed in the bosom of the Man Christ Jesus? Was ever subjection to parental authority so divinely perfect as His? And yet when the claims of service were to be responded to, when the integrity of true Naziriteship was to be maintained, He could say, "Woman, what have I to do with thee?" And again, "Who is My mother?" It was only the true and perfect Servant who knew how to adjust conflicting claims and keep each in its place. Hence from the same lips flowed forth the words of faithful Naziriteship at one time, and words of melting tenderness at another.

Abraham was hindered in his course by the tie of nature until that tie was dissolved by death, but the root of moral evil seems to have clung to him for a much longer period of time. What was that root? Regretfully, it was one which we can only too well understand – a little bit of unbelief, clothing itself in the form of humanly-prudent reserve in reference to his relationship to Sarah.

"What!" it may be said, "Unbelief in the heart of the father of the faithful?" Just so. It is a remarkable fact, illustrated in the history of the most eminent saints of God, that their most remarkable failure appears in the very thing for which they were most noted. Moses, the meekest man in all the earth, spoke unadvisedly. Job, the model of patience, cursed his day. Abraham, the father of the faithful, carried in his heart for many a long day and through many a changing scene, a root of unbelief. This root first sprouted in the land of Egypt where Abraham had gone to escape the famine that raged in the land of Canaan. And as might be expected, the sprouting brought trouble on himself and others. "And it came to pass, when he was come near to enter into Egypt, that he said unto Sarai his wife, Behold now, I know that thou are a fair woman to look upon: therefore it shall come to pass, when the Egyptians shall see thee, that they shall say, This is his wife: and they will kill me, they will save thee alive.

Say, I pray thee, thou are my sister, that it may be well with me for thy sake; and my soul shall live because of thee."

Reader, remember the Holy Spirit has penned this faithful record for our learning and admonition, and truly it is most solemn to think that such a man as Abraham could be so governed by the fear of personal danger as to expose the object of his heart's fond affections to loss of virtue and to deny his relationship to her. True, this conduct was the result of his being in a wrong position, for had he remained in the place to which God had called him, there would have been no need to deny his wife. But as it generally happens, one wrong step led to another, and having gone into Egypt through fear of the famine, he there denies his wife through fear of death.

"And the Lord plagued Pharaoh and his house with great plagues because of Sarai, Abram's wife." What marvelous grace to Abraham! God, who ever delights to rebuke his people's fears as well as to answer their faith, covered His erring servant with the shield of His powerful protection. Abraham's life and Sarah's virtue were both preserved in safety behind that impenetrable shield, and the house of Egypt's monarch was made to feel the heavy stroke of Jehovah's righteous rod. "And Pharaoh called Abram and said, What is this that thou hast done unto me? Why didst thou not tell me that she was thy wife? Why saidst thou, she is my sister? so I might have taken her to me to wife." Abraham had evidently exposed himself in all this matter. Hence, although God protects him, He yet allows Pharaoh to rebuke him.

It is well to see this. When the man of God steps off the path of faith and christian integrity, he at once exposes himself to the men of this world, and he need not marvel if they chastise him with an unsparing hand. Had Abraham remained in Canaan, he would not have been reproved by Pharaoh in Egypt. It is better far to starve, if it must be so, in the path of obedience than gain abundance by the sacrifice of faith and moral uprightness. May we have grace to remember this at all times! It is easy enough to put these things down on paper, but when the moment of temptation arises, it is another thing. Still we must remember that the Spirit of God has penned the history of Abraham for our profit, and it is well for us to ponder its holy lessons.

Now let us enquire as to the effect produced in Abraham by Pharaoh's sharp reproof. Did it prove effective in delivering him from the root of evil which had called it forth? Regretfully no. So far as the inspired history informs us, Abraham received the rebuke in silence and went on his way, but he carried the root along with him to sprout again. He received a fresh revelation from God; he obtained a splendid victory over Chedoraomer and his confederates and refused the tempting offer of the king of Sodom; he was comforted by fresh assurances and promises from God and manifested a child-like faith which was counted unto him for righteousness. In short, he passed through a variety of scenes and circumstances with varied exercises of soul no doubt, but all the while, the moral root to which we are directing the reader's attention, remained unjudged and unconfessed.

That root had sprouted and produced its bitter fruit, but as yet the sharp knife of self-judgment remained to be applied to it. It is not until we reach Genesis 20 that this root again appears above the surface in the matter of Abimelech, King of Gerar. Here we have the same scene enacted over again after years of rich experience of divine goodness and loving-kindness. The King of Egypt and his house had been brought into trouble before, and the King of Gerar and his house are brought into trouble now, for Jehovah reproved kings for Abraham's sake though the kings had reason to reprove Abraham because of his ways.

"Then Abimelech called Abraham and said unto him, What hast thou done unto us? and what have I offended thee, that thou hast brought on me and on my kingdom a great sin? Thou hast done deeds unto me that ought not to be done. And Abimelech said unto Abraham "What sawest thou that thou hast done this thing?" This was bringing the father to a point. There was no escaping such plain dealing. Therefore Abraham frankly opens his heart and unlocks that secret chamber which had been kept shut for so many years. He tells out all and exposes every fiber of the root which had proved the source of so much trouble to himself and others. Let us hearken to the unreserved confession of this dear and honored man of God. "And Abraham said, because I thought, surely, the fear of God is not in this place; and they will slay me for my wife's sake. And yet indeed she is my sister; she is the daughter of my father, but not the daughter of my mother; and she became my wife. And it came to pass when God caused me to wander from my father's house, that I said unto her, This is thy kindness which thou shalt show unto me at every place whither we shall come, say of me, he is my brother."

Here was the root of the whole matter. Why do we dwell upon it? Why seek to unfold it in such detail? Simply for the spiritual profit and moral health of the Christian reader. Have we not all our roots? Yes, verily, deep, strong and bitter roots – roots which have been the source of a world of sorrow and shame to ourselves and of trouble to those with whom we had to do. Well then, these roots must be reached and judged, for as long as they remain unreached and unjudged, it is utterly impossible that we can reach the higher stages of the path of devotedness. Need we remind the reader that it is not a question of life or salvation? Need we recall him to the thesis of our paper which is simply "What is devotedness?" Our one grand object is to raise the tone of devotedness in the soul of every Christian who may scan these lines. But we know that devotedness, to be true, steady and effective, must rest on the proper ground and breathe the proper spirit. That ground is faith; that spirit is worship; and though it be quite true that a soul may occupy, in the main, the ground of faith and breathe a spirit of worship while there are many roots in the heart unreached and unjudged, we are nevertheless fully persuaded that so long as there is any hidden root of evil in the heart, any chamber which we keep locked and refuse to have properly lighted and ventilated, the higher stages of practical devotedness are yet beyond and above us.

God knows we do not want to depress the heart of the reader. Indeed, if our lines have anything of a depressing tendency, their effect should be realized first and most of all by the writer himself. But we desire to encourage and exhort, and it is with a simple view to these desirable ends that we now turn directly to the reader and put this plain and pointed question home to him, Have you any secret reserve in your soul? Do you have any hidden root of evil deep down in your heart and mind? Is there anything you are keeping back from the action of the light and from the edge of the knife? Search and see! Search diligently! Do not deceive yourself nor let Satan deceive you. Deal honestly and truly with your own soul in this matter. Let no false application of the doctrines or principles of grace prevent you from exercising a most rigid censorship over your ways, your character and your heart with all its motive springs and hidden chambers.

Be assured of it, there is an urgent demand for real heart work on the part of all who long to tread the highest stages of the divine life. We live in a day which is earning for itself the title of "A day of shams." Yes, reader, *sham* seems stamped upon all around, whether in politics, commerce or manufacturing, and most assuredly, much of the Christianity of the day forms no sort of exception to the rule. Hence the demand for *reality* on the part of the true Christian. And, unquestionably, all reality must find its source in the heart. If the heart is not right and real with God, we cannot be real in anything.

There is another point to which we must refer in the life of Abraham before we close this part of our subject. It is presented in Genesis 21. The bondwoman and her son are cast out of the house. We do not dwell upon this point, but merely name it for the purpose of pointing out the deep moral conveyed to us in this portion of Abraham's history. The heart and the house had both to come under judgment before the call to Moriah fell on the patriarch's ears. God was about to call His beloved servant into the very highest position that man can occupy, to demand of him an expression of devotedness of the very highest order, to pass him through a crucible of the very highest degree of intensity. And, be it observed, before He did so, the root of moral evil had been reached in the heart and the legal element had been expelled from the house. All this is deeply practical.

God deals with moral realities. If we are to walk with Him along the high and holy pathway of pure devotedness, the heart and the house must be duly regulated. If the real desire of our hearts be after a closer walk with God, we must see to it that we are not retaining anything within or about us that would not agree with that nearness. Our God is infinitely gracious, merciful and patient. He can bear with us and wait upon us in marvelous tenderness, but at the same time, we have to remember that we forfeit present blessing and future reward through our lack of earnest devotedness. There is nothing of legality in this: it is but the just application of the principle of grace in which we stand.

"And it came to pass that God did tempt Abraham." Why is it we never read such words as "It came to pass that God did tempt Lot?" Alas! Lot was never in a moral condition to warrant his being so highly honored. *Sodom* tempted Lot, but it was no temptation at all to Abraham. What a contrast between Lot in the cave and Abraham on Mount Moriah! Yet they were both saved. But what a poor thing to be *content* to be saved! Ought we not to sigh after those spiritual heights which lie beyond? Should we not long to give expression to a more ardent devotedness? Oh! that our houses and our hearts were in a moral condition acceptable in the sight of God so we might enjoy habitual nearness to Himself and unbroken communion with Him. This is our privilege and we should never be satisfied with anything else.

It was a high honor conferred upon Abraham when God called him into the place of trial – when He asked him for "his son, his only son Isaac." It was an elevated point in the patriarch's career, and that he felt it to be such we may judge from the spirit in which he responded to the divine call and in the manner in which he traveled to the scene of sacrifice. "I and the lad will go yonder and *worship*." Here the true spirit of devotedness most blessedly unfolds itself. To give up his only son, the object of his affections, the channel of all God's promises, to lay this one as a victim on the altar and see him consumed to ashes, what was it all? Just an act of worship! This was real work indeed. It was no empty lip profession, no saying "I go, sir" and yet not going at all. "Abraham believed God." Here lay the secret of it all. He had learned to yield an unquestioning, implicit obedience to the Word of the Lord. Therefore when called to lay his Isaac upon the altar as a sacrifice – that Isaac for whom he had longed and waited and trusted – he bows his head and says, "I and the lad will go yonder and worship."

Thank God there lived such a man as Abraham, that there was enacted such a scene as that upon Mount Moriah, and that we have so vividly and forcibly presented to our hearts the ground and the spirit of true devotedness!

The more we ponder the question which has been occupying our attention, namely, What is devotedness? the more we are convinced of its immense practical importance. It puts the soul in immediate contact with the Lord Himself and opens a path for each one, along which he can move in calm and steady confidence, let his surroundings be what they may.

But just in proportion to the importance of the subject of devotedness is the need of clearness as to the true ground, spirit and object thereof. We have already sought to present to the reader the truth as to the first two points. Now it remains to dwell on

THE OBJECT OF DEVOTEDNESS

How much hangs on the answer which the heart gives to this question, "What is my object in life?" It is, undoubtedly, one of the very gravest questions which anyone can put to himself. It is the object which stamps the character. Let us remember this. What was it that gave character to Abraham's journey to Moriah and to his conduct when he arrived there? What was it that drew the attention of heaven to the scene? Was it the mere fact that a father was going to offer up his son as a sacrifice? No; thousands of fathers have done that. Thousands of sons have been sacrificed on the altars of false gods, and that too, in so°called devotedness. But what was it that distinguished the act of the father of the faithful? It was this: let us hear it and mark it with the heart's deepest attention. "Now I know that thou fearest God, seeing thou hast not withheld thy son, thine only son, from Me" (Gen. 22:12). Here we have Abraham's object, and on this point let us meditate for a few moments.

The heart may propose to itself a thousand objects. These objects may be good enough in themselves, yet not one of them be the object which characterizes Christian devotedness. We once knew a man who prayed for seven hours a day. We have seen him on his knees at four o'clock in the morning. And after the toils of the day we have seen him on his knees again till the midnight hour. We have seen him in agonies of devotion. His flesh was worn from his bones by constant kneeling. He was a blameless, friendly man. Those who marked the course of his daily life could not put their finger on a single moral blemish in his conduct as a man. And yet when we approached that man to speak some word about Christ, he shrunk from us and refused to listen. He was devoted to his religion *but he hated Christ.*

Again, a man may devote himself to philanthropy. He may devote his life and his fortune to the objects of benevolence and make the most splendid sacrifices to carry out his schemes. He may fix the wondering gaze of millions upon his career, yet be a total stranger to Christ.

Further, a man may devote himself to what may seem to be the work of the Lord. He may seem to be a laboring student of Scripture, an active, earnest, self-denying evangelist. He may go forth to the fields of foreign mission, leaving his country, his kindred and his home in devotion to his work. He may do all this and much more, and yet not exhibit one atom of true Christian devotedness simply because *Christ* was not his object in all that in which he was engaged.

All this is deeply solemn. We may be religions, devotional, benevolent, active in the Lord's work in all its departments, whether as evangelists, pastors or teachers, and yet not have Christ before our souls at all. A man may start in a work which, to all outward appearance, seems a real work of God. He may seem to be most simple in his devotion to that work and yet, it may turn out in the end that his heart was engrossed with the work to the total exclusion of Christ as an object. True Christian devotedness is embodied in this brief sentence, *"To me, to live is Christ."* Paul does not say, "To me to live is work," though where was there ever such a workman except the perfect Workman? He does not say, "To me to live is religion or benevolence or morality," though who more religious, benevolent or moral than Paul? It is not that he loved these things less, but he loved Christ more. This makes all the difference. I may wear myself out with religious exercises such as prayers, fastings and vigils; I may bestow all my goods to feed the poor; I may give my body to be burned, yet there may not be in all these things one particle of genuine devotedness to Christ.

Is not this a very weighty consideration in this day of religious activity, forms of piety and schemes of benevolence? Should we not, dear

Christian reader, look well to the question as to what is our real object? Is it not too true that one may spend a whole life in the exercise of religion and philanthropy, and yet live and die a stranger to that One who is God's only object, heaven's only center – Christ Jesus? Sadly, the truth of this is illustrated in the history of millions. The god of this world is blinding the minds of countless multitudes. And with what does he most effectively blind them? With schemes of benevolence and forms of piety. Oh! Christendom, Christendom, hear it: thy rituals, thy forms and thy schemes are blinding the minds, hardening the hearts and searing the consciences of untold millions.

It is not merely amid the haunts of vice in all its abominable forms, that God's faithful messengers are called to raise a warning voice, but on the broad and well-trodden highway of religious profession, along which multitudes are rushing to eternal doom. *The devil's grand object is to keep Christ out of the heart and he cares not by what means he attains this object.* He will use a man's lusts or he will use his superstitious fears. Forms of vice and forms of piety are all alike to him. *He hates Christ* and will seek by all means to keep souls away from Him. He will let a man be religious, benevolent, friendly, moral, but he will not, if he can help it, let him be a Christian. And when anyone has through grace become a Christian in reality, Satan's one aim is to draw his heart and turn his eye away from Christ. He will seek to engage him with objects professedly Christian to divert him from the only Object that really forms the Christian – Christ Himself. He will give him lots of work to do: he will *overwhelm* him with work and get him a name as a most wonderful workman. And yet, by means of this very work, he will sap the foundation of a man's Christianity and so deceive and pervert his heart that, in process of time, he will become occupied with *himself* and his doings instead of with Christ and His service!

Hence the importance of having the one object ever before the heart and that object is Christ. "To me to live is Christ." "Thou hast not withheld thy son, thine only son from Me." Christ is the great standard for everyone and everything. All must be measured by Him. Everything is to be regulated and valued with reference to Him. The question is not, how much work am I doing? but to whom is it done? Searching question! "Then shall the King say unto them on His right hand, Come ye blessed of My Father, inherit the kingdom prepared for you from the foundation of the world; for I was an hungered, and ye gave Me meat; I was thirsty, and ye gave Me drink; I was a stranger, and ye took Me in; naked, and ye clothed Me; I was sick and ye visited Me; I was in prison, and ye came unto Me... inasmuch as ye have done it unto one of the least of these My brethren, ye have done it unto Me" (Mt. 25:34-40).

Here lies the secret of all acceptable service and all true devotedness. We may feed the hungry, clothe the naked, visit the sick, but if the King cannot say, "Ye did it unto Me," it will be valueless.

Oh! what a privilege to be allowed to do any little thing for Christ! To be enabled to have Him ever before the heart! It is this which gives real value and true elevation to all we may be called to do in this world, whether it be sweeping a sidewalk or evangelizing a nation. Christian service is that which is done to Christ. Nothing else deserves the name; nothing else will be so esteemed in God's account; nothing else will pass as genuine gold through the fire of that great testing day which is rapidly approaching. All the thoughts of God center around Jesus. It is His eternal purpose to exalt and glorify that Name. The whole universe will yet be called upon to find in Jesus its central sun. The beams of His glory shall, before long, shine forth over the whole creation.

Thus it will be very soon. Now, the Christian is called to *anticipate* that day and to make Jesus his one absorbing, commanding object in all things. If he gives alms it is to be in the name of Jesus; if he preaches the gospel for the conversion and gathering of souls, it is to be with his eye fixed directly upon Jesus and for the glory of His Name. Will this restrict the sphere or measure of his benevolence? Will it lessen his interest in the work of evangelization? Quite the reverse; it will greatly enlarge the former and intensify the latter, and while it does all this it will elevate the tone of his spirit in the work and impart stability to all his service because it will ever keep his heart and mind occupied with the very highest object, even Jesus Christ, the same yesterday, today and forever.

I may enter upon a certain line of work under the influence of excitement or in imitation of others, or to get a name for myself– from all manner of motives. I may work with an energy and zeal which puts others to shame. I may be greatly looked up to get a great name among my fellows. I may be puffed, flattered and applauded. My name may appear as a celebrity in all the religious journals of the day. Yet, after all this, the Lord may not be able to say as to a single act of all my service, "You did it unto Me."

On the other hand a man may pursue a path of quiet, unobtrusive, unostentatious service, unknown and unnoticed, and not wishing to be noticed. The stream of his benevolence may flow abundantly, unknown to all except to those who are refreshed by its influence, and for the most part, not even by them. The lanes, the alleys, the courtyards, the prisons, the hospitals are visited; the widow's tear is dried, her sorrow soothed, her wants supplied; the orphan is thought of; the sons and daughters of toil and misery are looked after; the precious tidings of salvation are sounded in many a room; the gospel tract is slipped into many a hand; and all the while, little is heard or known down here of the doer of these precious, these most fragrant acts or service and self-sacrifice. But the odor goes up to the throne. The record is above: it is all engraved on the Father's heart. He remembers it all and will bring it all out in due time and after such a fashion that the doer would not recognize his own work.

Who knew what was in Abraham's heart when he started on that marvelous journey to Moriah – a journey which has only been exceeded in marvelous mystery by that from Gethsemane to Calvary? Who knew what he was going to do? Who would ever have known it if the Holy Spirit had not recorded it on the eternal page of inspiration? "I and the lad will go yonder and worship." "They went both of them together." "Thou hast not withheld thy son, thine only son from Me." Abraham was engrossed with God from first to last. From the moment he rose from his couch on that memorable morning, until he stretched forth his hand to take the knife, his soul was absorbed with the living God. It was this that gave holy elevation to the entire scene. It was done for God.

Thus it is always. Whatever is done for Christ will be remembered and rewarded; whatever is not will sink into eternal oblivion or be burned up in judgment. It is not the *quantity* but the *quality* of the work that will be tried and made manifest before the judgment seat of Christ. Look at the parable of the laborers in Matthew 20. What a seasonable lesson does that parable read out to our hearts! The laborers who were first hired were the only ones with whom an agreement was made; all the rest worked in the confidence that their Master would give them what was right. If any of the first set of laborers had been asked during the day, "What are you to get as a reward for your work?" they would have said "A penny." They were working for a penny. But if any of the others had been asked the same question, they would have said, "I don't know, but I am sure the Master will do what is right."

This makes all the difference. The moment I work for reward, it ceases to be Christian service. It is not that Christian service will not be rewarded: it most assuredly will, but just so far as it is Christian service, it will be rendered apart from all thought of reward. "The love of Christ," not the hope of reward, "constraineth us." Why did the wicked and slothful servant hide his talent in the earth? Because he did not know his Lord. Had he known Him, he would have loved Him and served Him for love's sake, which is the only service that Christ values.

It was, we may rest assured, joy to Abraham's soul to have a son to lay on the altar of God. And so with the true Christian now; it is his joy to be permitted to render any little service to that Lord whom he loves supremely. Nor will it be a question with him as to the kind of service or the sphere in which it is to be rendered, or the amount of the work; it is enough for him if his Lord can say, "You did it unto Me." "Why trouble ye the woman? for she hath wrought a good work upon Me." It does not matter in the least what we are doing, provided only it be done directly for Christ, with the eye fixed on Him and the heart filled with Him. It is this that imparts value to every little act of service, and if there be one thing more than another which the heart longs for, it is the ability to do all one's work, of whatsoever kind it is, with a single eye to Christ.

But ah! the heart is so treacherous and so prone to have mixed motives. We are apt to attach importance and interest to things because of *our* connection with them, to engage in service for service' sake, to be more occupied with our work than with the Master. May we have grace ever to remember that all that is not done directly to the Lord Himself is absolutely worthless, however showy it may be in the eyes of man; and on the other hand, that the smallest thing done in love to Jesus and in singleness of heart to Him, will never be forgotten.

It would be truly pleasant to the heart to dwell a little longer on this blessed theme, but we must close. Before we do, we desire to leave with the reader this one solemn question, "What is your real object?" We feel the weight of this question and we look to the Spirit of God to give it weight in the heart and conscience of the reader.

To everyone who can say in calm confidence and spiritual intelligence, "I am saved," the next grand point is to be able to say, "Christ is my object: to me to live is Christ." Alas, how few of us can say it. We stop short. We are occupied with our salvation, our peace and blessing, our comfort and liberty, or it may be we are taken up with our service. In a word, it is not Christ – it is not abiding in Him, feeding on Him and acting for Him. It is really self, and this is downright misery. We should never rest satisfied with anything short of having Jesus as a covering for our eyes and an Object for our hearts. This would be to understand experimentally the ground, the spirit and the object of true devotedness.

"THE WELL OF BETHLEHEM"
(2 SAMUEL 23)

"And David longed and said, Oh that one would give me drink of the water of the well of Bethlehem which is by the gate!" Such was the breathing of David's heart, a desire which met with a speedy and hearty response from three members of that devoted and heroic band which flocked around him in the cave of Adullam. "And the three mighty men broke through the host of the Philistines, and drew water out of the well of Bethlehem that was by the gate, and took it and brought it to David." There was no command issued. No one in particular was singled out and commissioned to go. There was the simple utterance of the desire, and this it was which afforded the opportunity for genuine affection and true devotedness. Had there been a specific command given to anyone, it would merely have afforded an occasion for ready obedience, but the utterance of a desire developed that ardent attachment to the person of David which is so lovely to behold.

And mark the actings of David in this most touching scene: "Nevertheless he would not drink thereof, but poured it out unto the Lord. And he said, Be it far from me, O Lord, that I should do this: is not this the blood of the men that went in jeopardy of their lives? Therefore he would not drink of it." It was a sacrifice too costly for any except Jehovah Himself. Hence David would not permit the sweet odor of it to be interrupted in its ascent to the throne of God.

How little did those three mighty men imagine that their act of loving devotedness would be recorded on the eternal page of inspiration, there to be read by millions. They never thought of this. Their hearts were set on David and they counted not their lives dear unto them so that they might gratify him or refresh his spirit. Had they acted to get a name or place for themselves, it would have robbed their act of all its charm and consigned it to its merited contempt and oblivion. But no; they loved David. This was the spring of their activity. They proved that he was more precious to their hearts than life itself. They forgot all in the one absorbing object of serving David, and the odor of their sacrifice ascended to the throne of God while the record of their deed shines on the page of inspiration and shall continue to shine so long as that page endures.

Oh! how we long for something like this in reference to the true David in this the day of His rejection. We do greatly covet a more intense and self-sacrificing devotedness as the fruit of the constraining love of Christ. It is not a question of working for rewards, for a crown or for a place, though we fully believe in the doctrine of rewards. No! the very moment we make rewards our object, we are below the mark. We believe that service rendered with the eye upon the reward would be defective. But then we believe also that every jot or tittle of true service will be rewarded in the day of Christ's glory and that each servant will get his place in the record *and his place in the kingdom* according to the measure of His personal devotedness down here. This we hold to be a great practical truth and we press it as such upon the attention of the Christian reader. We must confess we long to see the standard of devotedness greatly raised among us and this can only be effected by having our hearts more entirely consecrated to Christ and His Name. O Lord, revive Thy work!

DAVID'S LAST WORDS
(2 SAMUEL 23)

There is something deeply touching and most consolatory in the last words of "The sweet Psalmist of Israel." It is good and profitable to listen to the "last words" of any saint of God or servant of Christ. It is well to hearken to the mellow words of the white-haired and experienced, to those who have reached the final stage of life's rough journey. We all know that upon our first starting on our course, there is a degree of romance about us. We cherish large expectations from men and things. We fondly imagine that all is gold that glitters and we foolishly hope that all the promises and pretensions of the scene around will be fully realized. But alas! as we go on, we discover our mistake. Stern reality cures us of much of our youthful romance and the blasts of the desert heat carry away much of the bloom of our young days. The young believer is apt to confide in everyone who makes a profession; and this simple confidence is lovely. Would that it always met with a more worthy response. But it does not. One meets with much, even in an ordinary Christian career, to chill, to wither, to contract and repulse. Hence the weight and value of "last words," especially when we get them, not merely as the fruit of matured judgment, but as in David's case, by inspiration of the Holy Spirit.

"Now these be the last words of David, David the son of Jesse said, and the man who was raised up on high, the anointed of the God of Jacob, and the sweet psalmist of Israel, said, The Spirit of the Lord spake by me, and His word was in my tongue. The God of Israel said, the Rock of Israel spake to me, He that ruleth over men must be just, ruling in the fear of God. And he shall be as the light of the morning when the sun riseth, even a morning without clouds; as the tender grass springing out of the earth, by clear shining after rain."

Here, David sets up the divine standard of character for one called to rule over men. "He must be just"; and upon the basis of justice is erected a superstructure of cloudless light, richest blessing and abundant fruitfulness. All this will only be realized when the Son of David, now hidden in the heavens, shall ascend the throne of his Father and stretch forth His scepter over a restored creation.

Not only does David set up the divine standard; he compares himself with it, and it is in this comparison we have the great moral and practical truth which I desire to fasten on my reader's heart. "Although," says

David, "my house be not so with God; yet He hath made with me an everlasting covenant, ordered in all things and sure: for this is all my salvation and all my desire, although He make it not to grow."

The only way to get a right view of ourselves is by looking at Christ. This is what David does in these last words. He weighs himself in a perfect balance and declares himself light. He measures himself with a perfect rule and confesses himself entirely defective. He gazes upon the perfect model and exclaims, "I am not like that." He looks back over the past and sees his failings and faults. He turns over page after page of life's sad story and his eye, enlightened by beams of light from the sanctuary, sees the blots and the blemishes. But, blessed be God, he can fall back upon "an everlasting covenant, ordered in all things and sure," and in that well ordered covenant, finds "all his salvation and all his desire."

There is uncommon beauty and power in the connection between the "although" and the "yet" in the above passage. The former leaves a wide margin in which to insert the words of a convicted and chastened heart, the latter opens the floodgates to let in the full tide of divine mercy and loving kindness. "Although" puts man in the dust as a failing one; "yet" introduces God in all the fullness of His pardoning love. The former is the language of a soul that has learned itself; the latter is the breathing of a heart that had learned something about God.

Oh! beloved reader, is it not a great mercy that, when we reach the close of our history and review the past – when, as regards ourselves, we have only to say, "My house is not so with God" – we shall then fully prove the eternal stability of that grace in which we have found "all our salvation and all our desire!"

THE PRIEST'S PLACE AND PORTION
(READ LEVITICUS 6:14-18)

These verses show us three things in connection with "the law of the meat offering" – the priest, his place and his portion.

1. *The priest.* All the sons of Aaron were priests. They became such by birth. They were born into this highly-privileged position. They did not reach it by effort, but simply by birth. Being sons of Aaron, they *were* priests. They might be disqualified for the discharge of the functions of their position through bodily blemish or ceremonial defilement (Lev. 21-22), but as to the position itself, it was a necessary result of their being sons of Aaron. Position is one thing; ability to discharge the functions or capacity to enjoy the privileges thereof, is quite another.

A dwarf among the sons of Aaron was deprived of many of the higher priestly dignities, but a dwarf was to "eat the bread of his God, of the most holy, and of the holy." God would not leave the feeblest or most diminutive member of the priestly household without a holy portion. "Only he shall not go in unto the vail, nor come nigh unto the altar, because he hath a blemish, that he profane not My sanctuaries: for I the Lord do sanctify them." A dwarf could not attend the altar of God, but the God of the altar took care of the dwarf. The two things are divinely perfect. God's claims have been perfectly answered and the need of His priestly family perfectly met.

2. *The place.* The place where the priest was to partake of his portion teaches us a most valuable lesson of practical holiness. "With unleavened bread shall it be eaten in the holy place, in the court of the tabernacle of the congregation they shall eat it." That is to say, it is only in the power of personal holiness and in the immediate presence of God that we can really partake of our priestly portion. The *way* in which we get the place exhibits absolute grace. The *place* which we get demands personal holiness. To speak of effort in reaching the place is the fallacy of legalism. To think of unholiness in the place is the blasphemy of lawlessness. I reach the position only through grace. I occupy the position only in holiness. The pathway to the sanctuary has been thrown open by free grace, but it is to the sanctuary of God that grace has opened the pathway. These things must never be forgotten. We want to have them graven on the tablets of the conscience and hidden in the chambers of the heart.

3. *The portion.* And now as to the portion. "This is the law of the meat

offering: the sons of Aaron shall offer it before the Lord, before the altar. And he shall take of it his handful, of the flour of the meat offering and of the oil thereof, and *all* the frankincense thereof, and shall burn it upon the altar for a sweet savor, even the memorial of it unto the Lord. And the remainder thereof shall Aaron and his sons eat." The fine flour and oil typify Christ's perfect manhood, conceived and anointed by the Holy Spirit. This is the portion of God's priests to be enjoyed in the sanctuary of the divine presence, in separation of heart unto God. It is utterly impossible that we can enjoy Christ anywhere else but in the presence of God or in any other way than personal holiness. To speak of enjoying Christ while living in worldliness, indulging in pride, gratifying our lusts, giving a loose reign to our temper and passions, is a fatal delusion. "If we say that we have fellowship with Him and walk in darkness, we lie and do not the truth" (1 John 1:6). The two things are wholly incompatible. "Fellowship with God" and "walking in darkness" are as diametrically opposed as heaven and hell.

Thus the place of all true priests – all believers, all members of the priestly household – is to be within the sacred precincts of the sanctuary in the immediate presence of God, feeding upon Christ in the power of personal holiness. All this we are taught in "the law of the meat offering."

Let the reader note particularly that "all the frankincense" was consumed on the altar. Why was this? Because frankincense typified the fragrance of Christ's manhood as enjoyed exclusively by God Himself. There was that in Christ as a Man down here, which only God could duly appreciate. Every thought, every look, every word, every movement, every act of "the Man Christ Jesus" emitted a fragrance which went up directly to the throne of God and refreshed the heart of Him who sat thereon. Not a single atom of Christ's perfectness or preciousness was ever lost. It might be lost on a cold, heartless world and even upon carnal and earthly-minded disciples, but it was not lost upon God. It all went up to Him according to its true value.

This is a spring of joy and comfort to the spiritual mind. When we think of how the blessed Lord Jesus was not appreciated in this world, how little even His own disciples understood or valued Him, how the rarest and most exquisite touches and traits of His perfect humanity were lost upon a rude and unbelieving world and even upon His own people, what a comfort to remember that He was perfectly understood and appreciated by the One who sat on the throne! There was an unbroken line of communication kept up between the heart of Jesus and the heart of God.

343

The cloud of incense was continually ascending to the throne from the only perfect Man who ever trod this cursed and groaning earth.

Not a grain of the incense was lost because not a grain was entrusted even into the hands of the priests. All went up to God. Nothing was lost. The world might despise and hate, the disciples might fail to understand or appreciate; what then? Was a single ray of Christ's moral glory to go for nothing? Surely not; all was duly estimated by Him for whom it was designed and who alone could value it aright. This was true in every stage of Christ's precious life down here. And when we reach the end of that life and see the climax when one disciple sold Him for thirty pieces of silver, another cursed and swore he knew Him not, all forsook Him and fled, the world nailed Him to a cross between two thieves, God showed to the universe how much He differed from all the thoughts of men by placing the crucified One on the throne of the Majesty in the heavens.

Thus much as to the primary application of the incense which, unquestionably, is to Christ. We may also observe that it has a secondary application to the believer which he should seek to understand. True Christianity is the outflow of the life of Christ in the believer's practical ways and this is most precious to God, though it may be lost upon an unbelieving world and even upon a professing Church. There is not a movement of the life of Christ in the believer, not an expression of what He is, not the smallest manifestation of His grace that does not ascend directly as sweet incense to the throne of God. It may not attract the notice or elicit the applause of this world. It may not get a place in the records of men, but it goes up to God. This is enough for the faithful heart. God values all that is of Christ, nothing more, nothing else. There may be much that looks like service – much show, much noise, much that men make a great ado about – but nothing goes up to the throne, nothing is entered into the imperishable records of eternity but that which is the fruit of the life of Christ in the soul.

May God the Holy Spirit lead us into the experimental understanding of these things and bring forth in us, day by day, a brighter and fuller manifestation of Christ to the glory of God the Father!

THE BRAZEN SEA
(2 CHRONICLES 4)

"And Solomon made a molten sea of ten cubits from brim to brim, round in compass, and five cubits the height thereof; and a line of thirty cubits did compass it round about. And under it was the similitude of oxen which did compass it round about; ten in a cubit, compassing the sea round about. Two rows of oxen were cast, when it was cast. It stood upon twelve oxen, three looking toward the North, and three looking toward the West, and three looking toward the South, and three looking toward the East; and the sea was set above upon them, and all their hinder parts were inward. And the thickness of it was an handbreadth, and the brim of it like the work of a brim of a cup, with flowers of lilies; and it received and held three thousand baths .... *the sea was for the priests to wash in.*" (2 Chron. 4:2-6).

In order to a have a clear understanding of the doctrine taught us in this beautiful and significant figure, three things demand our attention – the material, the contents and the objects. May God the Spirit guide our thoughts and speak to our hearts as we dwell upon these things!

The material. Solomon's molten sea was made of brass, the apt symbol of divine righteousness demanding judgment upon sin (as in the brazen altar) or demanding judgment upon uncleanness (as in the brazen sea). The Lord Jesus is spoken of in Revelation 1 as having "His feet like unto fine brass as if they burned in a furnace." It is thus He is seen walking among the candlesticks. He cannot tolerate evil, but must, in the exercise of judgment, trample it beneath His feet. This will explain the reason why the altar where sin was expiated and the sea where defilement was washed away, were both made of brass. Everything in Scripture has its meaning and we should seek in a spirit of prayer to ascertain what that meaning is.

It is most comforting and establishing to the heart to be assured that the sin which God freely pardons and the uncleanness which He freely removes have been both fully and forever judged and condemned in the cross. Not a single jot or tittle of guilt, not a single trace of uncleanness, has been passed over. All has been divinely judged. "Mercy rejoiceth against judgment" and "grace reigns through righteousness" (James 2:13; Rom. 5:21). The believer is pardoned and cleansed: his guilt and uncleanness were judged on the cross. The knowledge of this most precious truth works in a double way. It sets the heart and conscience perfectly free and also causes us to abhor sin and uncleanness with an ever growing intensity. The altar of brass told forth in silent yet impressive eloquence, its double story: guilt had been divinely condemned, dear testimony to the fact that uncleanness had been divinely judged, and on that ground, could be divinely washed away.

What deep consolation for the heart in all this! And yet it is holy consolation. I cannot gaze upon the antitype of the altar and lightly commit sin. I cannot think upon the antitype of the molten sea and indifferently contract defilement. My consolation is deep and solid because I know I am pardoned and cleansed, but my consolation is holy because I know that Jesus had to yield up His life to procure my pardon and cleansing. God has been perfectly glorified; sin and uncleanness have been perfectly condemned; I am set eternally free; but the death of Christ is the basis of all. Such is the consolatory yet holy lesson taught us in the material of the brazen altar and the molten sea. Nothing is passed over by God, yet nothing is imputed to me because Christ was judged for all.

Let us now consider *the contents* of Solomon's molten sea. "It received and held three thousand baths" of water. If at the altar I see brass in connection with blood, at the sea I find brass in connection with water. Both point to Christ. "This is He that came by water and blood, Jesus Christ; not by water only, but water and blood" (1 John 5:6). "But one of the soldiers with a spear pierced His side and forthwith came there out *blood and water*" (John 19:34). The blood that expiates and the water that cleanses both flow from a crucified Savior. Precious and solemn truth! Precious, because we have expiation and cleansing; solemn, because of the way in which we get them.

But the brazen sea contained water, not blood. Those who approached thereto had *already* proved the power of the blood and therefore only needed the washing of water. Thus it was in the type and thus it is with the antitype. A priest under the law, whose hands and feet had become defiled, did not need to go back to the brazen altar, but forward to the brazen sea. He did not need to again apply the blood to constitute him a priest, but only to wash with water to enable him to discharge his priestly functions. So now, if a believer fails, if he commits sin, if he contracts defilement, he does not need to be again washed in the blood as at the first, but simply needs the cleansing action of the Word whereby the Holy Spirit applies to the soul the remembrance of what Christ has done. So the defilement is removed, the communion restored and the spiritual priest fitted afresh to discharge his priestly functions. "He that is washed needeth not except to wash his feet, but is clean every whit" (John 13:10). "The worshippers once purged should have had no more conscience of sins" (Heb. 10:2). Does this make little of defilement? The very opposite! Did the provision of a molten sea, with its 3000 baths of water, make little of priestly defilement? Did it not rather prove how much was made of it, what a serious matter it was in the judgment of God, how impossible it was to go on with a single soil upon the hands and feet?

Let my reader ponder this matter. Let him examine it in the light of Scripture. Let him make sure he really understands it. There is, in many cases, a great lack of clearness as to the doctrine set forth in the brazen altar and the molten sea. Hence, so many earnest Christians get into spiritual darkness and trouble as to the question of daily sins and daily defilement. They do not see the divine completeness of their cleansing by the blood of Christ. They therefore entertain the idea that they must, on every fresh occasion, go as at the beginning to the brazen altar as if they had never been washed at all. This is a mistake. When once a man is purged by the blood of Jesus, he is clean forever. If Christ has cleansed me, I am divinely, eternally clean. I am introduced into a condition to which perfect cleanness attaches and I can never be out of it. I may lose the *sense* of it, the *power* of it, the *enjoyment* of it. Peter speaks of some forgetting that they were purged from their old sins. If sin be trifled with and if self be not judged, it is hard to say what a Christian may come to. The Lord give us to walk softly and tenderly before Him every day so we may not come under the blinding and hardening influence of sin!

But be it remembered that the most effective safeguard against the working and the influence of sin is to have the heart established in grace and to be clear in the understanding of our standing in Christ. To be dark or doubtful as to these things is the sure way of falling into Satan's snares. If I am seeking to live a holy life in order to establish my position before God, I shall either be propped up in pharisaism or be plunged into some horrible sin. But when I know that all my sins and all my defilements were judged and condemned in the cross, and that I am justified and accepted in a risen Christ, then I stand on the true ground of holiness. And if I fail, as I do constantly, I can bring my failure to God in confession and self-judgment and know Him as faithful and just to forgive me my sins and to cleanse me from all unrighteousness.

I judge myself on the ground that Christ has been already judged before God for the very thing which I confess in His presence. If it were not so, my confession would be of no use. The only ground on which God can be "faithful and just to forgive and cleanse" is that Christ has already been judged on my behalf. And most assuredly, God will not execute judgment twice for the same thing. Blessedly true it is, I must confess and judge myself if I have gone wrong. A single sinful thought is sufficient to interrupt my communion. Every such thought must be judged before my communion can proceed. *But it is as a purged one that I confess. I am no longer viewed as a sinner, having to do with God as a Judge. I am now in the position of a child having to do with God as a Father.* He has made provision for my daily need, a provision which does not involve a denial of my place and portion or an ignoring of the work o£ Christ, but a provision which tells me at once of the holiness and grace of Him who made it. I am not to ignore the altar because I need the sea, but I am to adore the grace of Him who provided both the one and the other.

Having said thus much on the material and contents of Solomon's molten sea, a few words will suffice as to *the object thereof. "The sea was for the priests to wash in."* There came the priests from day to day to wash their hands and feet so they might always be in a fit condition to go through their priestly work. This is a striking type of God's spiritual priests – of all true believers whose works and ways need to be cleansed by the action of the Word. Both the brazen laver in the tabernacle and the brazen sea in the temple foreshadowed that "washing of water by the Word" which Christ is now carrying on by the power of the Holy Spirit. Christ in Person is acting up in heaven for us; by His Spirit and Word, He is acting in us and on us. Only thus are we enabled to get on. He restores us when we wander; He cleanses us from every soil; He corrects our every error. He ever lives for us. We are saved daily by His life. He maintains us in the full power and integrity of the position in which His precious blood has set us. All is secured in Him. "Christ loved the Church and gave Himself for it; that He might sanctify and cleanse it with the washing of water *by the Word*, that He might present it to Himself a glorious Church, not having spot or wrinkle or any such thing; but that it should be holy and without blemish" (Eph. 5:25-27).

Finally, one word as to the "oxen" which held up the brazen sea. The ox is used in Scripture as the symbol of patient labor. Hence their significant place beneath the brazen sea. From whatever side the priest approached, he was met by the apt expression of patient labor. It mattered not how often or in what way he came, he could never exhaust the patience that was devoted to the work of cleansing him from all his defilements. What a precious figure! And we have the substance in Christ. *We can never weary Him by our frequent coming. His patience is exhaustless.* He will not tire until He presents us to Himself without spot or wrinkle or any such thing.

May our hearts adore Him who is our Altar, our Laver, our Sacrifice, our Priest, our Advocate, our All!

THE GRAPES OF ESHCOL
(NUMBERS 13)

The grand principle of the divine life is faith – simple, earnest, whole-hearted faith that just takes and enjoys all that God has given, faith that puts the soul in possession of eternal realities and maintains it therein habitually. This is true in reference to the people of God in all ages. "According to your faith, so be it unto you," is ever the divine motto. There is no limit. All that God reveals, faith may have. All that faith can grasp, the soul may abidingly enjoy.

It is well to remember this. We all live very far below our privileges. Many are satisfied to move at a great distance from the blessed Center of all our joys. We are content with merely knowing salvation, while at the same time, we taste but little of holy communion with the Person of the Savior. We are satisfied with merely knowing that a relationship exists, without earnestly and jealousy cultivating the affections belonging thereto. This is the cause of much of our coldness and barrenness. As in the solar system the further a planet is from the sun the colder its climate and the slower its movement. So in the spiritual system, the further one moves from Christ, the colder will be the state of his heart toward Christ and the slower his movement for Christ. Fervor and rapidity will ever be the result of felt nearness to that central Sun, the great Fountain of heat and light.

The more we enter into the power of the love of Christ, the more we realize His abiding presence with us, the more intolerable we shall feel it to be away from Him. Everything will be dreaded and avoided which would tend to withdraw our hearts from Him or hide from our souls the light of His blessed countenance. The one who has really learned anything of the love of Christ cannot live without it; yes, it can part with all else for it. When away from Him, nothing is felt except the gloom of midnight and the chilling breath of winter, but in His presence the soul can mount upward like the lark as he rises into the bright blue heavens to salute with his cheerful song, the sun's morning beams.

Nothing exhibits more the deep-seated unbelief of our hearts than the fact that, while our God would have us enjoying communion with the very highest truths, few of us ever think of aspiring beyond the mere basics. Our hearts do not sigh after the highest walks of spiritual scholarship. We are satisfied with having the foundation laid, and are not as anxious as we should be to add layer after layer to the spiritual superstructure. Not that we can ever do without the foundation. This would be impossible. The most advanced scholar must carry the basics along with him, and the higher the building is raised, the more the need of a solid foundation is felt.

Let us look at Israel's case. Their history is full of rich instruction for us. It is "written for our admonition" (1 Cor. 10:11). We must contemplate them in three distinct positions – as sheltered by the blood, as victorious over Amalek and as introduced into the land of Canaan.

Now, clearly, an Israelite in the Land of Canaan had lost nothing of the value of the first two points. He was not the less shielded from judgment or delivered from the sword of Amalek because he was in the land of Canaan. No, the milk and honey, the grapes and pomegranates of that goodly land would but enhance the value of that precious blood which had preserved them from the sword of the destroyer and afford the most unquestionable evidence of their having passed beyond the cruel grasp of Amalek.

Still no one would say that an Israelite ought to have sought nothing beyond the blood-stained lintel. It is plain he ought to have fixed his steady gaze on the vine-clad hills of the promised land and said, "There lies my destined inheritance, and by the grace of Abraham's God, I shall never rest satisfied until I plant my foot triumphantly thereon." The blood-stained lintel was the starting post; the land of promise, the goal. It was Israel's high privilege not only to have the assurance of full deliverance from the hand of Pharaoh and the sword of Amalek, but also to cross the Jordan and pluck the mellow grapes of Eshcol. It was their sin and their shame that with the clusters of Eshcol before them, they could ever long after "the leeks, the onions and the garlic" of Egypt.

But how was this? What kept them back? Just that hateful thing which, from day to day and hour to hour, robs us of the precious privilege of treading the very highest stages of the divine life. And what is that? *Unbelief!* "So we see that they could not enter in because of unbelief" (Heb. 3:19). This caused Israel to wander in the desert for 40 tedious years. Instead of looking at Jehovah's power to bring them into the land, they looked at the enemy's power to keep them out of it. Thus they failed. In vain did the spies, whom they themselves proposed to send (Deut. 1:22*), bring back a most attractive report of the character of the land. In vain did the spies display in Israel's view a cluster of the grapes of Eshcol, so luxuriant that two men had to bear it upon a staff. All was useless. The spirit of unbelief had taken possession of their hearts. It was one thing to admire the grapes of Eshcol when brought to their tent doors by the energy of others, and quite another to move onward in the energy of *personal faith* and pluck those grapes for themselves.

And if "twelve men" could get to Eshcol, why not 600,000? Could not the same hand that shielded the one, shield the other likewise? Faith says "Yes." But unbelief shrinks from responsibility and recoils before difficulty. The people were no more willing to advance after the spies returned than before they set out. They were in a state of unbelief, first and last. And what was the result? That out of 600,000 which came up out of Egypt, only *two* had sufficient energy to plant their foot in the land of Canaan. This tells a tale. It utters a voice. It teaches a lesson. May we have ears to hear and hearts to understand.

It may be said by some that the time had not yet arrived for Israel's entrance into the land of Canaan inasmuch as "the iniquity of the Amorites was not yet full." This is but a one-sided view of the subject and we must look at both sides. The apostle expressly declares that Israel "could not enter in *because of unbelief.*" He does not assign as a reason "the iniquity of the Amorites" or any secret counsel of God with respect to the Amorites. He simply gives as a reason, the unbelief of the people. They might have got in if they would.

Nothing can be more unwarrantable than to make use of the unsearch-

---

* It is important to note that the proposal to send the spies originated with Israel. "And ye came near unto me, every one of you, and said, We will send men before us, and they shall search us out the land, and bring us word again by what way we must go up, and into what cities we shall come" (Deut. 1:22). An artless faith would have taught them that the One who had conducted them out of Egypt, through the Red Sea and across the desert, could and would lead them onward into Canaan, show them the way, and tell them all about it. But, alas! they wanted an arm of flesh. The chariot of Jehovah, moving majestically before the host, was not sufficient for them. They would "send men before them." God was not sufficient, Ah! what hearts we have! How little we know, and hence how little we trust God!

Some, however, may ask, "Did not the Lord command Moses to send the spies?" (Num. 13:1-3). True; and the Lord commanded Samuel to anoint a king over Israel (1 Sam. 8:22). Did this clear them of the sin of asking for a king and thus rejecting Jehovah? Surely not. Well, then, the same holds good with respect to the spies. The unbelief of the people led them to ask for spies, and Jehovah gave them spies. The same unbelief led them to ask for a king, and Jehovah gave them a king. "He gave them their request; but sent leanness into their soul "(Ps. 56:15). How often this is the case with us!

able counsels and decrees of God to throw overboard man's solemn responsibility. It will never do. Are we to fold our arms and lie back in the indolence of unbelief because of God's eternal decrees about which we know nothing? To say so can only be viewed as a piece of monstrous extravagance, the sure result of pushing one truth to such an extreme as to interfere with the range and action of some other truth equally important. We must give each and every truth its due place. We should not run one truth to seed while some other truth is not even allowed to take root. We know that unless God blesses the labors of the farmer there will be no crop at the time of harvest. Does this prevent the diligent use of the plough and the harrow? Surely not, for the same God who has appointed the crop as the end, has appointed patient labor as the means.

Thus it is also in the spiritual world. God's appointed end must never be separated from God's appointed means. Had Israel trusted God and gone up, the whole assembly might have delighted themselves on Eshcol's luxuriant clusters. This they did not do. The grapes were lovely: this was obvious to all. The spies were constrained to admit that the land flowed with milk and honey. But there was sure to be a "nevertheless." Why? Because they were not trusting in God. He had already declared to Moses the character of the land and His testimony ought to have been amply sufficient. He had said in the most unqualified manner, "I am come down to deliver them out of the hand of the Egyptians and to bring them up out of that land unto a good land and a large, unto a land flowing with milk and honey" (Ex. 3:8). Should not this have been sufficient? Was not Jehovah's description much more trustworthy than man's? Yes, to faith, but not to unbelief. Unbelief can never be satisfied with divine testimony, it must have the testimony of the senses. God had said it was "a land flowing with milk and honey." This the spies admitted. But hear the additions. "Nevertheless the people be strong that dwell in the land and the cities are walled and very great; and moreover, we saw the children of Anak there .... and there we saw the giants, the sons of Anak, which come of the giants; and we were in our own sight as grasshoppers, and so were we in their sight" (Num. 14:28).

Thus it was with them. They only "saw" the frowning walls and towering giants. They did not see Jehovah because they looked with the eye of sense and not with the eye of faith. God was shut out. He never gets a place in the calculations of unbelief. It can see walls and giants, but it cannot see God. It is only faith that can "endure as seeing Him who is invisible." The spies could declare what they were in their own sight and in the sight of the giants, but not a word about what they were in God's sight. They never thought of this. The land was all that could be desired, but the difficulties were too great for them. They had not faith to trust God. The mission of the spies proved a failure. Israel "despised the pleasant land" and "in their hearts, turned back again into Egypt."

This is the sum of the matter. Unbelief kept Israel from plucking the grapes of Eshcol and sent them back to wander for 40 years in the wilderness. These things, be it remembered, "were written for our admonition." May we deeply and prayerfully ponder the lesson! Out of 600,000 who came up out of Egypt, only two planted their foot on the fruitful hills of Palestine! Israel passed the Red Sea, triumphed over Amalek, but drew back in fear and retreated before "the sons of Anak," though these latter were no more to Jehovah than the former.

Now, let the Christian reader ponder all this. The special object of this paper is to encourage him to arise and in the energy of a full, unqualified trust in Christ, tread the very highest stages of the life of faith. Having our solid foundation laid in the blood of the cross, it is our privilege not only to be victorious over Amalek (indwelling sin) but also to taste of the old corn of the land of Canaan, to pluck the grapes of Eshcol and delight ourselves in its flowing tide of milk and honey: in other words, to enter into the living and elevated experiences which flow from habitual fellowship with a risen Christ with whom we are linked in the power of an endless life. It is one thing to know that our sins are cancelled by the blood of Christ. It is another thing to know that Christ has destroyed the power of indwelling sin. And it is a still higher thing to live in unbroken fellowship with Himself.

It is not that we lose the sense of the two former when living in the power of the latter. Quite the opposite. The more closely I walk with Christ, the more I have Him dwelling in my heart by faith, the more I shall value all He has done for me, both in the putting away of my sins and in the entire subjugation of my evil nature. The higher the superstructure rises the more I shall value the solid foundation beneath. It is a great mistake to suppose that those who move in the higher spheres of spiritual life could ever undervalue the title by which they do so. Oh! no; the language of those who have passed into the innermost circle of the upper sanctuary is, "Unto Him that loved us and washed us from our sins in His own blood." They talk of the love of Christ's heart and the blood of His cross. The nearer they approach to the throne, the more they enter into the value of that which placed them on such a delightful elevation. And so with us; the more we breathe the air of the divine presence, the more we tread in spirit the courts of the heavenly sanctuary, the more highly shall we estimate the riches of redeeming love. It is as we pluck the grapes of Eshcol in the heavenly Canaan, that we have the deepest sense of the value of that precious blood which shielded us from the sword of the destroyer.

Let us not, therefore, be deterred from aiming after a higher consecration of heart to Christ by a false fear of undervaluing those precious truths which filled our hearts with heavenly peace when first we started on our Christian career. The enemy will use anything and everything to keep the spiritual Israel from planting the foot of faith in the spiritual Canaan. He will seek to keep them occupied with themselves and with the difficulties which attend upon their upward and onward course. He knows that when one has really eaten of the grapes of Eshcol, it is no longer a question of escaping from Pharaoh or Amalek. Hence he sets before them the walls, the giants and their own nothingness, weakness and unworthiness. But the answer is simple and conclusive. It is this: trust! trust! trust! Yes, from the blood-stained lintel in Egypt to the rare and exquisite clusters of Eshcol, it is all simple, unqualified, unquestioning trust in Christ. "By faith they kept the passover, and the sprinkling of blood" and "by faith the walls of Jericho fell down" (Heb. 11). From the starting post to the goal, and at every intermediate stage, "The just shall live by faith."

But let us never forget that this faith involves the full surrender of the heart to Christ, as well as the full acceptance of Christ for the heart. Reader, let us ponder this deeply. It must be wholly Christ for the heart and the heart wholly for Christ. To separate these things is to be "like a rowboat with only one oar, which goes round and round, but makes no progress. It only drifts with the stream, whirling as it drifts. Or like a bird with a broken wing, whirling over and over, and falling as it whirls." This is too much lost sight of. Hence, the uncertain course and fluctuating experience. There is no progress. People cannot expect to get on with Christ in one hand and the world in the other. We can never feast on "the grapes of Eshcol" while our hearts are longing after "the flesh pots of Egypt."

May the Lord grant us a whole heart, a single eye, an upright mind. May the one commanding object of our souls be to mount upward and onward. Having all divinely and eternally settled by the blood of the cross, may we press forward with holy energy and decision "toward the mark, for the prize of our high calling of God in Christ Jesus."

"0 wondrous grace! 0 love divine!
  To give us such a home;
Let us the present things resign,
  And seek the rest to come;

And gazing on our Savior's cross,
  Esteem all else but dung and dross:
Press forward till the race be run;
  Fight till the crown of life be won."

THE TWO MITES
(MARK 12:41-44)

"And Jesus sat over against the treasury and beheld how the people cast money into the treasury; and many that were rich cast in much. And there came a certain poor widow, and she threw in two mites, which make a farthing."

How little did these people know whose eye was watching them as they cast in their offerings! How little did they think of being scanned by One whose eye could penetrate the deepest depths of their hearts and read the motives that actuated them in what they were doing. It may be the showy pharisee was there, displaying his wealth and making a pompous exhibition of his religiousness. Perhaps, too, the cold formalist was there, dropping in heartless routine, his stereotyped coin into the treasury. Jesus saw it all, weighed it all, judged it all.

It is well to think on this on every occasion in the which we are called to contribute to the Lord's cause. Well to remember, as the box or the basket is placed in my hand, that "Jesus is sitting over against the treasury." His holy eye rests, not upon the purse, but upon the heart. He weighs not the amount, but the motive. If the heart is right, the amount will be right, according to His judgment. Where the heart beats to His Person, the hand will be open to His cause. All who really love Christ will count it their high and happy privilege to deny themselves in order to contribute to His cause. It is most marvelous that He should condescend to ask us so to do. Yet He does so and it should be our deep joy to respond "according as God has prospered us," ever remembering that He loves a cheerful giver because that is precisely what He is Himself, blessed be His holy Name!

However, the point on which we specially want to dwell in Mark 12 is the act of the poor widow. Amid the crowd of contributors who pressed forward to cast their offerings into the treasury, there was one who particularly engaged the attention of our blessed Lord. "There came a certain poor widow and she threw in two mites, which make a farthing."

Now, that was a very small amount indeed if looked at from a monetary point of view. But think of the offerer. She was a "widow" – a "poor widow," the very impersonation of all that is desolate, helpless and lonely. A widow always gives us the idea of one deprived of every earthly stay and natural prop. "She that is a widow indeed, and desolate, trusteth in God, and continueth in supplications and prayers, night and day."

True, there are many so-called widows who are not of this stamp at all – many who look anything but lonely and desolate. But these are quite abnormal. They are entirely outside the sphere of true widowhood. The Holy Spirit has furnished us with a striking photograph of this class in 1 Timothy 5:11-13.

But the poor widow at the treasury belonged to the class of true widows. She was one according to the mind of Christ. "And He called unto Him His disciples, and saith unto them, Verily I say unto you, That this poor widow hath cast more in than all they which have cast into the treasury. For all they did cast in of their abundance, but she of her want did cast in all that she had, even all her living."

Doubtless, had these been the days of the public press, the princely offerings of the wealthy would have been paraded in the columns of some newspaper with flattering allusion to their large amount, while the poor widow and her offering would have been passed over in contemptuous silence.

But our adorable Lord thought differently. The poor widow's two mites outweighed in His balance all the offerings put together. It is a comparatively easy thing to give tens, hundreds and thousands from our accumulated treasures, but it is not easy to deny self of a single luxury or comfort, to say nothing of a positive necessity. But she gave all her living to the house of her God. It was this which threw her into such moral kindredness of spirit with the blessed Lord Himself. He could say, "The zeal of Thy house has eaten Me up." And she could say, "The zeal of Thy house has eaten up my living." Thus she was very near to Him. What a privilege!

Reader, did you ever notice the shape in which she had her living? Why does the Spirit take such care to say "Two mites, which make a farthing?" Why not be content to say, "She threw in a farthing?" Ah! this would never do. It would not have bought out the real point of exquisite beauty, the true touch of wholehearted devotedness. *If she had had it all in one piece, she must have either given all or nothing.* Having it in two, she had the option of keeping half for her own living. And truly most of us would judge it extraordinary devotedness to give to the Lord's cause half of all we possessed in the world. But this poor widow had a whole heart for God. This was the point. There was no reserve whatever. Self and its interests were wholly lost sight of and she flung her whole living into that which to her heart represented the cause of her God. May God grant us something of this spirit!

"HE FROM WITHIN"
(LUKE 11:7)

The Word of God judges the human heart with perfect accuracy and discloses all its most secret springs of thought and action. Indeed, this is one special way in which we may know that it is the Word of God. The poor Samaritan woman could say, "Come, see a Man that told me all things that ever I did: is not this the Christ?" She judged that a Man who could lay bare before her the deep secrets of her heart and of her life, must needs be the long expected Messiah, and she judged rightly. In like manner, we may say, "Come, see a book that told me all things that ever I did: is not this the Word of God?" No one can read the heart but God. No book can disclose the human heart but God's book. Inasmuch as the Bible perfectly discloses the human heart, we may know, even had we no other mode of judging, that the Bible is the Word of God.

Such an argument may be utterly condemned by an infidel, a skeptic or a rationalist who must, therefore, be met on other grounds. But it is impossible for any upright mind to ponder the simple fact that the Bible perfectly unfolds man's very nature, his thoughts, his feelings, his desires, his affections, his imaginations, the most secret chambers of his moral being, and not be convinced that the Bible is the very Word of God which is "quick and powerful, and sharper than any two-edged sword, piercing even to the dividing asunder of soul and spirit, and of the joints and marrow, and is a discerner of the thoughts and intents of the heart" (Heb. 4:12).

Nor is it merely in the Word of God as a whole that we observe this intense power of "discerning the thoughts and intents of the heart," but also in detached passages, in brief sentences, in a verse or clause of a verse. Look for instance at the three words which appear at the head of this article. What a revelation of the selfishness of the human heart do these words contain! What an expression of the narrow enclosure within which it lives! What a brief, pointed, concise commentary upon man's reluctance to be intruded upon when he has made arrangements for his personal ease! Who can read them and not see in them a perfect mirror in which the very pulsations of his own heart are reflected?

We do not like to be intruded upon when we have retired from the scene around us into the narrow circle of our personal or domestic enjoyment. When we have drawn the curtains, made ready the fire, opened the desk or the book, we do not like to have to respond to a call from without. It is at such times we can enter into the words, "He from within." They really contain a volume of profound moral truth. They graphically and vividly set forth an attitude of heart in which we are all far too frequently to be found. We are all too ready when a call comes, to send forth our answer "from within." We are too prone to say, "Dear me! this is a most inconvenient moment for that person to call, just when I am so particularly engaged." All this is precisely the attitude of heart set forth in the selfish words, "He from within."

And what answer is sure to be returned from the one who speaks "from within?" Just what might be expected. "Trouble me not." The man who has retired into the narrow circle of his own personal ease and enjoyment, closed his door and drawn his curtains around him, does not like to be "troubled" by anyone. Such an one is sure to say, even though appealed to as a "friend," "I cannot rise." And why could he not "rise?" Because "the door was shut and his children were with him in bed." His reasons for not rising were all selfish, and when he did rise it was only from a selfish desire to avoid further trouble. *Insistence* prevailed over a selfishness which was insensitive to the appeals of friendship.

How unlike all this was the blessed Lord Jesus Christ! His door was never shut. He never answered "from within." He ever had a ready response to every needy applicant. He had not time to eat bread or take rest, so occupied was He with human need. He could say, "I forget to eat My meat," so entirely was He given up to the service of others. He never murmured on account of the ceaseless intrusion of needy humanity. He kept no record of all He had to do, nor did He ever complain of it. "He went about doing good." His food and His drink were to do the will of Him who sent Him and to finish His work. To Him the poor and the needy, the heavy-laden and the heart-broken, the outcast and the wretched, the homeless and the stranger, the widow and the orphan, the diseased and the desolate, might all flock in the full assurance of finding in Him a fountain ever flowing and sending forth in all directions the abundant streams of living sympathy toward every possible form of human need. The door of His heart was always wide open. He never said to any son of want or child of sorrow, "I cannot rise and give thee." He was ready to "arise and go" with every needy applicant and His gracious word ever was "Give."

Such was Jesus when down here, and He is still "the very same, whose glory fills all heaven above." His door stands open so the vilest, the guiltiest and the neediest of sinners are welcome. They can have their crimson

360

and scarlet sins washed away in His atoning blood. They can have pardon and peace, life and righteousness, heaven and its eternal weight of glory, all as the free gift of grace divine. And while on their way from grace to glory, they can have all the love of His heart and the strength of His shoulder – that heart which told forth its affection on the cross and that shoulder which shall bear up the pillars of divine government forever.

Now, Christian reader, permit the word of exhortation. Remember that Christ is your life and that Christianity is nothing less than the living exhibition of Christ in your daily walk. Christianity is not a set of opinions to be defended or a set of ordinances to be observed. It is far more than these. It expresses itself thus, "To me to live is Christ." This is Christianity. May we know and manifest its power! May we be more occupied with Him who is our life! Then we too shall keep the door of the heart open to the sorrows, the miseries, the wants and the woes of fallen and suffering humanity. We shall be ready to "rise and give" to every case of real need. If we cannot give "three loaves" or the price of them, we shall at least give the look of love, the word of kindness, the tear of sympathy, the words of fervent intercession. And in no case shall we allow ourselves to get into the attitude of intense selfishness expressed in the words, "he from within." "For ye know the grace of our Lord Jesus Christ, that though He was rich, yet for your sakes He became poor, that ye through His poverty might be rich."

A MOTTO FOR THE NEW YEAR

Dear reader, we want you to accept a little motto for the year on which you have just entered. We think you will find it a precious motto for every year during which your Lord may see fit to leave you on this earth. It consists of two short but most weighty passages from the divine Volume. You will find them in Psalm 119. The first is this: "Forever, O Lord, Thy Word is settled in heaven" (v. 89). The second is, "Thy Word have I hid in mine heart, that I might not sin against Thee" (v. 11).

These are golden sentences for the present moment. They set forth the true place for the Word – "settled in heaven" and "hidden in the heart." Nor is this all; they also link the heart to the very throne of God by means of His own Word, thus giving to the Christian all the stability and all the moral security which the divine Word is capable of imparting.

We do not forget that to enter into the power and value of these words, there must be faith worked in the soul by the Holy Spirit. We would remember this. But our present subject is not faith nor yet the precious work of the Spirit of God, but simply the Word of God in its eternal stability and its holy authority. We esteem it an unspeakable mercy and privilege in the midst of all the strife and confusion, the discussion and controversy, the conflicting opinions and dogmas of men, the ever shifting sands of human thought and feeling, to have something "settled." It is a sweet relief and rest to the heart that perhaps has been tossed about for many a year on the troubled sea of human opinion, to find there is, in spite of all, that on which one may lean with all the calm confidence of faith and find therein divine and eternal stability.

What a mercy, in the face of the unrest and uncertainty of the present moment, to be able to say, "I have gotten something settled *forever* and *in heaven!*" What effect, we may ask, can the bold and insolent reasoning of infidelity or the sickly vaporings of superstition have upon the soul that can say, "My heart is linked to the throne of God by means of that Word which is settled forever in heaven?" None whatever. Infidelity and superstition, the two great agents of hell in this day in which we live, can only affect those who really have nothing settled, nothing fixed, no link with the throne and heart of God. The wavering and undecided – those who remain undecided between two opinions, who are looking this way and that way, who are afloat, who have no heaven, no anchorage – are in imminent danger of falling under the power of infidelity and superstition.

We invite the special attention of the young reader to all this. We would sound a warning note in the ears of such. The present is a moment of deep solemnity. The arch-enemy is putting forth every effort to sap the very foundations of Christianity. In all directions the divine authority and all-sufficiency of Holy Scripture is being called in question. Rationalism is gaining ground to a fearful extent at our seats of learning and polluting the fountains where the streams of religious thought and feeling are spreading over the land. Truth is discounted even among those who ought to be its guardians. We may now-a-days behold the strange sight of professing Christian teachers taking part at meetings where professed infidels preside. Sorrowfully, men who are professed infidels themselves may become pastors and teachers in that which calls itself the Church of God.

In the face of all this, how precious, how weighty is our motto, "Forever, O Lord, Thy Word is settled in heaven!" Nothing can touch this. It is above and beyond the reach of all the powers of earth and hell, men and demons. "The Word of our God shall stand forever." The Lord be praised for the sweet and solid consolation of this!

But let us remember the counterpart: "Thy Word have I hid in mine heart, that I might not sin against Thee." Here lies the great moral safe-guard for the soul in this dark and evil day. To have God's Word hidden in the heart is the divine secret of being preserved from all the snares of the enemy and from all the evil influences which are at work around us. Satan and his agents can do absolutely nothing with a soul that reverently clings to Scripture. The man who has learned in the school of Christ, the force and meaning of that one commanding sentence, "It is written," is safe against all the fiery darts of the wicked one.

Dear reader, let us earnestly entreat you to ponder these things. Let us remind you that the one grand point for the people of God at all times is *obedience*. It is not a question of power or of gift or of external show or of numbers; it is simply a question of obedience. "To obey is better than sacrifice." To obey what? The Church? No! The Church is a hopeless ruin and cannot therefore be an authority. Obey what? The Word of the Lord! What a rest for the heart! What authority for the path! What stability for the whole practical career! There is nothing like it. It tranquilizes the spirit in a wonderful manner and imparts a holy consistency to the character. It is a divine answer to those who talk of power, boast of numbers, point to external show and profess reverence for antiquity. Moreover, it is the divine antidote for the spirit of independence, so common at the present day, and for the haughty uprisings of the human will and the bold assertion of man's rights. The human mind is tossed like a ball from superstition to infidelity and can find no rest. It is like a ship without compass, rudder or anchor, driven here and there.

Thanks be to God for all those to whom the Holy Spirit has applied our mottos.

REASON AND REVELATION

Feeling as we do the deep solemnity of the present time and the danger which besets the Christian's path on every side, we press upon our readers the immense importance of the Word of God and implicit subjection to its holy authority in all things.

We do not exactly feel called upon to take formal notice of attacks upon the Word. We look upon such attacks as the direct and positive work of Satan who is seeking in every possible way to shake the foundations of our most holy faith and to pave the way for the march of infidelity and blasphemy which will before long darken the whole civilized world. It is surely most appalling to think that the professed pastors and teachers of Christianity should be the very men to rise up and lay impious hands upon the pillars upon which Christianity stands. May the Lord have mercy upon them and open their eyes that they may see their folly, guilt and danger, and flee for refuge to that precious blood which cleanses from all sin!

Still, though we do not deem it our place to review or expose infidel books, we will raise a warning cry against the influence of infidel principles. We see in all directions an effort to humanize everything divine and sacred; to bring everything down to the level of man's blind and perverted reason; to exclude all that is mysterious, all that is heavenly and divine; to exalt reason and insult revelation; to shut out God. Yes, beloved reader, this is the enemy's grand effort – to shut out God and upset God's revelation. We look in one direction and we see professedly Christian teachers seeking to undermine Christianity. We turn our eyes to another direction and behold a so-called Christian bishop sitting in judgment upon the Pentateuch and defiantly denying its divine inspiration. We look again and see some daring to approach the profound mystery of the cross, *to speculate as medical men upon the causes of the death of Christ!*

We shudder at the contemplation. We ask, where are we? What will come next? Is God to be shut out in everything? Must He not speak at all? Is He to be refused a hearing if He utters a word which man's stupid reason cannot understand? Does faith come by reason and reason by the word of man? It would seem so. The rare and exquisite touches of the pen of inspiration must be tried by the clumsy rules of arithmetic or the far more clumsy rules of the infidel's moral sense. The precious sacrifice of the Son of God must be treated more as a subject for a doctor's case-book than as a holy mystery revealed in the pages of the Book of God.

May God preserve His saints in these perilous times! May he fill our hearts with a very deep sense of the solemnity of the present moment and lead us to keep close to Himself and to His Word! Then shall we be safe from every hostile influence. Then shall we not regard the sneer of the skeptic or the arguments of the infidel. We shall know where all such things come and where they go. Christ will be our enjoyed portion, His Word and Spirit our guide, His coming the hope of our hearts.

"NEVERTHELESS"

The word which forms the heading of this paper occurs in Ephesians 5:33. It is a very important word, indicating what we are all so prone to forget, that there are two sides to every question, and in particular to the great question before the apostle's mind in this passage. He is speaking of the subject of marriage and of the relative duties of husband and wife, and he uses as an illustration, "The great mystery of Christ and the Church."

There are two sides to this subject. There is a heavenly side and there is an earthly side. We want them both. We cannot dispense with either, and the Holy Spirit has, in His infinite wisdom, bound them together by the little word "nevertheless." And what God has joined together let not man put asunder! It is blessedly true that the Church's relation to Christ is heavenly. The Church is called to know, rejoice in, feed upon, walk with, follow and be conformed to a heavenly Christ.

All this is vital and fundamental truth which cannot for a moment be given up or lost sight of, without giving up, so far, the heavenly side of Christianity.

But are we not in danger of forgetting the *practical application* of all this to our present walk on the earth amid the stern realities of actual life day by day? Are not husbands and wives, parents and children, masters and servants, *earthly* relationships? Unquestionably. True, they are formed upon a heavenly model and to be carried out after a heavenly pattern, as they also rest upon a heavenly base. Still they are relationships in nature, formed on the earth and to be carried out in daily life. There will be no such relationships in heaven. They do not belong to the resurrection-state. They belong to nature, to earth, to our time-condition, and we are called to walk in them as Christian men, women and children, and to glorify God by our spirit and temper and manner, our whole deportment therein, from hour to hour and day to day.

Thus, for example, of what use is it for a man to speak of lofty theories respecting the heavenly relationship of Christ and the Church while he fails every day of his life in his earthly relationship as a husband? His wife is neglected. She may be treated coldly or harshly. She is not nourished, cherished, sustained and ministered to according to the heavenly model of Christ and His Church.

No doubt, the same pointed question may be asked in reference to the wife and to all the other sacred relationships of our earthly and natural existence, for "there are two sides to every question."

Hence the very great importance of the apostle's "nevertheless." It has wide application. It is most evident that the Holy Spirit anticipated the need of such a qualifying, modifying, regulating clause when, having commented upon the heavenly side of the subject of marriage, He adds, "Nevertheless, let every one of you in particular so love his wife even as himself; and the wife see that she reverence her husband."

Christian reader, let us remember the two sides. Let us deeply ponder the inspired "Nevertheless." We may rest assured there is a need for it. There is the most urgent need of the practical application of divine and heavenly truth to our natural relationships and earthly ways. We have to remember that God recognizes nature, else why have we marriage? *Flesh is not recognized, but nature is,* and even admitted as a teacher (see 1 Corinthians 11:14). We are not yet *actually* in heaven. We are there, thank God, as to our standing, there in spirit, there in principle, there by faith. Our life, our portion, our hope, our home is there because Christ is there.

But we are here on this earth, called to represent Christ in this world as He represents us in heaven. God views us as men, women and children, called to tread the sand of the desert and to meet the positive realities of daily life. Life is a reality, an actual bona fide practical reality. And our God has provided for us in view of this fact, by the priestly ministry of Christ on high and by the ministry of the Holy Spirit and the teachings of Holy Scripture here below. We must have what is real to meet what is real. We are not called, thank God, to be occupied with visionary notions, with empty theories, with a powerless sentimentality, nor even with one-sided truth. No; we are called to be real, genuine, sound, practical Christian men, women and children. We are called to display in our daily history here on this earth, the practical results of that which we know and enjoy by faith in heaven. In one word, we must never forget that when the very highest truths are being unfolded before us, there is a healthful and holy *application* of these truths indicated by the inspired "Nevertheless."

HEADSHIP AND LORDSHIP

It is deeply interesting and most profitable to mark the varied lines of truth laid down in the Word of God and to note how all these lines stand inseparably linked with the Person of our Lord Jesus Christ. He is the divine Center of all truth. It is as we keep the eye of faith steadily fixed on Him that each truth will find its right place in our souls and exert its due influence and formative power over our course and character.

There is in all of us a tendency to be one-sided, to take up some one particular truth and press it to such a degree as to interfere with the healthy action of some other truth and hinder the growth of our souls. It is by *the* truth, not *some* truth, we grow; by the truth we are sanctified. But if we only take a part of the truth; if our character is molded and our way shaped by some particular truth, there can be no real growth, no true sanctification. "As newborn babes, desire the sincere milk of the Word, that ye may grow thereby" (1 Pet. 2:2). "Sanctify them through Thy truth; Thy Word is truth" (John 17:17). It is by the whole truth of God as contained in the Scriptures, that the Holy Spirit forms and fashions and leads in the Church collectively and in each individual believer. And we may rest assured that where some special truth is unduly pressed or some other truth practically ignored, there must be as a result a defective character and an inadequate testimony.

Take for example the two great subjects named at the head of this article – "Headship and Lordship." Is it not important to give each of these truths its due place? Is not Christ Head of His body the Church as well as Lord of the individual members? And, if so, should not our conduct be ruled and our character formed by the spiritual application of the former as well as the latter? Unquestionably. Well then, if we think of Christ as Head, it leads us into a very distinct and a very practical range of truth. It will not interfere with the truth of His Lordship, but will tend to keep the soul well balanced, which is so needful in days like the present. If we think only of Christ as Lord of His servants individually, we shall entirely lose the sense of our relationship one to another as members of that one body of which He is the Head. Then we shall be drawn away into mere independency, acting without the slightest reference to our fellow members. Each will stand out in his own intense individuality, practically disowning all vital connection with his brethren.

On the other hand when the truth of Christ's Headship gets its proper place in our souls – when we know and believe that "there is one body" and we are members one of another – then we will most fully own that each one of us, in our individual path and service, is responsible to the "one Lord." It will follow as a grand practical result that our walk and ways are affecting every member of the body of Christ on earth. "If one member suffer, all the members suffer with it." We can no longer view ourselves as independent, isolated atoms, seeing we are incorporated as members of "one body" by "one Spirit" and thus linked with the "one Head" in heaven.

This great doctrine is clearly and fully unfolded in Romans 12:3-8 and 1 Corinthians 12, to which we beg the reader's serious attention. Be it remembered that this truth of Christ's Headship and our membership is not a thing of the past merely; it is a present reality, a grand formative truth to be tenaciously held and practically carried out from day to day. "There is one body." This holds good today, just as thoroughly as when the inspired apostle penned the epistle to the Ephesians. Hence it follows that each individual believer is exerting a good or a bad influence upon other believers.

Does this seem incredible? If so, it is only to carnal reason and blind unbelief. Surely we cannot reduce the Church of God, the body of Christ, to a matter of geographical position. That Church, that body, is united by what? Life? No. Faith? No. By what, then? *By God the Holy Spirit!* Old Testament saints had life and faith, but what could they have known about a Head in heaven or a body on earth? Nothing whatever. If anyone had spoken to Abraham about being a member of a body, he would not have understood it. How could he? There was nothing of the kind existing. There was no Head in heaven and hence there could be no body on earth. True, the eternal Son was in heaven as a divine Person in the eternal Trinity, but He was not there as a glorified Man or as Head of a body.

Even in the days of His flesh, we hear Him saying, "Except a corn of wheat fall into the ground and die, it abideth alone." No union, no Headship, no membership, no vital connection until *after* His death upon the cross. It was not until redemption became an accomplished fact that heaven beheld that wonder of wonders – glorified humanity on the throne of God. The counterpart of that was God the Holy Spirit dwelling in men upon earth. Old Testament saints would have understood Lordship, but not Headship. This latter had no existence except in the eternal purpose of God. It did not exist in fact until Christ took His seat on high, having obtained eternal redemption.

Hence this truth of Headship is most glorious and precious. It claims the earnest attention of the Christian reader. We would solemnly and earnestly entreat him not to regard it as a mere speculation, as a matter of no importance. Let him be assured it is a great fundamental truth, having its source in a risen Christ in glory; its foundation in accomplished redemption; its present sphere of display, this earth; its power of development, the Holy Spirit; its authority, in the New Testament.

DAVID'S THREE ATTITUDES

In the course of David's most eventful and deeply instructive history, we find him presented by the pen of inspiration in three remarkable attitudes – lying as a penitent; sitting as a worshiper; standing as a servant. We also hear his utterances in these attitudes. The seeing and the hearing are full of deep moral instruction for our souls. May the Holy Spirit enable us to profit by it! May He guide our thoughts as we look at and listen to King David as a penitent, a worshiper and a servant! First, we have him:

LYING AS A PENITENT

"And David fasted, and went in and lay all night upon the earth" (2 Sam. 12:16). Here we have David lying upon the earth in the attitude of a true penitent. The arrow of conviction had entered his conscience. Nathan's pointed word, "Thou art the man," had fallen with divine power upon his heart. He takes his place in the dust, conscience-smitten and heart-broken before God.

Such is the attitude. Let us now listen to the utterance. We find it in Psalm 51. And what an utterance! How fully in keeping with the attitude! "Have mercy upon me, O God, according to Thy loving-kindness; according to the multitude of Thy tender mercies, blot out my transgressions." This is real work. The penitent places his sins side by side with the loving-kindness and tender mercy of God. This was the very best thing for him to do. The best place for a convicted conscience is the presence of divine mercy. When a convicted sinner and divine love meet, there is a speedy settlement of the question of sin. It is the joy of God to pardon sin. He delights in mercy. Judgment is His strange work. He will cause us to feel the sinfulness of sin, to judge it, to hate it. He will never work with untempered mortar or cry *peace* where there is no peace. He will send the arrow home. But, blessed be His name, the arrow from *His* quiver is sure to be followed by the love of His heart. The wound which His arrow inflicts will be healed by the precious balm which His love ever applies. This is the order: "Thou art the man," "I have sinned against the Lord," "The Lord hath put away thy sin."

Yes, beloved reader, sin must be judged in the conscience. And the more thoroughly it is judged the better. We greatly dread a superficial work of conscience – a false peace. We like to see the conscience probed to its deepest depths by the action of the Word and the Spirit of God. We want to see the grand question of sin and righteousness fully discussed and finally settled in the heart.

We have to bear in mind that Satan transforms himself into an angel of light, and in this dangerous character, it is quite possible he may endeavor to lead souls into a kind of false peace and happiness not founded upon the cross as the divine provision for the sinner's deepest need. We should deeply ponder those weighty words in the parable of the sower. "But he that received the seed into stony places, the same is he that heareth the Word and immediately with joy receiveth it: yet hath he no root in himself, but endureth for a while; for when tribulation or persecution ariseth because of the Word, by and by he is offended" (Mt. 13:20-21).

Mark the words, "Immediately, with joy receiveth it." There is no deep work of conscience, no moral judgment of self or of sin, and as a consequence, no depth of root, no power of endurance. This is very solemn and worthy of the most profound consideration at the present moment. We cannot too carefully ponder the connection between the expressions, "Immediately, with joy," "No root," "Withered away." There is great danger of a merely *intellectual* reception of the plan of salvation, apart from any spiritual work in the conscience. This is frequently attended with the most joyous emotions. The natural feelings are worked upon, but the truth has not penetrated the heart. There has been no furrow made by the action of the Word. Hence, when the time of trial comes, there is no power of continuance. It is found to be mere surface work which cannot stand the action of the sun's scorching rays.

Now, let not the reader suppose that we attach undue importance to conscience-work in the matter of conversion. We are fully persuaded that it is the Christ we reach and not the way we reach Him, that saves our souls. Moreover, the foundation of the soul's peace is not a certain process or exercise of any kind, whether of the heart, the conscience or the understanding. It is the divinely-effective sacrifice of the Son of God that purges the conscience and imparts peace to the convicted soul. It is the assurance on God's authority, received by the grace of the Holy Spirit, that the momentous question of sin was settled once and forever on the cross, that liberates the soul and gives a peace which nothing can ever disturb.

All this is so plain that if anyone were to say to us, "I have peace because I have passed through such deep exercises of conscience," we would without hesitation tell him he was self-deceived. It was not an exercise of conscience that ever satisfied the claims of God; therefore it is not an exercise of conscience that can ever satisfy the earnest cravings of a convicted soul. Christ is all, and having Him we want no more.

We deem it a thorough mistake for persons to build anything on the *mode* of their conversion. It is, in point of fact, affording the enemy an advantage over them which he is sure to use in shaking their confidence. The ground of the believer's peace is not that he was converted in such and such a manner – that he felt so deeply and wept so much, or struggled so hard or prayed so fervently. All these things have their place and their value. We do not suppose that Paul ever forgot the moment between Jerusalem and Damascus, but we are sure he never built his peace upon the remarkable circumstances of his conversion. Luther could never forget his two years in the monastery, but Luther never built his peace upon the profound exercises of those years. Bunyan could never forget the despondency, but Bunyan never built his peace upon the mental anguish which he tasted therein.

No doubt, the exercises through which these three remarkable men passed, exerted a very important influence on their future course and character, both as Christians and as ministers, but the ground of their peace was not anything they had felt or passed through, but simply what Christ had done for them on the cross. Thus it must ever be; Christ is all and in all. It is not Christ and a process, but Christ alone. Let souls ever remember this and let it be well understood that, while we press upon our readers the immense importance of a deep and thorough work of conscience, we do not want them to build upon the work *in* their conscience but upon Christ's work *on the cross.* It is the work accomplished *for* us and not the work done in us, that saves our souls. True, they are intimately connected and must not be separated, but they are thoroughly distinct and must not be confounded. We can know nothing of the work accomplished for us except by the work worked in us, but just in proportion to the depth and intensity of the work done in us, will be the clearness and fixedness of our rest in the work done for us.

But there is another point in reference to which we are anxious to avoid misunderstanding. Some might suppose that the object of our remarks on David *as a penitent* is to prove that unless we have passed through precisely the same exercises, we have no just ground for believing we are really regenerated. This would be a grave mistake. First, David had been a child of God long before that solemn moment on which we have been meditating.* Further, David found his relief, not in any exercises within, but in communications from without, not on the fact that the arrow had entered

---

* The reader will bear in mind that, in speaking of "David's three attitudes," we do not present them in their historical order, but simply view them as illustrating three grand points in the spiritual history of God's people.

his heart in the words, "Thou art the man" and drawn forth the penitential cry, "I have sinned against the Lord." No; but upon the precious truth conveyed to him in the words, "The Lord hath put away thy sin."

Finally, let not a damper be cast upon souls because the earliest moments of their spiritual history were characterized, not by profound penitential exercises, but rather by the most peaceful and happy emotions. It is impossible that the "glad tidings" of salvation can do anything else but gladden the believing soul. There was great joy in Samaria when Philip preached Christ to them, and the eunuch went on his way rejoicing when he learned that Jesus had died for his sins. How could it be otherwise? How could anyone believe in the forgiveness of sins and not be made happy by the belief? Impossible. "Glad tidings of great joy" must make the poor heart glad.

> "Forgiveness 'twas a joyful sound,
> To us when lost and doomed to die."

Surely it was. But does this fact interfere in the smallest degree with the value of a deep and thorough work of the Spirit of God in the conscience? By no means. A hungry man values bread, and although he will not think of feeding upon the pangs of hunger, yet the pangs of hunger make him value the bread. So it is with the soul. It is not saved by penitential exercises, but the deeper its exercises, the more solid its grasp of Christ and the more steady and vigorous its practical Christianity.

The simple fact, beloved reader, is this. We see in the present day a fearful amount of flippant, easy-going, airy Christianity, so called, which we greatly dread. We meet with many who seem to have attained a kind of false peace and frothy happiness without any real exercise of conscience or any application of the power of the cross to nature and its ways. These are stony-ground hearers. There is no root, no depth, no power, no permanency. And not only are such persons self-deceived, but the tone and aspect of their profession are, among other influences, forming the channel along which the tide of infidelity shall soon roll its poisonous and desolating waters. We believe that cold, powerless orthodoxy and flippant, formal, airy profession are, just as thoroughly as dark and degrading superstition, paving the way for that infidelity which shall yet cast its mantle over the whole civilized world.

This is a deeply solemn thought, but we dare not withhold it from our readers. We long to see a more effective testimony for Christ, a more earnest discipleship, a more thorough self-surrender and whole-hearted consecration to the name and cause of Christ. For this we sigh, for this we pray, but we certainly do not expect to find it amid the ranks of those who have never known much exercise of conscience or tasted the power of the cross of Christ.

However, we must not anticipate a line of thought which may come before us as we proceed with our subject. We shall, with God's blessing, see in David a noble illustration of personal devotedness. Meanwhile, let us contemplate him in the second of his remarkable attitudes:

SITTING AS A WORSHIPER

In the opening of 2 Samuel 7 we find David sitting in his house of cedar and surveying the many and varied mercies with which the hand of Jehovah had surrounded him. "And it came to pass, when the king sat in his house and the Lord had given him rest round about from all his enemies, that the king said unto Nathan the prophet, See now, I dwell in an house of cedar, but the ark of God dwelleth within curtains. And Nathan said to the king, Go, do all that is in thine heart: for the Lord is with thee."

David would build a house for God. But he was not the man, nor was it the time for that. Nathan is dispatched to correct the mistake. The service was well-meant, but that was not sufficient. It must be well-timed as well as well-meant. David had shed much blood. Moreover, there were enemies and evil at hand. There were also deeper lessons of grace in which David had to be instructed. God had done much for him, but all that had been done in the past was as nothing compared with what was yet to be done in the future. If a house of cedar was a great thing, how much greater was an everlasting house and kingdom. The Lord telleth thee, that "He will make thee an house." This was reversing the matter altogether. The doings of the past were full of grace; the doings of the future would be full of glory. The hand of electing love had lifted David from the sheepfold to place him on the throne of Israel. "And this was yet a small thing in Thy sight, O Lord God; but Thou hast also spoken of Thy servant's house for a great while to come." The past and the future are both brought in brilliant array before the vision of King David and he has only to bow his head and worship.

"Then went King David in and sat before the Lord, and he said, who am I, O Lord God?" Here we have David's second attitude. Instead of going out to build for the Lord, he went in and sat before the Lord. There is great moral beauty and power in this. To an unintelligent eye he might have seemed to be in a very useless attitude, but no one can ever stand as a servant who has not sat as a worshiper. We must have to do *with* the Lord before we can act *for* the Lord. Show us a man who has really occupied the place of a worshiper and we will show you one who, when he rises to his feet, will prove an effective servant.

Be it noted, it is one thing to sit before the Lord and another thing to sit before *our* work or service or preaching or circumstances or experiences – *our* anything. How often are we tempted to sit down and gaze at or think about *our* various exploits, even though these may be ostensibly in the Lord's work? This is sure to bring weakness. Nothing can be more miserable than self-occupation. It is right enough to feel thankful if the Lord has used us in any department of work, but let us beware of keeping self before our eyes in any shape or form, directly or indirectly. Let us not be found surveying the various things in which we are engaged, the different interests we have or the varied spheres of action in which we take part. All this tends to puff up nature, while it leaves the soul barren and impoverished.

Mark the difference! "Then went king David in and sat before the Lord, and said, who am I?" "I" is sure to fall into obscurity and oblivion when we sit before the Lord. We hardly know which to admire most, the attitude or the utterance. "He sat" and he said, "Who am I." Both are lovely, both in exquisite moral order. May we know more of their deep meaning and immense practical power! May we prove what it is to sit in the divine presence and there lose sight of self and all its belongings!

We do not attempt to enter upon an exposition of Psalm 51 which is David's utterance as a penitent, nor yet of 2 Samuel 7 which gives us his utterance as a worshiper. We merely introduce these precious Scriptures to the reader and pass on in the third place, to look at David's:

STANDING AS A SERVANT

"Then David the king stood up upon his feet" (1 Chron. 28:2). This completes the picture of this lovely character. We have seen him lying on the earth with the arrow of conviction piercing his conscience and the chastening rod of God held over him. We have seen him seated in the sanctuary, surveying the actings of grace in the past and anticipating the bright beams of glory in the future. And now we see him rising into the attitude of a truehearted servant to lay himself and his resources at Jehovah's feet. All is intensely real. The penitential cry, the aspirations of the worshiper, the words of devotedness and consecration – all is deep, fervent and genuine. "I have prepared with all my might for the house of my God." "Moreover, because I have set my affection to the house of God." What self-forgetting devotedness is here! David was not to have the honor of building the house, but what was that to one who had found his place in the sanctuary and learned to say, "Who am I?" It was all the same to David who was to build the home. It was the house of his God and that was enough. The strength of his hand, the love of his heart and the resources of his treasury were all willingly devoted to such an object.

We would like to pause here to enlarge, but we must close. May the Holy Spirit apply these things to our hearts by His mighty power. Christian reader, do you not long for more whole-hearted devotedness? Do you not sigh after a more lofty consecration of yourself and all you have to Christ and His cause in the earth? Well then, just get a little nearer to Him. Seek to be more in His presence. You have risen up from the attitude of a penitent, go now and sit and gaze and worship. Then when the proper occasion arises, you will be ready to occupy the position of an effective servant.

"GAIN TO ME"

"But what things were gain to me, those I counted loss for Christ" (Phil. 3:7). What a marvelous change! Saul had many sources of gain. He had gathered many honors around his name. He had made progress in Judaism beyond many of his equals. He had achieved a legal righteousness in which no man could find a flaw. His zeal, his knowledge and his morality were of the very highest order. But from the moment Christ was revealed to him, there was a thorough revolution. Everything was changed. *His* righteousness, *his* learning, *his* morality, all that could in any wise be gain to Paul, became as dung. He does not speak of open sins, but of those things that could justly be esteemed as gain to him. The revelation of the glory of Christ had so completely changed the entire current of Paul's thoughts, that the very things which he had once esteemed as positive gain, he now regarded as positive loss.

Why? Simply because he had found his all in Christ. That blessed One had supplanted everything in Paul's heart. All that belonged to Paul was displaced by Christ. Hence it would have involved actual loss to possess any righteousness or wisdom, holiness or morality of his own, seeing that he had found all these in divine perfectness in Christ.

If Christ is made of God unto me righteousness, is it not a loss to me to have any righteousness of my own? Surely. If I have gotten that which is divine, have I any need of that which is human? Clearly not. The more completely I am stripped and emptied of everything in which "I" could glory or which would be gain to "me," the better, inasmuch as it only renders me all the more entitled to a full and all-sufficient Christ. Whatever it be that tends to exalt self, whether it be religiousness, morality, respectability, wealth, glory, personal beauty, intelligence or philanthropy, it is a positive hindrance to our enjoyment of Christ as both the foundation of the conscience and as the object of the heart. May the Spirit of God make Christ more precious to us!

THE SUFFICIENCY AND
AUTHORITY OF THE SCRIPTURES

We agree with you in saying, "I recognize the voice of Jesus alone in His Word." Where else could we hear it? It is upon that blessed Word we are cast for everything. It is the solid foundation on which faith reposes. We want nothing else to give us full assurance but His faithful Word. No outward evidence, no inward feeling can possibly add to the truth and stability of the Word. How do I know I am a sinner? By the Word. How do I know that Jesus Christ came into the world to save sinners? By the Word. How do I know that my sins are forgiven? Is it by my feelings? No, but by the Word. That Word tells me that "Christ hath once suffered for sins." But how do I know He suffered for my sins? Because the Word says, "the just for the unjust, that He might bring us to God." I know I am "unjust" because the Word tells me so. Hence Christ suffered for my sins and I am forgiven according to the effectiveness of Christ's atoning suffering. I am brought to God according to the virtue and value of the Person and work of Christ. "He was delivered for my offenses and raised again for my justification." Thus, "being justified by faith, I have peace with God, through our Lord Jesus Christ."

Dear friend, you must lean like a little child on the Word. True, it is by the power of the Holy Spirit we believe in and feed upon the Word, but the Word is the solid foundation on which your precious soul must ever rest. May all your doubts and fears vanish in the pure and precious light of that Word which is "settled forever in heaven!"

You know from where such an infidel thought proceeds. It is from the father of lies. Treat it as such. Judge it and reject it utterly. It seems strange that after knowing the Lord for 40 years, you should even for a moment be troubled by the suggestion of one whom you know to be "a liar from the beginning." Ask a poor ignorant man how he knows the sun shines. Ask a simple believer how he knows the Bible is the Word of God. He will tell you he has felt its power. Has not the Holy Spirit given you to feel the power of the Word of God? If God cannot make me know that it is He who speaks to me in His Word, who else can?

Were we merely to believe in the divine inspiration of the Scriptures from human testimony – be that testimony ever so powerful – it would not be faith at all. I believe what God says because He says it, not because of any human authority. If all the fathers who ever wrote, all the doctors who ever taught, all the councils that ever sat, all the angels in heaven and all the saints upon earth, were to agree in declaring the Bible is the Word of God and we were to believe on their testimony, it would not be divinely-given faith. On the other hand, were all to agree in declaring the Bible is not the Word of God, it could not for a moment shake our confidence in that peerless revelation. Fling back, dear friend, at once into the enemy's teeth his foul and blasphemous suggestion and rest like a little child in the love and truth of that blessed One whom you have known for so many years.

We have not seen the book to which you refer, and judging from the extract which you have sent us, we have no desire to see it. We heartily and reverently believe in the absolute inspiration of the Holy Scriptures, given of God in the Hebrew and Greek languages. No doubt errors are found in various versions, copies and translations. We speak only of the Scriptures as given of God.

Oh, dear friend, what an unspeakable comfort to have a divine revelation! What should we do, where should we run if we were left to men's thoughts on the subject? What a poor affair it would be for us if we had to look to men to accredit the Word of God! They would very soon rob us of its authority and value. What impudent presumption for poor worms of the earth to dare to sit in judgment upon the Word of God, to pronounce upon what is and what is not worthy of God! If God cannot make us understand His Word, if He cannot give us the assurance that it is He Himself who speaks to us in Holy Scriptures, what are we to do? Can man manage the matter better? If God cannot make us understand His Word, no man can; if He does, no man need. We should earnestly counsel you, dear friend, to fling aside all such books, however highly commended.

Sadly, it seems to be the fashion today, in quarters where we should least expect it, to commend in most glowing terms all sorts of infidel books and blasphemous attacks upon the Word of God and the Person of Christ. We judge it to be a very great mistake indeed for Christians to read such books, unless they are called and fitted of God to expose them. Would you read a book entitled, "A treatise seeking to prove that two and three do not make five?" We hardly think you would. If God has graciously given you to rest by faith upon His eternal Word, what more do you want? Infidel books cannot help you. God is His own interpreter in Scripture as well as in providence. Would you think of turning to some skeptical or rationalistic book to help you in the solution of the mysteries of God's government? We trust not. Then why turn to such for a judgment as to inspiration? We cannot refrain from quoting for you that magnificent passage in 2 Timothy 3: "And that from a child thou hast known the Holy Scriptures, which are able to make thee wise unto salvation through faith which is in Christ Jesus. All Scripture is given by inspiration of God and is profitable for doctrine, for reproof, for correction, for instruction in righteousness; that the man of God may be perfect, thoroughly furnished unto all good works."

We greatly fear, dear friend, you were not under the cover of the shield of faith while reading this book of which you speak, but we earnestly pray that your precious soul may be enabled to fling off with calm decision any dark and skeptical suggestions which may be troubling you and to return to the eternal stability of divine revelation. God grant it in His infinite mercy.

The inspired Volume carries its own credentials with it. It speaks for itself. It comes to us with an overwhelming body of evidence, both internal and external. The Apocrypha, on the contrary, carried its own condemnation. It contains passages which you have only to read to be convinced that they were never inspired by the Spirit of God. We reject it on the ground of evidence, both internal and external.

The word in 1 Corinthians 11:2 should be rendered "traditions" or "directions." The apostle does not specify what they were, but thank God, we know that whatever ordinances, traditions or directions are essential for the Church to the end of time, are clearly laid down in the Scriptures of the New Testament. This is quite enough for us. Men have no authority whatever to set up rites and ceremonies in the Church of God; their doing so can only be regarded by every heart loyal to Christ as a daring usurpation of His authority which He will most assuredly judge before long.

We feel increasingly impressed, dear friend, with a sense of the urgent need of testing everything by the Word of God and of rejecting whatever cannot stand the test. It is not only deeply sorrowful, but most solemn to mark the way in which the authority of Christ as laid down in His precious Word is virtually set aside by those who profess to be His people and His servants. It never seems to occur to people that they are really responsible before God to judge by the light of His Word, the various things in which they are engaged. Hence they go on from week to week and year to year with a whole host of things having not a shadow of foundation in Holy Scripture. How appalling to think of the end of all this! It will not be with a scourge of small cords that all these things will be driven out of the temple! May God the Holy Spirit arouse by His mighty ministry, the whole Church to a more profound sense of the supreme authority and all-sufficiency of the Holy Scriptures!

May all the Lord's dear people be kept from the spirit of the age! We want to cultivate a truly humble contrite spirit, a spirit of lowly obedience, a spirit which shall lead us to bow down with unreserved submission to the authority of Holy Scripture. "It is written" is a sentence of commanding power. It is a sentence uttered by our blessed Lord and Master at the opening of His public career and referred to again and again in the course of His marvelous ministry. It was reiterated with solemn emphasis to His disciples as He was about to pass into the heavens. May this weighty sentence be engraved on the tablets of our hearts!

If we were asked to state what we consider to be the one grand need of the day in which our lot is cast, we would say without hesitation, we want to give the Word of God its true place as the basis of our individual peace and the sole and all-sufficient authority for our individual path. Let us unite, beloved friend, in earnest prayer to our God that He will give us grace so to do, to the praise of His holy name.

PRAYER

By all means persevere in prayer for the object you name. God may see it good to keep you waiting. The exercise is very healthful for the soul. There is a very encouraging word in Philippians 4, "Be careful for nothing; but in everything by prayer and supplication, with thanksgiving, let your requests be made known unto God." And what then? Does Paul say, "You shall immediately receive what you ask for?" No, but "The peace of God which passeth all understanding shall keep your hearts and minds through Christ Jesus." This is a most precious word. It presents a character of prayer so blessedly simple. We are encouraged by it to come to God about everything, no matter how small, without raising a question as to whether we have faith. We are to "make known our requests to God," though surely He knows them before. He loves to have us coming to Him about all our little matters and resting in the happy assurance that He will do what is right and give us what is good. Whether He gives or withholds, His peace shall guard our hearts and minds.

With regard to your difficulty in the matter of prayer, many are tried in the same way. It may be that you ask for things which would not be really good for you or it may be the Lord sees it right to exercise your heart by keeping you in the attitude of continued waiting upon Him. We have often been struck with the teaching of 1 John 3:21-22 and vv. 14-15. If we are in communion with God we shall ask for those things that are pleasing in His sight, we shall ask in faith and we shall assuredly get an answer. See also John 15:7, "If ye abide in Me and My words abide in you, ye shall ask what ye will and it shall be done unto you." This is very practical. May God Himself be your teacher.

It is regretfully possible that a Christian may find himself not in the spirit of prayer. When such is the case, he ought to judge himself and cry to God to lead him into a right state of soul. There is no value in form without power, but God is the abiding source of all power and freshness. And, blessed be His name, "He hath given us the spirit of power, and of love, and of a sound mind." Hence, when you find yourself not in a spirit of prayer, do not have recourse to a form but to the living God.

Our Lord does not forbid *frequent* repetition but "*vain* repetition." He Himself, blessed be His name, in His agony in the garden, prayed the same thing three times over. This is sufficient to prove that there may be repetition which is very far indeed from being "vain." An individual in the privacy of his closet, or a number of Christians in public assembly, may earnestly, fervently, perseveringly and importunately urge and re-urge a certain matter which presses heavily on the heart, without being open to the charge of "vain repetition."

In Romans 8:26-27 we are taught that the Holy Spirit makes intercession for us. He it is who is the Author of every true and right desire in our hearts. He teaches us to pray to the Father in the Name of Jesus. It is only by the Spirit that we can pray as we ought. As to the question of praying *to* the Holy Spirit, we do not think it intelligent. True, the Holy Spirit is God and is to be viewed in His own distinct Personality, but still the New Testament teaches us that He prays *in* us *to* the Father *by* the Son. A person praying to the Holy Spirit can hardly see with clearness the Spirit's indwelling.

In Acts 7:59 we have Stephen addressing prayer to the Lord Jesus. We cannot see how anyone could object to our doing the same. We must beware of being hyper-critical.

An intelligent worshiper will always address God in the character and by the name in which He is pleased to reveal Himself. His name to us is "Father." True, the One who is our Father was and is "the God of Jacob," "the Almighty God .... Jehovah," but to us He is Father. Precious title! May we ever live in the sunlight of His countenance! We would all readily say that it is not a question of bodily attitude in prayer, but rather of the state of the heart – the true attitude of the soul. At the same time we must confess we like to see people kneel down when they can. We say, "when they can" because in many cases, it is utterly impossible when people are so packed together as to be hardly able to move. There is no attitude which so aptly expresses prostration of soul as kneeling. It looks lazy and irreverent to see people always sitting while praying. But we must not judge one another in this matter. Many things have to be taken into account. The Lord looks upon the heart. May He ever find our hearts in the right attitude before Him! This is the grand point.

THE DIVINE CHARACTER OF FAITH

The inspired apostle James tells us that "Every good gift and every perfect gift is from above, and cometh down from the Father of lights." Does not this answer the question as to faith? Every perfect gift is from above and comes down from the Father of lights.

Some may have a difficulty as to Ephesians 2:8, "By grace are ye saved, through faith, *and this not of yourselves, it is the gift of God.*" But to us it is perfectly clear that "faith," like every other good and perfect gift, is from God. "All men have not faith," or as it should be read, "Faith is not of all." If faith be not the gift of God, it is only an exercise of the human mind and thus worthless.

Faith is a divine reality worked in the soul by the Holy Spirit. It grasps the revelation of God and thus links the heart with Him in a divine way. It is all of God from first to last. "All things are of God" in the new creation. Blessed be His holy name for the assurance! Were it not so – were there the weight of a feather or the movement of an eyelash of ours in the whole matter, it would spoil all.

THE LAW

Your question involves the very foundations of Christianity. We give you in reply, one brief but comprehensive statement of Holy Scripture. "For sin shall not have dominion over you: for ye are not under the law, but under grace." Again, "As many as are of the works of the law are under the curse" (See Rom. 7; Gal. 3). If we are to be taught by Scripture alone, then we learn that the believer is "dead to the law." He died in Christ as the New Testament teaches us in many places. Now, what has the law to say to a dead man? Or what has a dead man to say to the law? Is the law binding upon a dead man? The idea is absurd. "Wherefore, my brethren, ye also are become dead to the law by the body of Christ, that ye should be married to another, even to Him who is raised from the dead, that we should bring forth fruit unto God."

True it is that a Christian, walking in the Spirit, fulfills the practical righteousness of the law (Rom. 8:4). But if you put a Christian *under* the law, you put him under the curse, for the apostle declares that as many as are on that ground, not merely as many as have not kept the law, are under the curse. In short, *the entire teaching of Romans and Galatians is flatly opposed to the notion of putting Christians under the law whether for justification or as a rule of life.* So far from its being the ground of justification, it is the ground of condemnation. So far from its being a rule of life, it is a rule of death. See Romans 7:10 and 2 Corinthians 3.

Does anyone in his right mind need to be told that a Christian is not to steal or commit murder? Surely not. Let us remember that Christian morals rest on a *Christian* basis and not on a *legal* basis. The law was given to man in the old creation, to test him, prove him and cause the offense to abound. The Christian is not in the old creation but in the new (2 Cor. 5:17). He is not in the flesh but in the Spirit (Rom. 7:9).

Are these things mere figures of speech or are they divine statements concerning the very foundations of Christianity? Let us look well to it, dear friend. Let us see where we are. A person who, in his actual experience, is under the law, must be a stranger to the peace and liberty of the gospel. Moreover he must be wholly ignorant of the true character of Christianity.

If we trace the history and the writings of the great apostle of the Gentiles, we find there was nothing that so grieved and pained him – nothing he so strongly denounced – as the attempt to put Christians under the law in any shape or form or for any object whatsoever. When he

387

speaks of himself as "being under the law to Christ" (1 Cor. 9:21), any competent person understands that the word is "under rule or authority to Christ" and has nothing to do with being under the law of Moses, which the apostle everywhere denounces in the strongest terms. The law-teachers get no quarter whatever from Paul. This is as clear as anything can be. Hence, if we are going to submit to Scripture, the law question is easily settled. But if any man refuses to submit to that authority, we do not see there is much use in talking to him.

In 1 Corinthians 9:21 the expression "under the law" is one word which simply means *under the rule or authority of Christ.* Paul was not under the law of Moses, nor are we either, thanks be to God.

"The Jew" as such is bound to fulfill the law, or else to meet the curse pronounced upon "every man who continueth not in all things that are written in the book of the law to do them." But where is the Jew that can meet God on the ground of moral law or ceremonial law? Did you ever hear or know of one who could claim blessing on the ground of perfect obedience? It will be said, "There is mercy." Yes, but not under law. "He that despised Moses' law died without mercy." Law and mercy are two different things. If a man can fulfill the law, he does not need mercy; if he has not fulfilled the law, it has no mercy for him. What remains? Simply to take the place of a poor, ruined, self-destroyed, guilty sinner.

"0 Israel, thou hast destroyed thyself." What then? "In Me is thy help." But on whom has this help been laid? On One mighty to save, even the Messiah of Israel, Him of whom Isaiah speaks in the following well-known passage: "Behold, My Servant shall deal prudently, He shall be exalted and extolled, and be very high. As many were astonished at Thee; His visage was so marred more than any man and His form more than the sons of men. So shall He sprinkle many nations; kings shall shut their mouths at Him; for that which had not been told them shall they see, and that which they had not heard shall they consider. Who hath believed our report and to whom is the arm of the Lord revealed? For He shall grow up before Him as a tender plant and as a root out of a dry ground; He hath no form nor comeliness; and when we shall see Him, there is no beauty that we should desire Him. He is despised and rejected of men; a Man of sorrows and acquainted with grief; and we hid as it were our faces from Him; He was despised and we esteemed Him not. Surely He hath borne our griefs and carried our sorrows; yet we did esteem Him stricken, smitten of God, and afflicted. But He was wounded for our transgressions, He was bruised for our iniquities; the chastisement of our peace was upon

Him and with His bruising we are healed. All we like sheep have gone astray; we have turned every one to his own way; and the Lord hath laid on Him the iniquity of us all."

Here the repentant Jew may find the true ground of deliverance from the curse of the law. Christ was made a curse by hanging on a tree. "He suffered for sins, the Just for the unjust, that He might bring us to God." "And all who believe in Him are justified from all things, from which they could not be justified by the law of Moses." Nor this only; they are delivered from the law as a rule or principle, being counted dead to it by the death of Christ.

This in no wise interferes with Jeremiah 31:36-37 to which you refer. It has nothing to say to the question. If "the Jew embraces Christianity" he ceases to be a Jew and takes his stand on the new ground where there is neither Jew nor Greek, but all are one in Christ. This leaves wholly untouched the promises and purposes of God to Israel which shall all be literally and infallibly fulfilled in due time. "All Israel shall be saved." The Scriptures teem with the evidence of this grand truth. Not one jot or tittle of the promises made to the fathers can fail. To quote the proofs would demand a volume. If you will apply your heart to the study of Romans, Galatians and Hebrews, you will find a very full and satisfactory reply to your question, "What passages of Scripture tend to release the Jew from ceremonial observance?" If he believes in Jesus, he is dead to the law; if he does not, he will be damned by the law.

We cannot see how Galatians 3:19 can possibly negate the true reading of 1 John 3:4 which is "Sin is *lawlessness*." The two passages are in perfect harmony. "Wherefore then the law? It was added because of transgression." So also in Romans 4:15: "Because the law worketh wrath: for where no law is there is no transgression." Is it not obvious that to have transgression there must be law? Yes; and it is equally obvious that where there is a law there must be transgression because man is a sinner.

The law raised the question of righteousness and proved that man had none. Without law man was a lawless sinner. Under law, he was a wilful transgressor. From Adam to Moses, there was no law and therefore no transgression, though surely there was sin and therefore *death*, the wages of sin. "Nevertheless death reigned from Adam to Moses, even over them that had not sinned after the similitude of Adam's transgression" (Rom. 5:14). Adam had a law; therefore his act was transgression. So we read in Hosea 6:7, "They [Israel] like Adam, have transgressed." See margin. We are at a loss to understand the difficulties of some of our friends in reference to a matter so exceedingly plain.

We judge there is still a little confusion in your mind as to "the old husband" in Romans 7. We do not think it is the flesh any more than the law, though, assuredly, the flesh is to be reckoned dead, for such it is in God's account, and faith always takes God's view of matters. We are apt to get confused through not distinguishing in Romans 7 between the *illustration* of the marriage tie and the *application*. In the illustration the *husband* dies, but in the application it is *we* who have died. In short, death dissolves the tie – not the death of the law but *our* death. "Wherefore, my brethren, ye also are become dead to the law by the body of Christ." And again, "But now we are delivered from the law, being dead to that wherein we were held" (See Margin). In chapter 6 the question of "the flesh" is handled. In chapter 7 the question of "the law." Death delivers from both the one and the other.

We believe that in Romans 7 the apostle gives us the exercise of a quickened soul not knowing deliverance. It is, to use a figure, a man who has got out of a trap, describing his feelings when he was in it. Do you think Paul was a "wretched man" crying out for deliverance when he penned his epistle to the Romans? Most certainly not! He was a happy man rejoicing in full deliverance. But he is describing the exercise of a quickened soul still under the law and having no power against sin. This is not proper Christian experience. Can a Christian never do right? Must he always do wrong? Can a Christian say, "How to perform that which is good, I find not?" The fact is, in all this part of the chapter, you do not get the Holy Spirit in His indwelling power. There is new life but there is no power, no sense of full deliverance, no consciousness of victory. All this you have in chapter 8 which is proper Christian experience.

We believe many of God's beloved people have never gotten out of Romans 7. While we must admit that we should much prefer being honestly in chapter 7 to being falsely in chapter 8, yet we do not and cannot admit that chapter 7 is the proper place for one who ought to know the setting free power of these words, "There is therefore now no condemnation to them which are in Christ Jesus." It is very good for the soul to pass through Romans 7, but it is not for the glory of God that he should stay there. If it is right for all to remain in chapter 7, then for what end did the Holy Spirit pen chapter 8?

MARRIAGE

We do not feel free to offer any counsel in your case. You must wait only upon God. Each one must learn for himself, in communion with God, his proper path in this solemn matter. We have invariably found that those who were most forward in offering counsel were the most incompetent to give it. On the other hand, those whose counsel would be worth having were slowest to give it. Do not suppose, dear friend, that we do not sympathize with you in your exercise; we do most deeply. But we believe you must ask counsel of God.

1 Corinthians 7:32-34 teaches that the unmarried are the most free from care, but verse 7 as distinctly teaches that "every man hath his own proper gift of God." Each one must know for himself what his proper gift is. It is one thing to say, "Follow Paul's example' and quite another thing to have the "proper gift" to do it. It is a fatal mistake for anyone to expect to walk in a path for which God has not given him a call or given him the spiritual power. Remember in these days of ritualism and revived monasticism, that marriage is a holy and honorable institution, established by God in the Garden of Eden and sanctioned by His presence in Cana of Galilee. It is pronounced to be honorable in all by His Spirit in Hebrews 13:4. Thus much as to the general principle, but the moment you come to individual cases, each one must be guided of God. To Him we affectionately commend you.

We cannot understand why you should have occasion to seek a human opinion on a point where Hebrews 13:4 and 1 Timothy 4:1-4 are so clear. Oh! when will people learn to open their Bible and bow down to its holy authority in all things? We have an abhorrence of that mock spirituality, sanctimoniousness and transcendentalism so apparent in the remarks to which you call our attention. To us it seems to be simply holiness in the flesh, which we know is one of Satan's crafty wiles. As we said, marriage was instituted by the Lord God in the Garden of Eden. It was sanctioned by the presence of Christ in Cana of Galilee. It is pronounced honorable by the Holy Spirit in Hebrews 13. To forbid it is said to be a doctrine of demons in 1 Timothy 4. This is quite sufficient for us, let pious sentimentalists and hyper-spiritualists say what they will.

It must be entirely a question of individual faith. You must walk before God in happy loving fellowship. You should both wait upon God together and seek to be of one mind in the Lord. This is your happy privilege.

It is of the utmost importance for man and wife to cultivate the daily habit of waiting together on the Lord. It has a marvelous effect upon the whole range of domestic life. Bring everything before God, pour out your hearts together. Have no secrets, no reserve. Then will your hearts be knit together in holy love, and the current of your personal, conjugal and domestic life will flow peacefully and happily on, to the praise of Him who has made you one and called you to walk together as heirs of the grace of life.

We have often raised a voice of warning against the terrible evil of mixed marriages. We believe it to be a fatal step for anyone to marry an unconverted person, and a sad proof that the heart has departed from the Lord and the conscience has slipped from beneath the light and authority of God's Word. It is amazing how the devil succeeds in casting dust into people's eyes in this matter. He leads them to believe they will be a blessing to the unconverted partner, a lamentable delusion! How can we possibly expect blessing upon a flagrant act of disobedience? How can I, by going wrong, hope to set another right? Further, it frequently happens that persons, when bent on taking an unconverted partner, deceive themselves into the belief that the partner is converted. They claim to be satisfied with evidences of conversion which, under other circumstances, would utterly fail to command their confidence. The will is at work. They are determined to have their own way. Then, when too late, they discover their terrible mistake.

With regard to the question of how we should deal with persons who transgress in this matter, we are not aware of any direct instruction in the New Testament. Solemn remonstrance and faithful reproof there should be, most surely, but we judge it to be rather a case for pastoral dealing and personal discipline than for any action of the assembly.

In the painful case you name, we do not believe it to be the right thing for a son to "try and manage a reunion" between the father and mother. If the husband wishes to come back, the wife should receive him. This is clearly involved in 1 Corinthians 7:13. "The woman which hath an husband that believeth not, and if he be pleased to dwell with her, let her not leave him." If he wishes to come back, it is tantamount to "being pleased to dwell with her," and if she be told "not to leave him," it is tantamount to being told to receive him. At least, so we judge. It may be the Lord is about to bring the husband to Himself. If so, it would be very sad if a Christian wife should prove a stumbling-block by failing in grace. No doubt, he has greatly failed in his duty as a husband by leaving his wife,

392

even were there nothing more serious. But if he really desires – apart from any management or any influence brought to bear upon him – to come back, we cannot but judge it to be the duty of a Christian wife to receive him and to seek "by her chaste manner of life, coupled with fear," to win him for Christ. Should she refuse and he be then driven away into sin or hardness of heart, she could never forgive herself.

CHILDREN

The grand point in dealing with children is to insist upon obedience. It is of great importance. If this be carried out from the very first, it will save a world of trouble to both parents and children.

Children are called to yield implicit obedience to their parents. This is their divine role. Parents are to beware of provoking their children to wrath by arbitrary conduct, by exhibiting partiality towards one more than another, and by needless crossing of the will of the child merely to make a display of parental authority. The child should ever see that the parent has his real interest at heart and that true love is the motive spring of every act. But we must insist on the obedience of children, even in this age of independence – an age specially marked by disobedience to parents and by gross disrespect.

Many of the young people of the present day seem to regard their parents as belonging to the old school and being deficient in education. Hence, the readiness to contradict their parents and set up their own opinion. All this is unnatural and ungodly. It ought not to be tolerated. And we may also add a hint as to the very objectionable habit adopted by many young people of calling their father and mother by heartless, objectionable names. We would entreat all our young friends to watch against these things and against the spirit from which they proceed, and to cultivate a reverential spirit which will surely lead to a respectful manner towards their parents. It is a good proof of a good education when children respect their parents. Need we add that in all matters where God's authority is concerned, it must rise above all other claims! Oh, for the adjusting power of grace and truth!

We cannot understand how anyone calling himself a Christian parent can adopt a system of harsh and cruel treatment towards his children. It can only result in making them liars and infidels. They will tell lies to escape the strap. They will despise the religion which stands connected with such inordinate severity. Such treatment as you describe is more worthy of a cruel slavemaster than of a Christian parent. There are cases in which some discipline is necessary, but it should be administered in such a way as to convince the child that it is only for his good and not the fruit of bad temper or of arbitrary severity. The rod should be most reluctantly lifted. It should be the very last resource. In short, the Christian parent should ever keep before him as his model his heavenly Father's dealings with himself. Does *He* inflict punishment for confessed sin? The thought is blasphemy. He only chastens in love, to make us partakers of His holiness. It grieves Him to have to use the rod. "His soul was 'grieved for the misery of Israel." This should be the Christian parent's pattern.

We do not believe in the everlasting whipping system. It only hardens and brutalizes. And we would further add, dear friend, that the father and the mother should be wholly one in the administration of discipline. For a child to have to appeal to one parent to shield him from the other, reveals a condition of things in the domestic circle perfectly shocking to every well-regulated mind. The father and mother should not have a single divergent thought in reference to the system of training. They should appear before their children as one authority, one influence. The firmness of the father and the tenderness of the mother should be so sweetly blended that their joint action might be felt in the entire system of training. But how is all this to be realized? *By the parents being much on their knees together before God.* This is the true secret of domestic training. If the father and mother do not pray together, they will not act together; and if they do not act together, the education of the children must suffer. May the Lord in His infinite goodness help all Christian parents to discharge aright their high and holy functions so His name may be glorified in the households of His people!

We do not see any difficulty as to the term "children" in Ephesians 6:1. In the entire context, the Holy Spirit is exhorting Christians in their various relationships to discharge the functions given them therein. Only Christians are addressed or exhorted in the epistles. Hence it follows that the "children" here addressed are Christians. Christian parents are exhorted to bring up their children in the discipline and admonition of the Lord. This takes in *all* our children whom we are to train from the very beginning for the Lord, counting on Him for them, and He will never fail a trusting heart. We are to take God's ground for our children in the entire system of moral training from their birth. He will assuredly honor the faith that thus counts on Him for the children and trains the children for Him. He cannot deny Himself, blessed forever be His holy name!

1 Corinthians 7:14 stands in contrast with the Mosaic enactment which obliged men to put away, not only strange wives, but the offspring of mixed marriages. It is *now* not a question of the practical state of the children themselves – whether they are saved or not saved. The passage simply states that the children were sanctified by the fact of their relationship with the believing parent and need not therefore be put away. But

the idea of building upon such a passage the monstrous error that the children of Christian parents are saved, as such, without the quickening grace of the Holy Spirit, is too gross to need a moment's consideration.

We can assure you of our hearty sympathy and interest in the subject of your letter. Your path is very simple. You have only to train your dear children for God and count on God for your children. The Spirit of God alone can make a child understand divine things, and it is not for us to fix a limit as to the precise age at which a child can take in the truth of God. It is the Spirit's work. He can make babes as well as mature people understand. A little child is the very model on which every person must be formed who will enter the kingdom of God.

We believe that Matthew 18:10-14 furnishes the foundation of the precious truth of the salvation of infants. Do you not believe this? Are you not fully persuaded that all who die in infancy are saved? That inasmuch as their little bodies undergo the penalty of Adam's sin, their precious souls partake of the benefit of Christ's atonement! Well, if you believe this, why should your heart be troubled as to the destiny of your infant child in the event of the Lord's coming? Can you not fully trust that blessed One who, in the days of His flesh, said with such touching tenderness, "Suffer the little children to come unto Me and forbid them not; for of such is the kingdom of God?" Can your heart entertain for a moment the unworthy thought that your gracious Lord, when He comes for His people, could take the mother to be with Himself and leave her babe behind to perish?

You ask if we "can tell you of any Scripture which shows what becomes of the infant children of believers when the Lord takes His Church to Himself." We reply, Matthew 18: 10-14. "Take heed that ye despise not one of these little ones; for I say unto you, that in heaven their angels do always behold the face of My Father which is in heaven. For the Son of man is come to save that which was lost.* How think ye? if a man have an hundred sheep and one of them be gone astray, doth he not leave the ninety and nine, and goeth into the mountains and seeketh that which is gone astray? And if so be that he find it, verily I say unto you, he rejoiceth more of that, than of the ninety and nine which went not astray. Even so it is not the will of your Father which is in heaven, that one of these little ones should perish."

---

* In Luke 19:10, where it is not a question of infants, we read, "The Son of man is come to seek and to save that which was lost."

Now, dear friend, is not this a precious answer to your question? Is it not divinely calculated to hush all your anxiety in reference to your precious babe in the event of the Lord's coming? Do you think the loving Savior who uttered these words, will ignore them when He comes for His Church? The very thought is blasphemy. Ah! no; our loving Lord will be fully glorified in receiving to His bosom and taking to His home the infant children of His people, as well as the parents. It is not His will now, and it cannot be His will then, that one of these little ones should perish. May your heart find settled rest as to this question in the eternal truth of God and in the rich and precious grace which shines so brightly and blessedly in Matthew 18:10-14.

SERVANTS

The passage you quote at the opening of your letter contains the divine answer to your question and completely demolishes all your objections. The sentence, "They that have believing masters," proves that some had not. And yet you say, "But although the Word is clear as to this, I do not see that a servant" in a worldly family "can be really separate from the world." If the Word is clear, you ought to be able to see – and we doubt not you will be able to see it when you learn to bow your will to the supreme authority of Holy Scripture. We consider that when Scripture speaks on any subject, all discussion is closed for the humble, teachable soul. We certainly cannot understand any true Christian saying, "The Word is clear, but I cannot see it." Would you think of saying to your earthly master, "Sir, your directions are very clear, but I cannot see them?" If you were to speak so, we judge he would very speedily dismiss you from his service.

It seems to us, dear friend, you are completely mistaken as to the position and duty of a Christian servant in a worldly family. You say, "There may, it is true, be an opportunity of being a light for Christ by bringing the Word to bear upon their consciences." Now, we should judge that the very best possible way of being a light for Christ in any family, would be to fulfill with holy fidelity all the duties of your situation. It is not so much bringing the Word to bear on their consciences as letting it act on your own and proving that it does act by your cheerful temper, your humble deportment, your gracious manner, your earnest diligence at work, your faithfulness, your strict integrity, your unselfish devotedness to all the interests of your master. These lovely fruits of righteousness would bring more glory to your Lord and tell more powerfully upon the conscience of your master, than if you were preaching to him from morning till night.

Indeed we very much doubt the moral propriety of servants preaching to their masters. It needs special grace and wisdom to speak on divine things under such circumstances. The Lord may give an open door at times, but great tact is needed, owing to the unique position of a servant in relation to the master. The grand point is to let the *life* speak. "Exhort servants to be obedient to their own masters," whether converted or unconverted "and to please them well in all things; not answering again; not purloining; but showing all good fidelity; that they may adorn the doctrine of God our Savior in all things" (Titus 2:9-10).

The Word of God sets forth in the fullest and plainest manner "what should be the conduct and general bearing of Christian servants towards their employers." For example, "Servants, be obedient to them that are your masters according to the flesh, with fear and trembling, in singleness of your heart as unto Christ; not with eye service as menpleasers, but as the servants of Christ, doing the will of God from the heart; with good will doing service *as to the Lord* and not to men, knowing that whatsoever good thing any man doeth, the same shall he receive of the Lord, whether he be bond or free" (Eph. 4:5-8). Similar is the teaching of Colossians 3:22-25. Also in Titus we read, "Exhort servants to be obedient unto their own masters and to please them well in all things; not answering again; not purloining, but showing all good fidelity, that they may adorn the doctrine of God our Savior in all things."

We are not aware of any specific direction in Scripture as to the conduct of servants toward one another, but surely the general teaching as to Christian walk and character would bear upon that relationship as upon every other. If Christian servants will only study their model and seek to be formed thereon, it will regulate their conduct both towards their employers and toward one another. Further, Christian employers have to look well to the manner in which they conduct themselves in their relationship, for we may rest assured that to this question, as to all others, there are two sides.

BUSINESS

A man who puts pasteboard into shoes and sells them for leather is unworthy of the name of Christian; indeed he is not even an honest man. We may be told, "It is the custom of the trade." Well, how does this alter the matter for one who desires to walk in the fear of God and keep a good conscience? It may be the custom of the trade to put inferior yarn into cloth and to put water in the milk. But can a Christian or even an honest man do such things? Most assuredly not. The conscience of a Christian must be regulated, not by the custom of the trade, but by the Word of God. If this be lost sight of, there is an end to all practical Christianity in commercial life.

A Christian manufacturer could no more think of putting pasteboard into shoes and selling them as all leather, than he could think of picking a man's pocket. If indeed it be the custom to put pasteboard into shoes – if everybody does it and everybody knows it, then there is no deception in the matter. But if I sell a pair of shoes as all-leather when I know they are made of leather and pasteboard, then I am a liar and a thief. I am morally worse than a highway robber since he openly avows what he is, what he does and what he wants. A man who adulterates his goods is guilty of the very worst dishonesty.

Suppose a person is not a manufacturer but a salesman in a warehouse or shop. What is he to do? He does not adulterate, he merely sells. Is he dishonest? Is he untrue in selling adulterated goods? Unquestionably, if he sells them for genuine. How could a true Christian – any really honest man – declare an article to be genuine when he knows it is not? We heartily wish there were more honesty in commercial life.

But it will not do in the world. But what does this prove? Simply that the world is untrue and dishonest. If truth and uprightness cannot get on in the world, then what must the world be? Still, the Christian must be honest. His object is not to get on in the world or to make money, but to glorify God in his daily life. Can he glorify God by adulterating goods and telling lies?

We feel the immense importance, dear friend, of the subject which you have brought before us. We believe it demands the serious attention of all Christians engaged in manufacture and commerce. There is immense danger of being drawn away from the path of Christian integrity and falling into the wretched spirit of covetousness and competition so prevalent on all hands. We have to bear in mind that Christianity is a living reality. It is divine life coming out in all the practical details of our daily history. It is not confined to the benches of a meeting room. It has more ways of showing and expressing itself than by preaching, praying and singing – most precious as all these are in their place. It must come out in the factory, in the warehouse, in the shop, in the office, in the daily occupation, whatever that may be. How terrible to think of a man singing and praying on the Lord's day, and on Monday morning adulterating his bread and selling it as genuine!

Oh! let us be honest, come what may. Let us walk in the fear of God. Let us, like the blessed apostle, "exercise ourselves to have always a conscience void of offense toward God and man."

True, it may cost us something. We may have to suffer for righteousness' sake. But what is all this when compared with the deep joy of walking with God in that narrow path on which the blessed beams of His approving countenance ever shine? Is not a good conscience better far than thousands in gold and silver? Our God will take care of us. He will meet all our *real* need according to His riches in glory by Christ Jesus. Why should we ever devote ourselves to the contemptible "tricks of trade" in order to make money or make a living, when our Father has pledged Himself to care for us all the journey through?

It is very important that the Christian should be thoroughly clear and above-board in all his ways. There should be nothing questionable in any of his transactions – nothing hidden. We should not put our hand to a single thing which would not bear the strictest scrutiny. Hence, if this person "who works for a large firm in London" is doing anything which she would not wish the firm to know; if she is receiving anything which she wishes to hide from their knowledge, it is evident she is not acting uprightly. If she is perfectly clear in what she is doing, why send this question to us? Can she with a good conscience take the discount from the person who supplies her with the things? Should it be termed "discount" or "bribe"? "If thine eye be single, thy whole body shall be full of light." And again, "If our heart condemn us not, then have we confidence toward God." If it is an understood thing on the part of the firm that discount is given, it is all plain and right, but anything underhanded is utterly unworthy of one who is called to walk in the light of the divine presence.

It must be entirely a matter between your own soul and the Lord. We ought not do anything with a doubtful mind or anything on which we cannot, with perfect confidence, ask God's blessing. This is a great broad moral principle applicable to all Christians in all their circumstances. As to the special case which you have laid before us, we question how far you are responsible for the use which your customers make of the article you name. There are some things which could not possibly be made a good use of, as for instance, an infidel or immoral book. Hence we could not sell such, but we can see nothing wrong in the sale of the little flower you name. True, it may be turned to a superstitious use, but it need not be so and was not till lately. If people in business are to be held responsible for the use which may be made of their goods, the questions would be unending. Still, dear friend, it is of great importance that we should exercise ourselves to have always a conscience void of offense both toward God and man. May the Lord Himself be your teacher and guide! May He keep you walking in His presence and satisfied with Himself! Then all will be right.

It is a question for individual conscience. There is a very wide difference between a wine merchant and a keeper of a bar, at least so we judge, but it is not our province to lay down rules for other people's conscience. One thing is certain, the path of a true Christian is an exceedingly narrow one.

We thoroughly enter into your difficulty and sympathize with you. It would be to us a most serious question, were we engaged in printing or bookselling, as to what we printed or sold. But, dear friend, it is one of the many things as to which you must walk before God with a pure conscience. We certainly should not do anything that leaves a soil on the mind or a sting in the conscience, but no one can be a guide for another in such matters. The Lord is so good! He will guide and keep you.

We are of the opinion that you would be happier as a Christian and safer as a man of business, to work your present trade on sound principles, than to get into a large thing such as you describe which can only be carried on by a system of credit. We are fully convinced of the possibility of carrying on trade without going in debt and we strongly urge all our friends to do so. Why cannot a man in trade pay for what he buys as well as a private individual? True, he might not cover so large a surface, but he would have a more solid foundation. His trade might be small, but it would be safe and his mind would be in peace. "Let your moderation be known unto all men. The Lord is at hand" (Phil. 5:5). This is a seasonable word for Christians in this day of busy speculation and restless ambition.

There is urgent need, dear friend, for watchfulness lest we be ensnared by the money-loving spirit of the day. The devil is seeking to blind the eyes of professing Christians in various ways. He furnishes them with a thousand plausible reasons why they should push and grasp and scrape together. He will even misquote and misapply the Word of God to furnish a plea for money-making to those whose hearts are secretly set upon that object. But oh! the wretchedness of having before the heart such an object as to "make money." Surely as is the object so is the character. Only think of a saint of God, an heir of glory, hoarding up this world's miserable riches! Think of this in the face of so many of God's people in want and in the knowledge of the claims of the Lord's work at home and abroad! How can we suppose the existence of the life of Christ or the love of God in a soul that can lay by his hundreds and see his brother in need? Impossible. Oh! for a large heart!

The only counsel we can offer you is to wait on the Lord and ask Him to guide you. He has said, "I will guide thee with Mine eye," and "He cannot deny Himself." It may be He would have you plod on patiently with your present occupation. We are in a much safer position, morally, when our business is the burden on the back and not the idol of the heart.

One grand objection to a trades union is that it introduces a third party between master and servant which the Word of God nowhere recognizes. A master may dismiss his servant or the servant may leave his master if so disposed, but for any body of men to attempt to interfere and regulate terms between master and servant is a thing entirely opposed to the teaching of Holy Scripture.

Furthermore, the Christian master is taught in Scripture to "give unto his servants that which is just and equal," but the union interferes with this and insists upon his giving the same wages to an idle incompetent workman as to one who is really worth four times as much. *Finally, for a Christian to join a union or any other club is to be unequally yoked together with unbelievers.*

We look upon a trades union as a most unwarrantable interference with the rights of individual conscience. It usurps an authority without a shadow of Scripture foundation. The Word of God puts each in his right place and teaches him how to carry himself therein. If master and men would but listen to its holy teachings, there would be no need of unions. But sadly, they do not, and no doubt in many cases, the masters have not been as kind, as generous or a considerate as they ought, and the men have proved rebellious. Or – for there are two sides to every question – the men have proved idle and unprincipled and the masters have become severe and exacting. But the Christian, whether master or man, has to walk with God and to be governed by His Word, not by the demands of a trades union.

MONEY AND DEBT

We have read your later with deep interest and we can enter into your feelings. We believe the Christian is bound to provide for his family, day by day – bound to educate his children and put them in the way of earning an honest livelihood. All this is so plainly commanded in the New Testament as to admit of no question. But these sacred duties leave wholly untouched the question of hoarding up and of speculation. We do not believe in these latter at all. We believe that hoarding covers the soul with rust and speculation fills the heart and mind with care and anxiety.

We love and honor diligent and honest toil, but Scripture tells us that "the love of money is the [a] root of all evil" and we do not believe that God's blessing rests upon His children when they become *shareholders* in worldly companies. You yourself, dear friend, have proved this. We think you would have done better had you purchased a house, either to live in or rent, than to invest your money in such a company as you describe. But all these matters must be arranged between the Lord and one's own conscience. We merely add that there is a vast difference between committing actual sin and falling short of a high toned discipleship and personal devotedness. For ourselves, we earnestly long for the latter. We believe there is a sad lack of it in our day.

The tide of worldliness is rolling rapidly in upon us and we know of no more effective barrier with which to resist it than thorough heart-devotedness and consecration to Christ and His cause. Where the real bent of the soul is Christward, one is not troubled with questions as to the right or wrong of this or that; but where it is not, the heart can muster up a thousand plausible arguments. And it is labor lost to seek to answer such arguments, since there is no spiritual capacity to see the force of the answer. May God bless you, dear friend, and comfort your heart under your heavy loss. May your undivided confidence be in Him, and He will prove Himself better than ten thousand "limited companies."

We see nothing wrong in a Christian applying, in a becoming manner, for an advance of wages, provided it be not the fruit of covetousness, but simply for the support of his family. But we cannot attempt to lay down a rule. Very much will depend on the circumstances of the case.

We have long been in the habit of explaining Luke 16:9 by 1 Timothy 6:17-19. We consider it a very fine commentary on the passage. Worldly riches are not what properly belongs to us as Christians. Our riches are heavenly; our blessings spiritual, in the heavenlies, in and with Christ. Worldly riches belong properly to the Jew, but to the Christian they are the mammon of unrighteousness or the riches which do not rightly pertain to us. But if at our conversion, we happen to possess such riches, we are taught by Luke 16:9 to make friends of them by spending them in the Lord's service and for the poor, thus laying up in store a good foundation against the time to come.

The expression, "that they may receive you" is idiomatic and may be rendered as follows, "that they may be the means of receiving you." This is the true way to use riches, the very best mode of investing capital. It will yield a hundred fold, and where is the bank that can come up to this? Many of God's people have lately been called to taste the bitter fruit of seeking after what they considered profitable investments. It is a question if the tremendous crashing of banks and limited companies has not been the result of God's dealing with His children who were connected with them. The very best thing we can do with our money is to spend it for the Lord. Then, instead of being rust on our souls, it will be treasure in heaven. But we must remember that Luke 16:9 and 1 Timothy 6:17-19 are addressed to *disciples,* not to the unconverted. If this be lost sight of, we shall only cast dust in the eyes of men by leading them to suppose that the gift of God can be purchased with money. To one who thought this of old, Peter said, "Thy money perish with thee."

We take Romans 13:8 in its plain, broad sense. We believe it teaches us to owe no man anything. Would to God it were more fully carried out! It is painful beyond expression to see the sad lack of conscience among professors as to the question of debt. We would solemnly call upon all who are in the habit of going in debt, to judge themselves in this matter and get out of a false position at once. It is better far to sit down to a dry crust and to wear a shabby coat, than live well and dress well at our neighbor's expense. We regard it as positive unrighteousness. Oh! for an upright mind!

The first grand business of a person in debt is to get out of it. We must be just before we are generous.

INSURANCE

As to the question of insurance, it must entirely depend upon a man's faith. We assuredly believe it is much better to trust in the Living God than in an insurance policy. But then it must be a real thing. It is a poor affair for a man to say he is trusting in God and therefore he will not insure his life, if he is not really in the truth and power of what he is talking about. It may often happen that a man refrains from insuring his life so he will have more to spend on himself, while he deceives himself by the mere profession of faith without one atom of reality.

In the case of a mere man of the world, it is very commendable in him to curtail his personal expenses to secure something for his wife and family in the event of his death. But in the case of a Christian, he ought to be able to trust God. It is his privilege to do so, and God will assuredly answer faith. Insurance is not faith, but faith gives assurance. God is better than insurance, but God must be known in order to be trusted. There is no use talking about faith if one has not got it. Faith is reality; mere profession is a sham. May God make us real!

It must be entirely a question of individual faith. The Word is plain, "Lay not up for yourselves treasures upon earth." If anyone says you ought to lay up, he must settle the matter with the Lord Christ. Ephesians 4:28 teaches us that the object for which a man is to work with his hands is, not to lay up, but that he may have to give to him that needeth. It is a fine question to put to the heart – which would you rather have, a hoard of money or the living God? A genuine faith will not hesitate long about giving an answer.

GOING TO LAW

The question of going to law has been frequently discussed. If it be a matter between brethren, 1 Corinthians 6 is conclusive. If it be a matter between a Christian and a man of the world, we can only say that if the Christian goes to law, he is doing the very reverse of what God has done with him. He professes to have been forgiven ten thousand talents, yet he takes his fellow by the throat for a paltry hundred pence. Is this right? Is it pleasing to God? Is it yielding a true testimony to our heavenly Father? Is it representing Him? Is it imitating Him? God is not imputing trespasses. He is a pardoning God, delighting in mercy. If we go to law, we are not like Him; we are misrepresenting Him.

Why was the man in Matthew 18 called "a wicked servant?" Because, having been forgiven ten thousand talents, he took his fellow by the throat for a hundred pence. No doubt there are many questions raised on this subject. Persons may say, "What are we to do? How can we get on? We would be cheated on all hands if we did not avail ourselves of the law." To all this we say, "Is it right, is it consistent, is it like God for a Christian to bring a poor fellow sinner to the judgment seat on any ground whatever?" If not, why seek to defend it? We have nothing to do with results; we have only to do right and leave results with God. But even were we to look at results, we question if people make much by going to law. They very often find it to be throwing good money after bad. We know many Christian men in business who do not go to law and they are none the worse for it, even from a monetary point of view. But it is our business to judge the question in the light of the New Testament, and if so judged, we believe the answer will be easily had.

Surely, dear friend, if it be contrary to the Spirit of Christ for a Christian to go to law, it must be equally so to employ a society to do so on his behalf. If it be right to go to law, let it be done openly and honestly. If it be wrong, why attempt to do it by proxy?

THE LEADING OF THE SPIRIT

We consider that Joel 2:28 had a partial fulfillment at Pentecost. Its final accomplishment is still to be looked for in the history of God's ancient people. God *can* speak to men now by dreams or a vision of the night, but we consider that the true and proper way for a child of God to be guided is by the Word and Spirit of God. It is very unsafe ground indeed to be merely guided by dreams or by the *impressions* of a man's mind. We vastly prefer the solid imperishable Word of God.

It is greatly to be feared that many mistake their own inclinations for the movings of the Spirit of God – a terrible mistake! It needs much brokenness, self-emptiness and singleness of eye to discern and follow the precious leadings of the Holy Spirit. As a general rule, we should say that where the glory of Christ is the exclusive object of any act to which we feel led, we may conclude that it is the Spirit who moves us. The Lord is so gracious that we can fully count upon Him to guide and keep and use us where the heart is simple.

THE FATHER'S DISCIPLINE

The term "House of God" in 1 Peter 4:17 refers to the Church in its place of responsibility in this world. God judges His house *now*. He will judge the world by and by. Holiness becomes the house of God, and He must judge everything contrary thereto. A father rules and orders his house because it is his house and because he will have everything in his house agreeable to his tastes and suited to his dignity. Thus our God deals with us. It is not a question of the salvation of the soul or of the eternal security of the believer; all that is settled. But God disciplines His children and judges His house. It is a precious privilege to stand connected with God in this world, but it is a most solemn responsibility also.

1 John 5:16-17 refers to the case of a brother suffering under the chastening hand of God in government. Compare James 5:15. It might be for sin which was not unto the death of the body. In such a case one may be led to pray for the sufferer and receive an answer from God in his restoration to health. But the sin may be of such a nature that one could not possibly take it up in intercession at all, in which case the discipline must take its course and run on to the death of the body. Compare also 1 Corinthians 11:30.

We have repeatedly referred to 1 Corinthians 11:29-32. It teaches that God will assuredly chasten those who unworthily partake of the Lord's Supper. The passage applies to Christians *now* as well as in the early days of the Church. We are called to judge ourselves as we approach the Table of the Lord, else God will have to judge us in the way of present discipline, which may take the form of bodily sickness or even death itself. But, blessed be His name, He does this now so we may not be judged with the world by and by. It is truly blessed to hear the words, "No condemnation," amid the judicial dealings of 1 Corinthians 11, just as distinctly as amid the evangelic teachings of Romans 8.

You have solid reason, dear friend, to doubt the soundness of the teaching to which you refer, on 1 Corinthians 11:30: "For this cause many are weak and sickly among you, and many sleep." These persons had failed to judge themselves, failed to discern the Lord's body in the broken bread. They had eaten in an unworthy manner, though they were true Christians. Hence God, in His government of His house, had to chasten them by bodily sickness even unto death, so they might not be condemned with the world. How could any intelligent person teach that "the discipline here is not connected with those weak and sickly ones?" We say it was very closely connected with them! No doubt others were called to learn and take warning from the discipline exercised upon those erring members, but surely no father would think of chastening a good child for the sin of a bad one.

It would be a very grave mistake indeed to say "that all the trials and sufferings of Christians are punishments for some particular sin." Very often these things are sent as a preventive and to draw the heart nearer to Christ. Who would presume to say that the sickness of Epaphroditus in Philippians 2 was a punishment for some particular sin? The apostle expressly tells us that "for the work of Christ, he was nigh unto death." Were Timothy's frequent infirmities sent as a punishment for some particular sin?

We do not like the term "punishment" as applied to the dealings of our loving Father. There is nothing penal, in the strict sense of the word, even in His wise and faithful correction. *Christ our blessed Substitute exhausted on our behalf all that was penal.* God chastens His children to make them partakers of His holiness, as we learn in Hebrews 12. Moreover, the Father judges His house, as we read in 1 Peter 4:17. So in 1 Corinthians 11 we are told that many of the Corinthians were visited with bodily sickness and death because of their disorderly conduct at the Lord's table. But this we are told was so they might "not be condemned with the world."

In James 5 we read, "Is any sick among you? Let him call for the elders of the church and let them pray over him, anointing him with oil in the name of the Lord; and the prayer of faith shall save the sick, and the Lord shall raise him up; and if he have committed sins, they shall be forgiven him." The "if" shows that the sickness might not have been sent on account of any particular sin.

In 1 John 5 we read, "If any man see his brother sin a sin not unto death, he shall ask and he shall give him life for them that sin not unto death. There is a sin unto death, I do not say that he shall pray for it." For example, "Ananias and Sapphira" and the Corinthians! There may, in any given ease, be certain flagrant features attaching to some sin committed, causing those who look at things in the light of God's presence to feel instinctively that they could not possibly pray for restoration. We have to do with the government of God which is a very serious matter indeed. And it is one of the enactments of that government that "whatsoever a man" (no matter who) "soweth, that shall he also reap." But it is the Christian's happy privilege to view the actings of divine government through the atmosphere of divine grace.

410

Your case is painfully interesting. We are persuaded that if there be simple faith in waiting upon God, He will heal and restore. He is the Hearer and Answerer of prayer. We recommend you to retire from all creature confidences and cast yourself simply upon the Living God. You have been looking to human cisterns. We also judge you have been over-anxious to get well. Seek grace to lie passive in your Father's hands and know no will but His. When once your heart can say, "Thy will be done," the great moral end of the discipline is reached. We pray that you may reap a rich harvest of blessing from all the painful exercise through which you are now passing. May God comfort you, dear friend.

Hebrews 12:7 teaches us to leave ourselves wholly in God's hands, whatever be the character or measure of the chastening. It helps to this end to bear in mind that God is dealing with us as sons. *There is nothing penal in His chastening.* All is in perfect love, unerring wisdom and infallible faithfulness, and the purpose of God in it all is to make us partakers of His holiness. Hence, it would be a serious mistake for us to seek in any wise to take ourselves out of our Father's hand. We should rather desire that the chastening might produce the proper result and that God might be fully glorified thereby. Restless efforts to get out of trial prove we are not walking with God and that we do not see His hand or His end in the matter. Moreover, we shall find that all such efforts only increase our trouble while they rob us of the sweet consciousness that all we are passing through comes direct from the hand of our loving Father.

A SPIRIT OF LOVE AND GRACE

Romans 14:22, with the entire context, teaches us the necessity of walking tenderly in reference to the consciences of our brethren. A man may have faith as to certain things, perfect liberty in his own mind, whether as regards days or foods or many other minor things, but his faith or his liberty should not lead him to act in such a way as to stumble his weak brother. This is the spirit and teaching of this entire beautiful chapter – this lovely summary of Christian morals. Of course, if there were any attempt to impose the eating of herbs, abstinence from meats or observance of days as a yoke upon the necks of the disciples, it would be our place to resist with uncompromising decision.

Your most kind and Christian letter came to hand and we desire to give you our sincere thanks for the gracious spirit in which you write. Would that all who feel obliged in conscience to differ from us, were led to write in a like spirit and tone!

As to your first question, it might be well to ask the persons who use the language to which you refer what they mean by it. It certainly is possible to be occupied with mere doctrine apart from Christ, but we greatly fear that spirit of fault-finding which leads people to pick holes in everything and everyone except themselves. If we prayed more and talked less, we might be the means of doing some little good in our day and generation. We generally find that the fault-finding, hair-splitting generation are not the most blameless in their personal ways. The loudest talkers are generally the lowest walkers.

1 Corinthians 8:10-11 teaches us the solemn truth that if we, by a false use of our liberty, embolden a weak brother to act against his conscience, we, so far as in us lies, cause him to perish by destroying the action of his conscience toward God. It is of the utmost importance to allow Scripture to have its full play upon the soul and not to blunt its edge by the dogmas of systematic divinity. It is a good thing to open all the chambers of the heart and have them ventilated by the pure air of Scripture. We constantly find theology acting as a barrier to interrupt the rays of heavenly light and hinder their shining in upon the soul. The same authority that says "My sheep shall never perish" warns us against causing a weak brother to perish by a self-indulgent uncharitable use of our liberty. It will be our wisdom, as it most assuredly is for our moral security, to hearken to the one as well as to the other.

Matthew 18:23-35 does not refer to the question of "eternal life." Its primary application is to the Jew and his mode of dealing with the

Gentile. Notwithstanding the abounding mercy which God had shown to the Jew, he would not listen to the idea of mercy to the Gentile. The consequence is, as the apostle declares, "The wrath is come upon them to the uttermost" (1 Thes. 2:16, see the entire context). The apostate *nation* will never be forgiven. A *remnant* will be saved through grace and become the nucleus of the restored nation.

No doubt, we professing Christians have to learn a very important lesson from this scripture – the urgent necessity of cultivating a forgiving spirit. If we fail to act in grace, we are in danger of losing the sense of grace in our own souls. How dreadful for one who has been forgiven all his sins to drag a fellow sinner to the judgment-seat on account of a little money! Let us note particularly the closing words of our Lord, "So likewise shall My heavenly Father do also to you, if ye from your hearts forgive not everyone his brother their trespasses." This marks the application of the entire passage to our Father's governmental dealings with us from day to day.

It is a terrible thing for a professing Christian to harbor an unforgiving spirit. We do not see how it is possible for such to have any real sense of grace or any communion with God; nor should we wonder to find such given over to the most tormenting feelings as the expression of God's judgment upon a wrong state of heart. May we, beloved friend, ever cultivate a loving, genial, tender, forgiving spirit. We may rest assured our God delights in this. God loves a cheerful giver and a frank forgiver, because that is precisely what He is Himself, blessed forever be His name!

LENDING BOOKS

The following is an extract from a letter. "As one feeling much indebted to the good influence of books lent, allow me to say that believers might find 'a more excellent way' if, in a wise and loving manner, they lent their own books to those who are weak and uninstructed. I can but think of a dear Christian family at whose home my sister and I have often been taught the value and meaning of God's blessed Word, and of the exceeding kindness with which, on leaving, we have often been loaded with reading, which, at home, deepened the impression of what we had heard. Books we have wished to read and were unable to purchase, or those we had never known of till introduced to them by those dear friends who acted in this as though they counted not the things they possessed their own. Indeed, God has so blessed such reading to us that it has taken away the taste for much that we used to find great pleasure in."

"Even if a believer have but little means and yet wishes to help others in this way, it is wonderful how the Lord opens ways of doing so, for if everything is brought to the Lord, 'There is much food in the tillage of the poor' for others as well as for themselves, and 'if the eye be single, the whole body shall be full of light.' Perhaps the Lord may guide you to make some suggestion on the subject, for it is a way of serving the Master open to many. It pains my heart to see believers with well stored bookshelves unused for the Lord. I believe this is one way in which He is wounded in the house of His friends."

We heartily commend the foregoing weighty words to the attention of our readers. May we all seek grace to act on them! It will, perhaps, be said that there is another side of the question to be considered. No doubt there is. Books, when lent, are often not returned at all or returned so soiled and mutilated as to be unfit to be seen. Hence, there is a word for the borrower as well as for the lender. Surely if grace should rule the conduct of the lender, righteousness at least should rule the conduct of the borrower. Still, fully admitting the carelessness of many who get the loan of books, we should be very sorry indeed if this admission were allowed to blunt the edge of the most excellent suggestion of our correspondent.

ASSEMBLY FELLOWSHIP AND DISCIPLINE

We recognize no membership except that of the body of Christ – no society or association except the Church of God. But you must see this for yourself in the Word of God and then you will not need to ask your question.

We entirely agree with our beloved friend "W.K." as to receiving Christians at the table of their Lord. Any other mode or principle of action is not according to the truth of the unity of the body. There is a place at the Lord's table for every member of the body of Christ, *provided always that the proper discipline of the assembly does not call for exclusion.* There are two things which must never be lost sight of in connection with the question of reception at the Lord's table. These are, first, the *grace* which will not allow of the exclusion of any who ought to be admitted: secondly, the *holiness* which cannot allow the admission of any who ought to be excluded. If these things were allowed to act in the assembly, we should not have so much discussion and practical difficulty in the matter of reception.

The case to which you refer in 1 Corinthians 5 illustrates the nature and object of Church discipline. The man was put away from the assembly where the Holy Spirit ruled and delivered over to Satan, not that he might be lost, but "that his spirit might be saved in the day of the Lord Jesus." In the Second Epistle he is restored to the fellowship of the Church. We believe, most assuredly, that every assembly of Christians is solemnly bound to exercise discipline and put away evil from their midst. If they refuse to do so, they are not on the ground of the Church of God at all. We are most thankful for the blessing you have received through our pages. To God alone be all the praise! Continue to pray for us.

In 1 Timothy 1:20 the apostle delivers Hymenaeus and Alexander to Satan. It sets forth an act of solemn discipline by direct apostolic power. In 1 Corinthians 5 the assembly at Corinth is commanded to deliver the evil doer to Satan for the destruction of the flesh. In both cases we take it to be an act of discipline. A person put out of the assembly where the Holy Spirit ruled, was handed over to the power of Satan so that his flesh might be thoroughly judged and crushed – serious but needed work! May we learn, dear friend, to judge ourselves in secret before our God, so the assembly may not have to deal with us. If the *roots* of evil are judged in private, the *fruit* will not appear above the surface of our practical life.

John 20:23 refers to the administrative action of an assembly in discipline. See 1 Corinthians 5 for the regarding of sin and 2 Corinthians 2:6-

8 for the remitting of it. It is not official. It is not addressed to apostles, but to disciples. It does not touch the soul's eternal relation with God, but its present relation to the assembly.

The assembly is bound to put away a drunkard. If the excommunicated person is truly repentant, the assembly should receive him back. Both the putting out and the receiving back must be the act of the whole assembly and not of a part merely. It is of the utmost importance that none should attempt to interfere with the action of the assembly.

The greatest care, tenderness and wisdom are needed in cases such as you refer to. A man may be "overtaken in a fault" as in Galatians 6. In an unguarded moment a person may be led to take more stimulant than he ought, and perhaps he may seem to be the worse for drink. Should such an one be hastily thrust out of the assembly? Assuredly not. He should be lovingly and tenderly admonished by "the spiritual" who alone know how to do it. He should be carefully looked after, not for the purpose of finding accusation against him, but to "restore" and deliver him thoroughly from the effect of his "fault."

In short, there is a demand for the most tender, judicious, pastoral care in cases of this nature. The assembly should never be called into action except when there is no hope of restoration in any other way. Excommunication is the last sad act of the assembly, to be performed with broken hearts and weeping eyes, and only with a view to restoration. Salvation and not destruction is the object of the assembly's discipline.

The assembly should never be called to discuss cases. It is called to act in simple obedience to the Word of the Lord. The case should be so plain, so manifest, that all discussion is closed and nothing remains but solemn and unanimous action. If this were more understood and attended to, we should have fewer complicated "cases" of discipline. If the assembly be called to discuss, you will rarely if ever get a unanimous judgment. Hence if discussion be needed, the case is not fit to come before the assembly. The spiritual must still wait on God in prayer and watch the case in patient pastoral love. There should be no haste on the one hand, no indifference on the other.

Leviticus 13 is a fine study for all who are really interested in the condition of the assembly. We cannot dwell upon it here, but we earnestly commend it to the attention of our brethren. The priest was not hastily to pronounce judgment in any given case. The most patient care was needed lest anyone should be put out as a leper who really was not one, or lest any real case of leprosy should escape. There was to be no haste and no indifference.

It is of the deepest importance to understand the real object, nature and character of discipline in the Church of God. It is to be feared they are little understood. Some of us seem to look upon discipline as a means of getting rid of people whose ways may be displeasing or discreditable to us. This is a fatal mistake. The grand object of discipline is the glory of God as involved in the holiness of His Assembly and the real good of the soul towards whom the discipline is exercised.

As to the nature and character of discipline, we should ever remember that to take part in it according to the mind of Christ, we must make the person's sin our own and confess it as such before God. It is one thing to stand up in heartless formality and read a person out of the assembly. It is quite another for the whole assembly to come before God in true brokenness and contrition of heart to put away, with tears and confession, some evil that could not be got rid of in any other way. If there were more of this latter, we should see more divine restoration.

We feel the deep solemnity and interest of the subject which your question has brought to our notice and we trust it may receive more profound attention from the Lord's people everywhere.

We would affectionately suggest to you and the "many others" who feel with you in reference to those habits which you name, whether it would not be better to make them a matter of earnest prayer than to write about them to us. Christ is the Master of the Assembly. Appeal to Him. He never fails. "Where two or three are gathered together in My name, there am I in the midst." Is not He sufficient? Cannot He keep order? What should I say if one of my sons were to write to another to correct some disorderly conduct at my table? I should feel disposed to say to him, "What! my son, am not I competent to keep order at my own table? Must you needs write to a stranger to regulate my family?" Do we believe the Lord presides in the assembly? If so, we should look to Him to correct all abuses. If this were better understood, it would save a vast amount of trouble, avert a multitude of "cases," bring much glory to Christ and yield a rich harvest of blessing to our own souls.

You do not give us your address or even your name. Yet the nature of your communication is such as to demand some sort of guarantee. We feel strongly as to the practice of some of our correspondents in writing to us about the condition of assemblies and the walk and conversation of

417

individuals. We consider it quite wrong. We do not believe it to be according to the mind of Christ to make the failings of our brethren the subject of anonymous letters.

If it be a question of individual failure, the proper course is to go and speak tenderly and faithfully to the person himself. But this needs much grace and self-subjugation. Serious mischief may be done by approaching a failing or erring brother in a harsh, legal, knock-me-down spirit. If there be not moral power to act graciously in such a case, it is better to go and tell the Lord about it. So also as to what transpires in the assembly, if half the time spent in murmuring and complaining about this, that and the other, were spent in earnest prayer and loving intercession, how very different we should find it! We doubt not but that in very many cases, the deadness and lack of power complained of are caused by the wrong state of soul of the persons who complain.

In our experience and observation, we have always found that those persons who talked about the weakness and deadness of meetings had really need to look to themselves, whereas the really spiritual and godly members, instead of gossiping about such things, went to the Lord in prayer about them and thus brought down blessing on their own souls and on the assembly. We are not ignorant of the fact that there is everywhere much need of revival and bracing up, but we do not believe the remedy lies in anonymous communications to us.

We judge you have made a mistake in leaving the assembly because some of the members found fault with you. The discipline and surveillance of the assembly are very wholesome, though they may prove irksome to our proud and restless nature. We do not mean to say that the persons who found fault with you were right, inasmuch as we do not know the facts of your case. But speaking generally, it is a bad sign to see a person grow resistive under the exercise involved in walking in company with his brethren. You may rest assured it is far better to be rapped over the knuckles than to have our personal vanity fed by a flattering tongue. It may be that those who give the rap are wrong in how they do it. Further, it may be they also need a rap themselves. Be this as it may, we are thoroughly persuaded that the fellowship of the assembly is a safe and wholesome thing, and woe be to those who seek in pride or wilfulness to get rid of it! We strongly recommend you to humble yourself and seek to be admitted into the bosom of the assembly. "Humble yourselves under the mighty hand of God that He may exalt you in due time" (1 Pet. 5:6; James 4:10).

THE LORD'S SUPPER

Scripture is clear and definite on the subject of the Lord's Supper. The words are as distinct as possible, "As oft as ye eat this bread and drink this cup, ye do show the Lord's death till He come." Again, "This do in remembrance of Me." We remember Him in death – the basis, center and spring of everything to us. The apostle calls attention to the fact that it was in the same night He was betrayed that our blessed Lord, in His thoughtful, unselfish love for us, instituted the feast, and this is full of touching interest for our hearts. But as to the feast itself – its significance – its object – its place, Scripture is most precise: "ye do show the Lord's death," "Do this in remembrance of Me." We remember a Christ who was dead; we call Him to mind in that condition in which, thank God, He no longer is. All this can only be by faith through the power of the Holy Spirit. There is no need to enter into sensational details; indeed such things are most offensive to all true spiritual feeling. We cannot keep too close to the actual, perfect language of Holy Scripture.

It is quite true that the special object in the Lord's Supper is to remember Him and show forth His death, but John 14-16 clearly proves that after the Supper, our Lord spoke on various subjects. If He did so, surely His servants may do the same. It would be a serious mistake, therefore, to shut out all teaching and exhortation except such as had for its subject the fact of the death of Christ or the circumstances attendant thereon. We believe in this, as in everything else, the Holy Spirit must lead and order. There is always great danger in taking up a certain idea and running it to seed. We most fully enter into the thought of the true nature and object of the Supper itself, but we also believe that when the feast has been duly celebrated, then is a wide field for the action of the Holy Spirit in teaching and exhortation. "Let all things be done to edifying."

You ask, "If you found a young person who gave you the fullest assurance he was saved, enjoyed peace with God, enjoyed fellowship about the things of Christ, and whose conduct at home showed the power of it, if such an one expressed a desire to come to the Lord's table, would you receive him or would you keep him outside for a length of time if he were only 13 or 14 years old?" Most assuredly, we would gladly receive such an one and not keep him outside for a single hour. What has the question of years to do with the divine life? How old was Samuel when he first knew the Lord? or Josiah? or Timothy?

We regard your note as being anything but presumptuous, but we must persist in saying we see no foundation in Scripture for a person breaking bread alone. It is distinctly an act of *fellowship* to the integrity of which the presence of two is absolutely essential.

"Now when the even was come, He sat down with the twelve" (Mt. 26:20). So also Mark 16:17. Again, in Luke 22:14, "When the hour was come, He sat down and the twelve apostles with Him." Furthermore, Judas is distinctly mentioned as taking part in the feast and asking a question. And then not merely at the passover, but at the supper, our Lord says, "Behold, the hand of him that betrayeth Me is with Me on the table." We do not see how anyone can question the fact of the presence of Judas at the supper. His character was only known to the Lord. His fellow apostles did not seem to have any suspicion of him. But then to argue from this case that we ought to allow known evil at the Lord's table, is simply wicked. To say that we *may* have traitors at the table is to confess our own weakness, but to say that we *ought* to have known traitors, is perfectly shocking to any holy mind.

Where is there any warrant in Scripture for confining the Lord's supper to the first day of the week? No doubt the disciples did specially celebrate it on that day, but it was originally instituted on a week-day. We should rejoice to break bread at any time, provided people were up to the mark for it, and that all the circumstances of the case were according to the mind of God.

"The feast" in 1 Corinthians 5:8 is the antitype of the feast of unleavened bread which, as we learn from Exodus 12, was based upon and inseparably connected with the passover. The bloodstained lintel was not to be separated from the unleavened bread. Peace and purity, safety and sanctity, must always go together.

It would be a strange and miserable application of 1 Corinthians 5:8 to refer it to the matter of having bread without yeast or unfermented wine at the Lord's Supper. We believe, dear friend, the feast refers to the whole of our Christian life in this world. It should, from first to last, be a feast of unleavened bread, based on the great fact that "Christ our passover is sacrificed for us" – a life of personal holiness flowing out of accomplished redemption, known and applied by the power of the Holy Spirit.

420

SINGING

We regret that the friend who visited you did not seek to lead your souls to something more edifying than discussing the question of the Scripture authority for singing hymns at our meetings. Further, we marvel that a number of intelligent Christians should spend a moment in discussing such a question. You say "the question is at first sight startling." We cannot see anything "startling" in it except it be in its bearing upon those who raise it.

Let us see what Scripture says on the point. In Mark 14:26 we read, "And when they had sung an hymn, they went out into the Mount of Olives." You say that "Liddell and Scott tell us that the Greek word might equally correctly be rendered 'to praise.'" Here is what these learned lexicographers say: "to sing, laud, praise, sing of, tell of." And then they give the Latin "cano" which signifies *to sing.* But you say that some learned brother has informed you that "in no instance in Scripture does the word 'sing' refer to vocal music." If singing is not vocal, what is it? When Paul and Silas sang praises to God, was not that vocal? So also in Hebrew 2:12, we have the words of Christ Himself, "In the midst of the Assembly will I sing praise unto Thee." Is not this vocal? In 1 Corinthians 14:15 we have a different word. "I will sing with the spirit and I will sing with the understanding." Here the word stands in contrast with praying. Then in Revelation 5:9 we have another word. "They sung a new song." The same word occurs in chapter 14:3; 15:3 and in Colossians 3:16, "singing with grace in your hearts." And in Ephesians 5:19, "Singing and making melody in your heart to the Lord."

Now here we have three different Greek words rendered in our most excellent Authorized Version by the English word "sing." The question is, what idea do these words convey to the mind? Is it not that of audible praise or worship, whether rendered individually or collectively? Are not "Psalms and hymns and spiritual songs" divinely recognized? If so, for what are they designed? Is it not as a vehicle for the worship of Christians? We do not see how this can be called in question by any sober person. There is no analogy between *forms* of prayer and hymns. The latter are divinely recognized; the former are not. This is quite sufficient for us.

"But," you say, "there is danger of getting occupied with the tune or mere music." No doubt, and is there not danger in teaching, preaching, exhortation and even in praying of getting occupied with the language, with grammar, rhetoric or oratory? Must we therefore give up teaching, preaching, exhortation and prayer? Is there no remedy for the supposed evil except reducing our meetings to a senseless and miserable silence? It certainly is great evil in singing to forget the subject and object of our song and become occupied with the style and effect of our singing, and it is to this very evil that the revered writer to whom you refer applies the term "iniquity." But most certainly he never meant to teach that it is iniquity to use a hymn book or sing a hymn, for he has been doing both for the last forty years all over the world, and has contributed some precious hymns to help the worship of his brethren.

We have thus, dear friend, gone fully into your question. In taking leave of you we would affectionately entreat you to fling aside such foolish notions. When you come together, instead of discussing the rightness of singing, seek to have your hearts in tune *to* sing. We dread young Christians getting under the influence of a unhealthy sentimentality, transcendental notions or a higher spirituality, falsely so called. It is sure to lead to mischief. See that you keep clear of such. Cultivate simplicity, reality, soundness of mind and earnestness. There is no telling where we may find ourselves if we take up with every whim that comes in our way. Some would suggest our breaking bread alone, thus reducing the Church of God to a state of complete isolation. Others would rob us of our hymn books and reduce our meetings to a gloomy silence. From all such wild and foolish notions, may the good Lord deliver us! May He graciously fill our hearts with an intense desire for His glory, for the good of His beloved people and for the progress of His cause. May these realities so engage all our energies and fill up our every moment that we shall have no time or thought for the discussion of unprofitable questions.

As to the question of singing at funerals, it must entirely depend upon our spiritual power at the time. A person may be so bowed down with sorrow as to be wholly unable to sing, but you could not make such an one a model for others or hinder their singing on the ground of sympathy with him. We believe nothing can be more magnificent, more morally grand, than a hymn of praise, a song of triumph, chanted amid the very dust of death. To hear a congregation of saints singing at the grave of a brother or sister is a positive triumph over the enemy. But if anyone be so crushed under the sorrow as to be unable to sing, we feel assured the loving tender heart of Jesus feels the sorrow and puts the tears into His bottle. The one who wept and groaned at the grave of Lazarus would not rebuke the tears and groans of a crushed and desolate heart.

THE ROLE AND DEPORTMENT OF WOMEN

Scripture is very plain as to the place of the woman (1 Cor. 11:1-16). We do not believe it to be according to nature or according to revelation for a woman to be prominent either in the Church or in the world. It is our deeply cherished conviction that there is no sphere in which the woman can move with such grace and dignity as in the shade and retirement of the domestic circle. There she can prove herself the helper of the man in all good works. Home is preeminently the woman's place. The Holy Spirit has distinctly assigned her work when He declares that she is to "guide the house." There may be exceptional cases in which the Christian female, having no special home duties, may devote herself to outside work with real advantage to many, but such cases are few and far between. The general rule is as plain as possible (1 Tim. 5:14).

As to the question of "woman's rights," etc., we have nothing whatever to do with politics. It is our desire to be taught exclusively by Scripture, and most certainly we cannot find anything in the New Testament about women having a place in the legislature. In the history of Israel, it was always a proof of the nation's low condition when the female was thrown into prominence. It was Barak's backwardness that threw Deborah forward. According to the normal, the divine idea, the man is the head. This is seen in perfection in Christ and the Church. Here is the true model on which our thoughts are to be formed. So far as this poor world is concerned, it is all in confusion. The foundations are out of course. God has said, "I will overturn, overturn, overturn it, and it shall be no more until He come whose right it is; and I will give it Him" (Ezek. 21:27). There can be nothing right until "The kingdoms of this world are become the kingdoms of our Lord and of His Christ." Till then, the Christian must be content to be a pilgrim and a stranger on this earth, having his citizenship, his home, his portion, in heaven. May it be thus with all who belong to Christ!

We do not expect that persons who are bent on carrying out their own thoughts; whose will has never broken; who reason instead of submitting to the authority of Scripture; who say, "I think" instead of seeing what God thinks – we do not expect that any such will approve or appreciate what we have answered in reply to your question, but we must bow down to the authority of God in this as in all beside.

You have our fullest sympathy in all your mental exercises. We believe you are absolutely right in refusing to be present where a woman undertakes to speak or pray in public. The spirit and teaching of the New Testament are against any such practice. "Silence" is enjoined on the woman in public or in the presence of a man. As to 1 Corinthians 11, you have nothing about the assembly until verse 17 where a new subject is introduced, and as you truly remark, the Spirit of God cannot contradict Himself. He cannot in one place tell a woman to keep silence and in another, tell her to break it. It is both contrary to God and contrary to nature for a woman to come forward as a public speaker. She is to illustrate the proper place of the Church – subjection, not teaching. The Church ought not, does not teach: she is false if she does. "Thou sufferest that woman Jezebel, which calleth herself a prophetess, to teach." This is the spirit and genius of popery. To say that the Church has power to decree, enact or teach is apostasy. The Church is taught by the Word of God. She is to obey and be in subjection. She ought to be the pillar and ground of the truth – to *hold* and *maintain* the truth, but never teach. Such is the invariable teaching of the New Testament as to the Church of which the woman should be the illustration.

It will perhaps be said that God uses the preaching and praying of women for the blessing of souls. Well, what does this prove? The rightness of female preaching? No, but the sovereign goodness of God. Were we to argue from the fact of the divine blessing, what might we not be led to approve? God is sovereign and may work where and by whom He pleases; we are *servants* and must do what He tells us. In the time of the "awakening" souls were smitten in Roman Catholic chapels in the presence of the sacrifice of the mass. Does that prove popery to be right? No, it only proves that God is good. *To reason from results may lead us into the grossest error.*

It ought to be sufficient for everyone who bows to the authority of Scripture to know that the Holy Spirit strictly commands the woman to keep silence in public assembly. And truly we may say, "Doth not even nature itself teach" the moral unfitness of a woman's appearing in a pulpit or on a platform? Unquestionably. There are many and varied ways in which women can "labor in the gospel" without the unseemliness of public preaching. We are not told how "those women labored" with the blessed apostle, but most assuredly it was not by speaking in public.

As to the four daughters of Philip the evangelist "who did prophecy," it rests with the defenders of female preaching to prove that they exercised that gift in public. We believe it was in the shade and retirement of their father's house.

In conclusion, dear friend, we express our ever-deepening conviction that home is, preeminently, the woman's sphere. There she can move with moral grace and dignity. There she can shine as a wife and a mother to the glory of Him who has called her to fill those holy relationships. There the most lovely traits of female character are developed – traits which are completely defaced when she abandons her home work and enters the domain of the public preacher.

We believe it is plainly opposed to Scripture for a woman to speak in the Church or to teach or in any way to usurp authority over the man. But if there be a meeting of a private, social character, there is in our judgment an opening for the free communication of thought, provided always that the woman keep the place assigned her by the voice of nature and the Word of God.

Judging from the tone of your letter, we feel assured the Lord will guide you into the right path of service. We are not told in what specific way "those women labored with Paul in the gospel," but we know there are a thousand ways in which a woman may serve in the gospel without ever stepping out of that sphere which properly belongs to her. As to the married woman, we feel increasingly persuaded that home is preeminently her place; there she has a hallowed and elevated sphere in which she can serve in the full consciousness of being exactly where the hand of God has set her and where His Word directs her. May the Lord bless and keep you!

Scripture is very plain as to the manner in which Christian women should be attired, not only at the Lord's table, but at all times. Surely in this, as in all beside, there is urgent need of the exercise of a tender conscience, a godly subjection to the authority of God's Word. If Christians will not give heed to the exhortation of the Holy Spirit, they are not likely to pay much attention to these pages. One of the special needs of the moment is thorough submission to the true teachings of Holy Scripture. Where the heart is under the direct government of the Word all will be right; where it is not, there will be nothing right.

MINISTRY AND SERVICE

We entirely agree with your view of ministry. We believe that every member of the body has a ministry, and it is by each one knowing his place and his functions in the body, and working effectively therein, that the growth of all is promoted. On the other hand it is most disastrous for anyone to mistake his line of things, since he not only fails as to his own work but hinders others in theirs. May the Lord give us grace to know our niche and fill it! And may we learn to be content with a very little and a very humble niche. Someone has said, "I never was truly happy until I ceased to wish to be great." This is a wholesome saying and one which we would do well to ponder. It is immensely important for each one to know his own proper work. A man's whole life may be full of mistakes simply owing to his having never really fallen into his divinely appointed line of things. This is very deplorable. Not only does it involve a loss of time and labor on his own part, but it also of necessity interferes with the work of others.

May the Lord guide and keep us! And may our earnest breathing ever be "Lord, what wilt Thou have me to do?"

May God keep His servants humble and dependent! We are increasingly convinced that the quiet, shady, retiring path is the best and safest for the Christian workman. There is always immense danger when a man or his work becomes well known. When the fame of Israel was being spread abroad among the Canaanites, the Lord commanded Joshua to "make sharp knives and circumcise the people" (Josh. 5:2). Nature must be put in the place of death and kept there.

An evangelist is one who possesses a bona fide gift from Christ, the Head of the Church. If a man does not have this gift he is not an evangelist, though able to speak ever so fluently. We believe there is one feature which invariably characterizes a true evangelist – an intense love for souls and a thirsting for their salvation so Christ may be magnified. The glory of Christ must ever be the ruling object with every workman, whatever be his gift. We believe the evangelist ought to look for results and confidently expect them, just as the farmer looks for the fruit of his labor. He may have to exercise "long patience," but he should fully count on God for results. An evangelist is, of necessity, more or less a traveler. The *world* is his sphere, but the Lord will ever guide those who simply wait on Him, having no will of their own, no personal aim or object.

As to giving up our calling, provided it be a godly one, it is a most serious matter indeed, demanding grave consideration and most distinct guidance from God. If He calls us to this, He will most surely sustain us, for He will be no man's debtor. He never fails a trusting heart. But we must be very clear indeed as to the divine call, else we shall break down. We have known several who gave up their occupation to give themselves to the Lord's work, but the sequel proved in a very humiliating way that they were not called of God to enter upon that line of things. But no one can be a rule for another. Each one must walk before his Lord in this as in all besides. He is a most gracious Master, and even though we make mistakes we can cast ourselves in fullest confidence on His unfailing goodness. And where the heart is true to Him, all is sure to come right in the end.

May He guide and bless you, dear friend, and use you abundantly according to the earnest desire of your heart!

We cannot see what 2 Corinthians 11:8 has to do with the subject of "one man ministry" or how anyone could think of quoting it in defense of such a thing. Paul received help from the assembly at Philippi. He did not receive from the assembly at Corinth because they were not in good state. This was to their shame and loss. But what has all this to do with a humanly ordained minister receiving a salary from a congregation? There is no such thing in the Word of God.

It is difficult for one to judge for another in the matter to which you refer. Each one must act before the Lord and be guided of Him as to the best method of working. As a rule, it is the best way to study Scripture apart from the idea of having to preach. It is not good always to be reading for others; one is in danger of falling into the mere business of sermon-making which is very withering to the soul. It is well to go to the Word on the principle set forth in John 7:37, "If any man thirst, let him come unto Me and drink." We only speak of the principle, not the strict application of the passage. We should go ourselves to the fountain of Holy Scripture, not to draw for others, but to drink for ourselves. Then we shall be always full, always ready for the Master's use.

Far be it from us to encourage anyone in a random, haphazard way of speaking on Scripture. We believe such a habit to be ruinous to the soul of the speaker and worse than wearisome to the souls of the hearers. The apostle's advice to his son Timothy is important for us all, "Meditate upon these things; give thyself wholly to them, that thy profiting may appear to all. Take heed unto thyself and unto the doctrine; continue in them; for in doing this thou shalt both save thyself and them that hear thee" (1 Tim. 4:15-16). The "profiting" is sure to "appear" if the habit of meditation is diligently cultivated, but if one goes to a meeting with a sermon already prepared, it may not be the thing which the Lord would have spoken at all. No doubt, the Lord can and does guide His servants in study and preparation beforehand. He can fix their minds upon the right subject and teach the right method of handling it. He is so good that we can count on Him with fullest confidence in all things. But we have to watch against the habit of making ourselves up for an occasion on the one hand, and against idleness and indifference on the other. May the Lord bless you and help you in your work!

The special application of Ezekiel 34 is to the shepherds of Israel, though surely it conveys a solemn and needed lesson to all who undertake the work of a pastor in the midst of God's people.

In 1 Corinthians 13 the apostle sets forth the great motive spring of all true and effective ministry – love. In chapter 12 you have the *ground* of ministry; in chapter 13 the *motive spring*; and in chapter 14 the *object*. First, membership in the body; secondly, love; thirdly, edification. We cannot enter upon a detailed exposition of those portions.

UNITY

All who believe in Christ as dead and risen are sealed by the Holy Spirit and form part of His body. The body is viewed as on the earth. "There is one body." This is as true now as when the apostle penned the epistle to the Ephesians. This body is indissoluble. Its unity cannot be broken. There is no such thing as "rending the body of Christ" or "cutting off limbs." These are expressions which are used without due attention to Scripture. We are bound to recognize as a great foundation truth the unity of the body.

We are not called to *form* a unity, but to *own* the unity which God the Holy Spirit has formed. It is as contrary to the truth to set about forming a unity as to set about working out righteousness for ourselves. God reveals His righteousness on the principle of faith; we believe and possess it. So also, God reveals His unity; we believe and walk in the light of it. Sadly, men refuse to submit to God's righteousness and go about to establish their own. In like manner men refuse God's unity and go about to form their own, but both man's righteousness and man's unity must pass away like the vapors of the morning, whereas the righteousness and the unity which are of God shall endure through everlasting ages.

We most fully agree with you in saying that our motto should ever be, "Truth first; unity if you can, but truth." *If unity is attained by the sacrifice of truth, it cannot be "the unity of the Spirit."* Many fall into the mistake of thinking that unity is something which they themselves have to set up, whereas the unity of the body is a grand reality, a substantial truth in the light of which we are called to walk and judge ourselves and all around us. We are no more competent to form that unity than we are to atone for our sins or to work out a righteousness for ourselves. It is God's work from first to last. He has revealed His righteousness; we receive it by faith. He has revealed His unity; we receive it by faith. As it would assuredly be a grave error for us to attempt to work out our own righteousness, so it is a grave error to attempt to work out our own unity. Christ is the center of God's unity; the Holy Spirit is the power, and truth the basis.

As to man's unity, you will find all manner of centers – a man, an ordinance, a doctrine, something short of Christ. This unity may be maintained by the energy of the human will and is often based upon tradition, expediency or reason. In a word, it is not Christ or the Spirit or the truth. It is not of God, and if we do not gather with God, we must scatter.

SEPARATION FROM THE WORLD

The New Testament teaches in many places that the Christian is dead to the world; not merely to certain gross things in the world, but to the world in all its aspects. What then has a dead man to do with the world's politics? As Christians, we are sent into this world even as Jesus was sent into it. What had He to do with the world's politics? He paid tribute; so should we. He obeyed the powers that be; we should do the same. He suffered under this world's powers, and we may be called to the same.

We are instructed to pray for the powers and we are to do so quite irrespective of the nature or character of the power. In fact, when the apostle penned that principle, the imperial scepter was wielded by one of the worst men who ever lived. The Christian is taught to be subject to the powers that be; he is *never* taught to wield that power, but the very reverse. "Our citizenship is in *heaven*." We are only pilgrims and strangers in the world. The cross of our Lord has broken every link between us and this world. The resurrection has introduced us into a new world altogether. In the death of Christ we cleared the shores of the old world. In His resurrection we have landed on the shores of the new. "Ye are dead, and your life is hid with Christ in God." Therefore, "Set your affection on things above, not on things on the earth" (Col. 3). Oh! to know the formative, sanctifying power of this precious line of truth!

You are right in your judgment as to Genesis 9:6. It stands unrepealed. The law did not touch it; the gospel does not touch it. It abides in all its solemn force as an enactment of the government of God. If we in our wisdom or tenderness attempt to touch it, we simply make ourselves out to be wiser and more tender than God. *We must not confound the grace of the gospel with God's government of the world.* Christianity does not interfere with the arrangements of divine providence. It teaches Christians to act in grace toward all, but to apply the principles of the gospel to the government of this world would throw everything into confusion. Further, dear friend, what have we as Christians to do with sending petitions or remonstrances to the government? Nothing whatever. We have to pray for the government and to obey it; or to suffer if it calls upon us to disobey God.

But to interfere with the enactments of government is practically to deny our heavenly citizenship. And to attempt to hinder the course of justice is to fly in the face of God's own direct command, "Whoso sheddeth man's blood, by man shall his blood be shed." Where has this command been repealed? Nowhere. Hence let Christians beware how they attempt to tamper with it, under the influence of natural feeling or sentimentality. We dare not add, *of Christian principle,* because true Christian principle will ever lead us to bow to the authority of the Word of God, though we cannot exactly understand it or reconcile it with our own feelings.

We consider 2 Corinthians 6:14-18 a conclusive answer to your question. If that scripture does not govern a man's conscience, reasoning is worse than useless.

"Our citizenship is in heaven." "Ye are dead, and your life is hid with Christ in God." What has a dead man to do with politics? The Christian is one who has died in Christ – died to sin, died to the law, died to the world. Hence he has, in God's view of him, no more to do with these things than a man lying dead on the floor. He is alive in Christ – alive to God, alive to all that is spiritual, heavenly, divine. He is in the new creation. His morals, his religion, his politics are all in the new creation – all heavenly, all divine. He is done with the world in spirit and principle. He is in it, to walk as a pilgrim and stranger. He is *in* it to live as a Christian, as a spiritual, heavenly man. He is not *of* it to walk as a worldly, carnal, natural man. "If any man be in Christ, he is a new creation." May we live in the power of these things.

FALSE POSITIONS AND UNEQUAL YOKES

It was certainly very wrong of you to take a false oath and still more wrong of those who compelled you to take it for their gain. We do not believe it to be "the unpardonable sin," but you are bound to confess the sin and get out of a false position. Do not trifle with conscience, else you may get into a state which can only be compared to hell upon earth. No human power should have induced you to tell a lie, much less to swear one!

We feel deeply for you. You are evidently in a false and very trying position, but it is one thing to see this and another thing to know how to get out of it. *It is clearly wrong for a Christian to be yoked with an unbeliever for any object.* The fact of your having entered into this partnership in ignorance may account for your entrance, but it cannot justify your continuance therein. You have only to bow down before your Lord and confess your failure and look to Him to deliver you out of your false position. Beware how you act. Do nothing rashly. You must seek to act honorably toward your partner and toward all to whom you owe anything. God honors the bent of the heart and conscience in a right direction, and we must not do wrong things in seeking to get out of a position.

We need to know more of the circumstances of your case before attempting to give you any opinion. As you have put the matter, you seem to be in a false position. The sooner you get out of it the better. But then care must be taken to do things in a right way. It is certain that no worldly advantage should induce you to remain in a position which robs you of communion with God and His people. So far as you have informed us, it would seem to be distinctly an instance of the "unequal yoke." May the Lord give you grace to do the right thing in a right way.

We believe there are two evils involved in such membership as you name. In the first place, you are unequally yoked together with unbelievers, which you are expressly told not to be (2 Cor. 6:14). In the second place, you surrender your individual responsibility and become merged in an organization for whose every act you are morally responsible.

There is nothing in Scripture to hinder your being a *servant* of such a company as you name. To be a *partner* would be an "unequal yoke" which 2 Corinthians 6:14 expressly forbids.

We most assuredly judge it to be contrary to God's will for a Christian son to enter into partnership with an unconverted father, or vice versa. It is an unequal yoke in spite of the natural relationship. A son may serve under a father, but a deed of partnership involves an unequal yoke.

MILITARY SERVICE

Our Lord Jesus Christ has left us an example that we should follow His steps. Can we trace His footsteps into a field of battle? We are called to walk even as He walked. Is it walking like Him to go to war? True, we fail in many things, but if we are asked if it be right for a Christian to go to war, we can only answer the question by a reference to Christ. How did He act? What did He teach? Did He ever take the sword? Did He come to destroy men's lives? Did He not say, "He that taketh the sword shall perish by the sword?" And again, "I say unto you, that ye resist not evil." How do such words agree with going to war? But some will say, "What would become of us if all were to adopt such principles?" We reply, If all were to adopt those heavenly principles, there would be no more war and hence we should not need to fight. But it is not our business to reason as to the results of obedience; we have only to obey the Word of our blessed Master and walk in His steps. If we do so, we shall most assuredly not be found going to war.

Persons sometimes quote our Lord's words, "He that hath no sword, let him sell his garment and buy one," as giving sanction for going to war, but anyone can see that they have nothing to do with the question. They refer to the altered condition of things on which the disciples would have to enter when the Lord would be taken. While He was with them, they had lacked nothing, but now they would have to face in His absence the full brunt of the world's opposition. In short, the words have an entirely spiritual application. Again, much use is sought to be made of the fact that the centurion in Acts 10 was not told to resign his commission. It is not the way of the Spirit of God to put people under a yoke. He does not say to the newly converted soul, "You must give up this or that." The grace of God meets a man where he is, with a full salvation. *Then* it teaches him how to walk by presenting the words and ways of Christ in all their sanctifying and formative power.

Again it is said, "Does not the apostle in 1 Corinthians 7 tell us to abide in the calling wherein we are called?" Yes; with this powerfully qualifying clause, *"Abide with God."* This makes a great difference. Suppose a hangman is converted, could he abide in his calling? It will be said that this is an extreme case. Granted, but it is a case in point inasmuch as it proves the fallacy of the reasoning on 1 Corinthians 7. It proves there are callings in which one could not possibly "abide with God." So, as to your question, dear friend, we have simply to inquire, "Is it abiding with God or walking in the footsteps of Christ to go to war?"

If it be, let Christians do so; if not, what then?

You have only one question to ask yourself, namely, "Is the profession of arms one which a disciple of Christ can properly follow?" If not, your path is plain. You surely cannot think of placing your son in a position which he must abandon to follow a rejected Christ. No doubt, there are many of the Lord's beloved people in the army, but the question is not, Can I be saved and yet be in the army? Thousands have gone to heaven who have lived and died in that profession. But the real question for every loyal heart is, Can I follow the footsteps of my Lord while I remain in a position in which, at any moment, I may be called to take the life of my fellow and send a soul into eternity unprepared? This, dear friend, must be your one question. I cannot place my son, be he converted or unconverted, where I could not be myself. As for the discipline of the army being good for the purpose of bracing up the character, we must confess we have not much faith in it. The mess-room is not the place to which we should like to send a youth for discipline or training of any sort.

THE FUTURE STATE

The idea of departed spirits being in an unconscious state is as absurd as it is unscriptural. Has Paul been unconscious for nearly 2000 years? If there were any truth in this notion, could he have said, "To die is gain?" Would it be gain to be unconscious? Would it be "far better" than to enjoy Christ here and serve Him in the gospel and in the Assembly? When the Lord said to the dying thief, "Today, shalt thou be with Me in paradise," did He mean that he was to be unconscious? Why then say "with Me in paradise?" If he was to be unconscious, what difference would it make where he was to be? When the blessed apostle says, "Absent from the body, present with the Lord," does he mean a state of unconsciousness? Had Stephen nothing but a state of unconsciousness before him when he said, "Lord Jesus, receive my spirit?" It is most deplorable to find professed Christians holding such a miserable theory. Excuse our strong language. It is hard to speak in measured terms of such a baseless absurdity as a ransomed spirit asleep in the presence of Christ! May the Lord deliver His people from all vain and foolish notions!

Luke 23:43; Acts 7:59; 2 Corinthians 5:8 and Philippians 1:23 clearly prove that the moment the spirit of a saint leaves the body it is with Christ in Paradise. The "leading man" to whom you asked for information must be deplorably ignorant of the New Testament. Your letter shows that your mind has been sadly darkened by the cloud of skepticism which seems to be overshadowing thousands.

We have referred previously to the question of "everlasting punishment." We believe it so connects itself with the truth of the immortality of the soul and the infinite nature of Christ's atonement, that you cannot touch it without disturbing the entire arch of divine Revelation. The word "everlasting" occurs about seventy times in the New Testament and is applied to the life of the believer, to the Spirit of God, to the inheritance of the saints and to the punishment of the wicked. On what authority, therefore, can the word be said to mean eternal in one case and not eternal in another? All this reasoning is the fruit of positive infidelity, from which may God, in His mercy, deliver the children of His people! We believe that "hell-fire" is an awful and an eternal reality, nor should we be shaken in our belief by the absurd reasonings of ten thousand "leading men." "If the blind lead the blind, both shall fall into the ditch." Dear friend, ask God to guide you by His Word and Spirit, and place no confidence whatever in "leading men."

The last clause of John 3:36 is as simple as it is solemn. It tells us plainly that the wrath of God abides on all who refuse to believe on the Son. We have been much struck with the power of this entire verse as meeting and completely demolishing two fatal errors of the day, namely, *universal restoration* and *annihilation*. "Shall not see life." Here the universalist gets his divine answer. "The wrath of God abideth on him." Here the annihilationist gets his. If the unbeliever shall not see life, it is evident he cannot be restored. And if the wrath of God abideth on him, it is evident he cannot be annihilated. What living power, what overwhelming force in Holy Scripture!

You are absolutely right, dear friend, not to reason on the solemn subject of eternal punishment, but simply take Scripture as it stands. As to the statement that the word "everlasting" does not mean "forever" in the Greek, there are about 70 passages in the Greek Testament in which the word "aionios" occurs. It is applied to the "life" which believers possess, to the "habitations" into which they are to be received, to God, to the Spirit, to the kingdom of our Lord, and to the punishment of the wicked in hell. Now on what principle can anyone mark off seven or eight of these passages and say that in them the word does not mean forever, but in the remaining 62 passages it does?

Is it not most evident that if we deny the eternity of punishment we must deny the eternity of life, the eternity of God, of the Son and of the Holy Spirit? It is a serious thing to tamper with the truth of God or to mar the integrity of Holy Scripture. Truth is like a magnificent arch: if you touch the smallest stone in that arch, you mar the integrity of the whole. We feel persuaded, dear friend, that this question has a moral bearing as well as a theological. The denial of eternal punishment indicates a wrong condition of soul altogether. The will is at work; reason has not been subjugated; the heart is not broken; there is no real subjection to the authority of the Word. It is more "I think" than "Thus saith the Lord." All this is most serious and should lead us into deep exercise of soul and earnest prayer.

SELF-OCCUPATION AS OPPOSED TO THE TRUE GROUND OF PEACE AND HOLINESS

You may be thoroughly assured of this, dear friend, that you will never get peace by looking at your repentance or your anything. If such a thing could be, it would simply be satisfaction with yourself and this could never be right. Christ has made peace by the blood of His cross. God preaches peace by Jesus Christ. It is not by repentance, though we surely believe in the necessity of repentance! But what would you say, dear friend, to a person if he were to tell you that he had found peace because his repentance was of the right kind – because he hated sin as God hated it? You would say to him that his peace was a false one. Thanks be to God, the believer's peace rests on no such rotten foundation. The apostle does not say, "Having repented enough, we have peace with God." No, but "Being *justified by faith,* we have peace with God."

The believer's peace rests on a divine foundation. It is based on the glorious truth that God is not only satisfied as to the entire question of our sins, but He is actually glorified in respect to it. He has reaped a richer harvest in the matter of the putting away of our sins than ever He could have reaped in the fields of an unfallen creation. Nothing has ever glorified God like the death of Christ. The hearty belief of this must give peace to the soul. It is not the work done *in* us, whether repentance or anything else, that gives peace, but the work accomplished *for* us. It is not the work of the Spirit in, precious and essential as it is, that gives peace, but the work of Christ for us. This is a grand and most necessary truth for all anxious inquirers. It is well and right enough to judge ourselves, our state, our ways – to be humbled because of our shallow repentance, our coldness and indifference – but we shall never get peace by self-judgment. If we have not found peace before we sit down to the work of self-judgment, we shall find it very dismal work indeed.

It seems to us, dear friend, that you are too much occupied with the thoughts of men. One preacher tells you this; another preacher tells you that; and your own heart tells you something else. Would it not be well to listen to what *God* says? This is what faith does and thus finds settled tranquillity. The believer's peace can no more be disturbed than Christ can be disturbed from His seat on the throne of God. This seems strong, but it is true, and being true its strength is part of its moral glory. Let us entreat you to take up the lovely attitude of the soul in Psalm 85, "I will hear what God the Lord will speak" (not what this or that man will speak) "for He will speak peace unto His people and to His saints; but let them not turn again to folly." May the blessed Spirit lead you into the enjoyment of that peace which Christ has made by the blood of His cross, which God preaches in the gospel of His grace by Jesus Christ and which faith finds in the simple testimony of Holy Scripture!

You have our fullest sympathy. We have met many of God's dear children in precisely your condition. Indeed they have, in stating their exercises, used your very words. "This," you will say, "is poor comfort for me." And yet it may not be so. We know a very dear saint of God who was under exercise for years and the only thing that gave him the smallest comfort was Psalm 88. Why? Because there was not a single bit of comfort in it. Yet it was written by a saint of God. Therefore she might be a saint, though she was thoroughly miserable. We write not thus, dear friend, to lead you to be content in your present dark and unhappy condition. Far from it. We beseech you to look off from your feelings, your experiences, your evidences and your faith itself, and rest in Christ and His finished work. God is satisfied with Christ on your behalf. Is He not enough to satisfy you? Do you want to add something of your own to Christ? This is really the question. May God bless you!

We give you one sentence of Holy Scripture as an answer to your letter – Hebrews 12:2, "Looking off unto Jesus." If you could only lose sight of that troublesome, good-for-nothing, guilty, hell-deserving "I" and rest in Christ and His full salvation, you would be able to write a very different sort of letter. Your letter reminds us of Romans 7 by the predominance of "I." You must look simply to Christ. He has settled the entire question. You will never get anything except misery by looking at yourself and reasoning upon what you find there. People are always sure to be full of doubts when they are occupied with "I." It must be so, for how could "I" ever furnish a ground of peace? You may rest assured, dear friend, that until you learn to look outside of yourself and rest simply upon Christ, you will never know what solid peace really is.

We consider your mistake to be self-occupation. You are looking for evidences of your conversion as a ground of peace. This will never do. The true ground of peace is, not that you were converted six years ago, but that Christ died for your sins according to the Scriptures; that He was buried and that He rose again the third day, according to the Scripture." We do not think you have ever really laid hold of the true ground of peace in the presence of God. This is not to be found in yourself or in anything that you can do or think or feel or experience or pass through. It is wholly and exclusively in Christ. He has made peace by the blood of His cross. He is our peace. It is by Him God preaches peace, and being justified by faith we have peace with God. It is when your faith lays hold on God as the One who raised up Jesus our Lord from the dead that your peace will flow as a river.

Even though you could be sure you were converted six years ago, though you could see your name written in the book of life, that would not be the proper basis of your peace in the presence of God, but simply that Christ died for you and that God raised Him from the dead. Ponder this. You will never get any comfort by looking in at yourself or back at your past history. We could not think of building upon the most remarkable conversion that ever took place in this world. Even supposing you had all the feelings of which man is capable and all the feelings which attend upon true spiritual conversion, this would not be the proper ground for your soul to build upon: you must build upon Christ alone. You must commit your precious soul, absolutely, to the truth of God; you must believe what He tells you about Christ and not be looking for evidences in yourself. "Being justified by faith [not merely being sure of our conversion], we have peace with God."

It is not that we question your conversion. It is not that we do not believe in the reality and necessity of conversion and in the proper feelings attendant thereon. We most fully believe in all these things. But we do not believe in such things as the ground of a sinner's peace. If you ask us what gives us true settled peace, we reply, "Believing in Jesus." "Believing in Him that justifieth the ungodly." "Believing in Him that raised up Jesus our Lord from the dead." Read Romans 3 and 4. This takes us clean out of ourselves, and this is just what you want.

Why have you fallen away? Why have you gone back? Why have you been drawn into worse sins since your conversion than ever you committed before? *Because you have never really laid hold of Christ as your true ground of peace, as the One who is made of God unto us wisdom, righteousness, sanctification and redemption.* If He were a covering for your eyes and an object for your heart; if you were occupied with Him and not with yourself, you would have victory over your lusts, passions, tempers and tendencies; over habits, influences and circumstances. In short, to be occupied with Christ by the Holy Spirit is not only the true foundation of peace, but also the secret of strength and victory, and of all real progress in holiness.

Here is precisely where so many go astray. They are occupied with themselves – their conversion and its evidences, their experiences, what they have passed through, and the like. They take comfort from their likings and dislikings, from their loving what they once hated and hating what they once loved; all of which, though real enough in themselves, are not the ground of peace, the secret of liberty or the source of true spiritual power. These latter you must seek in Christ alone. The moment you take your eye off Him, you lose peace and power. "Looking off unto Jesus" must be the motto from the starting-post right onward to the goal. May God's Spirit make all this most real and precious to your soul!

You are entirely too much occupied with your own state and feelings. Seek to be more simple, to rest like a child in your Father's love and anchor your soul upon His faithful Word. It is of no possible use to "try" to be this or that. The more you dwell in calm sweet confidence on the love of Christ – the more you think of Him and feed upon His Word – the more you will grow into His likeness. "We all beholding .... are changed." May the Lord keep you, beloved, and make you very sound in His own precious truth! To His own loving pastoral hand we commend you.

PAUL AND THE TWELVE

There is a material difference between Paul's ministry and that of the twelve. To Paul was committed that precious mystery of the one body, composed of Jew and Gentile, united to the glorified Head in heaven by the Holy Spirit sent down to earth. "For this cause I Paul, the prisoner of Jesus Christ for you Gentiles, if ye have heard of the dispensation of the grace of God which is given me to youward: how that by revelation He made known unto me the mystery (as I wrote afore in few words, whereby, when ye read, ye may understand my knowledge in the mystery of Christ), which in other ages was not made known unto the sons of men, as it is now revealed unto His holy apostles and prophets by the Spirit; that the Gentiles should be fellow heirs and of the same body, and partakers of His promise in Christ by the gospel: whereof I was made a minister according to the gift of the grace of God given unto me by the effectual working of His power. Unto me, who am less than the least of all saints, is this grace given, that I should preach among the Gentiles the unsearchable riches of Christ; and to make all men see what is the administration of the mystery which from the beginning of the world hath been hid in God, who created all things by Jesus Christ" (Eph. 3:1-9). Compare also Romans 16:25-26 and Galatians 1:11-2:10.

The careful study of the above passages will open to you the nature and object of Paul's ministry, and the distinction between it and the ministry of the twelve. It formed no part of the latter to unfold the doctrine of the Church. They were called to preach the gospel. Starting from Jerusalem they were to go into all the world and preach the gospel to every creature. They were to teach all nations, baptizing them in the name of the Father and of the Son and of the Holy Spirit. But as to the special place, portion and prospect of the Church, we must take ourselves to the writings of the Holy Spirit by the pen of the Apostle Paul.

RECONCILIATION

The testimony of Scripture is as distinct as possible. It never speaks of God being reconciled to us. "If, when we were enemies, *we were reconciled to God* by the death of his Son" (Rom. 5:10). It does not say that God was reconciled to us. The death of Christ was essential to the reconciliation, but man was the enemy of God and needed to be reconciled. So we read in Colossians 1:21, "And you that were sometime alienated and enemies in your mind by wicked works, yet now hath He reconciled." The ground of this is stated in the previous verse to be "the blood of His cross." So also in 2 Corinthians 5:19, "God was in Christ reconciling the world unto Himself." It does not say "reconciling Himself to the world."

Thus to any who bow to Scripture, the truth is as clear as a sunbeam. "God so loved the world that He gave His only begotten Son." "It pleased Jehovah to bruise Him." It is of the utmost importance to maintain the true aspect of God's nature and character in the presentation of the gospel. To say that "Christ died to reconcile the Father to us" is to falsify the divine character as seen in the mission and death of His Son. God was not man's enemy but his friend. True, sin had to be condemned; God's truth, holiness and majesty had to be vindicated. All this was done in a divine way in the cross where we see both God's hatred of sin and His love to the sinner.

Atonement is the necessary basis of reconciliation, but it is very important to see that it is God who reconciles us to Himself. This He does, blessed be His name, at no less a cost than "the death of His Son." Such was His love to man, His kindness, His goodness, His deep compassion, that when there was no other way possible, sin being in question, in which man, the guilty enemy and rebel could be reconciled to Him, He gave His Son from His bosom and bruised Him on Calvary's cursed tree. Eternal and universal praise to His name!

RIGHTEOUSNESS

Christ is the believer's righteousness, as we read in 1 Corinthians 1:30, "Who of God is made unto us wisdom, righteousness, sanctification, and redemption." Again in 2 Corinthians 5:21, "For He [God] hath made Him [Christ] to be sin for us, who knew no sin, that we might be made the righteousness of God in Him." When we had no righteousness for God, He provided a righteousness for us, and that righteousness is Christ – a crucified, risen and glorious Christ. In the law, God was *demanding* righteousness from man. In the gospel, God is *providing* righteousness for man. This makes a vast and marvelous difference to anyone who is honestly struggling and toiling to work out righteousness for himself before God.

There was a great difference between Adam's apron and God's coat. God never set a stitch in the former, and man never set a stitch in the latter. There was nothing of God in the apron; there was nothing of man in the coat. Hence we find that Adam's apron proved useless in the hour of need. The very moment he heard the voice of the Lord God, he was afraid and fled to hide because, as he said, "I was naked." *He ignored his own apron!* It was of no use whatever to him. It could not even satisfy his own conscience. Not so, however, when he got on God's coat. He could then say "I am clothed" because God had clothed him. The coat he wore was of God's own making. Moreover, it was founded on the shedding of blood – an all-important cardinal truth. Divine righteousness rests on the basis of accomplished redemption. The cross is the grand foundation, the great central truth of Christianity.

ATONEMENT

The testimony of Holy Scripture is clear, explicit and abundant as to the grand cardinal truth that atonement is by the shedding of blood. The coats of skin which the Lord God made for Adam and Eve were procured from dead victims. The "more excellent sacrifice" of Abel consisted of blood and fat. So also in the history of Noah in Genesis 8 and in the history of Abraham in Genesis 15. Israel was screened from judgment in Egypt by the blood of the paschal lamb, as we read, "when I see the blood, I will pass over you" (Exodus 12). The whole book of Leviticus is one great stream tending to swell the tide of evidence on this vital question. The burnt offering, peace offering, sin offering and trespass offering were all based on blood-shedding. See also that famous passage in Leviticus 17. "The life of the flesh is in the blood: and I have given it to you upon the altar to make an atonement for your souls, for it is the blood that maketh an atonement for the soul" (v. 11).

Time fails us to bring forward the thousandth part of the Scripture proofs on this subject. We shall merely give two most pointed passages from the New Testament and then leave you to follow out the chain of evidence for yourself. "And almost all things are by the law purged with blood: and without shedding of blood is no remission" (Heb. 9:22). "Unto Him that loved us and washed us from our sins in His own blood" (Rev. 1:5, 9 with Acts 20:28). These passages speak for themselves. We desire to bow in reverent submission to the authority of Holy Scripture. We do not want to reason or argue. "Thus saith the Lord" is amply sufficient for us.

Your question as to John 1:29 and 1 John 2:2 is a very important one. It will help you much to distinguish between Christ as the *propitiation* for the whole world and as the *substitute* for His people. The two goats in Leviticus 16 typify Him in these two aspects of His work. The Lord's lot fell upon one. This was Christ the propitiation. The people's lot fell upon the other. This was Christ the substitute. John 1:29 refers to the former. "The Lamb of God that taketh away the sin of the world." See also Hebrews 9:26. Christ did a work on the cross in virtue of which every trace of sin shall yet be obliterated from the whole creation. The full result of this work will not be seen until the new heavens and the new earth shall shine forth as the eternal abode of righteousness. It is in virtue of Christ's propitiatory work that God has been dealing in mercy and goodness with the world and with man from the Fall down to the present moment. He has sent His sunshine and His rain upon the earth. He has filled men's hearts with food and gladness. He has been dealing in patience and longsuffering with the human family. And it is in virtue of the same propitiatory sacrifice that the evangelist goes forth with a world-wide gospel for the ears of every creature under heaven.

The evangelist cannot go and tell every creature that Christ died as his substitute, but he can tell him that He died as a propitiation; and when, through grace, the soul believes on the Lord Jesus Christ, he can learn the further calming truth that He died as a substitute and bore all his sins in His own body on the tree. See Hebrews 9:28, "So Christ was once offered to bear the sins of many" – all His people. In verse 26 we read, "He hath appeared to put away sin by the sacrifice of Himself." Christ is never said to have borne the sins of the world. It is utterly false doctrine; it is universalism. He bore the sins of His people, and He has done a work in virtue of which every trace of sin shall yet be abolished throughout the wide universe of God.

These distinctions, dear friend, are of the utmost importance. Scripture maintains them. Theology confounds them, and confounds souls as a result.

1 Peter 2:24 refers to the whole of Christ's sacrificial work. It is a quotation from Isaiah 53. The Septuagint version renders the word "stripe" by a singular noun. The atoning work of Christ is set forth in various ways throughout Scripture – "Death," "Blood shedding," "Stripes," "Cross," etc. There is always a distinct object in the use of any particular term. Accept, beloved friend, our warmest thanks for your truly kind and encouraging letter. May God bless you most abundantly!

THE SOVEREIGNTY OF GOD, THE RESPONSIBILITY OF MAN AND THE HEART OF GOD AS REVEALED IN THE GOSPEL

Matthew 20:16 sets forth the grand principle of divine sovereignty. "The last shall be first, and the first last: for many be called but few chosen." God has a right to do what He will with His own. Will anyone dare to question this? If so, it is plain he has never felt his true place as utterly lost. The only resource for a lost sinner is God's sovereign grace. There is no man who can stand before God on the ground of his own righteousness. All are guilty; hence the only resource is in divine mercy, but this mercy must be sovereign. To deny God's right to be sovereign is to deny His existence.

Does this touch for a moment the truth of man's responsibility? By no means. Both are true, and it is utterly impossible that two truths can ever clash. To attempt to reconcile divine sovereignty and human responsibility is worthless labor. They are reconciled already, being both set forth with equal clearness in the divine Word. It is wonderful how simple everything becomes when we fling aside the dogmas of one-sided theology and come like a child to Holy Scripture. Would that all the Lord's people would do this!

There is a lovely passage at the close of the book of Revelation. "Whosoever will, let him take the water of life freely" (Rev. 22:17). This is but one of a large number of passages which give us the other side of the subject.

The writer of the article to which you call our attention, rejects utterly the notion of man's free will. He believes that man is completely powerless; and not only so, but in a state of positive enmity against God so that, if left to himself, he never would come to Christ. All who come to the supper are compelled to come, else they never would be there. Moreover he most fully believes in the sovereignty of God and that the names of all who are saved were written in the Lamb's book of life before the foundation of the world.

But then, on the other side (for we must take both sides), let us ponder such words as these: "I exhort therefore, that first of all, supplications, prayers, intercessions and giving of thanks be made for all men; for kings, and for all that are in authority; that we may lead a quiet and peaceable life in all godliness and honesty. For this is good and acceptable in the sight of God our Savior; *who will have all men to be saved and to come unto the knowledge of the truth.* For there is one God and one mediator between God and men, the man Christ Jesus; *who gave Himself a ransom for all*, to be testified in due time" (1 Tim. 2:1-6).

And again, "The Lord is not slack concerning His promise, as some men count slackness, but is longsuffering to usward, *not willing that any should perish, but that all should come to repentance"* (2 Peter 3:9).

Now, if it be said that, in the above Scriptures, the words "any" and "all" refer to the elect, we reply that this is an unwarrantable liberty to take with the Word of God. If the inspired writer had meant "any of the elect" or "all of the elect," he would most assuredly have said so. But he says nothing of the kind. *It is not according to the desire of the heart of God that any should perish.*

But man is a responsible being, although your letter is totally silent on this very important question. In short, you seem to lose sight altogether of two weighty truths: first, the largeness of the heart of God – the fullness and freeness of His grace, the wide aspect of His salvation, that His righteousness is unto all, that the gospel is to be preached to every creature, that God commands all men everywhere to repent (Mark 16:15; Acts 17:30; Romans 3:22).

And, secondly, man's responsibility. Is the sinner responsible or is he not? If he is not responsible, then what mean such words as "Seeing it is a righteous thing with God to recompense tribulation to them that trouble you; and to you who are troubled, rest with us, when the Lord Jesus shall be revealed from heaven with His mighty angels; in flaming fire taking vengeance on them that know not God and that obey not the gospel of our Lord Jesus Christ; who shall be punished with everlasting destruction from the presence of the Lord and from the glory of His power!" And again, "For this cause God shall send them strong delusion that they should believe a lie; that they all might be damned who believed not the truth, but had pleasure in unrighteousness" (2 Thes. 6-9; 2:11-12).

Are men responsible to believe the gospel? Yes, truly, inasmuch as they shall be punished with everlasting destruction for rejecting it. Shall not the Judge of all the earth do right? People find difficulty in reconciling man's powerlessness with his responsibility. It is not one's business to reconcile things that are revealed in Holy Scripture. It is ours to believe. They are reconciled inasmuch as they are distinctly taught in the Word of God. It is

447

remarkable that we do not see the same difficulty in reference to the things of this life. Suppose a man owes you a thousand dollars but he has by unprincipled extravagance, rendered himself wholly unable to pay you. He is quite powerless. Is he responsible? And are you not perfectly justified, according to worldly principles, in taking legal proceedings against him? How much more will God be justified in His judgment of all those who reject the glad tidings of a full and free salvation sent to them on the ground of the atoning death of His only begotten Son!

We cannot at all agree with you in your remark that, "It appears a yes and no gospel" to call upon men to believe. Our blessed Master called upon men to "repent and believe the gospel" (Mark 1:15). And when asked by the men of His time, "What shall we do that we might work the works of God?" His reply was, 'This is the work of God, that ye believe on Him whom He hath sent" (John 6:28-29). Again, He challenges the Jews with this pointed question, "If I say the truth, why do ye not believe Me?" (John 8:46). Then, when we turn to the Acts of the Apostles we find Peter calling upon the Jews to repent and be converted. We find Paul telling the Philippian jailer to "Believe on the Lord Jesus Christ." He tells the Athenians that "God commandeth all men everywhere to repent." We read in 2 Thessalonians that our Lord Jesus Christ will take vengeance on those who obey not the gospel, and further that "God shall send them strong delusion that they should believe a lie, that they all might be damned who believed not the truth."

Now, it seems to us a very serious thing, in the face of all these passages, to call it "a yes and no gospel" to press upon men their responsibility to believe. But the fact is, dear friend, your difficulty is occasioned by the influence of a one-sided theology – a system which we can only compare to a bird with one wing or a boat with one oar. When we turn to the sacred page of God's Word, we find the truth, not one side of truth, but the whole truth in all its bearings. We find, lying side by side, the truth of divine sovereignty and human responsibility. Are we called to reconcile them? No, they are reconciled already because they are both set forth in the Word. We are to believe and obey.

It is a fatal mistake for men to frame systems of divinity. You can no more systematize the truth of God than you can systematize God Himself. Let us abandon, therefore, all systems of theology and schools of divinity and take the truth. There is not a single theological system under the sun that contains the truth. All may contain some truth, not one contains all. And very often you find that whatever little truth the system contains is misplaced and turned the wrong way, to the serious damage of truth as a whole and the stumbling and injury of souls. Every day we live we are more and more struck with the vast difference between the dogmas of divinity and the heart of the Christ of God.

The rendering of 1 Timothy 2:4 in our excellent Authorized Version is absolutely correct. Your difficulty arises from your not seeing the immense difference between theology and the heart of God. Theology consists of the conclusions of men's minds drawn from the facts of Scripture; and you may constantly find souls harassed and perplexed by the dogmas of conflicting schools of theology, instead of resting in child-like simplicity upon the plain statements of the Word of God.

In point of fact, what is called the high school of doctrine is right in what it holds and wrong in what it rejects. The low school of doctrine also is right in what it holds and wrong in what it rejects. The former holds predestination, election, divine sovereignty and the eternal security of all true believers, and herein it is right. But it denies the full offer of salvation to all men and human responsibility, and herein it is wrong. The low school of doctrine holds the freeness and fullness of salvation and the moral responsibility of the sinner, and herein it is right. But it denies the sovereignty of divine grace and the security of the believer, and herein it is wrong. You will bear in mind, dear friend, that when we use the terms "high school" and "low school," we do not at all mean to give offense; far from it; we merely speak of things as they are.

For ourselves we desire to be taught exclusively by Scripture and not by any school of divinity. We are sure that God never meant to puzzle, to repulse or to discourage poor souls. God is love, His grace has brought salvation unto all. "He willeth not the death of a sinner." "He willeth not that any should perish, but that all should come to repentance." "He will have all men to be saved and to come to the knowledge of the truth." Such is His gracious aspect toward all. Hence if any perish, it is not in pursuance of the will of God. But there is another side to this great question. Man is responsible. What mean those touching words of the weeping Savior, "How often would I have gathered you as a hen gathereth her chickens under her wing, *but ye would not!*" And again, "Ye *will not come* to Me that ye might have life."

Do you not see, dear friend, that Scripture as distinctly teaches divine sovereignty as it teaches human responsibility, and the permanency of salvation as distinctly as its freeness? Are we called upon to reconcile these things? No; they are reconciled by God Himself inasmuch as they are taught in His holy Word. We have only to bow our heads in believing and adoring reverence. It is a great matter to make one's escape from the labyrinths of systematic divinity and yield ourselves to the formative power of the whole truth of God.

We shall add that Scripture clearly teaches the doctrine of election, but diligently excludes the repulsive doctrine of reprobation. It teaches that all who reach heaven will have to thank God for it, and all who find their place in hell will have to thank themselves. 2 Corinthians 5:14 and many other passages of Scripture teach in the most distinct manner that Christ died for all. This aspect of the death of Christ, as also of the righteousness of God, is *unto all,* but when we came to the practical application, it is *"upon all them that believe."* All who hear are responsible to believe, for the message is sent into all the world and to every creature. "Whosoever will, let him take the water of life freely."

But what stumbles and perplexes so many people is that they are occupied with the dogmas of theology instead of the love of God, the atonement of Christ and the record of the Holy Spirit. The moment you take any doctrine of Scripture, whether it be election, predestination, final perseverance, or any other doctrine whatsoever, and detach it from the Person of Christ and the living and eternal reality of what God is, you instantly turn it into a stumbling-block. You may set it down as an absolute truth, dear friend, that our gracious God would never have people to be puzzled about their souls' salvation. Theology often puzzles people, but God never does. As to quibblers, it would be far more honest of them to declare plainly that they do not want to have anything to say to God, than to be seeking to find flimsy objections against His Word.

You must distinguish between Genesis 25:23 and Malachi 1:2-3. The former was uttered before the children were born; the latter, hundreds of years afterwards, when the conduct and character of each were fully manifested. It is important to mark this difference. And not only so, but we must seek to understand the object of the Holy Spirit in His use of the above Scriptures in Romans 9. The apostle is establishing the absolute sovereignty of divine mercy: God's right to do as He wills. He proves to Israel that to argue against divine sovereignty is to surrender all their privileges. For how did they get in? Was it by birth? No; for on that ground Ishmael and Esau had the precedence. Was it by works? No; for they made the golden calf. How then? Simply by God's sovereign mercy. Well then, if God is sovereign He can have mercy upon whom He will; and blessed be His Name, that opens the door for us poor Gentiles.

Like many others, you confound two distinct passages of Holy Scripture. "Jacob have I loved and Esau have I hated" was not said before the children were born, but hundreds of years after, when the real character and practical ways of each had been fully manifested. All that was said before the children were born was that "the elder shall serve the younger." It is more than a sad mistake to represent God as hating a man before he was born. In Amos 1:11 we read "For three transgressions of Edom [Esau] and for four I will not turn away the punishment thereof; because he did pursue his brother with the sword and did cast off all pity, and his anger did tear perpetually, and he kept his wrath forever." Have we not here ample grounds for the divine hatred? If you will carefully compare Genesis 25:23 with Malachi 1:2-3, you will see your mistake and you will better understand the apostle's use of both passages in his magnificent argument in Romans 9 – an argument so little understood by theologians.

You are fully warranted by the Word of God to entreat any sinner to come to Jesus at once. It is very evident that your mind is perplexed by the misapplication of Scripture. If you will only submit to the authority of the Word and not labor to reconcile things according to your own thoughts or the creeds of men, you will find that human responsibility is as distinctly taught in Scripture as human impotency. We must bow down with unquestioning submission to the teachings of divine inspiration.

We could not think of confining Matthew 11:28-30 in the way you suggest. We believe it refers to every weary, heavy laden, laboring sinner, Jew or Gentile. All such are made welcome to the "rest" which Jesus gives to those who come to Him.

We do not consider that John 9:31 has anything to do with the matter to which you refer. The Holy Spirit records what the blind man said to the Pharisees, but we believe that God is ever ready to hear the cry of any poor needy soul that looks to Him through Jesus. We are more and more convinced of the vast differences between the cold dogmas of theology and the loving heart of a Savior-God. There is a rigid, repulsive manner of using the letter of certain texts of Scripture, with which we have no sympathy. We believe it to be contrary to the spirit of the gospel and the mind of Christ. "God is love." Precious words! True, He has His counsels and purposes, but the activity of His nature is love and therefore all are welcome to come. He is a Savior-God and "there is one mediator between God and men, the Man Christ Jesus." Go on, therefore, beloved, to press upon your fellow-sinners, with all possible earnestness, their solemn responsibility to flee now from the wrath to come and lay hold upon eternal life.

You must remember there are two sides to every question. Hence, while it is blessedly true that salvation is free to all and the righteousness of God is to him who works not, but believes on Him who justifies the ungodly (see Rom. 4:5 and Titus 2:11), yet is the sinner most solemnly responsible to flee from the wrath to come and strive to enter by the narrow gate – the open door. To make use of the freeness of God's grace and of the gift of righteousness to set aside man's responsibility and the need of intense earnestness in the matter of the soul's salvation, is a fatal mistake. Hence the exceeding value of the passage to which you call our attention (Luke 13:24) In it we have the Lord's reply to a curious enquirer whom He would make anxious. He, as was His habit, answers the man, not his question.

2 Thessalonians 1:8-9 contains a distinct and clear answer to your question, "What will become of those who reject the gospel?" We most assuredly believe there will be no further offer of mercy to those who deliberately reject the gospel now preached – no mercy for baptized Christendom, the vine of the earth. "The everlasting gospel" shall go forth previous to the opening of the millennial kingdom, and a testimony will be given to those nations who have not heard the gospel, but all this leaves untouched the solemn fact that unmitigated warrior judgment shall overtake that terrible thing called Christendom – that dark and awful mass of baptized profession, the most dreadful moral blot in the universe of God. There is nothing for the false professing Church except the deep and dark delusion which God, in His judicial dealing, shall send upon all who obey not the truth. And after that comes the deeper and darker doom of the Lake of Fire.

Dear friend, should not the thought of this make us more solemn, more earnest, more real in our dealing with our fellow men? Ought we not be more alive to the awful condition and destiny of those who die in their sins? Are we doing all we might to rescue our fellows from impending danger? Is it right to fold our arms and say, with chilling indifference, "God will save the elect, we can do nothing?" We believe it to be simply absolute heartless cruelty to souls.

BAPTISM

Scripture gives us the simple fact that believers ought to be baptized. It says nothing as to whether it should be in public or in private. It does not tell us that it should be "In a place accessible to the public." It is left entirely open. Who witnessed the baptism of the eunuch? Where was Paul baptized? or Lydia? or the jailer? Where in the New Testament are we taught to contemplate the public, either in baptism or the Lord's supper? No doubt "the unlearned or unbeliever" may come into the place where Christians are assembled, but testimony to the world is not the object when Christians come together for communion or worship. Matthew 10:32 does not refer specially to the act of baptism. Our whole life should be a testimony for Christ. The Christian himself is "the epistle of Christ, known and read of all men."

We believe that Matthew 28:19 furnishes the proper formula for Christian baptism. We are not aware of any subsequent revelation on the subject. "In the name of the Father and of the Son and of the Holy Spirit." Here we have the full revelation of the Godhead, the true foundation of Christian doctrine. We see no reason for departing from the form of words prescribed by our Lord Jesus Christ. Is not His commandment more binding upon us than the example of any or all of His servants?

It is much to be desired that Christians see eye to eye on every subject, but this can hardly be expected, and most assuredly we should not allow our happy fellowship with the members of Christ's body to be hindered in the smallest degree by difference of judgment on the question of baptism. So long as a man is true to Christ – His name, His cause, His truth, His glory – I can love him with all my heart, though I may deem him mistaken as to his view of baptism. May the Lord bind us all more closely to Himself and to one another by the precious ministry of the Holy Spirit!

I am glad you have called my attention to my little book, *"Thou and Thy House."* I am aware of the use which has been made of it in a recent tract on the subject of "Baptism." With the theory of that tract I have no sympathy whatever; still less with its monstrous statements. I believe the course of some of our friends in urging on this question of baptism will, unless God in His mercy interpose, lead to most disastrous results. I complain not of any who conscientiously hold this or that view on the subject, but I do complain of those who, instead of preaching and teaching Jesus Christ, are disturbing the minds of God's people by pressing infant baptism upon them. For my own part – seeing the question has been forced upon me – I can only say I have for 32 years been asking in vain for a single line of Scripture for baptizing any except believers or those who professed to believe. Reasonings I have had – inferences, conclusions and deductions – but of direct Scripture authority not one tittle. There is not a word about baptism from beginning to end of my book, "Thou and Thy House."

THE COMING OF CHRIST

It must ever be the desire of the heart that loves Jesus to see Him as He is and be with Him and like Him forever. Hence, the proper cry of an affectionate heart is, "Come, Lord Jesus." But it is our privilege to have fellowship with Him in His longsuffering toward this poor world. "The longsuffering of our Lord is salvation." Blessed be His name, "He is not willing that any should perish, but that all should come to repentance" (2 Peter 3). We do not think there is any difficulty in reconciling the two things. A loving wife may mourn the absence of her husband and earnestly long for his return, but he is away preaching the gospel and she may have such full fellowship with him in his work as to be quite willing that he should prolong his absence if only a single soul should thereby be brought to Jesus.

As to your difficulty about the expression "falling away" in 2 Thessalonians 2, it arises, we judge, from your not seeing the distinction between the Lord's coming to receive His people and His coming to judge the world – between His coming as the Bridegroom and His coming as the Judge. "The day of the Lord" refers to the latter, and before that day comes, there will be a great apostasy or falling away and "the man of sin will be revealed." It is most needful to understand this distinction. The proper hope of the believer is the coming of the Lord, which may become reality at any moment, but when the Church has gone to be with her Lord, the man of sin shall be revealed, "whom the Lord shall consume with the spirit of His mouth and shall destroy with the brightness of His coming." This is far too weighty and extensive a subject to be handled in a short letter, but you might study prayerfully 1 Thessalonians 4:3-10 compared with 2 Thessalonians 2:12.

In 2 Thessalonians 2:1-2 the apostle is correcting a mistake into which the Thessalonian saints had fallen. They had been led to think that "the day of the Lord" had actually begun. In the first epistle, he had taught them to look for the Lord's coming and their gathering unto Him in the air, to be forever with Him. Further, he had taught them that "the day" was not to overtake them as a thief. Then, in the second epistle, the apostle exhorts them "by" or *on the ground of* Christ's coming, not to be agitated as to "the day." The former was their proper hope; the latter could not take place until after the manifestation of "the man of sin" which was then and still is future. Your difficulty arises from not distinguishing between "the coming" of Christ for His saints and "the day" of His manifestation in judgment upon the world. We are exhorted by the former not to be troubled about the latter. The two things are as distinct as possible. The one is the bright and blissful consummation of the Church's hope; the other, the death knell of all this world's glory. The distinction is very important.

We do not think that Matthew 16:27 and 1 Thessalonians 4:16 refer to the same thing. Matthew refers to the public manifestation, Thessalonians to the coming of Christ for His saints, according to John 14:3. The proper hope of the Church is her Lord's coming to receive her to Himself. She is called to wait for Himself, not for rewards. There will be rewards, but these belong to the manifestation of the kingdom and are neither our proper hope nor the true motive for service. The love of Christ is our true motive spring – Himself our hope.

As to the expression, "These my brethren," it refers to the messengers who shall go forth to the nations previous to the setting up of the kingdom. They will be from among the Jews. The entire scene refers to the judgment of the living nations. There is no such thing in Scripture as a general simultaneous judgment. There will be the judgment of "the quick" [the living] before the Millennium and the judgment of "the dead" after the Millennium, and the warrior judgment executed upon "the beast."

We judge that Philippians 4:5 refers to the Lord's coming. "Let your moderation [yieldingness] be known unto all men. The Lord is at hand." If our hearts are set upon the blessed hope of the Lord's coming, we shall not be standing up for our rights or grasping after the perishing things of this world. He may come tonight. Then we shall leave all these things behind forever. It is interesting to notice the two expressions in this passage. Our *moderation* is to be known unto men; our *requests* are to be made known unto God. Men are to see that we are perfectly content with our portion and prospect. We should never go to men with our wants. God is sufficient. Man is sure to disappoint us. God *never* fails a trusting heart, blessed be His holy name.

The judgment in Revelation 19 is what we may call the "warrior judgment." Most surely it is after the Church has left this scene. This is obvious from the fact that the saints come forth with the Rider on the white horse.

We believe the midnight cry has gone forth. We recognize the result of that cry in the large measure of attention which has been given since about the 1830's to the glorious truth of the Lord's coming. For centuries, not a sound was heard about the Bridegroom's return. "My Lord delayeth His coming" was the plain language of the professing Church. Christendom was asleep. But, through the mercy of God, the cry has gone forth – that soul-stirring cry, "Behold, the Bridegroom cometh; go ye out to meet Him." Are we ready? Have we got the oil in our vessels – the true grace of God's Spirit in our hearts? Solemn enquiry! Those who are "ready" shall go in with the Bridegroom. The rest shall be shut out into outer darkness – the awful region of weeping, wailing and gnashing of teeth; that place where hope can never come, where not one single ray of light can ever shine in upon the gloom of eternity.

Oh! may God's Spirit stir up all our hearts and make us thoroughly in earnest! May we be seen with girded loins and burning lights as men who are really waiting for their Lord! May we seek to sound a warning note in the ears of our fellow men as we pass along from day to day. Lord, make us serious!

THE BELIEVER'S SECURITY

You must ever remember that Scripture cannot contradict itself. Hence, when you read in John 10 such words as "My sheep shall never perish," your heart should rest in the full assurance of the eternal security of the very feeblest of Christ's blood-bought sheep. Many other scriptures establish the same precious truth. So 2 Peter 2:20-22 cannot possibly clash with John 10 and similar passages. But what does it teach? Simply that when *professors* of religion return to their old habits, they are in a worse condition than if they had never made a profession at all. It is obvious that true Christians are not in question here. A "dog and a sow" cannot be looked upon as "sheep," however they may profess "the knowledge of the Lord and Savior Jesus Christ." We desire to render hearty thanks to God for what you say as to the blessing and help received through our writings. To Him be all the praise!

As to John 15:2, the real secret of the difficulty felt by so many in this scripture is that they seek to make it a question of life and security, whereas it is simply a question of fruitbearing. If we do not abide in the vine we shall prove fruitless branches, and all such branches the gardener removes from the place of fruitbearing. The question of salvation is not touched.

You are perfectly right, because most thoroughly sustained by the Word of God, in saying to any soul, "Only believe God's testimony about His Son and you are eternally saved." This is an absolutely scriptural statement. The passages of Scripture in which you find difficulty (Rom. 14:15 and 1 Cor. 8:11) do not refer to the question of salvation or eternal life at all. It is not in the power of anyone to destroy eternal life, but if I interfere with the action of a brother's conscience – if I cause him to do what he feels to be wrong – then, so far as in me lies, I destroy him and cause him to make shipwreck of faith and a good conscience. In both the above passages, it is a question of personal responsibility and the integrity of conscience before God. This is most solemn. No man can touch the foundation on which a saved soul is built, but it is a most serious thing to wound any weak conscience. Let us therefore beware.

DISPENSATIONAL MATTERS

It was perfectly consistent for the disciples, previous to the day of Pentecost, to pray for the Holy Spirit since He was not given till that memorable day and could not be given until Jesus was glorified. Compare John 7:39; 16:7 and Acts 19:1-6. We believe the form of prayer given to the disciples was suited to the transition state in which they were until the coming of the Comforter. From that time it holds good that, "We know not what we should pray for as we ought, but the Spirit Himself maketh intercession for us with groanings which cannot be uttered." Where would be the force of this if the Church of God were confined to one definite form of prayer?

It is well for Christians to most attentively consider the vast difference between God's people – their standing, their calling, their hope – before and after the death and resurrection of Christ and the consequent descent of the Holy Spirit. This is very little seen or thought of; hence the low spiritual conditions, the darkness and doubt, the legality and distance, the cloudiness and mistiness so painfully observable among many of God's beloved people. How rarely do you find souls enjoying accomplished redemption and the indwelling of the Holy Spirit! There is everywhere a strong tendency to take merely Jewish ground. People are under law as to the state of their conscience. Little is known of the conscious possession of eternal life, sonship and the sealing of the Spirit. It is deemed presumption for anyone to have the full assurance of salvation. And yet, by a strange inconsistency, persons who speak thus deem it possible for some who have made great attainments in holiness and the divine life, to have assurance. This is presumption because it bases assurance upon something in us, even though 'that something be by the Holy Spirit, whereas Scripture bases our assurance and peace, not on anything in us, but upon accomplished redemption by Christ. This makes a grand and all-important difference.

The difficulty of your friend arises from not seeing that the Church as such is not before the apostle's mind in Galatians or Romans. He is speaking of believers and the ground on which they are individually justified before God. They are justified by faith, as Abraham was. Hence they are *morally* the children of Abraham. And though Abraham did not and could not belong to a body which had no existence except in the purpose of God until the Head ascended into the heavens, still most assuredly all the Old Testament saints will share in the heavenly glory. Many are perplexed as to this point because they make it a question of comparing individuals one with another. If it be a question of personal worthiness, holiness or devotedness, Abraham might stand above the most holy and devoted among us. But it is simply a question of God's dispensation arrangements, and if any be disposed to find fault with these, we are not going to argue with them. Some today have a way of turning the subject into ridicule which savors far more of wit than of spirituality or acquaintance with the Word of God. But we trust that we will never surrender the truth of God to escape the shafts of human ridicule.

The Church is on earth. It seems strange to have to affirm so obvious a truth. True, it is in ruins, but still earth is its sphere inasmuch as the Holy Spirit is on earth and He is the One who unites the members to the Head and to one another. Now, while it is true that the visible unity of the Church is gone, yet we are responsible to "endeavor to keep the unity of the Spirit in the bond of peace," and in order to do this we are to yield our souls to the action of the whole truth of God, whether that truth be found in 1 Corinthians or in 2 Timothy.

We have to recognize and mourn over the ruin, and confess our own share in that ruin, but we must not lower the divine standard or surrender a single tittle of divine revelation. It is our holy privilege to walk in the light of the very highest truths, notwithstanding the broken state of the professing body. "Where two or three are gathered together in My name, there am I in the midst of them" (Mt.18:20). These words set forth the real ground of the Assembly. They were uttered before the Church was set up and they will hold good to the end of time. "Scripture cannot be broken." "Forever, O Lord, Thy Word is settled in heaven."

Thanks be to our ever gracious God, He has not left us to walk according to our own vague and desultory thoughts or the commandments and doctrines of men. He has poured the heavenly light of His own Word upon our path, and that gives a certainty, a stability and a wonderful peace.

The Holy Spirit has given us the three grand distinguishing titles – "The Jew, the Gentile and the Church of God." Sadly, that which calls itself the Church of God has become a corrupt thing, a vast mass of baptized profession. But clearly that which is called Christendom is no longer viewed as being on Jewish *or* Gentile ground, nor will it be judged as such, but according to the profession which it takes up. Hence the appalling solemnity of Christendom's position. We believe it to be the most terrible moral blot in the wide universe of God, the master-piece of

Satan and the destroyer of souls. Oh! the awfulness of Christendom's condition; the awfulness of its doom! No human language can set it forth. May all who truly belong to the Church of God be enabled to yield a calm, clear, decided and consistent testimony against the spirit and principles and ways of that terrible thing called Christendom.

The "other sheep" of John 10 are those who are called from among the Gentiles to form, with those of the Jewish fold, the "one flock" under the one blessed Shepherd. In Ephesians 4 we have the further truth of the "one body" composed of Jew and Gentile and united by the Holy Spirit to the living Head in heaven and to one another on the earth.

In John 20 Mary illustrates the present relation of the Church with Christ. We do not know Him after the flesh. We are linked with Him, not as the Messiah on earth, but as a heavenly Christ. Thomas represents the Jew who must see to believe. Matthew 28 presents our Lord in His Jewish relations, and we find the women holding Him by the feet. This teaches us in the most blessed manner that He will yet resume His links with Israel according to the promises made to the fathers. We must remember that the Church forms no part of the ways of God with Israel and the earth.

The terms "kingdom of heaven" and "kingdom of God" are not always synonymous, though sometimes they are. Take Romans 14:17, "For the kingdom of God is not meat and drink, but righteousness, and peace, and joy in the Holy Spirit." We can easily see that "kingdom of heaven" would not do here. This latter is a great dispensational term, applying to the time during which the King is rejected and the kingdom, in consequence, in *mystery* instead of in manifestation. The term "kingdom of God" is sometimes applied in the same way (Mark 4:30; Luke 8:10). Also, it has *a moral and personal application* which distinguishes it from the phrase, "kingdom of heaven," which is unique to Matthew. Accept our warmest thanks for your most kind and interesting letter. Its tone and spirit are pleasing and refreshing in a day like the present. May God bless you very abundantly!

No passage could more distinctly teach the two resurrections than the very one which your friend has quoted in opposition, namely, John 5:25-29. There is "the resurrection of life" and "the resurrection of judgment." It may be that your friend bases his objection on the fact that the word "hour" is used, but this has no force whatever since in verse 25, the same word is applied to that period during which the Son of God is quickening dead souls – a period which has already extended nearly 2000 years. Now if the word "hour" be applied to a period of nearly 2000 years, what difficulty can there be in applying it to a period half that length? We consider that Revelation 7:1-8 refers to the saved remnant of Israel, the nucleus of the restored nation.

Ezekiel 37 refers to the future restoration and blessing of Israel. The closing chapters of Ezekiel shall, most surely, have their accomplishment in the nation's history. The temple will be rebuilt and the worship restored. The sacrifices, instead of being typical, will be commemorative. Thanks for your devotional lines. We greatly enjoyed their tone and spirit.

We take those charming passages in Isaiah in their full force and beauty, as setting forth the wonderful blessedness of that time when our beloved Lord shall reign from pole to pole and from river to the ends of the earth. How the heart longs for that time as we toil along through this sin-stricken world where all is so contrary to the Spirit and mind of Christ.

THE DOCTRINE OF CHRIST

The apostle John, by the Holy Spirit, teaches us that "He that hath the Son, hath life; he that hath not the Son of God hath not life." The person you describe has not the Son of God. Anyone who denies that Jesus is God, has not the Son of God. He is a blasphemer. As for his saying that "God was in Him more than in anyone else on earth," it is a blinding delusion and deceit of the enemy. If Jesus was not God, it is the merest absurdity to speak of His being a good man or the best man who ever lived, or of God being in Him. For any other than God to speak as Jesus did, would be blasphemy.

We must either confess the essential deity of the Man Christ Jesus or deny Him altogether. There is not the breadth of a hair of middle ground. But, blessed be God, Scripture is plain and emphatic. It claims for our adorable Savior not merely divinity but essential deity. This is demonstrated in a very singular and forcible manner by the fact that in Romans 1, where the apostle is speaking of the testimony of creation, he says, "For the invisible things of Him from the creation of the world are clearly seen, being understood by the things that are made, His eternal power and Godhead." In Colossians 2:9, in speaking of the Person of Christ, he says, "In Him dwelleth all the fullness of the Godhead bodily." In the original Greek of these two passages we have a different word for "Godhead." In Romans 1:20 the word is *divinity*. In Colossians 2:9 it is *deity*. The heathen should have learned that there was something superhuman, something divine in creation, but the Holy Spirit is not satisfied to claim divinity for the Person of Christ but absolute deity. This is magnificently striking.

We cannot understand you, dear friend, when you speak of a blasphemer of Christ as "a good living person, keeping God's commandments." What! "A good living man," yet denying the Godhead of Jesus! "Keeping God's commandments," yet blaspheming the Son of His love! Be not offended, dear friend, by our plain language. We must speak plainly. We utterly loathe and abhor the false liberality of the present day, a liberality which can lavish its compliments upon men, but deny the Christ of God. We hold it to be utterly impossible for anyone who lives and dies in the denial of Christ to be saved. Such an one has no Savior unless there is some other way of being saved than by Christ. May God open the eyes of your friend to see his guilt and danger – notwithstanding his "good living" and "keeping God's commandments" – and to flee by faith to the refuge provided for the lost in the precious atonement of our Lord and Savior Jesus Christ! We regret having to write in such a way concerning one who "is very near and dear to you," but we should either write as we have done or leave your letter wholly unnoticed. Our Lord Christ is more to us than all the friends in the world.

In Galatians 5:9 the apostle in speaking of bad doctrine, uses the very same form of words as in 1 Corinthians 5:6, which he applies to bad conduct. But the bad doctrine in question affected the very foundation of Christianity. So also in 2 John 10, the apostle calls upon the elect lady to shut her door against anyone who brought not the true doctrine of Christ. If a man denies Christ we cannot own him or salute him or wish him God speed. To do so would make us partakers of his evil deeds. What is the difference between a teacher of fundamental error and one who knowingly receives him or wishes him God speed? Does the law distinguish between a traitor and one who knowingly conceals the traitor? Could you have fellowship with a man who denies the Person or the work of Christ?

It is very striking to notice how much more alive people are to bad morals than bad doctrine. A person living in scandal is justly rejected, but a man may deny the deity or the eternal Sonship of Christ and be received and honored in the highest circles of so-called Christian society. A man who picks his neighbor's pocket is justly sent to prison, but a man may blaspheme the Son of God and yet be looked upon as a respectable Christian! How is this? *Because man thinks more of himself and his respectability than he does of Christ!*

But who would think for a moment of placing fundamental truth on a level with such a question as baptism or the interpretation of a text? To do so would be the very height of folly. If a man holds the truth as to Christ and is seeking to live according to it, we can give him the right hand of fellowship, although we may not agree with him as to baptism or many *minor* points. Difference of judgment on minor questions is a proof of human weakness, but if that difference be allowed to rise into undue prominence, it is a proof of Satan's power. When Christ is our absorbing and commanding object, all minor differences soon find their level.

JUDGMENT

Scripture distinctly teaches that the believer will never come into judgment at all. 2 Corinthians 5:10 declares that all shall be manifested before the judgment-seat of Christ, believers and unbelievers alike, although not, of course, at the same time. But how will believers be manifested? *In all the perfectness of Christ Himself!* Are they to be judged? Assuredly not. Their judgment is past forever. It was executed at the cross. If there was a single atom of sin or guilt left unatoned for in the death of Christ, a single question left unsettled, a single thing that has still to be judged, then, most assuredly, we shall be eternally damned. But no, dear friend, it is all settled – blessedly, divinely, eternally settled. All who believe on the Son of God have passed from death unto life and shall not come into judgment (John 5:24). It is as impossible that a believer can come into judgment, as that Christ Himself can. The members can no more be judged than the Head.

No doubt our works shall be tested. "The day shall declare it." Those works shall be tried by fire, and all the wood, hay and stubble will be burned up. Further, when we stand in the light of the judgment-seat of Christ, we shall look back with an enlightened gaze over the whole of our career and see as we never saw before, our mistakes, our follies, our sins, our infirmities, our mixed motives. But we shall see also, as we never saw before, the fullness of the grace of God and the effectiveness of the blood of Christ.

With regard to Matthew 12:36-37 it teaches us that "men will have to give account for every idle word." So also in Hebrews 9:27, we read, "It is appointed unto men once to die and after that the judgment." But the believer is taken completely off the ground of judgment since Christ was judged in his stead. Hence, instead of looking for judgment, the believer is looking for the Savior. Is all this precious grace intended to make us lax and careless? May we speak idle words because we are not to be judged? Far away be the horrible thought! No, dear friend, it is just because we believe that Jesus was judged in our stead and that we shall *never* come into judgment, that therefore we judge ourselves day by day and refuse to justify in ourselves a single sinful thought. "How shall we that are dead to sin live any longer therein?" It is our holy privilege to reckon ourselves "dead to sin." We have passed through death and judgment in the Person of our Substitute, so "we have boldness in the day of judgment because as He is, so are we in this world" (1 John 4:17). Here lies the grand secret of our peace – the secret of our deliverance from the power of sin – the secret of all holy living. May the Spirit of God expound and apply it in power to your heart. Then you will cease to be perplexed.

We quite agree with your view of the expression, "the terror of the Lord," and we trust your friend will be led to see the mind of God in the entire context. The believer can never come into judgment. In John 5:24 the word is "judgment" and not "condemnation." Every man's work shall be tested, but when the believer is manifested before the judgment seat of Christ, he will be perfectly conformed to the image of his Lord.

In 1 Corinthians 6 we are taught that the saints shall judge the world and even angels. They will be associated with Christ in that solemn work. It would be strange if the judges were to be arranged along with the judged. It is very sad to mark the confusion in people's minds in reference to a subject so plain and simple. It is, no doubt, the result of legal teaching and bad theology. There is no such thing in the New Testament as a general resurrection or general judgment. To maintain such a notion is to deny the very foundations of Christianity.

Scripture most certainly teaches that the unconverted shall stand before the judgment seat. 2 Corinthians 5:10 takes in all, both believers and unbelievers, though not of course at the same time or on the same ground. The expression "we all" in chapter 5:10 differs materially in the Greek from the "we all" in chapter 3:18. The latter refers only to believers; the former to both. Our Lord Christ will judge the living and the dead at His appearing and kingdom. In Matthew 25:31 we have the judgment of the living nations. Revelation 20:11 gives the judgment of the wicked dead. In the former, not one will have passed through death; in the latter, all will have done so. In neither scene have we the Church or Israel as the subjects of judgment.

THE INDIVIDUAL PATH OF FAITH: PRACTICAL ENCOURAGEMENT AND EXHORTATION

The life of faith in its every stage and every step must be intensely individual. No one can have faith for another, and no one ought to dare to intrude upon another's path. We may and ought to encourage one another to trust God – to strengthen each other's hands in God – but for anyone to counsel another to do this or that, unless there be distinct faith for it, is in our judgment a very grave mistake indeed. Hence, dear friend, if you are not thoroughly clear in your own soul as to whether it would be "faith or folly" to abandon your present position, we should strongly recommend you to pause. It is a serious thing to go beyond your depth, to feel the surgings of the tide of circumstances, if your feet are not on the rock. We have no fears on God's side of the question. He never fails a trusting heart. But from the style and tone of your letter, we have great fears for you.

Could you imagine Abraham asking anyone if it would be "faith or folly" for him to leave Ur of the Chaldees? Could you conceive Moses asking if it would be "faith or folly" for him to leave the court of Pharaoh? We most fully believe that your position would be a false one for us, and that to abandon it would be true wisdom, but you must see this for yourself. You must have it from God and act before Him, else it will all end in confusion and disaster. "Never go before your faith and never lag behind your conscience." This is a most excellent principle. May we all be enabled to act upon it! The Lord bless, guide and keep you!

We conclude from what you say that your own mind is ill at ease in reference to the matter about which you ask counsel. We would therefore recommend you not to do anything with a doubtful mind. "Whatsoever is not of faith is sin." Look to the Lord for guidance in this thing. See if you can do it to His glory, and if not, lay it aside. It must be between your own soul and the Lord. *Do nothing with a doubtful mind.* How precious to be able to bring everything, great or small, to Him!

The question you propose is one for your own conscience to weigh in the light of Scripture. It would be of no real use to you for us to say that we could not for worlds occupy such a position or stand in such a relationship as you describe, inasmuch as each one must act according to his light. We believe the servant of Christ ought to stand perfectly free from human influence. He should have to do only with His Lord, both as to his work and as to his support. But in all these things, the rule must ever be, "According to your faith." It is none of our business to judge others; each one must stand or fall to his own Master.

If your conscience is not clear before the Lord, do not move one inch in the matter. Let not the persuasive arguments of a thousand friends induce you to do anything with a doubtful mind. "Whatsoever is not of faith is sin." We do not offer any opinion on the abstract question which you have laid before us, but, judging from your own statements, it is very evident that your own heart would condemn you in taking such a step. On this ground, we solemnly counsel you not to move in the matter. May we be faithful to Christ! May we give Him an undivided heart!

The Lord alone can give you wisdom and grace to act in the painful circumstances you describe. If you really wait on Him, He will teach you when to speak and when to keep silence. There is danger of speaking in haste of temper rather than in a spirit of love, when replying to the godless remarks of the unconverted. This is to be guarded against. Further, we must remember there is very often far more powerful testimony in solemn and dignified silence than in talking for talking's sake. But the Lord will guide the lowly dependent heart. He will tell you when to speak and when to be silent. Then, you may rest assured, the speaking and the silence will each be fruitful in its season.

It is always well to watch our treacherous hearts, even in right things, lest they betray us. But in the matter to which you refer, we would remind you of the exceeding goodness and tenderness of our God. He most graciously allows us to pour out our hearts to Him in the freest manner. He perfectly understands our every feeling and He knows all about our relationships and the right affections which flow out of them. It would be unnatural not to feel unique earnestness in reference to the salvation of our relatives according to the flesh. Unquestionably, we should seek to be ruled in all things by the glory of God. But oh! let us ever abide in the sweet sense of His love and let us beware of a unhealthy analyzing of our poor thoughts and feelings. God bless you and keep you!

We fully sympathize with you in your dread of acting under mere impulse. It is always well to be sure of every step we take, to be able to give a "Thus saith the Lord" for whatever we do or whatever we refuse to do. Very much damage is done to the cause of truth and vital godliness by impulsive acting and by what we may term spasmodic devotedness. We greatly value calm, deeptoned decision for Christ – a decision produced by genuine love to His Person and profound subjection to the authority of His Word. These things are most needful in this day of man's will, man's judgment and man's reason. As to the matter which seems to exercise your heart, you must simply act before the Lord. It is entirely a question for your own conscience. Do not act on the judgment of another. If you feel free in conscience before God, it is better to continue as you have done for the sake of others. By all means, keep a good conscience, cost what it may.

We entirely agree with your remarks about the Church. The professing body is a ruin. The Body of Christ is one and indissoluble. It is our holy and happy privilege as it is our bound duty to have our feet on God's ground and our eyes on God Himself – to see and own our failure, but yet to hold fast the faithfulness of God. It needs a single eye to discern God's ground and a simple faith to occupy it, but He is always sufficient and His foundation stands sure. There is no reason why we should continue one hour in connection with what is wrong. "Let everyone that nameth the name of Christ depart from iniquity." This is conclusive. *Nothing can justify our remaining in connection with what we know to be false.* May the Lord Himself greatly bless you, beloved friend, and make you a blessing!

We see no other course open before you but one of plain decision for Christ, cost what it may. You must cease to do evil before you can expect to learn to do well. Trust Christ and act boldly for Him. "If thine eye be single, thy whole body shall be full of light." But if you are looking at circumstances, weighing consequences or conferring with flesh and blood, your eye is not single and you must be in darkness and perplexity. The Lord can very speedily provide you with a situation. Only wait on Him. Let your exclusive reference be to Him. He never fails a trusting heart. Do, dear friend, seek to prove the reality of sole dependence upon the living God. There is nothing like it. All human hopes are as a vapor that passes away. May the Lord undertake for you in His infinite goodness.

It is a most serious thing to trifle with the truth of God or to refuse the path which His Word plainly sets before us. Blessed be His name, He bears with us in our ignorance, our unbelief and varied infinities. But to sin against light is a fearfully solemn thing. "Give glory to the Lord your God before He cause darkness, and before your feet stumble upon the dark mountains, and while ye look for light, He turn it into the shadow of death and make it gross darkness" (Jeremiah 13).

Mark the words! "Before He cause darkness." Does God cause darkness? Yes, verily, and blindness, if people refuse His light. There is no darkness so profound, no blindness so awfully complete, as that which God sends *judicially* upon those who trifle with His Word. Look at 2 Thessalonians 2, "For this cause God shall send them strong delusion that they should believe the lie; that they all might be damned who believed not the truth, but had pleasure in unrighteousness." Here we have the future destiny of Christendom. God shall send strong delusion. He will turn their professed light into gross darkness and the shadow of death. All this is most solemn. It should make us tremble at the very thought of refusing to act up to the light which God graciously affords us.

Look at the blessed contrast to all this as given in Luke 11: "No man, when he hath lighted a candle, putteth it in a secret place, neither under a bushel, but on a candlestick, that they which come in may see the light." What does God give light for? That it may be quashed, quenched, hindered? Assuredly not; but that it may be seen. But how can it be seen if we do not act upon it? If we, for worldly gain, personal advantage, to please ourselves or to please our friends, refuse to obey the Word of God and thus hide the light under a bushel – what then? It may issue in "gross darkness," "the shadow of death," "strong delusion." How awful!

Our Lord continues, "The light of the body is the eye: therefore when thine eye is single" – that is, when you have but one object before you – "thy whole body also is full of light" (beautiful state!) "but when thine eye is evil, the body is full of darkness. Take heed, therefore, that the light which is in thee be not darkness. If thy whole body therefore be full of light, having no part dark, the whole shall be full of light, as when the bright shining of a candle doth give thee light."

How striking the contrast! Instead of stumbling on the dark mountains, the obedient soul not only has light for his own path, but he is actually a light-bearer for others. The moral progress in the above passage is uncommonly fine. There is first the single eye – the one simple, firm, earnest purpose of the heart to go right on in the path of obedience, cost what it may. Then the body is full of light. What more can there be? But there is something more, for assuredly there is no redundancy in Scripture. "If thy whole body therefore be full of light, having no part dark" – no reserve, no chamber of the heart kept locked up on account of friends, self-interest, worldly ease or anything else – "the whole shall be full of light." You become transparent and your light shines so others see it. Not that *you* think so, for a single eye never looks at self. If I make it my object to be a light-bearer, I shall get full of darkness and be a stumbling-block. When Moses came down from the mount, the skin of his face shone. Did he see it or know it? Not he. Others saw it; and thus it should be with us. "We all, with open face, beholding the glory of the Lord, are changed into the same image from glory to glory by the Lord the Spirit" (2 Corinthians 3).

Finally, dear friend, let us entreat you to yield yourself without reserve to the Word of your Lord. Do not permit your "friends" to stand in your way. Will your friends answer for you before the judgment-seat of Christ? Can they now fill your heart with that sweet peace which can only be found in the path of obedience? They do not deserve the name of *friends* if they stand in your way in following Christ. They are just like the swallows that flutter about us in the summertime, but on the first approach of autumn blasts they wing their way to sunnier climes. Obey, we beseech you, the Word of your Lord. Let no flimsy excuse, no worldly consideration, no thought of personal greatness weigh with you for a single moment. What will all these things be worth in the light of the judgment-seat of Christ? What will you think of them in eternity?

But you will tell us you are saved; you are a "Christian girl"; you have eternal life; you can never perish. Thank God for all this. But surely you do not mean to say that this is any reason why you should not obey what you know to be the Word of God. Is it not rather the very *ground* of obedience, and the love of Christ the constraining motive? What are all the friends in the world compared with Christ? Would they shed their blood to do you good? No, but they are making you miserably unhappy to please them. You would rather pain the heart of Jesus by neglecting His commandments than pain your friends by obeying Him.

May the Lord help you, dear friend, to lay aside every weight and your besetting sin, and run with patience and true purpose of heart the race that is set before you.

Few things are more solemn than to resist light. Look again at that most weighty passage in Jeremiah 13. "Give glory to the Lord your God before He cause darkness and before your feet stumble on the dark mountains, and while ye look for light, He turn it into the shadow of death and make it gross darkness" (v. 16). There is something very awful in the thought of *God* causing darkness and turning light into the shadow of death because of our not acting on the light when He graciously gave it. The contrast of all this we have seen in that lovely passage in Luke 11: 34-36. When we act on the light which God gives, we not only are full of light ourselves, but become lightbearers for others. This is very different from stumbling on dark mountains.

We do not wonder, dear friend, at the dim twilight of which you speak. The wonder is that it is not profound darkness. It would be so but for infinite grace. But we entreat you not to hesitate a moment longer. "How long halt ye? .... I made haste and delayed not to keep Thy commandments." "Let us go forth therefore unto Him without the camp, bearing His reproach." Let nothing cause you to linger. "To obey is better than sacrifice and to hearken than the fat of rams." It is a fatal mistake to refuse to act on divinely given light under the plausible pretext of usefulness. Our usefulness consists in doing what our Lord commands. Obedience is our work. May God give you grace to be decided for Christ! May He lead you forth into that blessed sphere in which you can walk with Him, lean on Him, work for Him and find all your springs in Him! To Him we earnestly commend you

FICTION

We do not see how you could sit in the presence of God and write fiction. "Speak every man truth with his neighbor" (Eph. 4:25). Fiction is not truth, and hence we judge that a Christian should neither speak it nor write it. True, you might be able to earn money by writing works of fiction and spend that money for the Lord, but does the Lord want money earned by writing what is not true? Are we to do evil that good may come?

It is evident, dear friend, that you have misgivings in your mind, and we do not wonder. We fully enter into your remark as to the numbers who are neglecting their Bibles for worthless and worse than worthless fiction. Indeed not only is the Bible neglected, but even works of solid information are laid aside for light and corrupting literature which is only fit to be thrown into the fire. We deeply feel the need of vigilance on the part of Christian parents, guardians and teachers to guard our young people from the demoralizing influence of much of the literature of the present day. We would feel bound to preserve our children's bodies from poisonous drugs; ought we not to preserve their minds from poisonous books?

"THE UNPARDONABLE SIN"

There are very false notions afloat as to the point to which you call our attention, and many like yourself are troubled thereby. We are continually asked about the "unpardonable sin" and the "sin against the Holy Spirit." If you read carefully Matthew 12:24-32 you will see that our Lord speaks of "blasphemy against the Holy Spirit" of which the apostate Jews were guilty. For this there was and could be no forgiveness. What could be done for those who not only rejected the Son but resisted the Holy Spirit and attributed His blessed operation to Beelzebub? They could neither be forgiven in the "age" of the law nor in that of Messiah. In short, it is wholly a question in this scripture of the apostate nation of Israel given over to hopeless perdition. We know that, just before the opening of the millennial age, there will be a repentant remnant for whom a fountain shall be opened and who shall be the nucleus of the restored nation. But this is far too wide a subject to enter upon here. We merely add that we judge it to be a temptation of Satan to lead you to imagine that you have committed "the unpardonable sin." You may rest assured, dear friend, that you have never been guilty of any sin which cannot be cancelled by that blood which cleanses us from *all* sin.

Many find difficulty in 1 John 5:16. "There is a sin unto death." This we believe to be a question of God's governmental dealings. We learn from 1 Corinthians 11 that God visits His people with sickness and even physical death because of their ways, but in neither of these passages is there any thought of "an unpardonable sin." We do not believe that any sinner in this acceptable year, this day of salvation, is beyond the reach of the pardoning love of God and the atoning blood of Jesus. Those who reject the gospel shall be given over to "a strong delusion" (2 Thes. 2:10-12). But that terrible moment has not yet arrived. "The day of vengeance" is held back in God's longsuffering mercy.

REPENTANCE AND CONVERSION

Repentance involves the moral judgment of ourselves under the action of the Word of God by the power of the Holy Spirit. It is the discovery of our utter sinfulness, guilt and ruin, our hopeless bankruptcy, our undone condition. It expresses itself in these glowing words of Isaiah, "Woe is me; I am undone," and in that touching utterance of Peter, "Depart from me, for I am a sinful man, O Lord." Repentance is an abiding necessity for the sinner, and the deeper it is the better. It is the ploughshare entering the soul and turning up the fallow ground. The ploughshare is not the seed, but the deeper the furrow, the stronger the root. We delight in a deep work of repentance in the soul. We fear there is far too little of it in what is called revival work. Men are so anxious to simplify the gospel and make salvation easy, that they fail to press upon the sinner's conscience the claims of truth and righteousness.

No doubt salvation is as free as the grace of God can make it. Moreover, it is all of God from first to last. God is its source, Christ its channel, the Holy Spirit its power of application and enjoyment. All this is blessedly true, but we must never forget that man is a responsible being, a guilty sinner commanded to repent and turn to God. It is not that repentance has any saving virtue in it. As well might we assert that the feelings of a drowning man could save him from drowning or that a man could make a fortune by a deed of bankruptcy filed against him. Salvation is wholly of grace; it is of the Lord in its every stage and every aspect. We cannot be too emphatic in the statement of all this, but at the same time we must remember that our blessed Lord and His apostles constantly urged upon men, both Jews and Gentiles, the solemn duty of repentance.

There is a vast amount of bad teaching on the subject, a great deal of legality and cloudiness whereby the blessed gospel of the grace of God is sadly obscured. The soul is led to build upon its own exercises instead of on the finished work of Christ – to be occupied with a certain process, on the depth of which depends its title to come to Jesus. In short, repentance is viewed as a sort of good work instead of the painful discovery that all our works are bad and our nature incorrigible. Still, we must be careful in guarding the truth of God. While utterly repudiating Christendom's false teaching on the important subject of repentance, we must not run into the mischievous extreme of denying its abiding and universal necessity.

Take a case. There are two men in a lifeboat; one was picked up after two hours' of terrible struggle with the waves, in the most awful mental agony through fear of death. The other was picked off the wreck a few minutes after she struck the reef and hardly had time to feel his danger. Both are in the lifeboat; both are safe, the one as safe as the other. They are saved by the lifeboat. It is not a question of their previous feelings, but simply of their being in the lifeboat.

No doubt, the former will have a deeper sense of the value of the lifeboat, but that is a matter of experience and not a question of salvation. There are hardly two cases of conversation alike. Some go through exercises of soul before they come to Christ, others after. It is the Christ I reach and not the way I reach Him, that saves my soul.

We cannot lay down a rigid rule. We believe that all must, sooner or later, learn what the flesh is, and the sooner and the more thoroughly we learn it the better. We have invariably found that those who have gone through the deepest ploughings at the first, make the steadiest and most solid Christians afterwards. But we are saved by Christ and not by experience. It often occurs to us that many of our young people who have been religiously brought up and led to make a profession, are much to be felt for when called to go out into the world. They are ignorant of their own hearts, ignorant of the snares and temptations of the world, ignorant of the devices of Satan. They have never proved what the world is. They were led perhaps gradually, imperceptibly, into the divine life, but have never been sifted and tested. Hence when brought face to face with the stern realities of life, when called to grapple with the difficulties of the day, to meet the reasonings of the infidel, the fascinations of ritualism or the allurements of the world – the theatre, the ballroom, the concert, the thousand and one forms of pleasure – they are not able to withstand these things. They are not decided for Christ; their Christianity is not sufficiently pronounced; they give way and fall under the power of temptation; and then they are most miserable, often brought almost to despair. But God in His mercy brings them back after their terrible conflict and overrules all the exercise for the deepening and consolidation of His work in their souls.

But, if there be not the germ of divine life; if it be merely the effect of religious training and home influence, then sadly the poor soul plunges with terrible eagerness into the vortex of sin and rushes headlong to destruction.

How many a lovely youth has gone forth from the parent's home, virtuous and unsophisticated, ignorant of the cruel ways of the world and ignorant of his own heart. The enemy lays some trap for him; he is caught in the snare; one thing leads to another; he goes from bad to worse, until at the last, he becomes the degraded victim of lust and vice, a moral wreck over which broken-hearted parents are called to shed many a bitter tear or by which their gray hairs are brought down with sorrow to the grave.

We are most thoroughly persuaded that what is needed for the day in which our lot is cast is whole-hearted, out-and-out, undivided consecration of heart to Christ. We need a thorough breaking with the world in its every phase and that perfect rest and satisfaction of heart in God Himself which renders a man wholly independent of all this wretched world has to offer. If there be not this, we need not look for any real progress in the divine life.

JUDGING

That the application of Matthew 7:1 to what you refer is incorrect will be evident to you if you refer to verse 15 of this chapter. How can we "beware of false prophets" if we are not to judge at all? We must not judge *motives*, but we are bound to judge conduct and doctrine. Look at 1 Corinthians 5:12-13. What does this mean? Clearly, that Christians are called upon to judge evil conduct and put away the impenitent offender. If the Corinthians had not done so, God would have judged them. Again, look at 1 John 4:1. What does this mean? Clearly, that Christians are called upon to judge the doctrine of any coming to them and to reject the false.